HISTORY OF LINGUISTICS 2021

STUDIES IN THE HISTORY OF THE LANGUAGE SCIENCES

AMSTERDAM STUDIES IN THE THEORY AND HISTORY
OF LINGUISTIC SCIENCE – Series III

ISSN 0304-0720

Founding Editor & General Editor (1973–2021)
E.F.K. KOERNER

General Editors

JEAN-MICHEL FORTIS (Paris) · KLAAS WILLEMS (Ghent) · OTTO ZWARTJES (Paris)

As a companion to the journal *Historiographia Linguistica* "Studies in the History of the Language Sciences" (SiHoLS) is a series of book-length scholarly works in the history of linguistic thought. Although its emphasis is on the Western tradition from antiquity to the modern day, it also includes, and welcomes, studies devoted to non-Western traditions. It comprises monographs, selective, thematically unified volumes, and research bibliographies.

A complete list of titles in this series can be found on
benjamins.com/catalog/sihols

Volume 133

Savina Raynaud, Maria Paola Tenchini and Enrica Galazzi (eds.)

History of Linguistics 2021.
Selected papers from the 15th International Conference on the History of the Language Sciences (ICHoLS 15), Milan, 28 August – 1 September

HISTORY OF LINGUISTICS 2021

SELECTED PAPERS FROM
THE 15TH INTERNATIONAL CONFERENCE ON
THE HISTORY OF THE LANGUAGE SCIENCES (ICHOLS 15),
MILAN, 28 AUGUST – 1 SEPTEMBER

Edited by

SAVINA RAYNAUD
MARIA PAOLA TENCHINI
ENRICA GALAZZI
Università Cattolica del Sacro Cuore

JOHN BENJAMINS PUBLISHING COMPANY
AMSTERDAM/PHILADELPHIA

The paper used in this publication meets the minimum requirements of the American National Standard for Information Sciences – Permanence of Paper for Printed Library Materials, ANSI Z39.48-1984.

DOI 10.1075/sihols.133

Cataloging-in-Publication Data available from Library of Congress:
LCCN 2024035524 (PRINT) / 2024035525 (E-BOOK)

ISBN 978 90 272 1815 5 (HB)
ISBN 978 90 272 4635 6 (E-BOOK)

John Benjamins Publishing Company · https://benjamins.com

Table of contents

Foreword & acknowledgments

According to the established schedule of previous conferences, the 15th International Conference on the History of the Language Sciences (ICHoLS XV) was planned to be held in Milan over the last week of August 2020, specifically from the 24th to the 28th. No surprises were expected; however, the organizers, hosts, and indeed the entire world were caught off guard by the outbreak of the COVID-19 pandemic in February 2020. Disoriented at first, the Scientific Committee and all involved institutions realized within a couple of months that we needed to postpone the event without hesitation. The postponement involved not only a shift in dates but also a transition from the originally planned venue in Milan to a fully digital format.

A considerable change in the organizational perspective became evident: different time zones required a different distribution of the plenary and parallel sessions (seven per day, morning and afternoon, each day). To ensure maximum accessibility for all participants worldwide, the plenary sessions were scheduled for the middle of the day according to the European time zone. This timing allowed participants to join either very early in the morning, for instance in Canada, or in the evening, e.g. in Korea.

At the same time, this new format encouraged many scholars, including first-time participants, to join the conference: over two hundred and fifty attendees from 30 countries, spanning Australia, Asia, Europe, Northern Africa, Canada, and both North and South America. ICHoLS XV was organized by the present editors and financially supported by their respective departments: the Departments of Philosophy and of Linguistic Sciences and Foreign Literatures at Università Cattolica del Sacro Cuore, with additional contributions from the Departments of Philosophy and of Literary, Philological, and Linguistic Studies at Milan State University. The event also received support from three learned societies affiliated with CISPELS (https://cispels.altervista.org/), a special contribution from the principal investigator of a PRIN (Projects of Relevant National Interest) funded by the Italian Ministero dell'Università, which organized two of the many workshops held during the conference, and – last but not least – several anonymous colleagues who believed in the scientific initiative and were ready to cooperate. The fees contributed by all participants were also essential for covering the expenses for the crucial technological assistance provided by Value People.

https://doi.org/10.1075/sihols.133.foreword

We would also like to extend our gratitude to the Organizing Committee, the widely international Scientific Committee, and its anonymous reviewers who ensured that each received abstract was reviewed two to three times. We thank the EasyChair platform team, as well as the competent and generous colleagues who provided additional readings and reviews of each full paper, now available in print. This would not have been possible without the valuable and long-lasting cooperation of Benjamins Publishing Company.

It is now time to acknowledge all the learned Societies that ensured the continuity of ICHoLS's history. They published our initial Winter 2019 call, supported its extension through time and space until the very end of its 2021 development, and ensured the success of the conference by presiding over sessions, listening, debating, and contributing to talks and workshops: the *Société d'Histoire et d'Epistémologie des Sciences du Langage*, France, founded in 1978; *the Henry Sweet Society for the History of Linguistic Ideas*, United Kingdom, 1984; the *North American Association for the History of the Language Sciences*, United States, 1987; the *Studienkreis "Geschichte der Sprachwissenschaft"*, Germany 1989; the *Società di Filosofia del Linguaggio,* Italy 1993; the *Sociedad Española de Historiografía Lingüística*, Spain 1995; the *Sociedad Mexicana de Historiografía Lingüística*, Mexico 2000; the *Giorgi Akhvlediani Society for the History of Linguistics*, Georgia 2010; and the young CISPELS (*Coordinamento Intersocietario per la Storia del Pensiero Linguistico e Semiotico*), Italy, 2021.

We greatly missed the message of Professor E.F.K. Koerner, the founder of ICHoLS, who was ill and unable to accept our invitation to greet the ICHoLS community at the beginning of the conference. He passed away on January 6th, 2022. We take this opportunity to remember him with deep gratitude.

We also wish to express our profound gratefulness to all the conference participants, and especially to the administrative and office workers, whose assistance was indispensable for making the 15th "COVID" edition of ICHoLS a reality.

The editors
Milan, Italy, 2024

Editors' introduction

To immerse our readers in the ambiance of ICHoLS XV, this time we cannot "compose one time and one place" for the event as we have done in the past. The grand halls of Potsdam, St. Petersburg, Vila Real, and Paris Sorbonne Nouvelle, just to remember the last events, have to leave space to distributed locations around the globe, linked through a network of computer screens and digital connections that made our talks and discussions possible.

Participants were scattered across numerous locations – whether in their hometowns or at holiday destinations. Some had their desk lamps switched on in the early morning hours, while others enjoyed sparkling daylight streaming through their windows, and some had to rely on artificial light as their rooms were gradually enveloped by darkness. We won't repeat what has already been mentioned about this special ICHoLS "COVID edition" in the previous pages.

After the usual opening greetings, just to ideally gather all of us, we decided to welcome everyone by sharing some noteworthy stories about our representative figures, serving as an introduction. First and foremost, we honored Agostino Gemelli (1878–1959), the first Rector Magnificus and founder of the Università Cattolica del Sacro Cuore, a medical doctor, psychologist, and phonetician. Through extensive archival research and lifelong study by one of our co-chairs, Enrica Galazzi, we were able to present a video, which can still be viewed here: https://www.youtube.com/watch?v=xgtzbuXYgoo. Similarly, we highlighted the contributions of Roberto Busa (1913–2011), a pioneer in computational linguistics, introduced by Marco Passarotti, another co-chair of the conference, along with Maria Patrizia Bologna (Milan State University), Rita Zama, and the three editors authoring this introduction.

Immediately after the opening ceremony, parallel sessions and/or thematic workshops began. There were seven sessions each day, running all day long except for a midday pause. We strategically scheduled all the invited talks in the middle of each day (CEST), as this was the most accessible slot for participants across different time zones. The first plenary session was held by Giorgio Graffi, and his text, titled *Can Linguistics and Historiography of Linguistics Profit from Each Other?* is the first entry in this volume, opening the first part: **General and Particular Issues in the History of Linguistics.**

The second invited talk was delivered by Giovanni Gobber, Dean of the hosting Faculty, on the topic *Konvergenz und Divergenz im Sprachwandel. Zum*

https://doi.org/10.1075/sihols.133.intro

Beitrag der italienischen Sprachforschung, mit besonderer Berücksichtigung der Auffassungen von Vittore Pisani. For those interested in a similar text, it is available in Italian in *Atti del Sodalizio Glottologico Milanese* V. 2020 N. 15 n.s. (2021): 73–92, under the title *La lingua nella riflessione di Vittore Pisani*; https://doi.org/10.54103/1972-9901/16698.

The third invited talk was presented by Patrick Sériot and is published in this volume under the title: *Type or Descent? The Philosophical, Romantic, and Biological Sources of Typology in Soviet Linguistics of the 1920s–1940s*.

The fourth and final invited talk was given by Marco Mancini (Sapienza Università di Roma) on *The Rise of Ancient and Middle Iranian Studies in Italy*. Unfortunately, due to his many public and professional commitments, the anticipated text has not yet been published.

Before mentioning the seventeen chapters published in this volume, which are divided into two further parts – **Antiquity** and **Sixteenth to Twentieth Century Works** – we wish to recall two additional key sources that contributed to the rich and intense scientific exchange made possible by the ICHoLS conference, despite the significant inconvenience of being confined to our respective countries and being physically distant from one another: the proposals of twelve thematic open workshops and the contributions by over two hundred scholars.

Here are the titles of the thematic workshops and the names of their organizers: 1. *Historiographical Studies: The Construction and Dissemination of Linguistic Knowledge within the Romance Languages Domain* (Ricardo Cavaliere); 2. *Saussure et l'école de Genève: Syntaxe et sémiotique* (Cercle Ferdinand de Saussure); 3. *Between Form and Meaning: The Structural Quest for "Gesamtbedeutungen"* (Lorenzo Cigana, Henrik Jørgensen); 4. *Grammars, Metalanguage, and Glossing on the Model Language as Reflection on the Target Language in the Middle Ages* (Paola Cotticelli, Diego Poli, Lucio Melazzo); 5. *The Meaningful Communicative Exchange from the Middle Ages to the Enlightenment* (same organizers); 6. *Linguistique grise. Le compte rendu et ses apports à l'histoire de la linguistique* (Giuseppe D'Ottavi, Silvia Piccini); 7. *Études saussuriennes aujourd'hui* (Núbia Faria, María Fausta Castro, Eliane Silveira); 8. *Horizons de projection – Histoire des représentations de l'avenir des savoirs linguistiques* (Jean-Marie Fournier, Christian Puech); 9. *German as a Foreign Language throughout the Centuries* (Rolf Kemmler, María José Corvo Sánchez); 10. *Language as a Specimen* (Floris Solleveld); 11. *The Crosslinguistic Application of Grammatical Categories and its Mechanisms from Antiquity to Modern Times* (Raf Van Rooy); 12. *Recursos digitales e información bibliográfica especializada para la Historia de la Lingüística hispánica: el proyecto BiTe-Ap1* (Eléna Battaner Moro).

Before plunging into the contents of this volume, which is highly representative of the various domains of inquiry, epochs, and international authors, we recall here the published outcomes (as far as known to us) of the whole conference, resulting of both the workshops first and from a couple of thematic sessions too.

Here they are, listed according to the corresponding workshop (WS) number: WS 2: three papers by Grazia Basile, Rosanna De Angelis, Emanuele Fadda resp., "Cahiers Ferdinand de Saussure" n. 74, 2021; WS 3: *Gesamtbedeutungen*, special issue ed. by Lorenzo Cigana & Henrik Jørgensen, "Acta Linguistica Hafniensia" International Journal of Linguistics vol. 55, 2023, https://www.tandfonline .com/toc/salh20/55/1; WS 4: *Metalanguage, Glossing, and Conceptualization in the Grammars of the Middle Ages*, ed. by Paola Cotticelli-Kurras, Nodus Publikationen, Muenster 2023; WS 5: *The Meaningful Communicative Exchange in the Middle Ages and in the Modern Age*, ed. by Paola Cotticelli-Kurras, "Beiträge zur Geschichte der Sprachwissenschaft" vol. 33, 1, 2023; WS 7: *Études saussuriennes aujourd'hui*, ed. by María Fausta Pereira De Castro, Núbia Rabelo Bakker Faria, Eliane Silveira, preface by Enrica Galazzi, Aracne, Roma 2023; WS 8: in the present volume are published the contributions by Dan Savatovsky, Jacqueline Léon, and Jean-Luc Chevillard; WS 10: the papers by Rebeca Fernández Rodríguez and by Floris Solleveld became part of a special issue *Language in the Global History of Knowledge*, "Berichte zur Wissenschaftsgeschichte" 46, 1, 2023, https://online library.wiley.com/toc/15222365/2023/46/1; WS 11: *The Crosslinguistic Application of Grammatical Categories in the History of Linguistics,* ed. by Raf Van Rooy, "Language & History" 66, 2, 2023, https://www.tandfonline.com/toc/ylhi20/66/2.

As regards to the thematic sessions, the volumes published so far are: *Insights into the History of Linguistics. Selected Papers from ICHoLS XV*, ed. by Maria Paola Tenchini and Savina Raynaud, Mimesis International, Milano-Udine 2024 (open access: https://mimesisinternational.com/insights-into-the-history-of-linguistics-selected-papers-from-ichols-xv/); *Texts and Ideas in the History of Language Learning and Teaching*, Quaderni del CIRSIL – 17, ed. by Giulia Nalesso and Alessandra Vicentini, Clueb, Bologna 2024, ebook available at: http://amsacta .unibo.it/.

Let us now delve into the first block of contributions (Part I, **General and Particular Issues in the History of Linguistics**), those which adopt a more epistemic, methodological, and multidisciplinary perspective. Giorgio Graffi's answer to the question *Can Linguistics and Historiography of Linguistics Profit from Each Other?* is a positive and pro-positive one. These fields *can* indeed benefit from each other, thereby preventing contemporary research from overlooking fundamental, albeit distant, theories (such as those concerning predication). This mutual benefit also helps avoid naive identifications between metalinguistic categories that, despite having similar denomination and temporal proximity, reveal themselves as theoretically definitely different. Graffi provides an exemplary caution against the temptation to superficially equate apparently related terms such as Bloomfield's 'immediate constituent' and Wundt's 'word group.' He suggests that accurately situating terms within their original theoretical and cultural contexts can prevent misleading and oversimplified interpretations. Last but not least, Graffi argues that, under certain conditions, linguistics and its history *should* mutually benefit, challenging Kuhn's claim of the incommensurability of theories. Instead, he encourages nuanced research that can yield clarifying and integrative results, fostering further development.

The issue of boundaries – geographical, cultural, disciplinary, and methodological – is at the core of Patrick Sériot's *Type or Descent? The Philosophical, Romantic, and Biological Sources of Typology in Soviet Linguistics of the 1920s–1940s.* The spatio-temporal coordinates of this topic are evident. However, Russian linguists often conceived themselves as fundamentally different from their Western counterparts. The author delves into the debate surrounding the following alternative: type or descent? In the Eastern context, descent from a common ancestor is rejected. Unlike European linguistics, Eastern comparative linguistics is not historic comparative: classification is replaced by typology. How, then, can the resemblance of forms be explained?

According to Jakobson and Trubetzkoy, the similarity of pure form, without any *contact* in time or space, suggests the existence of a plan, a design – a hidden teleology that governs these correspondences of form. Jakobson's idea of *contactless likeness* rests on European echoes from biological and philosophical debates. According to Sériot, linguistics in Russia is deeply rooted in the European cultural world, though the way of conceiving its identity proudly remains irreducible to any Western side of its Eastern profile.

In *Le futur antérieur des linguistes (fin 19e – début 20e siècle)*, Dan Savatovsky defines projection by distinguishing it from forecasting, prediction, and accommodation and demonstrates that the notion of projection involves linguistics as a discipline, not just as a body of knowledge. Savatovsky tries to understand what Saussure meant by the future tasks to be performed in linguistics and focuses on the proceedings of the first five editions of the International Congress of Linguists (1928–1939) to illustrate how early twentieth-century linguists conceived the future of their discipline.

Maria Paola Tenchini and Serena Cattaruzza's paper *Ethics and Language in (and around) Philipp Wegener* explores the relationship between language, speech, and ethics in Ph. Wegener's work and its recognition by later scholars such as A. Gardiner, K. Bühler, and S. Langer. Wegener distinguished himself by emphasizing ethics as a fundamental precondition for language acquisition and use, focusing on a dialogical dimension. The paper highlights three key points central to Wegener's thought: speaking as purposeful activity, language acquisition and use in children, and the development of language and linguistic structures. Although Wegener's ethical-sympathetic approach to communication has not entered the tradition of linguistic studies that succeeded him or that refer to him, it nonetheless prefigures not only the positions of A. Reinach but also, in a broader sense, some of the phenomenological perspectives of Th. Lipps, M. Scheler, and E. Stein.

Frank Vonk investigates *Walter Benjamin's Idea of Language*. In posthumously published fragments, the literary and art critic, philosopher, and explorer of the Judaic tradition inquires into the multifarious manifestations of language: from daily speech to tragedy, from Baroque literature to allegory, and from the basic human communicative function to Adamic language, which embodies the intensive *totality of language*. The theme of translation is also addressed in his inquiry.

In *Eléments pour une histoire de l'interprétation: considérations méthodologiques, enjeux et perspectives*, Elio Ballardini discusses how the emergence of schools for translators and interpreters after World War II fostered the development of Interpreting Studies alongside Translation Studies. Unfortunately, these areas of study long neglected other forms of interpreting, as they were predominantly conference interpreting–centered. Today, an increasing number of studies aim to reconstruct the global history of this millennia-old language practice. Initially West-centered, if not Europe-centered, this field is now expanding beyond its original geographical area. Ballardini examines this epistemological shift in the historiography of interpreting, the methodological problems it implies, and its challenges and perspectives.

In *"Computational Linguistics" as the Horizon of Projection of Early Machine Translation*, Jacqueline Léon traces the evolution from the initial goals of automatic translation by computers to recognizing the need for linguistics as a core discipline, specifically developing into computational linguistics. From 1949 to 1960, early attempts at machine translation (MT) yielded poor results. The subsequent ALPAC report (1960) recommended the development of Computational linguistics (CL). Thanks to the critical Y. Bar Hillel report (1960) and Chomsky's formal grammar and generative linguistics, the 1966 ALPAC report concluded that MT was still too expensive, but CL deserved to be potentiated. This shift marked a turning point for linguistics, emphasizing theory over practice and separating CL from direct computer application. The relevance of the relationship between institution and science during this period remains significant today.

Here begins Part II, devoted to **Antiquity** and focusing specifically on Sanskrit.

Declension and Description – The Ways of Sanskrit Grammarians by Émilie Aussant takes the reader back to antiquity (Sanskrit from the 5th c. BC to the 18th c. AD) and projects us in the extensive endeavor (twelve grammars) of not only describing but also teaching a language. One topic is focused on: the nominal declension. Sanskrit being a highly inflected language, declension has been often described by its own grammarians, from Pāṇini onward. While at the beginning only lists of *rules* were given in the corpus (within *syntagmatic* strings), in pedagogical grammars *paradigmatic sets* emerged. With one interesting exception, concerning non-metalinguistic approaches, there are, in fact, *mantras*, mainly verses extracted from Ṛgvedic hymns, which begin with a name, *Indra*, inflected in a different case, and they are recited together, *as a set*. The initial intent was certainly not grammatical: *Indra* being the name of a divinity, mentioning it in all its inflected forms was eminently a way to exalt the divinity in all its aspects and, then, to make the invocation more efficient.

Maria Piera Candotti and Tiziana Pontillo's paper, *Constituent-order in Sanskrit Bahuvrīhi Compounds. The Role of the Qualifier*, delves into a lively debate about Vedic and Sanskrit compounds, situated between morphological and syntactic processes. This study considers contrasting positions by Gillon (2008) and Lowe (2015), further discussed by the authors themselves (2014–2022). On the background of the most recent literature, Pāṇini's syntactic approach to compounding is confirmed for constituent order. However, explaining the specific order in Sanskrit bahuvrīhi compounds (a special case) requires the notion of 'qualifier.'

A further possibility to dwell on Sanskrit linking ancient with contemporary theoretical frameworks is offered by Davide Mocci's *The Internal Order of Sanskrit Compounds: A Dialogue between Pāṇini and Generative Grammar*. The study focuses on the internal order of Sanskrit noun–noun endocentric compounds. With the help of similar compounds in Western modern languages adopting different strategies, the reader is led to the discussion of categories such as the notion of 'head.' Pāṇini's grammar is then considered, with the notion of *upasarjana* proving explanatory, except for metaphorical compounds. Mocci then adopts a slightly revised version of Pāṇini's rule to account for those compounds. In conclusion, the notion relevant for determining the internal order of Sanskrit noun–noun endocentric compounds is the geometrically defined notion of 'embedded constituent,' stemming from generative grammar. This work well exemplifies how ancient and contemporary perspectives can help each other, through historiographical, metalinguistic, and linguistic research.

Part III includes **Sixteenth to Twentieth Century Works.**

"Loquimur cum vulgo, sed scribamus cum doctis" (Walther 1739): Chevillard's paper, entitled *How Far is the Horizon of Descriptive Linguistics?*, illustrates, with examples and comparisons, the diverse strategies adopted by European missionaries in describing sixteenth–eighteenth century Tamil language, in whose works the existence of Tamil triglossia ("vernacular," "formal," and "classic" Tamil) is reflected. The fate of these works is evoked, referring to their accessibility for modern readers or scholars. This accessibility has been made possible for some of these works (Beschi, Ziegenbalg, Henriques, and Da Costa) through the translation of the originals from Latin and Portuguese into English. However, there are still objective difficulties for others (fortunately, Chevillard himself is working on Proença's dictionary and Walther's grammar). The metaphor of the horizon used in the title of this contribution sounds like an invitation to explore new knowledge rather than just enjoying the already known.

In *Relevance of B. Delbrück's Work on Indo-European Syntax (A Century after his Death)*, Massimo Vai emphasizes the central role of Delbrück's works in the field of syntax. Through the definition of a basic order of the constituents of the sentence in Vedic – subsequently extended to Proto-Indo-European – and a movement rule correlated to the informative value of the constituents, Delbrück provides the essential foundations for a general syntactic analysis that remains indispensable today, as demonstrated by the recent reception of Delbrück's work. The numerous examples accompanying the theoretical clarifications particularly highlight the observations concerning the opposition between traditional and occasional word order, as well as the formal considerations that relate the variation of the order of constituents to the interface between the syntax and information structure of the sentence.

In *Three Documents Bearing on the Foundation of the Linguistic Society of America in the Age of Scientific Racism*, Margaret Thomas highlights the inward-looking nature of the LSA's establishment in 1924. The author accomplishes this through a close examination of three short texts – two letters and a short essay – all (co-)written by Leonard Bloomfield. The core question is whether, in an era of open racial discrimination, the LSA might have contributed to building a more equitable and inclusive society, where the scientific study of language is conducted with respect for the full scope of variation in all forms of human linguistic expression. According to Thomas, the evidence of an initiative to draw American linguists tightly together and to emphasize the scientific nature of their shared profession must be tested against a wider collection of texts, data, memoirs, and records of events.

Events directly involving some members of the LSA, such as Hockett's attempted resignation and the contested 1970 presidential election, are documented in Frederick J. Newmeyer's paper titled *Archival Resources for the Study of the Historiography of American Linguistics*. These and other significant events closely linked to the leading figures of American linguistics can be deduced from the analysis of the existing archives. Newmeyer provides an overview of the period roughly from the 1920s to the 1960s, and from the examples given, it is evident how material in these archives bears on debates in the historiography of linguistics.

Pierre-Yves Testenoire's paper, entitled *Courses in General Linguistics by Roman Jakobson at the École Libre des Hautes Études*, examines Jakobson's 1940s lectures in New York, particularly the general linguistics classes. It highlights how unpublished archival sources, alongside selected and retrospectively reedited documents, can deepen our understanding of Jakobson's theories and interpretations. Indeed, these sources offer more illustrations, clearer formulations, and richer bibliographical references than the published texts. Additionally, the course notes reveal the logic behind his teaching.

In *Contribution de Agostino Gemelli (1878–1959) à l'analyse des variations phoniques du langage*, Enrica Galazzi outlines how Agostino Gemelli, a medical doctor and psychologist, was involved in the study of phonic variations using avant-garde experimental methods. These innovative techniques allowed him to perform a multi-parametric analysis, which was unprecedented at the time. The results of his research, presented at the Third International Colloquium of Phonetic Sciences in Ghent in 1938, earned him international renown and recognition. A review of his findings enables us to assess the role that the Laboratory at Università Cattolica in Milan played in advancing research on the human voice, particularly in the emerging field of phonostylistics.

The Structuralist Quest for General Meanings: Mapping the History of Monosemy in Grammatical Semantics by Lorenzo Cigana and Henrik Jørgensen explores the development of the methodology known as "of general meanings," widely adopted in twentieth-century structural linguistics and grammatical semantics from the 1930s onward. The structural approach to the *Gesamtbedeutung* tradition involved reversing it, prioritizing the morphosyntactic definition of grammatical categories over semantic meaning. In particular, both Hjelmslev (1935) and Jakobson (1936) extensively discuss this tradition and the notions of *Grund-* and *Gesamtbedeutung*. The paper demonstrates how their models capture the same facts and where they overlap or differ. Jakobson and Hjelmslev's positions are further examined through later developments, highlighting a long-term challenge for the historiography of language science.

The wide scenario briefly outlined here and now ready to be explored will disclose different epochs, from the fifth century BC with Pāṇini's grammar to the most recent contemporary articles. It interweaves specific linguistic facts with enduring epistemological and methodological considerations and warnings. Thus, even non-specialist readers of a language or a specific epoch can gain valuable insights concerning methods and critical approaches.

Expressing gratitude once again to the present authors and all those who will disseminate these discoveries beyond their original context, we wish to conclude this shared, engaging commitment with a heartfelt farewell to our Parisian colleague Valérie Raby who unexpectedly passed away from a sudden illness on December 30, 2019, at the very beginning of the memorable ICHoLS XV enterprise.

The Editors
Milan, June 2024

PART 1

General and particular issues in the history of linguistics

CHAPTER 1

Can linguistics and historiography of linguistics profit from each other?

Giorgio Graffi
Università di Verona (Emeritus)

I offer support for an affirmative answer to the question in the title by means of two case studies. The first one is on the notion of predication. I compare two recent theoretical studies, arguing that one of them is less satisfactory than the other, since it does not consider the original Aristotelian notion of predication, which is necessary for an adequate treatment of natural language. The second case study deals with Immediate Constituent Analysis, which some scholars argue dates back to long before Bloomfield: this conclusion was drawn by implicitly equating 'constituent' with 'word group', while the two concepts actually differ. Our discussion leads to the issue of 'paradigm' in Kuhn's sense: to what extent are scientific notions formulated in different epochs and conceptual frameworks comparable? I maintain that they can be compared, by resorting to some approaches to the history of sciences that are different from Kuhn's.

Keywords: predication, constituent, word group, paradigm, research tradition

1. Introduction

The philosopher of science Imre Lakatos (1970: 91) opened one of his most famous papers by paraphrasing Kant's well-known dictum: "Philosophy of science without history of science is empty; history of science without philosophy of science is blind". Another contributor to the same volume where Lakatos' contribution appeared wrote:

> The history of science, by its nature as part of the history of ideas, has got to be a discipline which helps actual scientists to get a deeper insight into the real nature of their own science. If it does not do this, it becomes trivial – the activity of making a pedagogic collection of, in themselves, minor facts. (Masterman 1970: 88)

https://doi.org/10.1075/sihols.133.01gra

The easiest temptation would be to combine Lakatos' paraphrase of Kant's dictum with Masterman's remarks and to state that science without history of science is empty and history of science without science is blind. By applying this statement to our case, the question that gives this essay its title would be already answered, and in a strengthened way: not only *can* linguistics and history of linguistics profit from each other, but they also *must* be kept in strict contact with each other, if they both aim at adequacy.

Things are not quite so simple, however, since the relationship between any given discipline and its history cannot be directly equated with that between philosophy of science and history of science, or, more generally, with that of philosophy and its history. I think that if a mathematician, or a physicist, or a chemist, were asked if her/his discipline is empty without its history, s/he would undoubtedly answer negatively or would consider the question as meaningless. As far as I know, not many of today's scientists are interested in the history of their discipline. This also holds for linguists, most of whom are scarcely interested in the history of linguistic thought; on the other hand, a group of scholars has formed, especially over the last few decades, who have carried out a lot of very important research in the field of history of linguistics. Such scholars do not show, however, any particular interest in current problems of linguistics: the outcome has been that their research has an essentially "antiquarian" character; hence it has little hope of arising attention outside of its specific field. The attitudes of both groups (let's call them "pure" linguists and "pure" historians of linguistics) are respectable (especially the latter); but we may ask ourselves if they are correct.

Let's return for a moment to the difference between philosophy and other disciplines regarding their relationships with their respective histories. Of course, this is not the place to discuss the nature of philosophy, but I think I am not totally wrong in calling philosophy a "metadiscipline", hence its status is essentially different from that of any discipline, be it mathematics, physics, or even linguistics. The German philosopher Nicolai Hartmann once stated that it is impossible to do history of philosophy without having any philosophy as it would be impossible to do history of mathematics without knowing mathematics. To this statement, the Italian historian of philosophy Eugenio Garin (1990 [1959]: 39–41) replied that such a requirement cannot be exacted from a philosopher, since there is no "attained stage" in philosophy, contrary to mathematics and natural sciences. Garin's essay appeared in 1959: shortly after, Kuhn's notion of "paradigm" put the idea of "attained stage" in crisis even in natural sciences. The adoption of Kuhn's view of the history of the sciences would make any comparison between works belonging to different paradigms essentially meaningless: hence, it would bring about a complete separation between any science as it is presently carried out and its history.

Linguistics is not generally considered to belong to exact sciences, but to humanities; it is therefore uncertain if it has ever reached an "attained stage" (we can abstract, for the moment, from the question of whether such a notion is applicable to the natural sciences or not). However things may be, I think that most linguists are inclined to deny that their discipline has got such a stage, possibly because they adopt Kuhn's notion of 'paradigm' (I once read that, given the number of citations of *The Structure of Scientific Revolutions* found in linguistics books, Kuhn himself would have deserved to hold a honorary chair in any linguistics department). Such a position would have the effect quoted above, namely a complete separation of linguistics from its history.

To look for a possible solution to the dilemma, it may be useful to investigate some concrete cases of possible relationships between linguistics and history of linguistics. I will discuss two case studies. The first case study deals with the notion of predication; the second, with the history of the notion 'immediate constituent'. Both aim at showing that linguistics and history of linguistics can profit from each other: the first should show that history of linguistics is useful in contemporary linguistic research, the second, that it is advisable to know contemporary linguistics in order to better evaluate some issues in the history of linguistics. After examining these case studies, I will try to put their analysis into the more general framework of the relationship between sciences and their history.

2. Two case studies

I will deal with two recent papers on the notion of predication, by David Gil (2012) and by Andrea Moro (2019), respectively. According to Gil (2012: 303), "[...] there do indeed exist languages whose grammars make little or no reference to the notion of predication". According to Gil, an example of languages that lack predication is his hypothetical "IMA" (Isolating – Monocategorial – Associational) languages; other languages (such as Riau Indonesian) show a limited degree of predication; and languages such as English have a full-fledged predication. Predication also gradually developed through phylogeny and ontogeny of language. At any rate, predication is not a linguistic universal:

> Clearly, predication must play a central role in any theory of grammar [...]. However, as evidenced by Riau Indonesian, predication is not universal in the sense that it receives grammatical expression in all languages [...]. That most formal logics in use today draw heavily on a primitive irreducible notion of predication may actually be no more than a reflection of some contingent facts about grammar. (Gil 2012: 303–330)

What are the "contingent facts about grammar" that Gil alludes to? They would consist in the influence of the Greek language on Aristotle's thought. About this subject, Gil refers to a passage by the philosopher Fritz Mauthner: "The whole logic of Aristotle is nothing but a consideration of Greek grammar from an interesting point of view. Had Aristotle been speaking Chinese or Dakota, he would have had to arrive at a completely different logic" (Mauthner 1913: 4).[1] We can note, by the way, that the thesis that Aristotle's logic is molded by the structure of the Greek language was held not only by Mauthner, but also by several people before as well as after him: e.g., by Adolf Trendelenburg in the first half of the 19th century or by Emile Benveniste in the second half of the 20th. More importantly, it has been shown to be essentially untenable by the Italian scholar Walter Belardi (1985: 147–165). But this discussion would take us too far.

Moro does not engage himself in a debate with Gil, but he holds a quite different view of predication: "Predication constitutes the defining property of clause structures in all (but only) human languages and is one that has never been dismissed since it was established in the canonical models of Ancient Greek linguistics" (Moro 2019: 1). He therefore maintains the universality of the predicative relation and gives an opposite value assessment of Ancient Greek linguistics: while Gil suggests that it had a negative influence on later linguistic thought, Moro stresses its continuing relevance. It is not surprising that his view of predication is quite different from Gil's. It may be interesting to trace a comparison between the two papers, which are placed within two different frameworks: Gil's is in cognitive-typological linguistics while Moro's is in generative grammar. However, both essentially resort to the same pair of notions, i.e., headedness and thematic-role assignment: this makes their comparison significant. I will sketch the essential features of both Moro's and Gil's analyses, without going into detail and referring the interested readers to the original papers and to the literature quoted there.

In Gil's view, predication is a headed structure, i.e., an *endo*centric configuration, which "involves an asymmetric relationship between a predicate and its argument or arguments" (Gil 2012: 307). It consists of "the convergence of thematic role assignment and headedness in a particular configuration," namely "of the identification, within a single meaning element, of the two notions of thematic role assigner and head [...]. Thus, a predicate is a thematic role-assigner head, while its arguments are its thematic role-bearing modifiers" (Gil 2012: 310). The

1. "Die ganze Logik des Aristoteles ist nichts als eine Betrachtung der griechischen Grammatik von einem interessanten Standpunkte aus. Hätte Aristoteles Chinesisch oder Dakotaisch gesprochen, er hätte zu einer ganz anderen Logik gelangen müssen, oder doch zu einer ganz anderen Kategorienlehre".

head of the predicative structure, hence of the clause, is the verb (cf. Gil 2012:318, 322). Attribution is not derived from predication, as was often assumed, but it is its "near mirror-image counterpart": while in a predicative structure such as *the chicken is eating*, *eat* is both the head and thematic role-assigner, in the corresponding attributive, *the eating chicken*, the role assigner is still *eat*, but the head is *chicken* (cf. ibid). According to Gil, therefore, predication 1) is a headed structure and 2) a case of thematic-role assignment.

On the contrary, Moro assumes that predication 1) is a headless, or *exo*centric structure, and 2) is not always a case of thematic-role assignment, since "thematic link can be manifested in a predicative link but it is not necessary" (Moro 2019:3). A cornerstone of Moro's view of predication is his analysis of copular sentences, whose underlying structure he assumes to be the following one:

(1) copula [$_{SC}$ NP NP]

SC means 'small clause,' namely a clause without features of tense, aspect, mood, person and number. A movement transformation applies to structure (1), bringing about structure (2a) or (2b), depending on which NP (the first or the second one) is the displaced one (as indicated by the symbol *t*, 'trace'):

(2) a. NP copula [$_{SC}$ t NP]
b. NP copula [$_{SC}$ NP t]

Moro names (2a) "canonical copular sentence" and (2b) "inverse copular sentence": in the former, the moved NP is the subject, in the latter the predicate. They are exemplified by (3a) and (3b), respectively:

(3) a. A picture of the wall was the cause of the riot
b. The cause of the riot was a picture of the wall

Moro (2019:4), relying on his previous work on the topic of copular sentences (Moro 1997), shows that, despite their similarity, (3a) and (3b) have two different structures, (2a) and (2b), respectively. According to Moro, 1) the predicative structure is a SC, hence a symmetrical, headless structure (the two NPs are sisters and neither of them belongs to the category SC); 2) as the case of copular sentences shows, the thematic-assigner is not always a verbal head: in such sentences, the copula *be* (as well as its equivalents in other languages) is simply the "spelling-out" of the features of tense, aspect, mood, person and number, and the subject NP is assigned a thematic-role by the head of the predicate NP; 3) if the clause contains a lexical verb, this assigns a thematic role to the subject as well as its other arguments, as in (4a), e.g., where *Mary* and *John* receive the role of agent and patient, respectively. However, these roles are due to the properties of the lexical head *portray*, which can be both verbal and nominal, as shown in (4b):

(4) a. $[_S [_{NP}$ Mary] $[_{VP}$ portrayed John]]
b. $[_{NP}$ Mary's portrait of John]

Furthermore, predication is not always a case of thematic-role assignment; consider, e.g., the following case:

(5) $[_{NP}$ This] is $[_{NP}$ Mary's portrait of John]

In (5), the lexical head *portray* assigns the same thematic roles to *John* and *Mary* as in (4a) and (4b), but in (5) the preverbal NP *this* does not receive any such role (recall that copula *be* is not a role assigner); nevertheless it "is clearly subject of the sentence" (Moro 2019:3). Hence, Moro concludes, "thematic assignment can be manifested in a predicative link but it is not necessary." In synthesis, "predication can carry thematic information but the identification of subject and predicate cannot be derived from it" (namely, from thematic information; Moro 2019:2). The syntactic functions of subject and predicate derive from the symmetrical relation that exists between the two NPs within SC, in the case of copular sentences (cf. structure (1)), or between NP and VP, when the verb is lexical, as in (4a). Structure (4a) is that found in early generative works, such as Chomsky (1957:26, 111). In the subsequent developments of generative grammar (especially since the second half of the 1980s), such representation of clause structure was replaced by others, but this change involved the loss of "[t]he specificity of the configurational relation of predication" (Moro 2019:3). Such relation occurs in (4a), but not in (4b) which is an NP, i.e., a headed, asymmetrical structure.

I will now try to assess whether Gil's or Moro's approach to the notion of predication is the more adequate and whether history of linguistics can help us to settle this question. The two scholars clearly refer to two different conceptions of predication. Gil's starting point is predication in the sense of first-order predicate-calculus, to which he makes some important changes, deriving it from the notions of headedness and thematic-role assignment, as has been seen; this conception is often labeled (not quite rightly, in my view), as "Fregean". Moro, instead, adopts the so-called "Aristotelian" view. Roughly, a sentence such as (6a) could be represented as (6b) according to the first conception and as (6c) according to the second one:

(6) a. Mary loves John
b. f (x, y), where f = *loves*, x = *Mary*, y = *John*
c. $[_S [_{NP}$ Mary] $[_{VP} [_V$ loves] $[_{NP}$ John]]]

The opposition of a "Fregean" to an "Aristotelian" conception suggests that the former was developed as an explicit alternative to the latter. In fact, this is not entirely accurate, since they represent two different schemes which developed over the centuries in an independent way and were not opposed to each other for a long time: the "speech-act scheme" (in a sense only loosely connected with that of J. L. Austin's theory) and the "participant scheme," to employ the terminology of Elffers-van Ketel (1991: 198). According to the first scheme, the subject denotes what the predicate states something about; according to the second one, the subject denotes the thematic (or semantic) role of a given entity (prototypically, so to speak, the agent, but it could also be the experiencer, or the undergoer, etc.). As remarked by Elffers-van Ketel (ibid.): "[...] the subject is opposed to the predicate in the 'speech-act scheme' only. According to the participant-scheme the subject is rather opposed to other participants of the predicate, like the direct object and the indirect object." In principle, therefore, the two schemes are not alternative to each other: "a grammarian may fully recognize the 'participant' relationship between subject and direct object, while *at the same time* conceiving the sentence as primarily a combination of subject and predicate, in a wider sense of 'predicate'" (Elffers-van Ketel 1991: 199; original emphasis).

Chronologically, the speech-act scheme was the first to be proposed, as is shown, at least, from Aristotle's definition of the predicative relationship and of *rhêma*. "Whenever one thing is predicated of another as a subject (*héteron kath'hetérou kategorêtai hōs kath'hypokeiménou*), all things said of what is predicated (*katà toû katēgorouménou*) will be said of the subject also" (*Categories*, 1b 10–12, translation Ackrill). "A predicate (*rhêma*) is [...] a sign of things said of something else" (*De interpretatione*, 16b 6). I slightly modify Ackrill's translation of the latter quotation, rendering *rhêma* as 'predicate,' not as 'verb': *rhêma*, as used by Aristotle, does not simply mean 'verb,' but 'predicate' in general, and the best translation of *ónoma* would be 'subject.' This is shown, for example, by the fact that Aristotle quotes examples of what we would now call 'pure nominal sentences,' namely sentences without any verb, as instances of *lógoi* containing a *rhêma*.[2] It is the synthesis of subject and predicate that gives the statement its assertive value: "for not even 'to be' or 'not to be' is a sign of the actual thing (nor if you say simply 'that which is'): for by itself it is nothing, but it additionally signifies some combination (*sýnthesín tina*), which cannot be thought of without the components" (*De interpretatione*, 16b 22–25, transl. Ackrill). Finally, note that

2. I have maintained this for more than thirty years (see Graffi 1986; English translation in Graffi 2021: Chapter 1). I did not really propose anything new, but I was just following a tradition that dates to Steinthal (1890: 239) at least: "So *rhêma* is not just our verb, nor just our adjective, but also a noun, insofar as it is in the predicate; *rhêma* is predicate in general" ["Also ist ῥῆμα nicht bloß unser Verbum, auch nicht bloß unser Adjectivum, sondern auch Substantivum, insofern es im Prädicate steht; ῥῆμα ist Prädicat überhaupt."]. De Rijk (1996) also recognizes that the main meaning of *rhêma* is '(grammatical) predicate.'

many of Aristotle's examples consist of nominal predicates: hence it is difficult to label the subject as 'agent' or 'patient' (or 'undergoer').

Let us now turn to the participant scheme. Possibly, a germ of it can be found in the Stoics' analysis of the sentence. The Stoics do not establish a dyadic opposition between *ónoma* and *rhêma*, but they distinguish between three different kinds of 'predicates' (*katēgorémata*): *orthá* ('straight'), *ýptia* ('inverse') and *oudétera* ('neuter'):

> [...] some predicates are direct (*orthá*), some reversed (*ýptia*), some neither (*oudétera*). Now direct predicates are those that are constructed with one of the oblique cases, as 'hears (*akoúei*)', 'sees (*horâ*),' 'converses (*dialégetai*)'; while reversed are those constructed with the passive voice, as 'I am heard (*akoúomai*),' 'I am seen (*horômai*).' Neutral are such as correspond to neither of these, as 'thinks (*phroneî*)' 'walks (*peripateî*).'
> (Diogenes Laertius, *Vitae philosophorum*, VII, 64–5, translation Hicks)

Greek and Latin grammarians ignored the speech-act scheme: the notions of subject and predicate are unknown to them (see, e.g., Graffi 2021: Chapter 3). On the other hand, they distinguished, as did the Stoics, between active, passive and neuter (i.e., intransitive) verbs, hence showing some hints of the participant scheme. At any rate, the difference between the two schemes remained virtually unnoticed for the most part of history of linguistics,[3] since the standard examples of verbal predicates only contained intransitive verbs: *Socrates wins*, *Socrates runs*, etc. Therefore, both schemes (accidentally) matched with each other: what is spoken about coincided with the agent, or the undergoer, etc. The two schemes began to be considered as alternative when the logically-based model of syntax entered its crisis in the second half of the 19th century and attempts were made to replace it with a "psychologically-based" model. The issue had different outcomes. Two of them are especially significant. On the one hand, some scholars, like Carl Svedelius or Theodor Kalepky, abandoned the speech-act scheme

3. Modists, especially Thomas of Erfurt, seized the difference between the two schemes, at least in part, in terms of *constructio* vs. *perfectio*. Not every construction is perfect, but only that containing a subject (*suppositum*) and a predicate (*appositum*); cf. Thomas of Erfurt in Bursill-Hall (1972: 286, 314). This construction is a case of composition *secundum distantiam* (which the translation rather loosely renders as "by means of a verb"), as, e.g., *homo est albus* vs. *homo albus*, the latter being a case of composition *secundum indistantiam* (cf. id: 314; it may be interesting to note that, in the immediately following lines, Thomas refers to the notion of synthesis in Aristotle's *De interpretatione*; cf. above). Lacking the notion of Verb Phrase, and therefore identifying *appositum* with the verb, Modists analyze sentences with a transitive verb as formed by two constructions: that between subject and verb, and that between verb and object, labeled *constructio intransitiva* and *constructio transitiva*, respectively (cf. id., 286, 300).

and only preserved the participant scheme: according to them, the subject has no special status (for more details, cf. Elffers-van Ketel 1991: 295–299; Graffi 2001: 90–94). This was also the solution adopted by Tesnière some decades later. Vice versa, some other scholars (like Otto Jespersen) preserved the speech-act scheme in a purely grammatical form: namely they described it as interdependence relation which also occurs in structures which apparently have no-sentential nature (Jespersen's notion of 'nexus'). Jespersen was possibly also the first one to explicitly reject the idea that the attributive connection is derived from the predicative connection, contrary to what was mostly assumed before him. As we have seen above, Gil also recently rejected such a derivation, stating that "attribution is a mirror-image of predication." Jespersen's solution was different, however: nexus (i.e., the predicative structure) and 'junction' (i.e., the attributive structure) are fundamentally different from each other, the only point they share being the fact that both present the so-called "three-rank hierarchy" (namely, they both contain a 'primary,' a 'secondary' and a 'tertiarty;' cf., e.g., Jespersen 1924: 97).[4] The logicians of the time independently came to the same conclusion as Tesnière:[5] in a sentence with a transitive verb, such as *John loves Mary*, there is no difference in status between the subject and the direct object, since both are arguments of the dyadic predicate *love*.

Our quick historical survey shows the independent origin as well as the fortunes of the speech-act scheme and of the participant scheme. Gil does not consider the first scheme, nor does he criticize it, differently from grammarians and logicians between the 19th and the 20th centuries. Any terminological choice is of course free: hence, if Gil likes to label thematic-role assignment as predication, there is no problem at all. But there are good reasons for keeping the two notions distinct: our look at the history of linguistics showed us how they had an independent origin and concern two different aspects of the clausal syntax, as also shown

4. An interesting paper by Cigana (2020) argues for an opposed view: "The refusal of predication and of the standard subject-predicate relation is a feature Jespersen shared with Tesnière" (Cigana 2020: 223, n. 9). I find this statement too drastic. Possibly, Jespersen's views on the matter were somewhat wavering, but one cannot forget that Jespersen (1924) devotes a whole chapter to "Subject and Predicate", which is far from maintaining the usefulness of these notions, and analyzes the nexus into a 'subject-part' and a 'predicate-part'. Cf. also the immediately following footnote.

5. I say "independently" because, apparently, grammarians and logicians had no knowledge of each other's results. For example, a logician (Næs 1932: 27) criticizes Jespersen, and grammarians in general, for assigning a particular status to the subject with respects to the other arguments. For his part, Tesnière (1959: chap. 49; keep in mind that this posthumous book largely dates to the years 1930s-1950s) states that the analysis of the sentence into subject and predicate derives from "a priori formal logic": subject and object are 'participant roles' on the same plane.

by Moro's analysis (see the discussion of (3) and (4), above). It seems therefore preferable to reserve the label 'predication' for the speech-act scheme; but what is important is not to see the participant scheme as an alternative to it.

Let us now turn to our second case study, the history of the notion immediate constituent. I start from a quotation by Percival (1976 [1967]: 239): "That Wundt's linguistic theory is the origin of Bloomfield's theory of immediate constituents is too obvious to require further demonstration." I do not intend at all to employ Percival's paper as "the whipping boy": this would be quite unfair, since it dates to over fifty years ago; furthermore, it was just this paper that stimulated me to deal with the history of the notion immediate constituent. However, since Percival's thesis of a derivation of Bloomfield's theory from the analyses of the German psychologist Wilhelm Wundt was later endorsed by several linguists and historians of linguistics as well, I think that it would be meaningful to assess it.

Let us first take a closer look at Wundt's analysis (cf. Wundt 1912, Part II: 329–333). Wundt analyzes the German sentence (7)

(7) *Ein redlich denkender Mensch verschmäht die Täuschung*
"An honest-thinking man spurns the deception"

as formed by a subject (*ein redlich denkender Mensch*) and a predicate (*verschmäht die Täuschung*); as can be seen, Wundt, differently from other scholars of his epoch, still adopts the speech-act scheme. In his view, both the subject and the predicate also contain a subject and a predicate:

(8) *ein Mensch denkt redlich*
"A man thinks honestly"

and

(9) *die Täuschung wird verschmäht*
"The deception is spurned"

According to Percival, this is an authentic example of immediate constituent analysis in Bloomfield's sense.

Let us now consider Bloomfield's exemplification of IC-analysis:

> Any English-speaking person who concerns himself with this matter, is sure to tell us that the *immediate constituents* of *Poor John ran away* are the two forms *poor John* and *ran away*; that each of these is, in turn, a complex form; that the immediate constituents of *ran away* are *ran*, a morpheme, and *away*, a complex form, whose constituents are the morphemes *a-* and *way*; and that the constituents of *poor John* are the morphemes *poor* and *John*. (Bloomfield 1933: 161)

The two analyses differ in a fundamental way. Wundt's analysis is based on the generalization of the predicational scheme to all kinds of word-groups. Bloomfield's analysis is strictly distributional and does not resort in any way to the subject-predicate structure; this is shown by the fact that it is applied both to syntax and morphology: in the latter, the subject-predicate dichotomy has no role. Hence Wundt's analysis cannot be considered "the root" of Bloomfield's. Of course, strict connections do exist between Wundt and Bloomfield, as expressly admitted by Bloomfield in the preface to Bloomfield (1914). This volume also contains a decidedly "Wundtian" analysis of a sentence:

> In the sentence *Lean horses run fast* the subject is *lean horses* and the horses' action, *run fast*, is the predicate. Within the subject, there is the further analysis into a subject *horses* and its attribute *lean*, expressing the horses' quality. In the predicate *fast* is an attribute of the subject. (Bloomfield 1914: 61)

However, this analysis only shows the closeness between Wundt's views and those expressed in Bloomfield's first book, not between Wundt's analysis of the sentence and IC-Analysis as presented in Bloomfield's *Language* and developed first by American structuralists (Nida, Wells, or Harris) and later by generative grammar.

3. Some possible objections to our approach

One could object that our approach is somewhat contradictory: discussing the notion of predication we have compared two of today's linguists (Gil and Moro) with those of earlier periods (like Jespersen or even Aristotle); investigating the history of the notion of immediate constituent, we have apparently concluded that Wundt's and Bloomfield's analyses are fundamentally different from each other. In a few words: can contemporary linguistic theories and analyses be meaningfully compared with those of earlier epochs? If the answer is negative, the profit that linguistics and historiography of linguistics could make from each other would be very little, if any. Such a negative answer would also be suggested by Kuhn's notion of 'paradigm': if taken in its strictest interpretation, concepts or theoretical frameworks belonging to different paradigms are incomparable with each other. As Kuhn (1970: 149) writes: "Within the new paradigm, old terms, concepts, and experiments fall into new relationships one with the other. The inevitable result is what we must call, though the term is not quite right, a misunderstanding between the two competing schools." A "Kuhnian" attitude would therefore legitimate our treatment of the history of immediate constituent analysis, but not that of predication.

A possible answer would be that linguistics is still in a "pre-paradigm" state, so it is possible to compare definitions and analyses of linguistic phenomena formulated by different scholars at different epochs. A similar solution was suggested by Simone (1992). I have developed this suggestion in a paper of around a quarter of century ago by suggesting that linguistics has not yet experienced "a scientific revolution, in the authentic Kuhnian sense of the phrase" (Graffi 1995: 181; now also in Graffi 2021: 155). This would render our approach to the history of the notion of predication quite legitimate. Against such a solution, however, other objections could be raised. One of such objections could be that we are not really doing history of linguistics, but we are simply adding more references to our topic. This kind of objection was made by Kragh (1987: 200, fn. 1) towards the physicist and historian of rational mechanics Clifford Truesdell, who said he had "been led to new results in rational mechanics through the study of Cauchy's works, dating back to 1820". Kragh (1987: 33) objects that "the works of Cauchy are not, in themselves, history of science. Their possible importance for modern research is not due to the historian of science but to Cauchy." A similar remark, specifically concerning the relationships between linguistics and history of linguistics, was also made by Elffers-van Ketel (1991: 64): "we discuss earlier work in the same way as we discuss contemporary work". This being the case, our discussion of predication would not be history of linguistics in the proper sense. Another (and possibly even stronger) objection would be that we consider linguistics as being in a pre-paradigm situation when we deal with the notion of predication, whereas we consider Wundt's and Bloomfield's theories as incomparable with each other, so ascribing each of them to a different paradigm (at least implicitly). Hence, it could seem that we apply the Kuhnian approach in two contradictory ways. Furthermore, the essential incomparability of Wundt with Bloomfield would render our research only relevant for history of linguistics, so virtually useless for linguistics.

Actually, Kuhn's ideas are more about *philosophy* than *history* of science. After all, his main critics were philosophers, not historians of science: Popper, Lakatos and Feyerabend (see Lakatos, Musgrave 1970). Hence, I think that a possible solution to these difficulties can be found in some approaches to the history of sciences that are different from Kuhn's approach. One of such approaches was proposed by Holton (1973; 1978), according to whom a key role in the history of sciences is played by what he calls 'themata', which "persist through revolutionary periods" (Holton 1978: 23). One example of thema in Holton's sense is "the physical concept force", which, in a sense, constantly recurs throughout the history of physics:

> [..] throughout history there has existed in science a "principle of potency." It is not difficult to trace this from Aristotle's *enérgeia*, through the neo-platonic

> *anima motrix*, and the active *vis* that still is to be found in Newton's *Principia*, to the mid-nineteenth century when "Kraft" is still used in the sense of energy (Mayer, Helmholtz). (Holton 1973: 58)

Holton describes the features of thematic analysis as follows:

> Thematic analysis allows discernment of some constancies or continuities in the development of science, of relatively stable structures that extend across supposed revolutions and among apparently incommensurable rival theories [...].
> Techniques analogue to the thematic analysis that I have applied to science have worked well before in other fields, for example, in content analysis, linguistic analysis, and cultural anthropology. (Holton 1978: ix–x)

This last quotation is especially significant: Holton does not only see the recurrence of themata across alleged "revolutions" as a feature of the history of natural sciences, but he also sees the existence of themata as a property shared by both natural sciences and humanities.

Another alternative to Kuhn's views can be found in Laudan (1977). Laudan (1977: 71–72) remarks that the word "theory" is employed with two different senses: according to one of these senses, we speak about Maxwell's theory of electromagnetism, or Wegener's theory of continental drift; in the other sense, we speak of "evolutionary theory", or "atomic theory", etc. "Theory" in this second sense is labeled "research tradition" by Laudan, who defines it as follows: "*A research tradition is a set of reasonable assumptions about the entities and processes in a domain of study, and about the appropriate methods to be used for investigating the problems and constructing the theories in that domain*" (Laudan 1977: 81; original emphasis). According to Laudan, therefore, research traditions run across paradigms. Laudan (1977: 140; original emphasis) also says: "Where discontinuities occur is not so much at the level of first order problems as at the level of explanation or problem solution. [...] *it is basically the shared empirical problems which establish the important connections between successive research traditions*."

Of course, Holton's and Laudan's perspectives and theoretical tools are not to be confused, least of all equated. Nevertheless, they share an important point: even if the development of science is characterized by "revolutions" which replace paradigms with other paradigms (and independently from the tenability of such a view), approaches belonging to different paradigms can also be compared. Let us now to apply Holton's or Laudan's conceptions to our case studies.

Predication as intended within the speech-act scheme can be qualified as a thema (in Holton's sense) or as a research tradition (in Laudan's terms) throughout the history of linguistics. Of course, such thema was dealt with in quite different perspectives and by quite different scholars in the different epochs: so, for example, Aristotle's analysis was a necessary precondition for the definition of the *lógos apofantikós*; on the other hand, Jespersen's notion of nexus is simply grammatical and also extends to subordinate and apparently non-sentential structure; Moro's approach to the question is framed in the more general debate on the form of syntactic configurations. Specific historical contexts and different explanatory goals therefore interact with the same thema. This legitimates our (obviously partial) comparison of the three different approaches. What is the relationship of this thema with the participant scheme? Borrowing a concept from Holton again, we could label this an 'antithema' to the speech-act scheme. Svedelius', Kalepky's and, finally, Tesnière's proposals are a clear instance of such 'antithema'; Gil's definition of predication gives to the antithema the label traditionally assigned to the thema.

Let us now turn to the history of the notion immediate constituent. Continuing to use Holton's terminology (and resorting to a somewhat musical metaphor), we can say that the different approaches by Wundt, on the one hand, and by Bloomfield, on the other, are instances of variations on a same theme, namely that of word group. This latter thema surfaced much later than that of predication: possibly, the first one to see the existence of a linguistic unit intermediate between the word and the sentence was Comenius in the 17th century (see Oniga 2016). This theme was developed in the following century, especially by Girard (1747). During the 19th and the first decades of the 20th century the research focused on the structure of word groups and their analogies or differences with sentences: the idea most largely widespread throughout the 19th century was that of deriving the attributive relationship from the predicative one. Once this idea became superseded, some other interesting analyses of word groups were proposed in the early decades of the 20th century, especially by Ries (1928), Sechehaye (1926), and Meriggi (1933), the last of whom even proposed that the label 'isolating' languages be replaced with that of 'grouping' languages. One can also observe some strict analogies between some aspects of Ries' and Bloomfield's (1933) analyses, especially Ries' notion of *Kern* that almost exactly matches with Bloomfield's 'head'. Nevertheless, if immediate constituent analysis is a theory of word groups, not any theory of word groups is equivalent to immediate constituent analysis (cf. Graffi 2021: 117). In a nutshell: Wundt's and Bloomfield's accounts can be compared with each other since they belong to the same thema (or to the same research tradition); but the roots of the analysis of the latter cannot be found in that of the former.

I will end this section by discussing another objection I have hinted at above, namely that, even if the resort to the notions of thema or of research tradition can legitimate the comparison of such different approaches as Aristotle's, Jespersen's, or Moro's, I am not really practicing history of linguistics, but I am rather simply developing theory of grammar within a wider spectrum of intellectual references. To such an objection, I would answer that we can recognize the same thema across different epochs in the history of linguistics, although, in many cases, it is not dealt with in the same way. Vice versa, the same label can often designate two (or more) different notions. To ascertain this is, in fact, historical research.

However, I think that Kragh is right when he distinguishes between history of *science* and *history* of science:

> Science (S_1) can be regarded as a collection of empirical and formal statements about nature, the theories and data that, at a given moment of time, comprised accepted scientific knowledge. [...] The science (S_2) that is historically relevant consists of the activities or behaviour of scientists, including factors of importance to this, in so far as these activities have been connected with scientific endeavours. Thus, S_2 is science as human behaviour whether or not this behaviour leads to true, objective knowledge about nature. S_2 encompasses S_1 as the result of a process but the process itself is not reflected in S_1. Usually S_2 cannot be found in articles or books, but has to be pieced together with the use of historical sources. [...] If history of *science* is meant then the science concerned will be often science in the S_1 sense, consisting mainly of a technical analysis of the contents of scientific publications placed in a historical framework. *History* of science, however, will be science in the S_2 sense. (Kragh 1987: 22–23)

I will come back to this objection in a moment.

4. Concluding remarks

My aim was to show that linguistics and history of linguistics not only *can*, but they also *should* take profit from each other. In particular, our first case study shows that the two different schemes of sentence structure that were formulated throughout the history of linguistics (the speech-act scheme and the participant scheme) are not alternative, but complementary. Our second case study shows how the same theme (i.e., the nature of word groups) has been dealt with according to different frameworks throughout the history of linguistics: hence, different theoretical analyses, such as by Wundt or by Bloomfield, cannot be equated.

Turning now to the Kragh-style objection quoted at the end of the preceding section, I admit that what I have presented here is relevant (if it is) to history of *linguistics*, not to *history* of linguistics; and I also admit that the second kind of history can be much more interesting, from a general point of view. My aim was simply to argue for the usefulness of history in the former sense also for "pure" linguists, and for the usefulness of the knowledge of contemporary linguistics for a better understanding of the history of the discipline.

Acknowledgments

I would like to thank Els Elffers-van Ketel, Lia Formigari, Andrea Moro and Alfredo Rizza for kindly reading some earlier versions of the present paper, of which, in any case, the responsibility is solely mine.

References

Belardi, Walter. 1985. *Filosofia, grammatica e retorica e nel pensiero antico.* Roma: Edizioni dell'Ateneo.

Bloomfield, Leonard. 1914. *An Introduction to the Study of Language.* New York: Henry Holt & Co. (New edition, with an introduction by Joseph F. Kess. Amsterdam & Philadelphia: John Benjamins, 1983.)

Bloomfield, Leonard. 1933. *Language.* Holt: New York.

Bursill-Hall, G.L., ed.. 1972. *Thomas of Erfurt. Grammatica speculativa.* London: Longman.

Chomsky, Noam. 1957. *Syntactic Structures.* The Hague: Mouton.

Cigana, Lorenzo. 2020. "Some Aspects of Dependency in Otto Jespersen's Structural Syntax". *Chapters of Dependency Grammar. A Historical Survey from Antiquity to Tesnière* edited by András Imrényi & Nicolas Mazziotta, 215–252. Amsterdam & Philadelphia: John Benjamins.

Elffers-van Ketel, Els. 1991. *The Historiography of Grammatical Concepts. 19th and 20th-Century Changes in the Subject-Predicate Conception and the Problem of their Historical Reconstruction.* Amsterdam & Atlanta: Rodopi.

Garin, Eugenio. 1990. *La filosofia come sapere storico.* Bari: Laterza.

Gil, David. 2012. "Where does Predication Come from?". *Canadian Journal of Linguistics/Revue canadienne de linguistique* 57.303–333.

Girard, Louis-Gabriel. 1747. *Les vrais principes de la langue françoise.* Paris. Mercier (reprint Genève : Droz, 1982).

Graffi, Giorgio. 1986. "Una nota sui concetti di *rhêma* e *lógos* in Aristotele". *Athenaeum*, n.s., 74.91–101.

Graffi, Giorgio. 1995. "Old Debates and Current Problems: *Völkerpsychologie* and the Question of the Individual and the Social in Language". *Historical Roots of Linguistic Theories* edited by Lia Formigari & Daniele Gambarara, 171–184. Amsterdam & Philadelphia: John Benjamins.

Graffi, Giorgio. 2001. *200 Years of Syntax. A Critical Survey.* Amsterdam & Philadelphia: John Benjamins.

Graffi, Giorgio. 2021. *From Aristotle to Chomsky. Essays in the History of Linguistics.* Münster: Nodus Publikationen.

Holton, Gerald. 1973. *Thematic Origins of the Scientific Thought. Kepler to Einstein.* Cambridge (MA) – London: Harvard University Press.

Holton, Gerald. 1978. *The Scientific Imagination. Case Studies.* Cambridge: Cambridge University Press.

Jespersen, Otto. 1924. *The Philosophy of Grammar.* London: Allen & Unwin.

doi Kragh, Helge. 1987. *An Introduction to the Historiography of Science.* Cambridge: Cambridge University Press.

Kuhn, Thomas S. 1970. *The Structure of Scientific Revolutions*, 2nd ed. Chicago: The University of Chicago Press.

doi Lakatos, Imre. 1970. "History of Science and its Rational Reconstructions". *PSA 1970. In memory of Rudolf Carnap* edited by Roger C. Buck & Robert S. Cohen, 91–136. Dordrecht: Reidel.

doi Lakatos, Imre & Alan Musgrave, eds. 1970. *Criticism and the Growth of Knowledge.* Cambridge: Cambridge University Press.

Laudan, Larry. 1977. *Progress and its Problems. Towards a Theory of Scientific Growth.* Berkeley-Los Angeles-London: University of California Press.

doi Masterman, Margaret 1970. "The Nature of a Paradigm." *Criticism and the Growth of Knowledge* edited by Imre Lakatos & Alan Musgrave, 59–89. Cambridge: Cambridge University Press.

Mauthner, Fritz. 1913. *Beiträge zu einer Kritik der Sprache. III: Zur Grammatik und Logik.* Stuttgart und Berlin: Cotta.

Meriggi, Piero. 1933. "Sur la structure des langues «groupantes»". *Journal de Psychologie* 30.185–216.

doi Moro, Andrea. 1997. *The Raising of Predicates.* Cambridge: Cambridge University Press.

doi Moro, Andrea. 2019. "The Geometry of Predication: a Configurational Derivation of the Defining Property of Clause Structure". *Phil. Trans. R. Soc. B* 375: 20190310.

Næs, Olav. 1932. "Das grammatische Begriffssystem im Lichte der Neuen Logik". *Norsk Tidsskrift for Sprogvidenskab* 6.5–28.

doi Oniga, Renato. 2016. "The Emergence of the Syntactic Concept of Phrase in Comenius". *Historiographia Linguistica* 43.285–299.

doi Percival, W. Keith. 1976 [1967]. "On the Historical Source of the Immediate Constituent Analysis". *Notes from the Linguistic Underground* edited by James D. McCawley, 229–242. New York, San Francisco, London: Academic Press.

Ries, John. 1928. *Zur Wortgruppenlehre.* Prag: Taussig & Taussig.

doi Rijk, Lambertus M. de. 1996. "On Aristotle's Semantics in *De Interpretatione* 1–4". *Polyhistor. Studies in the History and Historiography of Ancient Philosophy Presented to Jaap Mansfeld on his Sixtieth Birthday* edited by Keimpe Algra, Pieter W. v. d. Horst & Douwe (David) Runia, 115–134. Leiden: Brill.

Sechehaye, Albert. 1926. *Essai sur la structure logique de la phrase.* Paris: Champion.

Simone, Raffaele. 1992. *Il sogno di Saussure.* Bari: Laterza.

Steinthal, Heymann. 1890. *Geschichte der Sprachwissenschaft bei den Griechen und Römern*, 2nd ed. Berlin: Dümmler.

Wundt, Wilhelm. 1912. *Völkerpsychologie. I. Die Sprache*, 3rd ed.. Leipzig: Engelmann.

CHAPTER 2

Type or descent?

The philosophical, romantic, and biological sources of typology in Soviet linguistics of the 1920s–1940s

Patrick Sériot
Université de Lausanne

Either science aims at universal validity, or it is no science. The idea that science can be culturally or nationally determined is unanimously considered as an outdated Romantic cliché. Nonetheless, it is usual to speak of the Western thought, without wondering where its Eastern limit is to be found. In the history of linguistics, Russian science of language is often proclaimed by Russian thinkers as being "fundamentally different" from Western linguistics. This paradox is examined here after R. Jakobson's works in the interwar period and their links to Goethe's and *Naturphilosophie* research in biology: idealistic morphology appears to be a way towards typology.

Keywords: function, Goethe, Jakobson, metaphor, metonymy, Naturphilosophie, Russian linguistics, teleology, tradition, typology, Western thought

1. Introduction

It is so usual in North America and Western Europe to speak of the Western thought, Western philosophy, Western metaphysics, Western culture, that an obvious question remains unnoticed: nobody seems to wonder where the Eastern limit of the so-called Western thought is to be found, or even if it exists at all. If it seems to go without saying that Japan, China, or India do not belong to the Western world, what about Russia? Or is Eastern Europe a part of Europe? For the Czech writer Milan Kundera, Russia is not in Eastern Europe but in Western Asia.

This question is vast, it is a part of political sciences, cultural studies, or the theory of ideologies. It receives different answers in architecture, literature, or

https://doi.org/10.1075/sihols.133.02ser

religion. A field where this Eastern border of the so-called "West" is seldom considered is the history of linguistics.

For modern scientists, the question of "national traditions" in science is epistemologically irrelevant. The Pythagorean theorem is valid regardless of the culture where it is stated. This principle is slightly different, nonetheless, for linguistics, where it is usual to speak of different *traditions*: the Indian linguistic tradition (Panini) has another history and another origin than the Greco-Latin tradition (Apollonius Dyscolus, Varro) (see e.g. Lepschy, 1990). In this latter work, a chapter is devoted to the Orthodox Slavia (vol. II: 256–275), which is but a part of medieval linguistics in general, on the same level as Roman Slavia. Picchio (1972), Garvin & al. (1963) present substantial and precise aspects of grammatical and linguistic thought in Eastern Europe, but they do not ask if Russian linguistics (or linguistics in Russia) is part of Western linguistics or an autonomous domain *per se*. In other words: is there a *specific* Russian tradition in linguistics, *different* from the Western tradition? For Western Marxist thinkers, Russian, or Soviet linguistics belongs to another culture, though in a political, not cultural, sense.

2. Absolute Russian specificity

It is poorly known in the "West", nonetheless, that in Russia a direct answer is commonly given to this identity query: the Russian tradition is presented as the direct heir of the Greek tradition, which itself is fundamentally *different* from the Latin tradition. V. Kolesov (1991) explains that in the 16th Century translations from Latin grammars written in the West, i.e. "from an entirely foreign tradition", began to appear in Russia:

> In many ways, these terms came into conflict with terms already familiar to the East Slavic reader, at least from the *Dialectics* of Damaskin in Slavic translation [...]. This translated text is already included in another tradition associated with translations of other scholarly books: from the Latin language (*Rhetorics* and *Logics*).
>
> A dynamic contradiction, which provoked an active reaction from official religion and philosophy, manifested itself in connection with the translation into Russian of grammars of Latin orientation, especially Donat's *Ars Minor* in 1522 [...]. From that time on, the grammatical (and, more broadly, social, cultural) ideas of the Greek orientation came into conflict with the ideas of a completely different culture, Roman, Catholic, bringing to life profound changes at all levels of the cultural and social life of Russia in the 16th Century. [...] Now, in the subtext of any scientific investigation, including linguistics, there was a confrontation between two cultures and between two philosophical and religious orientations. The ideological basis for the inclusion of a new cultural structure in the national tradition

> was the idea of "Moscow is the third Rome"; there was a need for a critical examination of the achievements of both civilizations – Hellenic and Roman. Translations of sacred books from Latin [...] provided the theological basis for the subsequent two-century discussion regarding the "Latinism" in the Orthodox culture, which they sought to pass for the culture of the Russian people.
> (Kolesov, 1991: 219)

This clear-cut opposition between a Western and a specific Russian tradition in linguistics has to be discussed. If a 'Sonderweg' exists in linguistics in Russia, it has to be proven, not just claimed.

We should begin by deploring the lack of translations from Russian into Western languages: *rossica non leguntur.*[1] I insist that linguistics in Eastern Europe (especially in Russia) is rich, interesting, heterogeneous, and that the history of linguistics in Europe would not be complete if linguistics in Russia were neglected and not sufficiently translated. Let us take as a point of departure that Eastern Europe is in Europe and not in Western Asia and explore the consequences of this principled stand.

The first thing that stands out when reading linguistic texts from Russia is a constantly repeated statement, an insistent Russian discourse on the specificity of Russian linguistics, on its thorough *difference* from the Western 'tradition'. Here are some examples from various periods of time:

> Thanks to the tireless linguistic work of the academician N. Marr, creator of the Japhetic theory, in our country, in the Soviet Union the science of language is built on completely different bases, has a radically different way of approaching linguistic problems, has different development prospects, totally unlike the current state of Indo-European linguistics. (Serdiuchenko, 1931: 167)

> Various objects of study in Russian and European linguistics caused their different interpretations, revealed different initial attitudes, a qualitatively different description of the relations existing between the elements of the described object.
> (Berezin, 1976: 6)

These quotes from Soviet linguistics could be seen as mere clichés from the cold war about the philosophical basis of dialectical materialism. But it is important to note how this claim of fundamental difference was shared by Russian émigrés in the West. Let us take an unexpected and unsuspected example of this attitude in R. Jakobson, who is often presented as "an American scholar". But this "American

1. "What is (written) in Russian is not read". The origin of this expression is *Graeca sunt, non leguntur*, common in the Middle Ages about monks who quoted Greek without understanding it, or refused to read it. It was diverted to Russia in the 19th Century to regret that works written in Russian are not read and known in the "West".

scholar" had this epitaph carved (in Russian) on his grave in Harvard: *Roman Jakobson – russkij filolog*. What did that mean for him to be a Russian philologist? Unlike in the previous excerpts, Jakobson gives, if not proofs, at least arguments.

In 1929, Jakobson, being a very active member of the Prague linguistic circle, wrote an astonishing paper for the journal of the German university in Prague *Slavische Rundschau*,[2] in which he defined the specificity and difference of Russian linguistics and Russian thought in general. For Jakobson, there is no doubt about the Russian *Sonderweg*: "the Russian ideological tradition" is the same in the Soviet Union and in the emigration, Marxism is a political opinion, which has no impact on the Russian (and Slavic) science of language. "Die Tradition der russischen Wissenschaft", "eine tief traditionelle Erscheinung der russischen Wissenschaft" (Jakobson, 1929: 53) do exist. "Russian theoretical thought has always been characterized by a number of specific tendencies'" (*ibid.*). These "tendencies" rely on a complete opposition to Western science:

"The general principles of research elaborated by Romano-Germanic scholarship cannot be mechanically transplanted to another soil" (*ibid.*: 66). He affirms "the inapplicability of the starting points of Western science to the treatment of other types of materials" (*ibid.*). He stands for "a revision of Russian folkloristics, renouncing uncontrolled transplantation of the practices of Western science", and Russian philological studies "can provide a certain fruitful corrective to the one-sided westernism of some Western Slavic scientific disciplines" (*ibid.*).

If Russian science is so specific, it is because Russia itself is a *world apart*:

> The historical unity and inseparability, the peculiarity and originality of this world appear ever more clearly in consciousness; the thesis arises more and more clearly: Russia is a specific geographical world. (*ibid.*: 53)

And this specific object of knowledge creates a specific point of view:

> The tendency for the avant-garde of Russian scientific thought was always decisive to encompass the entire Russian world at a glance and to consider the individual spatial and temporal expressions of this world from the perspective of this whole. (*ibid.*: 53)

Russia *is a structural object in itself*: "die Auffassung Rußlands als eines strukturalen Ganzen"; "Recent ethnographic studies (Zelenin, Trubetzkoy) reveal step by step the uniformity of the Eurasian cultural cycle and its differences from the cultures of other countries in the world"" (*ibid.*: 53).

---

2. "Über die heutigen Voraussetzungen der russischen Slavistik" (1929): "On the Present Presuppositions of Russian Slavic Studies", cited here after the 1988 reprint by E. Holenstein. All translations from German are mine, *PS*.

For Jakobson, Russian culture is a 'structural totality, a system of correlative series (which are to be explained in a non-genetic and non-causal, but functional way)", its history is a "nomogenesis",[3] an "immanent evolution conforming to laws", since nothing else could be expected from "the traditionally teleological attitude and structuralism of Russian science" (*ibid.*: 55, 56).

3. The enigma of similarity

This Russian science is characterized in the following way: "the category of mechanistic causality is alien to Russian science"; "The Russian milieu can be described as hostile to positivism"; "The aversion to positivism is characteristic of all expressions of life in Russian thought, as much for Dostoevsky as it is for Russian Marxism"; "Like a red thread runs through the Russian natural philosophy, the anti-Darwinist tendency"; "the harmonious doctrine of nomogenesis [is] permeated through and through by the idea of purposefulness (*Zielstrebigkeit*)"; "The following is characteristic of the fundamental, most peculiar line of Russian science, namely of today's science: the correlativity between individual series is not thought of in terms of causality: one series is not derived from the other; the basic picture with which science operates is a system of correlative series, an immanent structure to be considered, which is endowed with an internal law (*Gesetzmäßigkeit*)" (*ibid.*: 55, 56).

Jakobson eventually addresses the question of language by stressing an original feature of the linguistic situation in the Russian (called "Eurasian") world: "the structural commonality of the originally unrelated languages of Russia", "the symbiosis of the Russian language with neighboring offspring of other language families". This peculiar symbiosis between the Russian language and unrelated languages of the Soviet Union gives rise to the idea that "the genetic problem must give way to the functional problem" (*ibid.*: 66).

These numerous quotes from Jakobson were necessary to underscore my position: the specificities of Russian science called for by Jakobson find their source not in an epistemological universe apart from the Western one, but precisely in this latter, albeit in its claimed opposition to it. These peculiarities *are* interesting, as they enable us to see Western linguistics with the eyes of another ourselves, from "the other Europe".

What is at stake here is the following: if unrelated languages in the Soviet Union present similarities of structure, is this phenomenon due to pure chance or does it reveal a *hidden order*? This was the question raised by R. Jakobson and

3. On *nomogenesis* see the next section.

N. Trubetzkoy in their studies on the Eurasian union of languages (*die eurasische Sprachbund*).[4] And here comes an interesting moment in the history of linguistic typology. What is at stake is the enigma of similarity without a common ancestor, *i. e. without contact* in time.

In the interwar period Jakobson and Trubetzkoy refute the dominant paradigm which explains any similarity between phenomena only through descent from a common ancestor.

> The Mordovian and Russian phonological systems are so similar to each other that the Mordovians use the Russian alphabet for their language without any additions and changes, without experiencing the slightest difficulty.
> (Trubetzkoy, 1932 [1987: 63][5]

Precisely in the same period in the Soviet Union, all linguists who worked directly or indirectly with N. Marr were interested in analogies, comparisons, parallels, similitudes, links, convergences, and connections between objects and domains apparently distant in time and space, the same concern as Jakobson! Here and there the keyword is *uvjazka*: "link". Two outstanding women, Rozalia Shor (1894–1939) and Olga Frejdenberg, (1890–1955) tried to draw parallels between the mythical subjects of ancient India and those of medieval European literature. An inestimable linguist, Solomon Katsnelson (1907–1985), unfortunately totally unknown and not translated in the West, a pupil of N. Marr and I. Meshchaninov, laid the foundation of typological studies in the Soviet Union, on the principle of comparing linguistic structures independently from their genetic relationships. The object of knowledge became *type*, and not *class*:

> The doctrine of morphological classes of languages should now have given way to the doctrine of morphological types of languages. Classification was replaced by typology. (Katsnelson 1983 [2001: 735])

4. On this question see the following translations in English: Trubetzkoy 1991, Jakobson 2023, and also Sériot 2014.

5. Mordovian is a Finno-Ugric language, without any common origin with the Indo-European family.

4. On the sources of typology: Similarity without a common ancestor

In the 1930s Jakobson has an explicit target: "naturalism" in linguistics. What does that mean?

> The doctrine of Schleicher, the great naturalist in the field of linguistics, has been undermined for a long time, but one can still find many traces. (1938 [1971: 234])

> Is it necessary today to remind that language belongs to the social sciences, not to natural history? Is it not an obvious truism?. (*ibid.*)

Jakobson's target is "orthodox evolutionism":

> It is the tendency to explain the grammatical and phonetic similarities of two languages by their descent from a common ancestor-language, and to consider only the similarities which may be explained in such a way that remains without any doubt the most stable element of this doctrine. (*ibid.*)
> The similarity of structure is independent from the genetic relationship of the languages in question and can connect either the languages of the same origin or of different ancestry. (*ibid.*: 236)

Now, we can pose the problem in the following terms: what is the value, or the explanatory power of the resemblance of form? Does it rely on *chance?* on *cause?* on a *hidden plan?* or: why are similar things similar?

A way of tackling this puzzling question is a close reading of the way the so-called "bourgeois science" was presented in the Soviet Union in the 1920–1930s. Was it, strictly speaking, idealistic or materialistic?

A first step on the way of solving the problem in our linguistic field is the notably interesting paper which Ernst Cassirer (1874–1945) wrote in New-York a few days before he died (Cassirer, 1945). He drew attention to the striking similarity between the French naturalist Georges Cuvier (1769–1832) and Jakobson's and Trubetzkoy's structuralism. His argument relies on the common epistemological attitude they shared: the "law of correlation of the parts in a whole". What is true for the organs in their relation to the organism they belong to is also true for the phonemes inside the phonemic system of a given language. Willingly or not, Cassirer had the intuition that the implicit way of reasoning for Jakobson and Trubetzkoy was the very naturalistic model they explicitly refused.

We shall now go a little bit further.

The great German writer Goethe is known abroad mainly for his literary works. Nonetheless, he saw himself essentially as a scientist-naturalist (see Goethe, 1830). His anti-Newtonian *Farbenlehre* (Theory of colors) was for him more important than his *Die Leiden des jungen Werthers (The Sorrows of Young Werther).*

Goethe was a promoter of *idealistic morphology*, the main theses of which can be summarized as follows:

- two forms may be similar without any contact either in space or in time
- no similarity in form can be due to *chance*
- everything fragmentary is blameworthy.[6]

The consequence of these principles is that there exists a *hidden plan* to be discovered and exposed. I will try now to show how this idealistic morphology is a useful clue toward figuring out some features of Jakobson's work that distinguish him sharply from "classical" structuralism.

5. The theory of types

How can we explain and justify the similarity of objects which look like one another?

There are three main possibilities:

1. a common ancestor
2. teleological convergence
3. harmony and transcendence

Jakobson and Trubetzkoy chose the last two and rejected the first.

The reason, for them, is that similarity with a mechanical cause does exist but is *meaningless*. On the contrary, similarity of pure form, without any *contact* whether in time or space, means that there is a plan, a design, a hidden teleology which governs these correspondences of form.

Here we are confronted with an important and irreconcilable opposition between a positivist attitude, which considers that a similarity without contact does not have the slightest interest, and idealist morphology, which, on the contrary, strives to unmask the hidden reason of similarity.

The first approach, for instance, will not be interested in the phenomena of doppelgangers, these people who look like each other, without having a common origin: their resemblance is due to pure chance, therefore not bringing any information on the only issue which has a value for them: reconstructing the common origin. The French linguist Antoine Meillet, in his covert polemics against Jakobson, is a concrete example of this epistemological attitude:

6. "Alles Vereinzelte ist verwerflich", Goethe 1887: 108, cited after Nisbet 1972: 68.

> The classification according to the general traits of structure was found to be devoid of any practical or scientific usefulness; it is just a form of entertainment, of which no linguist could ever take advantage. (Meillet, 1921: 76–77)[7]

By contrast, the Soviet biologist Aleksandr Liubishchev (1890–1972), who during his whole life professed a very explicit Platonism without ever getting into political troubles, constantly maintained the opinion that no similarity of form can be due to chance: if frost flowers on a frozen window-pane look like tree leaves, if the form of a sea-shell resembles the form of a galaxy, all these phenomena can be summed up by a common reflection: *Eto ne sluchaino!* ["It is not by chance! "].[8]

In the 1920s Jakobson was deeply interested in a non-Darwinian biology which was becoming increasingly popular in the Soviet Union: the nomogenesis of L. Berg (1876–1950). Nomogenesis is a theory which claims that evolution is governed, determined and regulated by *laws* (in Greek: *nomos* = law); it is a variant of *orthogenesis*, a general view of biological evolution which rejects any randomness.

In a letter to V. Shklovsky dated February 26, 1929, Jakobson wrote: "I read Berg's book on nomogenesis with passionate interest. "[9] In later years he recommended this work to Noam Chomsky[10] several times.

In *Nomogenez*, published in 1922, Berg explicitly rejected Darwinian theory. Drawing support from Owen's theories, he emphasized the notion of *convergence*, i.e. the independent acquisition of similar characteristics by unrelated organisms.[11] But whereas Owen was trying to understand homologies, Berg overturned the value scale. The focus of his research was *analogies*, and he sought to show that in diametric opposition to Darwinian theory, evolution did not proceed by divergence from a common ancestor but rather by the convergence of unrelated organisms living in the same environmental conditions.

Another unforeseen source of Jakobson's ideas in the interwar period is the theory of types of N. Danilevsky (1822–1885) (see MacMaster, 1965). Danilevsky was an extreme nationalist and anti-Western thinker, both a historian and a biologist. He is known in Russian intellectual historiography for his book against Darwin (1885) and his book against Europe (1869). Both are extremely aggressive.

7. "Il [ce classement d'après les traits généraux de structure] s'est trouvé dénué de toute utilité soit pratique, soit scientifique; c'est une amusette dont aucun linguiste n'a pu tirer parti".

8. Liubishchev's works were reprinted by Y. Lotman in the Tartu semiotic journal *Trudy po znakovym sistemam* in 1977.

9. Letter published in Toman 1994: 61.

10. *Ibid.*: 23.

11. Berg 1922: 105.

Jakobson ranked Danilevsky among the "wonderful fruits" of Russian philosophy due to his anti-positivism (Jakobson 1929 [1988: 55]).

N. Danilevsky proposed a theory of *closed types*. In this domain, he followed very closely the French naturalist Georges Cuvier (1769–1832), who maintained that the living kingdom was divided into four *types* ("embranchements"), which are totally different from one another and impenetrable to one another.

This theory of closed types was important for Jakobson and Trubetzkoy, who used it in their linguistic work to prove that the Russian (or Eurasian) culture was totally alien to the European one. Thus, for Trubetzkoy there is a clear opposition between the continuous and the discontinuous in languages. We saw his claim that Russian and Mordovian, which are totally unrelated genetically, present a phonemic *continuity* (they belong to the *same type*), whereas Russian and Czech, linked by an obvious kinship, display a discontinuity (they are the members of two *different* phonemic types).

Goethe, the main representative of idealistic morphology, thought that all the plants go back by "metamorphosis" to an ideal, primordial proto-plant (*Urpflanze*), which is not a common ancestor, but an ideal prototype. Trubetzkoy and Jakobson share Goethe's concept of archetype, but they add to it the very different principle of closed type, borrowed from Cuvier.

6. Metaphor and metonymy

In our quest for the poorly known sources of Jakobson's way of thinking, another unexpected candidate appears: Paracelsus (1493–1541).

In the Renaissance, a way of curing headaches was to eat walnuts. What is the *link* between both? It is the *similarity* between the form of a walnut and the form of the human brain. If one thinks that no similarity of form is due to chance, then it is evident that there is something superior which links walnuts and the brain. This kind of medicine thus makes sense (and receives its delusional efficiency), provided that one admits the premise that form *is* a content. It is called *sympathetic medicine.*

My point is that Jakobson took this question of similarity of form very seriously. Let us take his well-known definition of poetry:

> The poetic function projects the principle of equivalence from the axes of selection to the axes of combination. (Jakobson 1960: 358)

In this very famous but very intriguing formula Jakobson stresses the very high role he assigns to similarities and contiguities in verbal art. A clue to understand this enigmatic formula is given surreptitiously by Jakobson in a paper from 1956 where he writes:

> The principles underlying magic rites have been resolved by Frazer into two types: charms based on the law of similarity and those founded on association by contiguity. [...] This bipartition is indeed illuminating.
> (Jakobson, 1956 [1971: 258])

What Jakobson found in the British anthropologist James Frazer (1854–1941) is the principle of *sympathetic magic* in primitive cultures, divided into magic by contact and magic by resemblance.

Here is the passage from Frazer's *The Golden Bough* which is decisive for our discussion:

> If we analyze the principles of thought on which magic is based, they will probably be found to resolve themselves into two: first, that like produces like, or that an effect resembles its cause; and second, that things which have once been in contact with each other continue to act on each other at a distance after the physical contact has been severed. The former principle may be called the Law of Similarity, the latter the Law of Contact or Contagion. From the first of these principles, namely the Law of Similarity, the magician infers that he can produce any effect he desires merely by imitating it: from the second he infers that whatever he does to a material object will affect equally the person with whom the object was once in contact, whether it formed part of his body or not. Charms based on the Law of Similarity may be called Homoeopathic or Imitative Magic. Charms based on the Law of Contact or Contagion may be called Contagious Magic. (J. Frazer, 1911: 52–53)

Little by little, we begin to piece together the parts of the puzzle:

> similarity → metaphor (syntagmatic axis)
> contiguity → metonymy (paradigmatic axis)

A next step in this reconstitution of the origins of Jakobson's ideas in the interwar period could be the *Naturphilosophie* of the first half of the 19th Century.

The notion of *function* was soon to emerge. It was on this basis that the British anatomist Richard Owen (1804–1892) developed the opposition between *homology* and *analogy* that from then on dominated comparative anatomy, especially after it was redefined in the theory of evolution.

In 1843 Owen systematized the *Naturphilosophie* opposition between *affinity* and *analogy,* except that the word *affinity* was replaced by *homology.* Organs or body parts that had the same *function* in different animals regardless of their origin (e.g., wings in birds and wings in insects) were *analogous* while organs of the same origin in different animals and regardless of form or function were *homologous* (e.g., birds' wings and whales' pectoral fins).

I wish to draw attention on the striking parallelism of argumentation in Jakobson and Richard Owen: the opposition between homology and analogy in the philosophy of nature in the middle of the 19th Century is used by Jakobson to support the idea of difference between language families and language unions.

In this regard, his booklet "K kharakteristike evraziiskogo iazykovogo soiuza" (1931) [For a characterization of the Eurasian language union] is of primordial importance.[12] The main idea of Jakobson is that language unions are more important, or more real, than language families in order to explain the existence of Eurasia. Jakobson goes further than Trubetzkoy. Thus, despite the obvious genetic link between Russian and Czech, these two languages belong to two completely different cultural worlds, and this difference is based on the fact that Czech does not have the hard/soft phonological correlation, whereas all the languages of Eurasia possess it. For him, it is also a way of contrasting Rumanian and Moldavian.

This opposition is reinforced by a fascination for symmetry. Here, like in Platonism, geometry is a means of interpreting geography. For him, symmetry lays in the idea of resemblance between edges or "peripheries". The *center* was a compact, continuous mass defined by a positive category: the phonemic softness of consonants, and a negative characteristic: the absence of polytony. So, it cannot be "by chance" that the Eurasian space is surrounded by two phonemic zones of polytony (the Baltic union in the North-West and the South-East union):

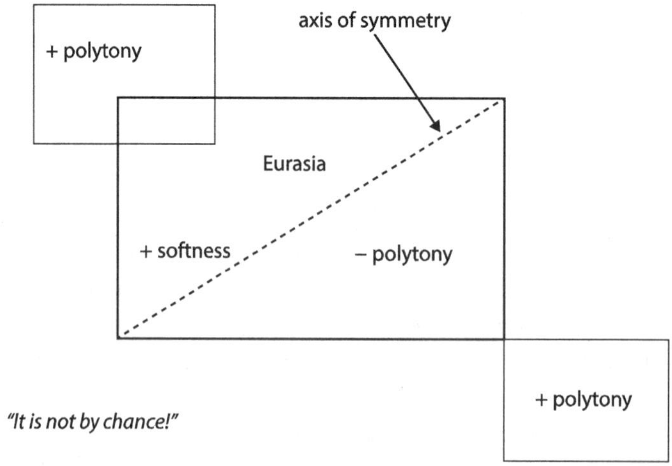

12. An English translation has just been published in McElvenny 2023: 159–204.

Another example of this overwhelming role of geometry and symmetry is Jakobson's interpretation of the place of the articles in Western European languages:

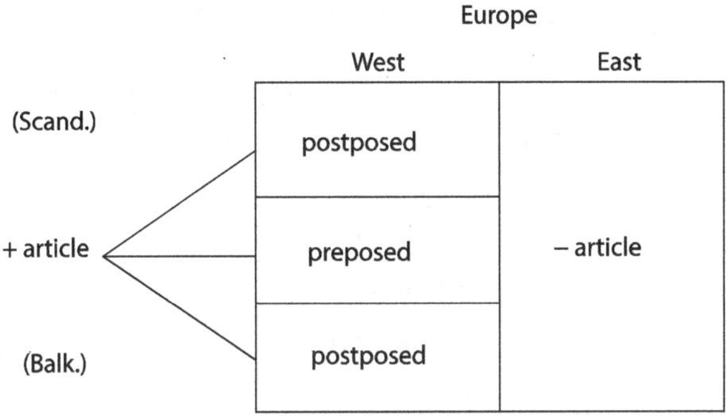

In order to link Jakobson's interest for symmetry with similarity, we have to turn now to Greek philosophy, more exactly to Empedocles' formula: τὸ ὅμοιον τοῦ ὁμοίου ἐφίεσθαι.

This formula receives different translations according to each language. In English it reads: *like is only known by like / like produces like.* But in French it is: *seul le semblable attire le semblable.* The Russian version is also different: *podobnoe stremitsja k podobnomu* ["like strives to like"]. I think a more or less adequate translation of ἐφίεσθαι would be "refers to", or "is linked to".

This philosophical principle leads to a dispute in physics in the 17–18th Centuries about "action at a distance". According to the concept of action at a distance, bodies act on each other with no material mediator, through the void, and at any distance. An example of a force considered as exerting a direct action at a distance is Newton's force of universal gravitation. On the contrary, in the conception of short-range interactions, they are transmitted only by special material intermediaries.

The subject of the dispute is contactless action. Jakobson transposes the dispute from physics to linguistics: action without a contact in space becomes for him similarity without a contact in time.

It is now possible to understand that Jakobson strove to build a synthesis, or an ambiguous mix between:

a. the Romantic values of the *Naturphilosophie*
   and
b. the principles of anti-positivistic and anti-Darwinian natural sciences.

His emphasis on *function* masks a fascination with the necessary relation *form / content,* which was the "mainstream" of Russian intellectual thought in the inter-war period (from Losev to Stalin through Marr). If *a form without content is not a form*, one understands the impossibility of the arbitrariness of the sign for Jakobson. In addition to quoting Joseph de Maistre – "Let us therefore never speak of chance and arbitrary signs"[13] – Jakobson relies heavily on the neo-Platonic principle of the *link*, which he calls *metod uvjazki* ("the linking method").

Thus, we can rebuild Jakobson's axiological scale of values:

– Metonymy	*+ Metaphor*
Horizontal axis	Vertical axis
Syntagmatical axis	Paradigmatical axis
Combination	Selection
Contiguity	Similarity
Prose	Poetry
Pasternak	Maiakovsky
Realism	Romanticism
Language family (Sprachfamilie)	Language union (Sprachbund)
Magic by contact	Magic by similarity
Divergence from a common ancestor	Convergence from a difference
Mechanics	Function
Causality	Goal
(Phylogenesis)	Nomogenesis
Randomness / Chance	Zakonomernost' (*Gesetzmäßigkeit*)
Chaos	Order

We can now conclude this long story. The basis of Jakobson's unity of thought in the 1920–1930s is the idea of *contactless likeness*:

- cause is replaced by purpose
  therefore language unions are more real than language families
- magic by similarity underlies the metaphor
  therefore contactless links are more important than "mechanical" links.

13. De Maistre 1821 [1980: 103]. Jakobson frequently cited this line from *Les Soirées de Saint-Pétersbourg* in his 1930s writings, and he came back to it in the *Dialogues with K. Pomorska* at the end of his life (1983: 88).

The general premise is that any form of similarity is significant.

The texts by Jakobson in the interwar period are at the crossroads: they are both echoes of an anti-Darwinian biology and an attempt at synthetizing the idealistic morphology of German romanticism with Neo-Platonism.

As far as linguistics is concerned, Russia is not another planet, linguistics in Russia is deeply rooted in the European cultural world, which could greatly benefit from a thorough comparison with this other ourselves: the Eastern part of the West.

References

Berezin, Fedor M. 1976. *Russkoe iazykoznanie kontsa XIX – nachala XX v.* [*Russian linguistics of the late XIX – early XX century*]. Moskva: Nauka.

Berg Lev. 1922. *Nomogenez, ili èvoliuciia na osnove zakonomernostei*, Petrograd: Gosudarstvennoe izdatel'stvo. English translation: *Nomogenesis, or evolution determined by law*, London, 1926.

Cassirer Ernst. 1945. "Structuralism in modern linguistics", *Word*, vol. 1, n°2: 99–120.

Danilevsky, Nikolai. 1869. *Rossiia i Evropa, Vzgliad na kul'turnye i politicheskie otnosheniia slavianskogo mira k germano-romanskomu* [*Russia and Europe: a view of cultural and political relations between the Slavic and Germano-Roman worlds*]. Sankt Peterburg: Tipografiia bratiev Panteleevykh.

Danilevsky, Nikolai. 1885. *Darvinizm: kriticheskoe izsledovanie* [*Darwinism: a critical study*], 2 vols. Sankt Peterburg: Komarov.

Frazer, James G. 1911. *The Golden Bough*, vol. I, London: MacMilan.

Garvin, Paul; Lunt, Horace & Stankiewicz Edward. 1963 (19802). *Current Trends in Linguistics. Vol. I: Soviet and East European Linguistics.* The Hague; Paris & New York: Mouton.

Goethe Johann Wolfgang. 1830. "Principes de philosophie zoologique", *Schriften zur Anatomie, Zoologie, Physiognomik.* Reprint 1962. München: dtv: 151–178.

Goethe Johann Wolfgang. 1887. *Goethes Werke*, vol. I, Weimar: Weimarer Ausgabe.

Jakobson, Roman. 1929. "Über die heutigen Voraussetzungen der russischen Slavistik", *Slavische Rundschau*, 1: 629–646. Reprint in Elmar Holenstein (ed.): *Roman Jakobson. Semiotik. Ausgewählte Texte 1919–1982*, Frankfurt a/M: Suhrkamp, 1992: 50–70.

Jakobson, Roman. 1931. *"K kharakteristike evraziiskogo iazykovogo soiuza"*, Paris: Evraziiskoe izdatel'stvo. English transl. 2023. "The Eurasian language union", *The Limits of Structuralism*, J. McElveny (ed.), Oxford: Oxford University Press: 159–204.

Jakobson, Roman. 1938. "Sur la théorie des affinités phonologiques entre les langues", *Actes du IVe Congrès international des linguistes tenu à Copenhague du 27 août au 1er septembre 1936*, Copenhague: Einar Munskgaard: 48–58; reprinted in a modified version in Jakobson, 1971: 234–246.

Jakobson, Roman. 1956. "Two aspects of language and two types of aphasic disturbances", *Fundamentals of Language*, The Hague: Mouton: 55–82; reprinted in Jakobson, 1971: 237–259.

Jakobson, Roman. 1960. “Linguistics and Poetics”, in *Style in Language*, edited by T. Sebeok. Cambridge MA: MIT Press: 350–377.

Jakobson, Roman. 1971: *Selected Writings*, II, The Hague: Mouton.

Jakobson, Roman & Pomorska Krystyna. 1983. *Dialogues*. Harvard: Cambridge Univ. Press.

Katsnelson, Solomon. 1983. “Lingvisticheskaja tipologiia” [Linguistic typology], *Voprosy iazykoznaniia* 3: 9–20; 4: 19–34. Reprint in Katsnelson, S. 2001. *Kategorii iazyka i myshlenia* [*The Categories of Language and Thought*]. Moskva: Iazyki slavianskoi kultury: 713–755.

Kolesov, Vladimir. 1991. “Razvitie lingvisticheskikh idei u vostochnykh slavian epokhi Srednevekoviia” [The development of linguistic ideas among the Eastern Slavs in the Middle Ages]. *Istoria lingvisticheskikh uchenii. Pozdnee Srednevekovie* [*History of linguistic theories. Late Middle Ages*], edited by A. Desnickaia. Sankt-Peterburg: Nauka: 208–254.

Lepschy, Giulio. 1990. *Storia della linguistica*, vol I. Bologna: Il Mulino.

Liubishchev, Aleksandr. 1977. “Ponjatie sistemnosti i organizovannosti (predvaritel’nyj nabrosok)” [The concept of consistency and organization (preliminary outline)], *Trudy po znakovym sistemam*, 9: 134–141.

MacMaster, Robert. 1965. *Danilevsky: A Totalitarian Philosopher*. Harvard: Harvard University Press.

Maistre de, Joseph. 1821. *Les soirées de Saint-Pétersbourg*. Reprint 1980: Paris: Ed. de la Maisnie.

McElvenny James (ed.). 2023. *The Limits of Structuralism. Forgotter Sources in the History of Modern Linguistics*, Oxford: Oxford University Press.

Meillet, Antoine. 1921. “Le problème de la parenté des langues”, in Id. *Linguistique historique et linguistique générale*. Paris: Champion: 76–101.

Nisbet H. B. 1972. *Goethe and the Scientific Tradition*, University of London, Institute of Germanic Studies.

Picchio, Ricardo. 1972. *Studi sulla questione della lingua presso gli Slavi*. Roma: Ateneo.

Serdiuchenko, Georgii. 1931: “Staroe i novoe v nauke o jazyke” [The old and the new in the science of language], *Na podieme*, 4: 156–175.

Sériot, Patrick. 2014. *Structure and the Whole. East, West and non-Darwinian Biology in the Origins of Structural Linguistics*. Boston & Berlin: Walter de Gruyter.

Toman, Jindřich, ed. 1994. *Letters and Other Materials from the Moscow and Prague Linguistic Circles*, 1912–1945. Ann Arbor: Michigan Slavic Publications / Cahiers Roman Jakobson 1.

Trubetzkoy, Nikolai. 1932. “Das Morwinische phonologische System verglichen mit dem Russischen”, in *Charisteria Guilelmo V. Methesio quinquagenario a discipulis et Circuli Linguistici oblata*, Prague: svmptibvs “Pražský linguistický kroužek”, 21–24. Reprint in Russian translation: N. S. Trubetzkoi. *Izbrannye trudy po fonologii* [*Selected works on Phonemics*]. Moskva: Progress, 1987: 63–66.

Trubetzkoy, Nikolai. 1991. *The Legacy of Genghis Khan and Other Essays on Russia’s Identity*, Anatoly Liberman (ed.). Ann Arbor: Michigan Slavic Publications.

CHAPTER 3

Le futur antérieur des linguistes (fin 19e–début 20e siècle)

Dan Savatovsky
Université Sorbonne Nouvelle | UMR CNRS 7597 *Histoire des théories linguistiques*

Cette contribution porte sur la notion de *projection disciplinaire*, en vigueur en histoire/épistémologie de la linguistique. On s'attache d'abord à la distinguer des notions de *prévision*, *prédiction* et *accommodation* (cf. Horkheimer, Hempel et/ou Popper). On montre que la projection implique la linguistique comme *discipline* et pas seulement comme savoir. Puis on cherche à comprendre ce que Saussure entendait par "la tâche" à réaliser en linguistique (*Cours de linguistique générale*, chapitre II). On s'intéresse enfin au corpus constitué par les *Actes* des cinq premières sessions du Congrès international de linguistes (1928–1939) pour rendre compte de la manière dont ceux-ci ont conçu les développements à venir de leur discipline, s'agissant notamment des échanges et de la délimitation des frontières avec les disciplines connexes ; des interventions dans le champ de la politique de la langue ; de l'adoption de méthodologies communes dans l'enquête linguistique et l'exposé de ses résultats.

Mots clés : horizon de projection disciplinaire, prédiction, prévision, accommodation en linguistique, Congrès international de linguistes (1928–1939)

1. Introduction

À l'ère du savoir positif, s'attacher à définir l'*horizon projectif* ou *prospectif* d'une discipline scientifique conduit à raisonner en termes de *programme(s)*, une approche fréquente dans les écrits de linguistique générale parus à la fin du dix-neuvième et dans la première moitié du vingtième siècle – période à laquelle cet article est plus particulièrement consacré. Un mot revient souvent alors: celui de "tâche(s)" à réaliser. On trouve l'un de ses emplois les plus connus dans le chapitre II du *Cours de linguistique générale* (= CLG), qui a pour titre "La tâche de la linguistique". Je m'y attarderai un instant, notamment pour faire un sort à ce singulier (*la* tâche) – qui est en effet assez singulier.

https://doi.org/10.1075/sihols.133.03sav

Au-delà de Saussure, des linguistes de renom se sont employés, à la même époque et dans la même configuration épistémique – celle d'une réflexion sur la manière de concevoir la *généralité* en linguistique – à prévoir, anticiper, programmer, bref à *projeter* son développement en termes de "tâche(s)" à entreprendre. Contentons-nous ici d'énumérer quelques-uns de leurs noms : Jan Baudouin de Courtenay (1963 [1889]), Victor Henry (1896), Albert Sechehaye (1908), Otto Jespersen (1922), Joseph Vendryes (1933), Leonard Bloomfield (1933).

Après avoir tenté de cerner les notions de *projection disciplinaire* et *d'horizon de projection*, j'en viendrai à un exemple : de quelle manière les participants au Congrès international des linguistes – instance collective – ont cherché à leur tour à tracer le devenir de leur discipline. Je me restreindrai aux cinq premières sessions de ce Congrès, organisées tous les deux ou trois ans jusqu'à la Seconde Guerre mondiale, depuis celle de La Haye (1928), jusqu'à celle de Bruxelles – prévue pour septembre 1939 et qui n'a pas pu se tenir, on imagine pourquoi (mais dont préparatoires ont été publiés) – en passant par les sessions de Genève (1931), Rome (1933) et Copenhague (1936).

2. Prédiction, accommodation, prévision et projection

Quelques éclaircissements de nature terminologique, pour commencer. L'expression *horizon de projection* est empruntée au lexique de la géographie, où elle désigne l'aire de validité d'une représentation cartographique. La philosophie des sciences a retenu certains traits de cette origine : la projection, telle qu'on l'entend dans ce domaine, est à la fois un dessin et un dessein. En usant d'une métaphore spatiale, on vise à montrer comment une discipline se figure son déploiement temporel, comment elle tente de planifier, de cartographier ses propres contours (ses frontières internes ou externes), ses lignes de force, ses terrains à défricher, ses points aveugles, etc. Et, en même temps, on conçoit ce déploiement comme un projet concerté et délibéré : le projet d'une communauté professionnelle qui se dote d'institutions (chaires, revues, sociétés savantes, congrès...) permettant de le mettre en œuvre grâce au cumul des connaissances dans des cadres théoriques relativement stables (ceux d'une science "normale"), grâce aussi à l'enseignement et à la diffusion de ces connaissances.

En quoi une projection se distingue-t-elle d'une *prévision*, d'une *prédiction* et d'une *accommodation* ? Dans la philosophie des sciences exactes, c'est surtout le couple formé par ces deux dernières notions qui a prévalu, notamment chez Popper (1963) et Hempel (1966) : si un phénomène est connu avant la formulation de la théorie qui en rend compte, alors cette théorie accommode le phénomène ;

si le phénomène n'est observé qu'après la formulation de la théorie à partir de laquelle on l'infère, alors la théorie le prédit.

À la différence d'une accommodation, une prédiction est donc la conséquence empirique d'une théorie, qui n'a pas encore pu subir l'épreuve de la falsification quand cette théorie a été construite. On dit d'une théorie qu'elle est bonne lorsqu'elle est consistante et qu'elle est dotée d'une grande puissance prédictive.[1] Ainsi, Newton a prédit le retour de la comète de Halley, Einstein la courbure des rayons lumineux par le soleil, etc. L'histoire des réussites scientifiques serait alors l'histoire des prédictions qui se réalisent. Les exemples que je viens de donner, qui sont parmi le plus souvent cités, proviennent de l'astronomie et de la physique ; quel en serait l'analogue dans les sciences humaines, en particulier dans les sciences du langage ? Ce qui pourrait équivaloir à la prédiction telle qu'on la conçoit dans les sciences exactes répond à trois cas de figure :

(1) un phénomène non observable, faute de données, un fait de langue non attesté, mais dont l'existence est hypothétiquement requise pour rendre compte de certains observables : la théorie des laryngales établie par Saussure dans son *Mémoire* de 1879 – c'est un cas bien documenté – présuppose ce type de phénomènes. Il faut attendre 1927 pour que Kuryłowicz vérifie que le hittite, déchiffré pour la première fois en 1915 par l'orientaliste Hrozný, avait conservé ḫ comme trace des phonèmes $*h_2$ et $*h_3$. Il s'agit là d'un hapax : le hittite est la seule langue indoeuropéenne ayant gardé une pareille trace de laryngales. On peut donc bien considérer l'existence d'une langue telle que le hittite comme étant, chez Saussure, de l'ordre de la prédiction.

(2) Deuxième cas de figure : la prédiction caractérise une loi permettant de déduire des changements qui ont affecté une langue donnée ceux qui se produiront dans son évolution future. Cette loi peut être de type probabilitaire. Elle portera alors sur un niveau donné de l'analyse linguistique. Ainsi, dans la linguistique contemporaine, la variation diachronique fait l'objet d'une approche statistique, fondée sur une modélisation bayésienne, c'est-à-dire sur une méthode d'inférence permettant de calculer la probabilité d'un changement à partir de l'observation d'événements linguistiques connus. Cette modélisation a été principalement mise à contribution dans le domaine de la morphologie. Mais, en droit, elle peut aussi porter sur d'autres niveaux d'analyse d'une langue donnée.

1. Ces deux traits ont été dégagés par le positivisme : "[l]a perfection spéculative d'une science quelconque doit se mesurer essentiellement par ces deux considérations principales : la coordination plus ou moins complète et la prévision plus ou moins exacte. Ce dernier caractère nous offre surtout le criterium le plus clair et le plus décisif comme se rapportant directement au but final de toute science." (Comte 2014 [1835]: 332) "Axiome fondamental : *toute science a pour but la prévoyance*, qui distingue la science réelle de la simple érudition, bornée à raconter les événements accomplis, sans aucune vue d'avenir." (*Ibid.* : 28).

Il en va ainsi également des langues artificielles. Pour les linguistes partisans de la création d'une langue internationale auxiliaire (Baudouin de Courtenay, Schuchardt, Jespersen…), les langues modernes "analytiques" représentent un moment supérieur de l'expression linguistique parce que la morphologie y est simplifiée (ce qui renforce la tendance à l'économie des moyens), que la syntaxe y est plus régulière, que l'ordre des mots y est fixe. Ces tendances une fois identifiées, il est possible de les mener à leur terme. L'évolution des langues n'est pas promise à la dégénérescence et à la dialectalisation tendancielle, comme le pensaient les premiers comparatistes. Elle peut être imaginée, programmée, planifiée,[2] comme un progrès qu'une langue internationale conçue comme la langue la mieux aboutie viendrait consacrer, après qu'on en aurait explicité et régularisé les facteurs. À ces conditions, les projets de création d'une langue internationale sont bien des projections de type prédictif relevant d'une politique de la langue et peuvent faire partie des tâches de la linguistique.

(3) La prédiction en linguistique peut enfin correspondre à une règle de généralisation permettant de calculer la productivité d'un phénomène d'après une procédure récursive. C'est le cas chez Chomsky : une grammaire générative est un ensemble de règles à partir desquelles on doit pouvoir engendrer toutes les phrases des langues naturelles, dispositif comparable à la capacité prédictive d'un système hypothético-déductif dans les sciences exactes.[3]

On pourrait objecter que les exemples ici donnés relèvent des *théories* linguistiques et non de leur épistémologie, qu'elles ont trait aux faits empiriques que ces théories ont pour fonction d'ordonner et d'expliquer, et nullement à leur histoire — domaine auquel la notion d'horizon de projection appartient au premier chef ; qu'ils n'appartiennent donc pas au domaine de la linguistique *générale*, pour en rester à la problématique des "tâches" à prévoir, telles que les envisageaient les linguistes au tournant du 20e siècle. Mais précisément : nous pouvons ici poser que la capacité d'un linguiste de cette époque (de toute époque ?) à se projeter dans l'avenir est le plus souvent pensée par lui comme étant le redoublement réflexif de la puissance prédictive des théories qu'il élabore.

C'est pourquoi, pour plus de clarté, il convient d'associer au couple prédiction / accommodation un second couple notionnel que j'emprunte à Max Horkheimer : la prédiction (*Voraussage* ou *Vorhersage*), qui se rapporte à des événements

2. En allemand, on parle de *Plansprachen*, en anglais de *language planning*.

3. À cette réserve près que, comme les autres sciences humaines et à la différence des sciences de la nature, la linguistique, bien que réputée "science galiléenne" par certains linguistes d'obédience chomskyenne, comme Jean-Claude Milner (1989: *passim*), ne peut pas expérimenter, c'est-à-dire isoler les phénomènes étudiés en vue de les soumettre à la falsification, ce qui restreint la valeur prédictive de leur explication.

ou à des faits, est à dissocier de la *prévision* (*Vorausicht*), qui se rapporte à des modèles abstraits (*Typen*), c'est-à-dire à des lois dont on peut inférer des hypothèses. La prévision détient une forme conditionnelle : lorsque certaines conditions déterminées sont données, certains événements déterminés doivent se produire. L'approche d'Horkheimer a trait à la sociologie et, bien entendu, se pose la question de savoir si elle peut s'étendre à d'autres *Geisteswissenschaften*, comme les sciences du langage. "[L]a possibilité de prévoir est, pour toute science, la pierre de touche du vrai [*Wirklichen*]" (Horkheimer 1933: 407) dans la mesure où elle s'inscrit toujours dans un espace-temps déterminé : on prévoit des événements. La dimension temporelle est ici fondamentale ; c'est de son inscription dans une histoire que la prévision tire son efficace. Or cette temporalité est bidimensionnelle: une prévision ne se transforme en prédiction que parce qu'il y a eu saisie rétrospective au préalable. "Le sens des propositions abstraites doit s'accomplir en des propositions concrètes et celui de chaque *prévision* en des *prédictions*.[4] Si la signification des abstractions n'est pas elle-même contrôlée par une application pratique continue et modifiée selon les circonstances, elles doivent nécessairement devenir étrangères à la réalité et finalement devenir non seulement inutiles, mais même fausses" (*Ibid.* : 409–410). Horkheimer rejoint ici Hempel : certes, les lois scientifiques rendent compte de phénomènes attestés – distincts à ce titre des phénomènes prédictibles – mais les deux types de phénomènes sont structurellement identiques et logiquement équivalents.

Même si tous ces cas, on le voit, ont trait au plan des phénomènes eux-mêmes et à leur rapport avec les théories qui les prédisent ou qu'ils accommodent, s'ils n'ont trait que médiatement aux domaines de recherche, c'est-à-dire au plan métadiscursif auquel renvoie aussi la notion d'horizon de projection, il y a donc isomorphisme entre les deux plans. Cette notion implique non pas, de manière directe, les faits de langue dans leurs rapports avec les théories, mais la linguistique comme *discipline*, pas seulement comme savoir – on y reviendra.

3. La *tâche* de la linguistique

Dans quelle mesure la projection disciplinaire correspond-elle alors à la *tâche* programmée par Saussure ? Il faut s'attarder ici sur le second chapitre du CLG, c'est-à-dire sur la leçon d'ouverture du 3e cours (28 octobre 1910):

4. *Prévision* et *prédictions* sont ici en français dans le texte.

> La tâche de la linguistique sera :
>
> a. de faire la description et l'histoire de toutes les langues qu'elle pourra atteindre, ce qui revient à faire l'histoire des familles de langues et à reconstituer dans la mesure du possible les langues mères de chaque famille ;
> b. de chercher les forces qui sont en jeu d'une manière permanente et universelle dans toutes les langues, et de dégager les lois générales auxquelles on peut ramener tous les phénomènes particuliers de l'histoire ;
> c. de se délimiter et de se définir elle-même.[5] (Sausssure 1968–1974, p. 99)

La tâche unique, mais qui se décline en trois volets (ces volets sont donc intimement imbriqués), cette tâche est singulière à plus d'un titre et pas seulement parce que le mot est employé au singulier dans l'intitulé du chapitre.[6] Qu'est-ce donc que cet avenir imaginé par Saussure, cette organisation prévisionnelle, sinon la continuation du programme déjà en grande partie réalisé, celui de la grammaire comparée du 19e siècle ? En imaginant ainsi le "devant-soi" de la discipline, Saussure récapitule pour les extrapoler les trois grandes étapes de son développement révolu :

i. poursuivre et mener à son terme ce que les comparatistes de la première génération (Bopp, Rask ou Grimm) ont envisagé pour la famille indoeuropéenne, mais à l'échelle de toutes les familles de langues : "reconstituer" leur langue mère (généralisation typologique) ;

5. D'après les notes de cours de Constantin, Saussure se pose la question de savoir ce que la linguistique "a devant soi : 1° comme matière 2° comme objet ou tâche [?]. 1°) une étude scientifique aura pour matière toute espèce de modification du langage humain [...]. 2°) La matière, la tâche ou l'étude scientifique des langues, ce sera si possible <1°)> faire l'histoire de toutes les langues connues (...). Mais en second lieu <2°)>, ce qui est fort différent, il faudra que de cette histoire de toutes les langues elles-mêmes se dégagent les lois les plus générales (...)". (Saussure & Constantin 2005, Cahier I : 85)

6. Il convient cependant de noter qu'ailleurs Saussure use du pluriel, distinguant *la* tâche, quand il s'agit de la linguistique en tant que telle, *des* tâches dès lors qu'il faut examiner dans une acception *plus spéciale* ses rapports avec les sciences connexes (correspondant au troisième volet dans le CLG). "Il y a des tâches plus spéciales qu'on pourrait rattacher, elles concernent les rapports que la linguistique pourrait avoir vis-à-vis de certaines sciences. Les unes sont en rapport pour lui emprunter des renseignements, des données, et les autres, au contraire, pour lui en fournir et l'aider dans sa tâche. Il arrive souvent que le domaine respectif de deux sciences n'apparaît pas avec une grande clarté dès le premier moment ; en tout premier lieu, il faut citer les rapports entre la linguistique et la psychologie – qui sont souvent difficiles à délimiter. C'est une des tâches de la linguistique de se définir, de reconnaître ce qui est de son domaine. Dans les cas où elle dépendra de la psychologie, elle en dépendra indirectement, elle restera indépendante." (Saussure & Constantin, *ibid.*: 3–4).

ii. poursuivre le programme de la seconde génération (Schleicher) : "dégager les lois générales auxquelles on peut ramener tous les phénomènes particuliers de l'histoire" des langues. Cette généralité des lois permet de ranger la discipline – dans certains de ses domaines du moins, comme la phonétique – parmi les sciences de la nature (généralisation régulatrice) ;
iii. respecter les lois de limitation (au sens de Kant) ou de prohibition édictées par les comparatistes de la troisième génération – les néogrammairiens, dont Saussure lui-même fait partie : "se délimiter (et se définir) elle-même". Cela suppose notamment qu'on assigne la place de la linguistique parmi les autres sciences,[7] qu'on l'inscrive ainsi dans une taxinomie disciplinaire. Les thèmes prohibés, comme celui de l'origine du langage, ne sont pas interdits à d'autres types de recherches, celles de la psychologie ou de la physiologie, comme V. Henry (1896: 48) l'avait souligné. Mais le respect des lois de limitation vaut aussi comme principe empirique ; il revient à s'interdire toute assomption ontologique, toute hypothèse réaliste, toute "restitution" dans les reconstructions de formes indoeuropéennes : "on ne restitue pas l'indo-européen"[8] (généralisation méthodologique).

Aucune perspective nouvelle ? Pas vraiment, en réalité, dans la mesure où

iv. il est question d'étendre les postulats de la grammaire historico-comparative à toutes les langues "qu'on pourra atteindre" : c'est la première acception de la *généralité* de la linguistique – premier volet ;
v. en matière de "lois générales", il s'agira d'identifier les "forces" qui sont en jeu "de manière universelle et permanente dans toutes les langues", c'est-à-dire de passer d'une conception *mécanique* de la légalité aveugle (l'*Ausnahmlosigkeit* des lois phonétiques) à une conception *dynamique* (les *forces* qui *expliquent* le changement linguistique, et pas seulement les mécanismes qui les *décrivent*) – second volet.

Ces deux premiers volets de la tâche tripartite assignée par Saussure sont, on le voit, de l'ordre de l'accommodation. Seul le dernier volet correspondrait donc à une *projection*, telle qu'on vient de tenter d'en circonscrire la notion : il s'agit pour la linguistique de "se définir elle-même". Parler d'horizon de projection, ce n'est donc plus la considérer comme un domaine empirique (les phénomènes) ou théorique, mais comme une entité disciplinaire.

7. Clairement indiquée dans son titre complet : "Matière et tâche de la linguistique ; ses rapports avec les sciences connexes."

8. Meillet, 1903: 26. Comme pour Henry, et conformément aux principes du criticisme kantien auxquels répondent les lois de limitation, l'irrestituable indoeuropéen doit être pensé comme une chose-en-soi, un objet transcendantal (voir Savatovsky 2004).

Ce n'est pas ici le lieu d'énumérer tous les traits qui distinguent la notion de science de celle de discipline, qui permettent de considérer un savoir comme une discipline.[9] Je n'en retiendrai qu'un : l'organisation de la communauté des savants, le partage international du travail au sein de cette communauté, un partage qui s'opère en linguistique à partir de la fin des années 1920 dans le cadre du Congrès international et du Comité International Permanent des Linguistes [= CIPL], chargé du suivi des résolutions adoptées lors de chacune des sessions du Congrès et de la préparation de la suivante.

4. Le congrès international de linguistes

Un mot d'abord de la première session, à la préparation de laquelle Meillet a pris une part importante. Si le programme de travail à prévoir par le Congrès relève de la constitution de la science en discipline, l'idée de discipline est ici associée à celle d'une certaine clôture de la science à un moment donné de son développement, souvent conçue comme un aboutissement lié à l'exhaustivité des phénomènes étudiés et des résultats obtenus. On la trouvait ainsi exprimée chez Meillet dès son premier ouvrage de synthèse, vingt ans auparavant:

> Il n'y a pas de langue, attestée à date ancienne ou récente, qui puisse être ajoutée au groupe indo-européen ; il ne vient plus à la grammaire comparée des langues indo-européennes de matériaux vraiment neufs. (Meillet 1903: 411)

Dans cette première acception, parler d'horizon de projection consiste alors à inscrire les tâches assignées à la communauté savante dans des cadres conceptuels et empiriques prédéfinis et relativement rigides.

C'est en effet le cas dans l'esprit de Meillet : le congrès de La Haye devait être à ses yeux "un congrès non d'exposition de résultats partiels mais d'organisation du travail commun" (1927: xl), en matière de géographie linguistique tout spécialement. Exigence d'autant plus forte qu'il s'agissait de faire progresser un chantier qu'il avait ouvert lui-même juste avant la Grande Guerre, rouvert après 1918, et qui avait débouché sur une importante publication collective, *Les langues du monde* (Meillet & Cohen (dir.), 1924). Un chantier qu'il fallait poursuivre, qui exigeait pour cela la mobilisation d'un grand nombre d'autres linguistes "de terrain" et – en termes d'ouverture des frontières disciplinaires – la collaboration des linguistes et des ethnographes. La Société de linguistique de Paris avait déjà accueilli plusieurs d'entre eux en son sein, notamment Paul Rivet, l'un des pionniers en France de la linguistique amérindienne, qui avait participé à l'entreprise

9. Voir Savatovsky 2021.

des *Langues du monde*. Toutes les sessions du Congrès international de linguistes antérieures à la seconde guerre mondiale reviendront sur cet objectif, notamment à travers la question de la *fiche* qui occupera une partie des discussions – question de la standardisation des méthodes d'enquête, question même de la réorientation de l'investigation linguistique comme travail "de terrain". Question où, à nouveau, la projection disciplinaire exige ou entraîne une rétrospection à nouveaux frais, un retour à la fois sur les conditions les plus anciennes dans lesquelles le comparatisme s'est constitué et sur le nouveau regard que la description des langues du monde a permis de porter sur la description des langues indoeuropéennes.[10]

L'autre projection qui transparait dans les documents préparatoires au congrès de Genève (1931) touche à la discipline elle-même, à sa "définition" (pour reprendre l'expression de Saussure), c'est-à-dire à son autonomie par rapport aux disciplines connexes et aux échanges qu'elle peut avoir avec elles. D'où le bilan de la session de 1928 dressé par le comité d'organisation de la future session de 1931 : "pour la première fois, des linguistes ont pu débattre en commun des questions de linguistique sans se couvrir de l'autorité des philologues classiques, des néo-philologues ou des orientalistes. Par là, ils ont affirmé l'autonomie que leur science avait depuis longtemps acquise de droit." (*Actes du 1er Congrès…*, s. d.: 10).

D'autre part, il convient de distinguer entre les questions susceptibles d'être abordées par le Congrès et celles que les organisateurs identifient comme "techniques" et qui feront l'objet de simples "vœux".

> Les questions purement techniques ne peuvent – cela va sans dire – être tranchées dans le Congrès lui-même. Mais son intervention dans ce domaine n'en est pas moins très efficace. Il peut émettre des vœux, contrôler ou sanctionner les propositions émises par des experts, nommer des commissions chargées de poursuivre les questions amorcées. Ainsi le Congrès de Genève entendra et discutera des rapports exécutés par le CIPL, conformément aux décisions prises à La Haye.
> (*Actes du 2e Congrès…*, 1933: 10)

Il convient aussi de différencier les tâches à programmer à court terme et celles qu'il faut projeter à long terme. À court terme, on trouve les questions vives qui feront l'objet d'appels à communications en vue des sessions suivantes. Ainsi, à Genève (1931), une "large place [aura été accordée] à la linguistique générale. C'est aux congrès spéciaux (de romanistes, de slavistes, de phonéticiens, etc.) d'aborder des sujets qui relèvent uniquement de telle discipline particulière." (*Actes du 2e Congrès…* 1933: 9). À plus long terme, un des rôles de la projection est de réaffirmer ou redessiner l'architecture générale de la discipline, ses rapports avec d'autres disciplines, etc.

10. Comme Benveniste le montrera *ex post* (1966: 6).

Enfin, la préparation de chaque session aura fait l'objet d'un questionnaire adressé à tous les participants, avec notamment trois questions d'ordre général, dont certaines sont formulées *ne varietur* d'une session à l'autre et auxquelles ils auront largement répondu :

- Quelles suggestions seraient à faire sur "l'organisation du travail linguistique, sa technique, son outillage? [...], sur la manière de recueillir, d'enregistrer et de classer les matériaux, sur la terminologie, la bibliographie, les publications à entreprendre, etc."
- Quel rôle attribuer, "dans le devenir et l'évolution des langues (en particulier dans la constitution des langues unifiées), d'une part aux phénomènes spontanés et à l'inconscient et, de l'autre, aux interventions de la volonté et de la réflexion? Subsidiairement, que pensez-vous de l'adoption d'une langue artificielle comme langue auxiliaire ?"
- Enfin, il est question de la manière d'articuler la description de chaque niveau d'analyse linguistique avec celle des autres niveaux. Ainsi : "les systèmes phonologiques envisagés en eux-mêmes et dans leurs rapports avec la structure générale de la langue."

Mais la lecture des actes du Congrès, d'une session à l'autre, tout au long de cette dizaine d'années d'avant-guerre montre aussi que certaines de ces questions ne trouvent pas de réponse. La projection est alors aporétique. C'est ainsi le cas de celles qui portent sur la *Schallanalyse*[11] ou sur les expériences de terrain du dialectologue.

Pour résumer, de manière longitudinale (d'une session à l'autre), il apparaît que, conformément aux préconisations initiales de Meillet, les problèmes de méthode prévaudront sur la divulgation des résultats empiriques (lesquels doivent être réservés prioritairement aux revues). Cette exigence est réitérée dans la préparation des sessions suivantes: "[é]tant donné que dans un congrès scientifique international, la science qui se fait doit primer la science acquise et que, d'autre part, il s'agit de rendre plus intime la collaboration entre spécialités trop isolées les unes des autres, [il faut] choisir des sujets qui comportent une démonstration ou discussion de méthode ou qui se prêtent à un commentaire méthodologique." (*Actes du 4e Congrès...*, 1938: 9). On sait bien que cela n'a pas toujours été le cas, comme l'atteste la présentation de résultats nouveaux et prometteurs par les phonologues pragois en 1928, mais cette visée méthodologique a dans l'ensemble prévalu, ce que montrent les projets d'unification de la terminologie linguistique[12] ou de création d'une notation phonétique standardisée.

11. Qui marque le "tournant mélodique" de l'analyse du son. Voir Sievers (1924).

12. Voir Chevalier 2001.

Parmi ces problèmes de méthode, on trouve aussi des questions très pratiques : en particulier tout ce qui touche à la rédaction et à la publication des travaux de recherche, comme la standardisation des abréviations, la manière de citer ou l'ordre des données à enregistrer. Il s'agit aussi d'harmoniser la composition des index d'ouvrages ou d'autres outils paratextuels et de créer une bibliographie unifiée du domaine. La visée ici est triple : transmissibilité et cumul des connaissances d'une génération de chercheurs à une autre ; homogénéisation des échanges d'information ; intérêt didactique – il est question de promouvoir la formation des chercheurs.

Enfin, se projeter ainsi, c'est se doter d'une organisation du travail scientifique qui institue la communauté internationale des linguistes en instance de régulation : le degré de satisfaction des vœux émis à chaque session fait l'objet d'une évaluation lors de la session suivante. Elle devra aussi jouer ce rôle pour tout ce qui a trait à la politique de la langue et qui suppose que le congrès s'institue porte-parole des linguistes auprès des pouvoirs publics de leurs pays respectifs. Deux thèmes prédominent alors : l'adoption d'une langue internationale auxiliaire (un vœu dont l'expression est reconduite sans grand changement de 1931 à 1939) ; la préservation des langues en danger, une préoccupation alors émergente. Les congressistes de La Haye votent une résolution pour "obtenir des divers gouvernements un effort rapide pour l'étude des langues et des civilisations qui meurent."[13]

5. Conclusion

La prévision, la prédiction et l'accommodation caractérisent des théories scientifiques ; la projection, des disciplines. Les champs de validité respectifs de ces opérations paraissent donc clairement distincts. Il n'en demeure pas moins que le développement des théories fournit un modèle à celui des disciplines, tout comme la science en fournit un à l'épistémologie: il y a isomorphisme dans les deux cas. L'exemple du Congrès international de linguistes le montre clairement : l'horizon de projection de la linguistique relève au premier chef de son organisation comme discipline. Elle présuppose sous cet aspect l'institution des praticiens en communauté organique qui vise à parler d'une seule voix, principalement orientée – du moins jusqu'à la seconde guerre mondiale – vers la linguistique générale, s'attachant à clarifier des questions de méthode plus qu'à susciter des résultats, à délimiter les frontières avec les disciplines connexes, à peser sur les décisions à prendre en matière de politique de la langue.

13. Voir sur ce point le compte rendu de Rivet (1928: 416).

Références

Sources primaires

Bloomfield, Leonard. 1933. *Language.* New York : Holt, Rinehart & Winston.

Baudouin de Courtenay, Jan [= Boduèn de Kurtenà, Ivan Aleksandrovič]. 1963 [1889]. "O zadačax jazykoznanij" [Les tâches de la linguistique]. *Izbrannye trudy po obščemu jazykoznaniju* [Travaux choisis de linguistique générale], vol. 1, 203–222. Moskva : Akademija nauk SSSR.

Comte, Auguste. 2014 [1835]. *Cours de philosophie positive*, vol. 2. *La Philosophie astronomique et la philosophie de la physique.* Paris : Bachelier.

Congrès international de linguistes. sd. *Actes du 1er Congrès… tenu à La Haye, du 10 au 15 avril 1928.* Leiden : Sijthoff.

–. 1933. *Actes du 2e Congrès… tenu à Genève… du 25 au 29 août 1931*, Paris : Maisonneuve.

–. 1935. *Atti del III Congresso internazionale dei linguisti (Roma, 19–26 sett. 1933).* Firenze : Le Monnier.

–. 1938. *Actes du 4e Congrès de linguistes, tenu à Copenhague, du 27 août au 1er septembre 1936.* Copenhague : Munksgaard.

–.1939. *5e Congrès de linguistes* [prévu à] *Bruxelles du 28 août au 2 septembre 1939. Rapports exposant les questions inscrites au programme. Réponses aux questionnaires. Résumés des communications.* Göteborg : Elanders.

Henry Victor. 1896. *Les antinomies linguistiques.* Paris : Hachette.

Jespersen, Otto. 1922. *Language, its Nature, Development, Origin.* London : Allen & Unwin.

Kuryłowicz, Jerzy. 1927. "ə indo-européen et ḫ hittite", *Symbolae grammaticae in honorem Ioannis Rozwadowski*, vol. 1, edited by W. Taszycki & W. Doroszewski, 95–104. Kraków : Gebethner & Wolff.

Meillet, Antoine. 1903. *Introduction à l'étude comparative des langues indo-européennes, suivie d'un Aperçu du développement de la grammaire comparée.* Paris : Hachette.

Meillet, Antoine. 1927. "Le Congrès international des linguistes". *Bulletin de la Société de Linguistique de Paris* XVII:2 : xxxix–xl.

Meillet, Antoine & Marcel Cohen, dir. 1924. *Les langues du monde.* Paris : H. Champion.

Rivet, Paul. 1928. "Premier Congrès international de linguistes." [Compte-rendu], *Journal de la Société des américanistes* 20 :416.

Saussure, Ferdinand de. 1968–1974. *Cours de linguistique générale.* Édition critique par R. Engler, Wiesbaden : Otto Harrassowitz.

Saussure, Ferdinand de & Émile Constantin. 2005. "Ferdinand de Saussure : Notes préparatoires pour le cours de linguistique générale 1910–1911. Émile Constantin : Linguistique générale. Cours de M. le professeur de Saussure 1910–1911". *Cahiers Ferdinand de Saussure* 58 : 83–289.

Sechehaye, Albert. 1908. *Programme et méthode de la linguistique théorique.* Paris : H. Champion.

Vendryes, Joseph. 1933. "Les tâches de la linguistique statique". *Journal de psychologie normale et pathologique*, n° spécial, "Le langage" : 172–184.

Sievers, Eduard. 1924. *Ziele und Wege der Schallanalyse.* Heidelberg : Winter.

Sources secondaires

Benveniste, Émile. 1966. "Tendances récentes en linguistique générale". *Problèmes de linguistique générale*, vol. 1 : 3–17. Paris : Gallimard.

Chevalier, Jean-Claude. 2001. "La terminologie linguistique dans les premiers congrès internationaux des linguistes", *Métalangage et terminologie linguistique*, dir. par Bernard Colombat & Marie Savelli, vol. 1 : 513–526. Leuven : Peeters.

Hempel, Carl. 1966. *Philosophy of Natural Sciences*. Englewod Cliffs, N.J. : Prentice–Hall.

Horkheimer, Max. 1934 [1933]. "Zum Problem der Vorraussage in den Sozialwissenschaften". *Zeitschrift für Sozialforschung* 2 : 407–412.

Milner, Jean-Claude. 1989. *Introduction à une science du langage*. Paris : Le Seuil.

Popper, Karl. 1963. *Conjectures and Refutations. The Growth of Scientific Knowledge*. New York : Routlege & Kegan Paul.

Savatovsky, Dan. 2004. "Les cinq antinomies de Victor Henry : une épistémologie kantienne de la linguistique". *Linguistique et partages disciplinaires à la charnière XIXe-XXe siècle: Victor Henry (1850–1907)* dir. par Christian Puech : 77–97. Leuven : Peeters.

Savatovsky, Dan. 2021. "De quoi les *Sciences-du-langage* sont-elles le nom?". *Les Sciences du langage face au défi de la disciplinarisation et de l'interdisciplinarité. Actes du colloque ASL de 2019* dir. par Guy Achard-Bayle, Marina Krylyshin & Malika Temmar, 25–46. Limoges : Lambert-Lucas.

Abstract

This paper deals with the notion of *disciplinary projection*, as it is (or should be) used in the history and the epistemology of linguistics. First, we define *projection* by distinguishing it from *forecasting*, *prediction*, and *accommodation* (cf. Horkheimer, Hempel and/or Popper). We show that the notion of projection involves linguistics as a *discipline* and not only as a knowledge. Then we try to understand what Saussure meant by the future "task" to be performed in linguistics (*Cours de linguistique générale*, Chapter II). Finally, we focus on the proceedings of the first five sessions of the International Congress of Linguists (1928–1939) in order to show how they conceived the future of their discipline, emphasizing four themes: exchanges and the delimitation of borders with related disciplines; interventions in the field of language policy; adoption of shared methodologies in linguistic investigation and the presentation of its results.

Keywords: disciplinary projection, forecasting, prediction, accommodation in linguistics, International Congress of Linguists (1928–1939)

CHAPTER 4

Ethics and language in (and around) Philipp Wegener

Maria Paola Tenchini & Serena Cattaruzza
Università Cattolica del Sacro Cuore | Università di Trieste

In the logical-psychological-linguistic contributions of the German area between the nineteenth and the twentieth century, Philipp Wegener is the scholar who stresses the role of ethics as the precondition for the acquisition and use of language. His considerations are embedded in a theoretical framework that focuses on the concrete acts of speech in situational context, as well as on the active interaction between speaker and hearer for the construction of meaning. Within this dialogical approach, sympathy should be considered as the "most fundamental prerequisite" for understanding speech (Wegener 1885: 68). Wegener's view never gained unanimous coeval fame either in linguistics or in the psychology of language; nonetheless he was appreciated later by scholars of the caliber of Karl Bühler and Alan Gardiner. Our paper investigates the attention Wegener pays to the connection between language, speech, and ethics and considers how this concept may have paved the way for a social notion of language.

Keywords: Ph. Wegener, ethics, sympathy, language, speech

1. Introduction

At the core of our paper are Philipp Wegener's reflections on the connection between language and ethics, which in turn are related to the nature of language and to the mechanism of speaking and understanding. In the logical-psychological-linguistic contributions of the German–Central European area between the nineteenth and the twentieth century, Wegener was the only scholar who stressed the role of ethics as the 'precondition' for the acquisition and use of language. His considerations are embedded in a theoretical framework that focuses on the concrete acts of speech in situational context and on the active (asymmetrical) interaction between speaker and listener for the construction of meaning.

https://doi.org/10.1075/sihols.133.04ten

Wegener describes language both as a cognitive means of exchange (*Verkehrsmittel*) among the members of a specific language community and as the activity of speaking (*Tätigkeit des Sprechens*) (Wegener 1921: 1). Both functions include the idea of interaction, of a continuous exchange "bei dem der Einzelne bald der Sprechende, bald der Hörende ist, bald dem Ambose, bald dem Hammer gleicht" (*ibidem*).[1] The accomplished speaker has learned the way in which to connect groups of sounds to form a definite meaning only "aus dem Zusammenleben mit anderen Individuen" (Wegener 1885: 63),[2] namely through long practice in a continuous intercourse. In Wegener's theoretical apparatus, speaking is a listener-directed activity: his notion of language is a dialogical one, both in its genesis and development, and in the function of the linguistic signs. He claims "dass nicht die Form des Ausdrucks als solche, sondern die Art der Verknüpfung in der Seele des Hörenden bestimmend ist für die Bedeutung und den Inhalt der Worte" (Wegener 1885: 14).[3] Within his social approach, sympathy should be considered as "die fundamentalste Voraussetzung alles Sprachverständnisses" (Wegener 1885: 68).[4]

According to Robert Musil, in his comment on Goethe's *Harzreise im Winter* (1922), ethos is internal to an order of sentiments and ideas which, as such, is "rational", but not in conflict with the "spirit". In this sense, the ethical order reconciles "subjective" and "objective", because the aim of its order is an overall view of relationships, of the constantly fluid meanings of human activities: it is a representation of life. And its fundamental instrument is language. This definition by Musil is useful for a first framing of the refined, non-obvious interplay between ethics and language that, as we will see, Wegener proposes.

In the Preface to his *Sprachtheorie*, Karl Bühler declares that language belongs to life's indispensable instruments and constitutes a powerful "geformter Mittler" (Bühler 1934: XXI).[5] The analysis that he goes on to develop in this regard is, in its most important topics, indebted to the work of the great linguists, from the Ancient Greeks to Wegener and Gardiner.

In this respect, it is interesting to recall here Susanne K. Langer's shrewd observation (in her documented work *Philosophy in a New Key*, 1941) about assigning a

1. "in which the individual is sometimes the speaker, sometimes the listener, sometimes the anvil, sometimes the hammer" (if not stated otherwise, translations are ours).

2. "from living together with other individuals" (transl. Abse, 1971: 171, slightly modified).

3. "that it is not the form of expression as such, but rather the way in which it is related to the mind of the listener which is decisive for the meaning and content of the word" (transl. Abse, 1971: 175).

4. "the most fundamental prerequisite for understanding speech" (transl. Abse, 1971: 175).

5. "a formed intermediary" (transl. Goodwin & Eschbach 2011: XXV).

leading role to Wegener's *Untersuchungen*. Langer chooses the example of the *word sentence* (Wegener's *Wortsatz*) as a paradigmatic case of compassion, goodwill, and the well-disposed in general, which are essential for the natural development of linguistic communication. The ethical nature of the sympathetic value – according to Langer – is connected to the Wegenerian basic assumption that the distinctive human attitude towards things and events is shared by our neighbor.

Based upon these inputs, this paper is structured as follows: in Section 2, we will analyze Wegener's contribution to the role of ethics in language development, use, and understanding. In Section 3, we will consider the assessments of some scholars on such an issue. Section 4 concludes the paper.

2. The ethical dimension in language and speech

To highlight the importance of this dimension for Wegener, let us start with one of his conclusive considerations in the last chapter of his *Untersuchungen*:

> Die Sprache beruht auf dem Verkehr der Menschen untereinander, auf den egoistischen und sympathischen Gefühlen, ihr Leben ist auf das tiefste in den ethischen Bedingungen der Gesellschaft und des Einzelmenschen verwurzelt. Die Sprache ist Verkehr der Menschen unter einander und nur die sprachlichen Vorgänge, welche wir als Hörende verstanden haben, können uns beim Sprechen als Sprachmittel dienen. (Wegener 1885: 182)[6]

According to Wegener, no linguistic investigation can be separated from the problem of understanding (cf. *ibidem*).

Language and language as activity have the characteristics of social practice.[7] This conception leads Wegener to state that the nature of language is dialogical

6. "Language is based upon human intercourse, upon egoistical and sympathetic feelings. Its life is deeply engrained in the ethical conditions of society and of the individual. Speech is human intercourse, and only those linguistic processes which we as listeners have understood can serve us in our speaking" (transl. Abse 1971: 272, slightly modified).

7. As Knobloch clearly points out in a thorough analysis of the issue (cf. Knobloch 1988), the psychological approaches to language in Germany between 1850 and 1950 had different beginnings and outcomes: for Steinthal, language is primarily a representation of sensory impressions (*Darstellung der Sinneseindrücke*) and a step in the evolution of the mind; for Wundt, a stage in the psychological evolution of expressive movements (*Ausdrucksbewegungen*); for Gerber, a technique for the processing (*Kunsttechnik zur Gestaltung*) of thoughts, messages and knowledge; for Noiré, a tool for guiding and organizing social life; and for Wegener, it is a system of mechanized means of communication, in which *actio* comes before *repraesentatio*.

and not monological (64),[8] as only in dialogue are the groups of sounds the means of speech and it is only in dialogue that all speaking has a social purpose (66).

Wegener claims that the foremost purpose and intention of speaking is to influence the listener's will or knowledge (*den Willen oder die Erkenntniss*) in a way that seems valuable to the speaker: "So soll im Imperativ und Wunsche der Wille des Angeredeten zum Handeln bestimmt werden, in der Frage zur Aufklärung über eine dem Sprechenden wertvolle Vorstellungsgruppe" (67).[9] Imperative and question stem from the speaker's interest, but they change the world of both speaker and listener because "[d]as geforderte Handeln und die geforderte Antwort ist so wenig immer Selbstzweck, wie die Speise, die wir fordern; vielmehr ist beides häufig Mittel eines höheren Zwecks" (*ibidem*).[10]

The basis of the intrinsically dialogical nature of language (and speech) is to be looked for in its ethical conception. When the speaker wants the listener to do something for him/her – through an act of whatever kind – and the listener reacts properly, then an ethical factor enters the development of language (*Sprachentwicklung*) and speech (cf. 13). This ethical conception pervades all of Wegener's model, so much so that observations in this direction are found scattered throughout his work. While the current authors are aware that an action of this type necessarily entails simplifications, to present Wegener's conception in some detail, three aspects are mentioned here: speaking as purposeful activity; language acquisition and use in children; and development of language and linguistic structures. These aspects are to be intended as deeply rooted in the Wegenerian conception of communication and understanding.

2.1 Speaking is a purposeful activity

Starting from the idea that we speak to communicate, Wegener wonders what we communicate and why. Claiming that we communicate thoughts and that the purpose of all speaking is the communication of thoughts is "too narrow" (*zu eng*) for him as, for instance, influencing one's mind by means of an imperative is not the same as communicating a thought, and a request does not appear to the listener as communication of ideas. Moreover, the literal content of our message

8. Hereafter, any quotes from Wegener (1885) will be indicated by page number only.

9. "Thus, in forms of commanding and wishing, the mind of the addressed person is to be primed for action; in the form of questioning, it is to be primed for an explanation about groups of thoughts valuable to the speaker" (transl. Abse 1971: 174).

10. "the demanded action and the requested answer are no more a purpose in themselves than the food which we require; they are rather a means to a higher purpose" (transl. Abse 1971: 174, slightly modified).

does not always coincide with the purpose of our speech (cf. 66–67). Actually, as mentioned above, according to Wegener the foremost purpose and intention of speaking is to influence the listener's mind or knowledge. He describes in detail the nature of the speaker's purposes, which are arranged like the feelings of value (*Wertgefühle*) in an infinitely graduated system (67), and divides them into two large classes, "ethisch and psychisch untereinander verknüpft" (68):[11] the selfish purposes and the altruistic purposes. The former aim at arousing sympathy or interest for one's own ideas or value judgements, while the latter aim at showing sympathy and interest for the ideas and values of others.

Wegener points out that "es beginnt die Welt der Werte mit der elementaren sinnlichen Lusterregung, durchläuft die grosse Reihe der höheren Lustempfindungen zur reinsten Lust, der inneren ethischen Befriedigung [...] Diese Werte sind die Zwecke der sprachlichen Mittel..." (67).[12] Wegener adds that a selfish purpose can become the means to a selfless purpose (for example, the acquisition of money can become the means for charity, orders and demands can be the means for education) and vice versa (the support of people in need can turn out to be the means for one's own advance) (*ibidem*).

Both selfish and selfless purposes are necessary for understanding, and sympathy is all-important:

> Die Wichtigkeit der Sympathie für die grundlegendste aller menschlichen Tätigkeit die Sprache [sic] ist ein starker Beweis, dass der Mensch im Zusammenleben mit dem Nebenmenschen notwendig zur Ausbildung des sympathischen Triebes und damit zur Ausbildung der Grundlage aller Sittlichkeit gelangen muss, eine Entwicklung des Menschen, die in der Gesellschaft sich mit gleicher Sicherheit und Notwendigkeit einstellt als die Entwicklung räumlicher und zeitlicher Anschauung (69).[13]

After remarking that in the same way that society would deteriorate if its members were ruled purely by selfish purposes, so too would the language depending upon society deteriorate (68), Wegener adds that understanding would be impossible if the selfish instinct were lacking. Indeed, thanks to the selfish instinct, a

11. "both ethically and psychically related to each other" (transl. Abse 1971: 175).

12. "the world of values begins with the elementary sensual desire-stimulation, continues through the whole series of sensations of desires to the purest desire of all, inner ethical gratification [....]; these values are the aims of the linguistic means..." (transl. Abse 1971: 174–175).

13. "The importance of sympathy for the most basic of all human activities, that is, speech, clearly demonstrates that man, in living together with his fellow human beings, must cultivate his sympathetic instincts and, thereby, attain a basis for all morality. This is a development in man that occurs with the same certainty and necessity in society as does the development of temporal and spatial perception" (transl. Abse 1971: 176, slightly modified).

speaker can regard another's speech as purposeful, whereas thanks to sympathy, the speaker reflects on the other's speech. A speaker would not be in a position to recognize the means to a purpose in somebody else's utterance if this ethical basic factor were lacking and if s/he did not assume from her/his own example that someone undertakes a certain action, also a verbal one, only because s/he wants to attain something; also lighthearted chatting (*das leichte Geplauder*) and the strait-laced fulfilment of an obligation in a conversation (*die steife Pflichterfüllung der Unterhaltung*) can be determined by the aim to realize something valuable (68). In Wegener's theory the psychological process of analogy offers a positive reading of the selfish purposes as well. He highlights throughout the *Untersuchungen* the huge importance of this process in understanding. Of course, analogy is not the sole means of understanding: Wegener recognizes that speech comprehension is based primarily upon inferences (*Schlüsse*) of different kinds.

2.2 Language acquisition and use in children

In Wegener's theory, speaking is a purposeful action from the very beginning. He states that during the first two years of its life, a child uses words as a means to obtain relief for/satisfaction of a need/desire. Indeed, these words are embedded in her/his mind primarily in the series of sensations of pain or discomfort (e.g., hunger). For the mother (or the caretaker), any word uttered by her baby functions as an imperative: she is called upon to do something, and accordingly, she gives something (e.g., the bottle) to the child. Consequently, the child may now associate words with a sensation of pleasure or relief (12–13).

Wegener interprets this kind of intercourse between mother and child in ethical terms: "[d]er Grund aber, dass diese Form des Ausdrucks vom Hörenden als Imperativ gefasst wird, ist in erster Linie ein ethischer, das Gefühl der Verpflichtung, dem hülfebedürftigen, leidenden Menschen zu helfen, also das Gefühl der Sympathie" (13).[14] According to him, it should be evident that it is not the form of the expression as such that is decisive for the meaning and the content of a word, but rather the way in which it is related to the mind of the listener (cf. Bühler 1909). Understanding is guaranteed because the listener is aware of the child's need, as the tone is congruent to the situation. At this point, an ethical factor enters the development of language (*Sprachentwicklung*) and the sound shaping of the word (*Form der Lautgebung*) (13): for instance, an echo of the baby's crying remains in the whining sound of requests/pleas in adults.

14. "The reason that this form of expression will be understood by the listener as an imperative is an ethical one, the feeling of obligation to help the needy or suffering, the feeling of sympathy" (transl. Abse 1971: 129).

On the basis of the listener's iterated reactions to one of his/her utterances, the child in turn associates a function with that word and learns to use it correctly to achieve a goal (primarily selfish). Over time, this single word loses its primary function of imperative, and children may use the same word to perform other acts of speech, such as the representative one (to use a current term), by incorporating the idea of the verbal tense into the expression (14–15). Once again, if the same word can be used for various sentence forms and various tenses, it goes without saying that "nicht das Wort als solches, nicht der Wortkörper bildet den Satz, neben diesem ist der Ton oder die Art des Vortrages, die *actio*, wie es die römischen Rhetoren nennen, ein zweites wesentliches Element dieses Wortsatzes" (15–16).[15] For example, in a child's speech the concept of the subject that the predicate is concerned with is not expressed in words but is solely indicated by the tone.

Wegener proceeds to make very interesting observations on the use of tone, intonation, and rhythm; on the different modulations, their regularity, and their possible modifications; and on the gestures that accompany speech. Wegener concludes that the fundamental ethical views have a key role in understanding these prosodic modulations both as means of linguistic expression (*als Mittel sprachlichen Ausdrucks*) and for the configuration and application (*Verwendung und Ausgestaltung*) of these means and that "[d]er Ton bildet erst den Schlüssel zum Verständnisse des Wortes oder Satzes, nicht blos in der Kindersprache" (18).[16]

This ethical component, which from the very beginning governs the interchange between speaker and listener, between needs and their satisfaction, between performatives and answers, will govern every interactional dynamic, even in adult life where single words used as sentences (*Wortsätze*) in each situation will be replaced by articulated and complex speeches/texts.

2.3 Development of language and linguistic structures

This is a very broad topic, which Wegener spreads out over multiple passages, and we can only touch on it here in its main aspects.

---

15. "It is thus not the word as such, not the body of the word alone which builds the sentence. Along with this is the tone or the manner of delivery, the *actio*, as Roman rhetoricians called it, which is a second important element of this word-sentence" (transl. Abse 1971: 130).

16. "The tone, first of all, provides the key for the understanding of words and sentences, and not only in the language of children" (transl. Abse 1971: 133).

According to Wegener, the primigenial speech form is the word sentence (*Wortsatz*):[17] that is, a sentence (we would say an utterance) composed of a single word with a predicative function, for example: *linden, excellent!, nice, out!*

In Wegener's theoretical framework, speech always consists of an exposition (*Exposition*) and a predicate (*logisches Pradikat*). The exposition, or logical subject, is the "uninteresting known", the ground that prepares for the appearance and understanding of the predicate; the logical predicate is the new and interesting part of the message (20–21). In the case of word sentences, the exposition of the predication act is not verbalized but can be inferred from the context shared by the interlocutors, actually from the so-called situation of visual perception (*Situation der Anschauung*) in which the utterance *linden* may stand for *this tree is a linden*, or from the so-called situation of the remembrance (*Situation der Erinnerung*), in which *excellent* may stand for *the wine is excellent* if someone is removing a glass of wine from their lips.[18]

But if interlocutors cannot rely on perception or remembrance, the support for understanding is offered by the verbalized exposition (i.e., by the verbal context in which the assertion is made). Wegener (cf. especially Wegener 1911) states that a verbal exposition is always necessary for the listener when the situation does not directly contain expositional elements. The speaker, or writer, in her/his turn, knows that s/he has to add the most details the less the listener knows about a situation. An ethical disposition to make oneself understood is inherent in the message structure.

It is worth noting that according to Wegener, the grammatical form of subordinate clauses can be interpreted this way too. Appositive and relative clauses give us an insight into the development of the expositional form: both are forms of postposed exposition and represent supplementary corrections of representation (*nachträgliche Correcturen der Darstellung*, 34). In addition, main clauses can be used as a supplementary explanation of an incomprehensible word (*als nachfolgende Erklärung eines unverständlichen Wortes*, 36): this happens, for example, in the free use of parenthetical clauses. Understanding drives our speech actions; therefore, if we see that our interlocutor cannot grasp our message and thus the purpose of our speaking, we add a supplementary correction.

So, the postposition of elements with expositional value serves as supplementary correction of a message without sufficient exposition. The speaker under-

17. Wegener dedicated an entire essay to the topic, published posthumously (cf. Wegener 1921), as well as several passages in the *Untersuchungen*. He defended the idea, particularly *contra* Wundt, that the word sentence was the primordial form of communication (cf. Wegener 1902). For further details, see Tenchini 2020.

18. On this point cf. Brugmann (1904) and Bühler (1934); for an overview see Tenchini 2008.

stands that s/he needs to intervene to fill this deficiency, starting from the listener's facial expressions or questions. This can also explain the genesis of demonstratives and deictic elements in the situation of perception and the development of their textual function (from *look over there* (*sieh hin*) to *that is …* (*das ist …*) to *the linden* (*der Linden*)). And this explains how all words, which originally were general predicates, have evolved and become congruent to specific situations and have been able to assume the textual function of logical subject designating a substance in every circumstance. Wegener states that all words have arrived at the capacity of being logical subjects and constituting exposition through the process of semantic fading that occurs during their repeated predicative use, therefore thanks to "mechanization". Before having faded words to designate the logical subject, language was not able to designate the situation except through direct indication in the situation of visual perception (cf. 54 and *passim*).

Based on the fact that the *Wortsatz* was the primary form of expression, according to Wegener it seems reasonable to assume that the predicate remained for a long time not only the sole but, in more complex utterances, also the first uttered word and that

> [e]rst die Ausbildung der Sprache zur Kunst und zur Lehre schärft die Verpflichtung ein, die Exposition dem logischen Prädicate vorauszustellen. Diesem Streben nach vorausgehender Exposition ist es zu danken, dass in fortgeschrittenen Zeiten, z. B. denen der klassischen Latinität[,] der relative Expositionssatz so massenhaft dem Hauptsatze vorausgestellt wird; und bei dem Gefühle, dass das logische Prädicat das Verbum sei (und allerdings ist das häufig der Fall), tritt das Verbum an das Satzende, also hinter all die Bestimmungen, welche als Exposition erscheinen (40).[19]

Let us report two passages to conclude this (selective) presentation of Wegener's reflections on the development of linguistic structures intended as the outcome of corrective actions aimed at guiding and facilitating understanding. In the first passage, our scholar states that the history of language reflects the progress of the spirit (*des Menschengeistes*) and this fact has led to putting the expositional elements first:

19. "Only the development of verbal language in art and science impresses on us the duty to place the exposition in front of the logical predicate. It is this striving for a preceding exposition which accounts in enlightened times, for example, in the classical Latin period, for the relative expositional sentences being placed in front of the main clause. Thus, with the feeling that the logical predicate should be the verb (and indeed this is often the case), the verb came at the end of the sentence: that is, behind all the determining factors which appear as exposition" (transl. Abse 1971: 151, slightly modified).

> Man darf hiernach wohl sagen, dass uns die Sprachgeschichte ein Bild von dem allgemeinen Fortschritte des Menschengeistes entrollt: die ruhige, vernünftige Ueberlegung und Berechnung der Verständnissfähigkeit des angeredeten Nebenmenschen gewinnt die Oberhand über die elementare Gewalt des Gefühls und des Strebens (43).[20]

In the second passage, Wegener reiterates that these 'mature' structures, which are now perceived as congruent, actually derive from earlier structures that reflected the speaker's naive assumption that the listener was aware of the same representations:[21]

> Selbstverständlich empfindet das Sprachgefühl der entwickelten Sprachstufen auch nicht die leiseste Spur von Unvollkommenheit bei diesen einmal festgewordenen Satzformen, sie erscheinen vielmehr als der wirklich logische adäquate und congruente Ausdruck des Gedankens. Und trotzdem sind sie hervorgegangen aus der täglich zu beobachtenden naiven Voraussetzung des Sprechenden, als müsse der Hörende genau dieselben Vorstellungen bewusst haben und vergleichen wie der Sprechende, als wäre der Massstab des Sprechenden ein allgemein bekannter und absoluter (45).[22]

3. Assessments

Wegener does not say whether and how much his ethical approach was influenced by the ideas of Steinthal, author of a volume entitled *Allgemeine Ethik*, which appeared in 1885, although Wegener openly acknowledges Steinthal's value in his *Untersuchungen*.[23] In fact, the two scholars give a different weight to the notion

---

20. "One may certainly say hereafter that the history of language unveils a picture of the general advance of man's mind: sober, reasonable reflection, and calculation of the comprehensive ability of the addressee, wins the upper hand over the primitive power of feeling and striving" (transl. Abse 1971: 153, slightly modified).

21. Here Wegener refers, with plenty of examples, to the verbal and nominal declension through different suffixes and to the word order of the ancient Indo-Germanic stages.

22. "It is self-evident that one's language feeling at the most developed stages of language does not sense the least trace of defect in these sentence forms once they have become firmly established. Rather, they appear to be the really logically adequate and congruent expression of thought. Nevertheless, these sentence forms have arisen from the naive assumption of the speaker that the listener must be aware of the same representations as he himself is and be able to compare, as if the criterion of the speaker were a generally known and absolute one" (transl. Abse 1971: 155, slightly modified).

23. As Eisler's classic *Wörterbuch der Philosophischen Begriffe und Ausdrücke* (1899: 750) attests, sympathy is a source of inspiration for ethics according to many philosophers, especially mod-

of sympathy, which for Steinthal is secondary to benevolence (*Wolwollen*: cf. Steinthal 1885: 114–119).[24]

Among the coeval reviews of the *Untersuchungen*, only two refer to Wegener's ethical approach in explaining linguistic facts: Uphues' review ultimately criticizes this aspect because it does not take into account other factors occurring in speech comprehension and child language acquisition (Uphues 1885: 1624), while Ziemer's positively underlines the close relationship between ethical conditions, language development, and the structuring of speech with the anteposition of the exposition (Ziemer 1886: 182–183).

In his *Theory of Speech and Language* (1932), dedicated to the German scholar, Gardiner acknowledges Wegener's contribution to the ethical prerequisite of verbal interaction by stating that "this point is rightly stressed by Wegener", and ascribes self-seeking, altruism, and sympathy to "the human attributes from which speech obtains its driving force" (Gardiner 1932: 68). He sums up Wegener's ideas about the purposes that move speaking and understanding as follows:

ern ones, from D. Hume and A. Smith up to E. Platner and A. Bain. Moreover, the role of sympathy in the mechanism of linguistic communication, so essential in Wegener, is already present in Steinthal.

24. For instance, Steinthal points out: "Ganz ungeeignet zur Bezeichnung unserer Idee [eines wohlwollenden Menschen] wäre Sympathie. Diese ist Mitgefühl mit dem Wol und Wehe, den Freuden und Leiden des Andren, kann also nur eintreten, wo das Befinden des Andren so lebhafte Gefühle in demselben mit so offenem Ausdrucke erzeugt, dass man durch Warnehmung dieses Ausdruckes sympathisch ergriffen wird; es zeigt sich nur dann und wann. Das Wolwollen aber wartet ja nicht, das der Andre jauchze oder schluchze, um mit ihm zu jubeln oder zu weinen; es ist immer da, schon vorher und auch ohne solche vorübergehende Ausnahmen. – Auch ist Sympathie ganz ohne Willen, eine psychologische, ganz unwillkürliche Regung unserer seelischen Natur, die müßige nachahmende Wiederholung (der Reflex) eines Gefühls des Andren; also ist sie ganz pathologisch, und folglich nichts etisches in ihr. [...] Der Wolwollende hat Mitgefühl; aber er hat es, von ethischer Einsicht beherscht und geleitet und erzeugt" (Steinthal 1885: 114–115). [Sympathy would be unsuitable to describe our idea [of a benevolent person]. Sympathy is the feeling of compassion towards the joys and sorrows of others and can only occur when the other person's feelings are so vividly expressed that one is moved by the perception of this expression; it only occurs every now and then. Yet benevolence does not wait for the other person to rejoice or weep in order to celebrate or mourn with them; it is always present, even before and without such temporary exceptions. Moreover, sympathy is entirely involuntary, a psychological reflex of our emotional nature that mimics the feelings of others; therefore, it is entirely pathological and consequently not ethical. The benevolent person has compassion, but it is guided and directed by ethical insight]. Leitzmann (1916: 248) recalls in his obituary of Wegener that the latter had invited him to read Steinthal's *Ethics*.

> [...] brief mention must be made of the human attributes from which speech obtains its driving force. These are the twin, but contrary, attributes of self-seeking and altruism. The former impels us to enlist the brains and muscles of our fellows for our own advantage, while the latter, born of sympathy, causes us to study the interests of others – interests often well-served by information, persuasion, or even commands". (*ibidem*)

Gardiner, like Wegener and Bühler (1934), develops an instrumental theory of language. Bühler intervenes by simplifying the formulas and sometimes adding new ones. The quintessence of linguistic theory, in fact, requires visual-intuitive indications in addition to conceptual abstraction. Thus, Bühler's contribution to the study of the indication field and deictics is to be understood as a completion of the work produced by Wegener (1885) and Brugmann (1904), whom he acknowledges as forerunners (cf. Bühler 1934: 232).

Modern linguists, in analyzing the concrete event of speaking, have already given space to situational moments, but only Wegener and Brugmann described the function and role of indexical words from a more general point of view: namely that of the signal. The term *signal* is Bühlerian, as Bühler considers it fundamental both in human and animal communication, but his method of determination corresponds perfectly to that employed by the two above-mentioned scholars. Moreover, according to Bühler, linguistic signs acquire certain "field values" in everyday communicative exchange.[25] The indicative terms, devoid of a symbolic field or "context", in turn require a field, the situational one, since they must be projected onto a surrounding field or background (*Umfeld*), a concept extrapolated from the color theory formulated by Hering and connected to the investigations on the "Gestalt" promoted, among others, by E. Rubin up to K. Lewin. Wegener, similarly to Brugmann, lists the circumstances that, in the concrete situation of speaking, can converge in determining the exchange value of sound signs (cf. Wegener 1885: especially 21–27). Finally, in Bühler's opinion, Wegener is the most consistent language theorist in defining the expositional elements of the proposition (cf. Bühler 1934: 375).

As anticipated in Section 1, Langer assigns a leading role to Wegener's *Untersuchungen* in her (1941) work based on the study of the most relevant logical-psychological-linguistic contributions of the German–Central European area between the nineteenth and the twentieth century. According to her, the ethical nature of the sympathetic value is connected to the Wegenerian basic assumption that the distinctive human attitude towards things and events is shared by our

25. From a theoretical-linguistic point of view, it should be necessary to further investigate this undeniable fact, already emphasized by Wegener in his *Untersuchungen* (cf. especially p. 19 and f.). For more details see Cattaruzza 2008.

neighbor, and that compassion, goodwill and being well disposed in general are essential for the natural development of linguistic communication (cf. Langer 1941: 111). The "one-word phrase" (as she called the word sentence) constitutes an elementary but crucial stage in the language, which Bühler, in Wegener's footsteps, defined as "empractical" in his *Sprachtheorie* (1934): the word is inserted in the speaker's situation with a diacritical function. "Empractical" or "sympractical" is defined the use of linguistic signs in case the surrounding field (*Umfeld*), in which the sign is activated, is a praxis, i.e., the sign is connected to perceptual phenomena. According to Bühler empractical utterances may be both deictic and symbolic signs. For Wegener, this use of a single word which designates our thinking in the context of the situation, is happily implemented until uncertainties and ambiguities may arise that may lead to misunderstandings. Thus, one must then add deictics to the word, such as "this", "here", and "now", which enrich the original expression and accentuate gestures and behaviours. In this manner, a logical-grammatical structure naturally develops from the primitive sentence for further amendments,[26] which disambiguate and enrich the relational modules of the situation. The mature outcome of this process not only manifests an amazing cognitive structure, but it is also the result of a need, as Wegener says, of a duty – the duty to pursue completion (cf. Wegener 1885: 40).

Langer argues that the specific acquisition of each language is the result of a natural process arising from practical needs of a social and communicative nature but simultaneously supported by a generative ethical drive for the amending and generalizing of expositive and enunciative syntactic forms (cf. Langer 1941: 111–112).

26. For further insights into this aspect, see Innis (1984), who aptly titled one essay on Wegener "Articulation as Emendation". He writes: "Articulation proceeds through increased and complexified predications, with previous predications themselves passing into the status of 'subjects'. The motive and matrix for this increased complexification are first of all failures of attempted linguistic understandings, failures traceable to many sources. A defective and hence incomplete utterance must always be 'emended', supplemented. When the listener indicates failure to understand, whole or in part, the speaker must add to the utterance, by making explicit what was either implicit and not shared, or by breaking the prior, relatively compact utterance into even more signifying units, with the 'routes of reference' or systematic connection running either to novel units in the various 'situation fields' or to parts of the linguistic expression itself, giving rise to demonstrative pronouns and all sorts of intralinguistic referring devices, rooted in anaphora quite generally. Bühler took up themes such as these, which Wegener argued with a wealth of examples, in his *Sprachtheorie...*" (Innis 1984: 582). Cf. also Juchem (1984).

4. Conclusion

In this paper, Wegener's contribution to the role of ethics in language development, use, and understanding has been analyzed. He concludes his *Untersuchungen* by saying that if he has succeeded in demonstrating that the keys to the solutions to all the questions addressed in the text lie in the hands of ethics and psychology, then he believes he has achieved something (Wegener 1885: 183). As shown in Section 3, Wegener's explicit and insistent position on this point has not entered the tradition of linguistic studies that succeeded him or that refer to him. However, it is undeniable that the effects of Wegener's ethical approach regarding the development and use of language and linguistic structures have been taken up, primarily by Gardiner and Bühler. Levelt signals an ideal connection between Wegener and Reinach and the modern speech act theorists precisely on this basis: "A final point that Wegener makes is that the dialogical use of language has an ethical dimension, precisely because it serves the function of influencing the will of another person. These ethical, quasi subtleties of speech acts are recognized and extensively treated in the speech act theorists. But a first formulation had already been provided by the philosopher (Husserl's student) and lawyer Adolf Reinach (1883–1917) in 1913" (Levelt 2013: 284).[27]

But the ethical-sympathetic enhancement within the communicative mechanism proposed by Wegener not only anticipates the positions of Adolf Reinach, a member of the Munich school led by Theodor Lipps, but also, in a broader and more general sense, the aesthetic-experimental investigations of Lipps himself; the philosophical anthropology (especially regarding the ethical-affective determination of the nature and forms of sympathy) of Max Scheler; and above all, the exemplary contribution of Edith Stein, who assigns an eminently communicative and cognitive function to ethical-empathetic performance within the context of Husserlian phenomenology (cf. Cattaruzza 2003).

Can Wegener's idea of language as a means of exchange among the members of a specific language community, as well as the activity of speaking, both including the idea of interaction, and the idea of acquisition and development of language as the outcome of a long practice in a continuous intercourse, be considered a clue for a social notion of language? The answer can only be positive.[28] He was

27. Here Levelt refers to Adolf Reinach, *Die apriorischen Grundlagen des bürgerlichen Rechtes* (1913).

28. For instance, referring to Wegener's framework, Innis (1984) writes: "A praxeological instrument first of all, spoken language is a species of social action, 'based upon human intercourse, upon egoistical and sympathetic feelings' (272), and is aimed at modifying or directing the consciousnesses of the hearers or listeners, whose 'material' or 'spiritual' needs are primary

not the first to hold this position, but it seems to us that he is the first to systematize and illustrate it in such detail.

Going back to Musil, the basic question is the following: "As for the 'humanistic spirit' of which we are making such extensive use, are we sure that he knows how to use the comparative method and to bring out the vital elements? Namely, is it 'ethical'?" (Musil 1922 [1978]: 1153). The exclusively and reductively historical method risks neglecting the essential value of the objective, systemic content of the humanistic investigation. It must also pursue a certain precision and order that will not obliterate the vital phenomena (connections, relationships, fluid and plurivocal meanings) of human activity but will describe its texture with an adequate ethical and phenomenological discipline. Furthermore, it has to be said that the Wegenerian sensitivity to the ethic-gnoseological-linguistic theme could already have had its roots in the university years, in particular those in Berlin, as Rosanna Sornicola notes in the interesting contribution *Mathesius, Wegener e le fasi dello storicismo* (1995). Therefore, the science and art of language are well within this research program. And the work of Wegener – which came a few years after the pioneering work of William D. Whitney, *The Life and Growth of Language* (1875), but many years before the Musilian observations – addressed with farsighted psychological-analytical ability the study of the linguistic phenomenon, identifying in the dialogue cell the vital driving force and describing its development in a way that is as complete as it is precise.

Thus, Wegener anticipated and promoted the inspiration of subsequent authors and schools – primarily Karl Bühler and his school, Alan Gardiner, but also Roman Jakobson and the Prague school and, in Bühler's footsteps, Agostino Gemelli and the Milan school.

References

Abse, Wilfred. 1971. *Speech and Reason. Language disorder in mental disease.* With a Translation of *The Life of Speech* [by] Philipp Wegener. Charlottesville: The University Press of Virginia.

Brugmann, Karl. 1904. *Die Demonstrativpronomina der indogermanischen Sprachen. Eine Bedeutungsgeschichtliche Untersuchung.* Leipzig: Teubner.

in determining the trajectories and structures of the linguistic action: Now, to succeed as a social action any linguistic utterance has to be subject to certain conditions – modern days: rules – and one of Wegener's main claims to fame is his insistence upon the necessity of a shared 'situation' between speaker and listener, a point taken up and given extensive development by Gardiner and Bühler ..." (Innis 1984: 578).

Bühler, Karl. 1909. "Über das Sprachverständnis vom Standpunkt der Normalpsychologie". *Bericht über den 3. Kongreß für experimentelle Psychologie vom 22.-25.4.1908 in Frankfurt*, 94–130. Leipzig: J. A. Barth.

Bühler, Karl. 1934. *Sprachtheorie*. Jena: Fischer. Engl. transl. by Donald Fraser Goodwin with Achim Eschbach, 2011, *Theory of Language. The representational function of language*. Amsterdam & Philadelphia: John Benjamins.

Cattaruzza, Serena. 2003. "Theodor Lipps – Edith Stein: sull'empatia". *Discipline filosofiche* XII:2.275–286.

Cattaruzza, Serena. 2008. *L'indicazione della realtà. Teoria dei segni e della conoscenza in Karl Bühler*. Milano-Udine: Mimesis.

Eisler, Rudolf. 1899. *Wörterbuch der Philosophischen Begriffe und Ausdrücke*. Berlin: Verlag der Königlichen Hofbuchhandlung von E. S. Mittler & Sohn.

Gardiner, Alan H. 1932. *The Theory of Speech and Language*. Oxford: Clarendon Press.

Innis, Robert E. 1984. "Articulation as Emendation: Philipp Wegener's Anti-Formalist Theory of language". *Semiotics* edited by John Deely, 577–587. Lanham & New York & London: University Press of America.

Juchem, Johann G. 1984. "Die Konstruktion des Sprechens. Kommunikationssemantische Betrachtungen zu Philipp Wegener". *Zeitschrift für Sprachwissenschaft* 3:1.3–18.

Knobloch, Clemens. 1988. *Geschichte der psychologischen Sprachauffassung in Deutschland von 1850 bis 1920*. Tübingen: Max Niemeyer Verlag.

Langer, Susanne K. 1941. *Philosophy in a New Key. A study in the symbolism of reason, rite, and arts*. New York: Mentor Book – New American Library.

Leitzmann, Albert. 1916. "Philipp Wegener". *Indogermanisches Jahrbuch* IV.246–250.

Levelt, Willem J. M. 2013. *A History of Psycholinguistics. The Pre-Chomskyan Era*. Oxford: Oxford University Press.

Musil, Robert. 1978 [1922]. "Das hilflose Europa oder Reise vom Hundertsten ins Tausendste". *Ganymed. Jahrbuch für die Kunst, in Gesammelte Werke* edited by Adolf Frisé, vol. II, 1137–1154. Reinbek bei Hamburg: Rowohlt.

Reinach, Adolf. 1913. "Die apriorischen Grundlagen des bürgerlichen Rechtes". *Jahrbuch für Philosophie und phänomenologische Forschung* 1:2.685–847.

Sornicola, Rosanna. 1995. "Mathesius, Wegener e le fasi dello storicismo". *Lingua e Stile* XXX:1.159–174.

Steinthal, Heymann. 1885. *Allgemeine Ethik*. Berlin: Druck und Verlag von Georg Reimer.

Tenchini, Maria Paola. 2008. *Aspetti funzionali e pragmatici nel pensiero linguistico di Philipp Wegener. Con la traduzione antologica di Philipp Wegener, Untersuchungen über die Grundfragen des Sprachlebens*. Brescia: La Scuola editrice.

Tenchini, Maria Paola. 2020. "Wegener's Wortsatz and the notion of sentence". *History of Linguistics 2017: Selected papers from the 14th International Conference on the History of the Language Sciences (ICHoLS XIV) Paris, 28 August–1 September* edited by Émilie Aussant & Jean-Michel Fortis, 49–64. Amsterdam & Philadelphia: John Benjamins.

Uphues, Goswin K. 1885. [review to] "Ph. Wegener, *Untersuchungen über die Grundfragen des Sprachlebens*". *Wochenschrift für klassische Philologie* 51.1618–1624 (columns).

Wegener, Philipp. 1885. *Untersuchungen über die Grundfragen des Sprachlebens.* Halle: Niemeyer.

Wegener, Philipp. 1902. [review of] "Delbrück, B., *Grundfragen der Sprachforschung mit Rücksicht auf W. Wundts Sprachpsychologie erörtert,* Strassburg, 1901". *Literarisches Centralblatt* 12(22. März). 401–410.

Wegener, Philipp. 1911. "Exposition und Mitteilung. Ein Beitrag zu den Grundfragen des Sprachlebens". *Wissenschaftliche Aufsätze zur Feier des 350-jährigen Jubiläums des Gymnasiums und der Realanstalt zu Greifswald,* 3–21. Greifswald: Julius Abel.

Wegener, Philipp. 1921. "Der Wortsatz". *Indogermanische Forschungen* 39.1–26.

Whitney, William D. 1875. *The Life and Growth of Language: an outline of linguistic science.* New York: D. Appleton and company.

Ziemer, Hermann. 1886. [review of] "Ph. Wegener, *Untersuchungen über die Grundfragen des Sprachlebens*". *Berliner Philologische Wochenschrift* 6 (6. Februar 1886).181–185.

CHAPTER 5

Walter Benjamin's idea of language

Frank Vonk
HAN University of Applied Sciences

The German literary critic, art critic and philosopher of language Walter Benjamin (1892–1940) has in many ways struggled with the question how language *manifests* itself in art, epistemology or literature. In posthumously published fragments, Benjamin shows how his restless mind has produced texts in which he has tried to connect the religious (Judaic) tradition with the ruinous appearance of an ideal language in names, trying to understand and explain the imperfection of language, also in translations between languages. Benjamin has covered this ruinous world in an allegoric view of language as it was done in Baroque allegories (the *vanitas*) showing itself in mourning plays,, hoping for a new, better world. In a way Benjamin's concern with language shows how language is fragmentized in daily speech in which only the communicative function has survived. The 'divine' dimension or word can only allegorically be considered to be relevant to this communicative function.

Keywords: language, name, word, world, translation

1. Introduction

In Benjamin's works we discover a different way of dealing with typically human conceptualizations and their different effects on human life, in its particularity as well as from a more general point of view. In discussing and describing several cultural aspects of human life, in different cultural dimensions the effect of this fragmentary *mer-à-boire* is that any science can pick out relevant ideas which have influenced modern thought. Benjamin's work also has a systemic dimension which is often overlooked and has to do with the underlying coherent ideas which Benjamin takes up in his work. One of these systematic undertows is Benjamin's idea(l) of language and how it is semantically connected to being human, in a material and mental way.

https://doi.org/10.1075/sihols.133.05von

2. On the German mourning play: The role of language

In his *Habilitationsschrift, Der Ursprung des deutschen Trauerspiels* (1924–28), it was Baroque literature and the ways in which the world as such was depicted and transformed in allegorical concepts which quite early drew Benjamin's attention. In two fragments on "*Trauerspiel* and Tragedy" (1916) and "*The Role of Language in* Trauerspiel *and Tragedy*" (1916) he gave some insights into what must have been his main ideas on seventeenth-century literature in its different forms of appearance in historical time. Later on, these insights also influenced the main ideas for a *Habilitation* thesis in the mid-1920s. In the first article Benjamin mentions the notion of historical time: historical time "passes over into tragic time" (Benjamin 1996: 55) by "actions of great individuals". This idea of "greatness" appears in history as well as in tragedy, especially in art:

> Historical time is infinite in every direction and unfulfilled at every moment. This means that we cannot conceive of a single empirical event that bears a necessary relation to the time of its occurrence. For empirical events time is nothing but a form, but, what is more important, as a form they are unfulfilled. The event does fulfil the formal nature of the time in which it takes place. For we should not think of time as merely the measure that records the duration of a mechanical change. [...]. Historical time, however, differs from this mechanical time. [...:] the determining force of historical time cannot be fully grasped by, or wholly concentrated in, any empirical process. Rather, a process that is perfect in historical terms is quite indeterminate empirically; it is in fact an idea. (Benjamin 1996: 55)

Being "unfulfilled" and "unnecessary" in historical time, empirical events show something provisional which, therefore, could have been otherwise and thus presuppose necessary possibilities which sometimes for some reasons do occur and sometimes do not. "Fulfilled time" is a biblical concept, the idea of messianic time which does not match with individual, experienced time (cf. Benjamin n.y.). The individual time of the tragic hero in tragedies is a "magic circle" of the hero's deeds and existence. In the tragedy "the hero dies because no one can live in fulfilled time. He dies of immortality" (Benjamin 1996: 56). Ironically, this quotation refers to the "individually fulfilled time" (Benjamin 1996: 56). The sense of fulfilment very often happens in moments of utter tranquillity or passivity, when the tragic hero paradoxically reaches his fulfilment and individuation this moment enables us to connect history and tragedy: "The time of the mourning play in Baroque literature is not fulfilled, but nevertheless it is finite" (Benjamin 1996: 57). It is a "hybrid form". The form in which a higher, tragic life is individuated in the "restricted space of an earthly existence" (Benjamin 1996: 57):

> [...] the mourning play presents us not with the image of a higher existence but only with one of two mirror-images (*Spiegelbilder*), and its continuation is not less schematic than itself. The dead become ghosts. *The mourning play exhausts artistically the historical idea of repetition.* Consequently, it addresses a problem that is completely different from the one dealt with in tragedy. In the mourning play guilt and greatness calls not so much for definition – let alone overdetermination – as for expansion, general extension, not for the sake of guilt and greatness, but simply for the repetition of those situations. (Benjamin 1996: 57)

Concerning messianic and historical time in his early thoughts, what has been visualised in his *Theologico-Political Fragment* (cf. Hamacher 2011; Benjamin n.y.) outlines his main idea about the historical, profane time which aims at creating a particular order, and the messianic or a-historical time, which is concerned with the status and function of a messiah moving reluctantly towards the empirical and individual time. Thus, the empirical event and the historical time meet in the tragic hero, exceeding fulfilled time and becoming immortal. The same tension Benjamin discovered in the phenomenon of creative, untimely or pure language and its appearance in multiple materializations or specific forms of spoken and written human languages.

3. Benjamin's theory of language: "On language as such and on the language of Man"

If we focus more on Benjamin's intention concerning his theory of language he outlines a couple of layers in the creation of the world as we perceive it. The use of language realizes an epistemological point of view, as a *medium* not an *instrument*, enabling human beings to conceptualize reality by not naming the "integral" meaning of words as it was part of the created wor(l)d or the names given to what came to be man's presence, but by naming aspects of experienced reality in "the language of man". Thus, the "original" created language has diversified itself in time and space (reflecting the narrative of the Tower of Bable).

Benjamin distinguishes the following stages of language in mental being and its development over time, starting from the creation of the world in the word of God:

1. the creating language, in which the word directly creates the objects and recognizes itself in names;
2. the Adamic language, which is a language of pure knowledge in name giving;
3. the present human language, the so called language of judging (*urteilend*);
4. the silent language of objects. (cf. Witte 1985: 28; Eden 1999: 90f)

The third category is the degenerated human language we nowadays use and which is meant for communication and thus has become an instrument and less a medium of words. This in fact does no longer represent the creative dimension of words and names but only shows aspects of what once has been created by God in saying and named by Adam using *pure* names – the pure names have been diversified or plurified in the *historical* development of human languages as well.

The "nameless language of things" passes through translation – at once reception and conception – into the "name-language" of man, which is the basis of knowledge. As a specifically human inheritance, naming incorporates both intensive and extensive tendencies of language, the communicable and the communicating, and thus constitutes the "language of language". To illuminate the function of naming and its intrinsic relation to perception, Benjamin turns to the opening chapters of the biblical book of Genesis, not as revealed as authority but as an index to "the fundamental linguistic facts", taking language in the biblical sense "as an ultimate reality, approachable only in its unfolding, inexplicable and mystical". [...]. The task of naming would be impossible were not the nameless language and the naming language related in God, released from the same creative word. Our knowledge of things – generated in the names with which we allow their language to pass into us – is essentially creativity relieved of its divine actuality, the knower is made in the image of the creator. "Man is the knower in the same language in which God is creator" (Eiland/Jennings 2014: 89).

However, human languages in the present still have the possibility to connect one way or another with the former, more pure stages in which man still uses names and is able to discover the creative dimension of language: the utopian or messianic stage which is not embedded in how language functions right now. In art, poems and literature for instance, we still encounter the spontaneous or creative dimension of 'an' "original" language: this is the search for the frontier, the incommensurable, which presupposes a leap towards the messianic stage: "[In the name as a frontier] contemporary language participates in the Adamic language, in which the *intensive totality of language* is given" (Witte 1985: 28).

From this point of view, one needs a form of *critique* as a translation of the contemporary language into the more perfect Adamic language. One needs the symbolic, divine language of the non-communicable. Benjamin's research on language is focussed on the possibility of saying or expressing the unsayable or inexpressible.[1]

1. An interesting aspect of this dimension of names, the magical, is to bring it back to "infancy". Children do have a playful attitude towards language, names and words, which presupposes a particular, innocent view on language which has not been taken over by the way language is instrumentally used by adults and thus represents a transcendental experience (cf. Agamben 2001: 7ff.).

4. The moment of "beginning"

Essential to Benjamin's method is the *moment of beginning*, when any concrete experience comes in and becomes part of man's experienced world. Having experiences – also the experience of the fact that language exists, the *experimentum linguae*, as Agamben (2001: 7ff.) maintains – is the source of knowledge as the main dimension of language. To enable knowledge of the created world by the medium of language which communicates itself as it were, this leads Benjamin to the following conclusion: "The linguistic being of all things is its language" (cf. Benjamin 2019: 11).

The study of language goes beyond the empirical or experimental and gives Benjamin the possibility to study the mystical or mythical dimension of language (cf. Menninghaus 1995; Heil 2011). To surmount experiment and observation, i.e. the empirical aspect of language, the representational and epistemological functions of language are far more relevant to understanding what language *actually*, in its presence to living human beings, is and what its contribution is to philosophy and the thematization of the origin of language.[2]

If one connects the historical continuum and the event of the origin of language, then it is rewarding to see how Benjamin deals with the biblical narrative of the creation of the world, of its inhabitants, of man and of his capability of naming (*benennen*) which God has bestowed upon man near the end of His task of creating the world as it is and probably is the best possible world in time.[3]

2. Since the beginning of the philosophy of language the 'origin of language' is a recurrent topic. We could refer to Plato's *Kratylos* or jump straight to Johann Gottfried Herder's (1744–1803) contribution to one of the questions put forward by the Prussian Academy of Sciences in 1769 concerning the origin of language. Finding and discussing the origin was omnipresent in the 19th century. In 1772 Herder published his contribution, *Abhandlung über den Ursprung der Sprache*, in which he reflected on the "inseparability" of language and thought, language being the tool, the content and form of human thinking (cf. Robins 1967: 166f.). The divine origin of language, based on the first book of the Old Testament was mainly suggested in Jewish philosophy. Founding themselves on Neoplatonist thinking and the idea of emanation and returning, medieval Jewish philosophers, like Ibn Gabirol (Avicebron, 1020–1058), suggest a model of steps connected with a biblical creator-God which stands above the cosmic intellect:

> as the absolute unity of matter and form he is the creator of the world, the forms of which are determined by his will and the matter of which he brings forth from his being (*Wesen*). In the sense of the Bible God brings forth the world by his being and his will out of nothing and "moves and orders all things." (Höffe 2005: 120; translation fv)

3. Nothing is said about the meaningful sounds in animal communication and in what way God has taken this into account in his creation of animals and their capacity to communicate with each other; this obviously shows the biblical focus on human beings and not on animals and their capacity to utter meaningful sounds.

Nevertheless, considered as plurified signs, names enable human communication: sharing thoughts, making appointments, commanding others, etc. From its pure origin, it is hard to understand how and why language, names, words, sentences, have this possibility of communication, next to designing and creating an integral connection between the language of things, the language we use in daily life, and the originally created "words" and their meaning(s).

If we look for an origin of language it is obvious that for some reason it was not there before this very beginning and did not play any role in the *history* of human life – if we could be sure at all of an emergence of language at any moment in time (or assume a prehistory of language, a *before-language*) and the need of it to *represent* the world (for whatever reason) and thus be able to build up knowledge of it. We assume that *language, as a medium, was already there*, before we created the individual sciences of the created objects but then again, although language has its function in daily life it is unclear how any science took up words, sentences and concepts to create its own world of scientific discourse representing the world of objects, processes or laws in their own way. The moment of arbitrariness is by far the greatest challenge in creating scientific languages and ruling out the subjective or mystic dimension, which seems to be essential to the linguistic acts by which God created the world. In a letter to Martin Buber (1878–1965) from 17 July 1916 Benjamin outlines his conceptualisation of the concept of magic in his idea of language; he linked this idea to his rejection of a possiblc contribution to Buber's journal *Der Jude*: "[Benjamin] criticizes political writing, which uses language only as a [means] of a more or less suggestive *dissemination* of the motifs which determine within the inner mind [*Innern der Seele*] of the person acting [...]" (Heil 2011: 13; translation fv).

Benjamin consistently rejects the instrumentalization or indirectness of language which would make it hardly acceptable that language has a foundational role to play in representation and knowledge of what must be true. Language offers a human, indirect way of gaining knowledge of the real wor(l)d of objects which suggests an indirect approach towards truth – considering language as a system of signs which arbitrarily link the acoustic sounds or the written letters in the conceptualization of this world of objects. Therefore, Benjamin assumes a deeper layer which cannot be part of language as a system of signs but resides in the essence of linguistic, artistic, literary or in general cultural expressions of what the world in reality is, the world's own language (or language of things). Thus, it is not a reduced view on language which Benjamin is interested in in his study of language: words refer to a concrete integrated creation (*Geschaffenheit* not *Beschaffenheit*) to which given Adamic names only partially refer. Names only become relevant in human discourse, where communication is indirectly used to make oneself understood, not to represent the created objects or enable knowledge of them.

The essence of language (words) is its creative power; although it still has remnants from the past, its original created being:

> Language is [...] a means for knowledge of something, which is already there, but it is "medium of knowledge", where it is also a "creative word". This identity was given by God, who – as it has been described in *Genesis* – creates by the word. This unity of creation and knowledge on the side of God goes hand in hand with the unity of spontaneity and reception on the side of man.
> (Roselli/Lorenz 2017: 32; translation fv)

Creating by reception, as Benjamin maintains, is the activity of the artist and for instance the silent objects which are received by the artist and creatively rearranged in his works of art. Not unlike God created the world and all the objects in it by his word, he created man and did not subsume man under his word or language – he was given this ability: God gave Adam the ability or the power by which he himself, without any help, could give names to the objects which were created by God and thus gaining knowledge of them: "[God] did not want to subsume man under language, but in man God released language, which served him as a medium of creation, freely out of himself. [...]. In naming man corresponds (*ent-spricht)* to the objects by translating the "nameless into names", whereas God guarantees the objectivity of this translation (Roselli/Lorenz 2017: 33f.; translation fv).[4]

4. "Objectivity" here means that the created things, animals, trees etc. have been separated from its creator and show a plurality which can only be perceived or experienced as a "unity" on a higher level of abstraction, for which man has been given the capability of abstraction. In our daily, ordinary world, however, where we have more than just one name-giver, it becomes harder to understand the meaning of this initial idea of creation (although it has been implemented in many "idealistic" philosophies, in which for instance spontaneity and receptivity are connected, like in Immanuel Kant's *Critique of Pure Reason*). But then again, this connection resides inside the subject, the I, which excludes an immediate access to "objective" entities which are considered the created world by words. An interesting aspect here is that Adam, when busy giving names to created things, was a person in isolation, living alone and not in a community of human beings where the names were *used* between he members to communicate themselves. So, what is the use at all of "having" names without any community in which these names might have any particular purpose. Words and names, therefore, were only there to serve as marks to refer to and perhaps give meaning to a created world and everything in it. It needs further reflection to understand this conceptual framework. Without any further qualifications things exist and only become useful in human communities after the Fall. In them man will not be able to communicate (*mit-teilen*) creative word as such (which seem to be imitated by Adam), if man was not given the task to give names to created objects, although this

Therefore, to Benjamin language cannot be an arbitrary system of signs, as it would be in its instrumental use after the Fall: in postlapsarian times the connection between the naming language of mankind (especially of the individual Adam) and the creative word of God were disconnected or became arbitrary (cf. Roselli/Lorenz 2017: 34) gives the following consequences of this disconnection:

1. Language becomes arbitrary signs;
2. The arbitrary sign forms itself the "directing word", the judgment (*das Urteil*; which has direct knowledge of good and evil);
3. Abstraction becomes the "capability of the linguistic mind";
4. This capability brings about the plurality of languages and the confusion of languages (which is visible in the "prattle" (*Geschwätz*) of language users.

There is a fundamental change in how man perceives, experiences and thinks the world in language: by using the names man had originally given to all things (animals etc.) in his world he no longer "grasps" the linguistic essence or being of things but there is a sense of taking naming too far (*Überbenennung*): The proper name of the created things, their truths, is no longer recognized by man and the proper names are replaced by a plurality of arbitrary names in different languages which reveal a certain sadness or sorrow, concepts in Baroque literature which Benjamin further explored in his *Habilitationsschrift.*

5. An example: On translating (the consequences of Benjamin's theory of language)

Benjamin gives a lot of attention to the problems of translating a literary work into another language. Considering the "Task of the Translator" (1923) Benjamin maintains that there is a kind of pure or ideal language on the level of semantics (*meaning*) which is fragmentary in its realization in spoken or written language but contains an integral dimension if connected to the pure words used to create the world. In the development of languages over time these words have been materialised in different languages we nowadays know – and (have) know(n) of

task and possibility to do so as an isolated name giver must have been a capability derived from a / the divine word creator. Furthermore, "the Adamic giving of names is far away from being a play or arbitrariness, that rather in giving names the paradisiac situation confirms itself as such, in which man did not have to struggle with the communicative dimension of words" (Fuld 1979: 76; translation fv). In paradise, Adam did not have to take the communicative dimension of language into account, although his ideas about the objects named need a contemplation on their connection with the objects on the one hand and the created objects by means of divine words on the other hand.

in earlier stages and forms of appearance in historical time –, and can also be linked to a created world which as such is not given in language but in our observation of the real mental or materialised objects. These are not part of language at all but belong to the realm of Ideas (*zum geistigen Wesen*). Thus, a sheep will be perceived as such by man but this perception as such is not specific for any particular language. In a way, translating is connecting the intention of a word in poems or novels – or even in communication – into a different language by connecting the intention with the way of giving meaning to words, sentences, texts language used in a particular, original literary work within the other language; at the same time an approximation to a pure language underlies or surmounts the continuum of all existing languages.

> Fragments of a vessel that are to be glued together must match one another in the smallest details, although they not be like one another. In the same way a translation, instead of imitating the sense of the original, must lovingly and in detail incorporate *the original's way of meaning*, thus making both the original and the translation recognizable as fragments of a greater language, just as fragments are part of a vessel. For this very reason translation must in large measure refrain from wanting to communicate something, from rendering the sense, and in this the original is important to it only in so far as it has already relieved the translator and his translation of the effort of assembling and expressing what is to be conveyed. In the realm of translation too, the words *En arkhēi ēn ho logos* ["In the beginning was the word"] apply. On the other hand, as regards the meaning, the language of a translation can – in fact, must – let itself go, so that it gives voice to the *intentio* of the original not as a reproduction but as harmony, as a supplement to the language in which it expresses itself, as its own kind of *intentio*. [...]. A real translation is transparent; it does not cover the original, does not block its light, but allows the pure language, as though reinforced by its own medium, to shine upon the original all the more fully. This may be achieved, above all, by a literal rendering of the syntax which proves words rather than sentences to be the primary element of the translator. For if the sentence is the wall before that language of the original, literalnesss (*Wörtlichkeit*) is the arcade.
>
> (Benjamin 1996: 260)

Here, the role of the "word", its specific role in rendering thoughts and ideas, and the supplementary character of the specific language to express the pure language is Benjamin's concern. The issue here is that reality cannot be represented in language but the words as such (also in the translation constructed by the translator from the original into the target language) help the translator to co-create the translation. Thus it is impossible to translate the aspects which constitute the words (or names) in the original and target language (if compared to Gottlob Frege's (1848–1925) concepts of sense and reference, *Sinn* and *Bedeu-*

tung) but there is an ontological dimension which has a link to the pure language which is presupposed in the possibility to construct a *correct* translation of one language into another, whatever correctness here may be. What Benjamin is concerned with are the ways in which the linguistic inventory on the level of words (or "arcades") refers to the real world of objects and the ways in which words or names as highlighting aspects of this objective world are represented (*dargestellt*) in the words or names of every single language. In a way, Benjamin takes up ideas from Johann Gottfried Herder (1744–1804) and Wilhelm von Humboldt (1767–1835) concerning the way in which world views are represented in the national languages. Words refer to one and the same object but differ in their ways of meaning (cf. Eilenberger 2018: 119f.). What is relevant here is the role and form of an ideal or pure language which is the "language of God", a language in which the aspect character of language does not exist.

The true language is, so to say, the ideal goal of speaking: a speaking, in which every object as such would reveal itself in its complete clarity and sophistication and determination. It would be, as Benjamin meant in his 1916 essay, a situation in which for everything which exists, the word or name God has given to all created objects can be found. The task of the translator is the task of man himself: "Man is the naming, from which we recognize, that from him the pure language speaks. All nature, as far as it communicates itself, communicates itself in language, and finally in man himself." (Eilenberger 2–18: 121; translation fv)

6. Finally

However, language in general (language which fulfils its proper function, being a connector between users of language) and particular languages as such are not primarily means of communication – although in the postlapsarian era language, words and names have drifted away from the authentic correlation with the created world and words of objects and in their own way of meaning enable possible understanding as well as a particular knowledge of what is represented in language; although this seems to be rather fragmentary in one's own national language. This representation or *Darstellung* characterizes the magical dimension of language in that it reveals reality but only in an ideal way, being related to its mental being.

There is a connection between our dealing with objects in their concrete, realistic and their nominalist appearance, as words or names being part of my own, particular spoken and written language where the epistemological dimension has necessarily disappeared.

References

Agamben, Giorgio. 2001. *Kindheit und Geschichte. Zerstörung der Erfahrung und Ursprung der Geschichte* translated. from Italian by Davide Giuriato. Frankfurt/M.: Suhrkamp.

Benjamin, Walter. n.y. *„The Theologico-Political Fragment"*. Retrieved from: https://platypus1917.org/wp-content/uploads/2011/12/benjamin_theologicopolitical.pdf, 29 June 2021.

Benjamin, Walter. 1996. *Selected Writings. Volume 1, 1913–1926*, edited by Marcus Bullock, Michael W. Jennings. Cambridge/Mass.: The Belknap Press.

Benjamin, Walter. 2019. *Über Sprache überhaupt und über die Sprache des Menschen* edited by Fred Lönker. Stuttgart: Reclam.

Eden, Tania. 1999. "Walter Benjamin". *Philosophie der Gegenwart in Einzeldarstellungen von Adorno bis v. Wright* edited by Julian Nida-Rümelin, 89–94. Stuttgart: Kröner.

Eiland, Howard & Michael W. Jennings. 2014. *Walter Benjamin. A Critical Life*. Cambridge, Mass., London: The Belknap Press.

Eilenberger, Wolfram. 2018. *Zeit der Zauberer. Das große Jahrzehnt der Philosophie 1919–1929*. Stuttgart: Klett-Cotta.

Fuld, Werner. 1979. *Walter Benjamin. Zwischen den Stühlen. Eine Biographie*. München, Wien: Hanser Verlag.

Hamacher, Werner. 2011. „Das Theologisch-politische Fragment". *Benjamin Handbuch. Leben – Werk – Wirkung* edited by Burkhardt Lindner, 175–192. Stuttgart, Weimar: J.B. Metzler.

Heil, Alexander M. 2011. *Die Verletzbarkeit sprachlicher Wesen. Die frühe Sprachphilosophie Walter Benjamins in Kontext von Sprache und Gewalt*. Baden-Baden: Deutscher Wissenschafts-Verlag.

Höffe, Otfried. 2005. *Kleine Geschichte der Philosophie*. München: Verlag C.H. Beck.

Menninghaus, Winfried. 1995. *Walter Benjamins Theorie der Sprachmagie*. Frankfurt/M.: Suhrkamp.

Robins, Robert Henry (1967 [1990]): *A Short History of Linguistics*. London, New York: Longman.

Roselli, Antonio & Ansgar Lorenz. 2017. *Walter Benjamin. Philosophie für Einsteiger*. Paderborn Wilhelm Fink.

Witte, Bernd. 1985. *Walter Benjamin*. Reinbek: Rowohlt.

CHAPTER 6

Eléments pour une histoire de l'interprétation

Considérations méthodologiques, enjeux et perspectives

Elio Ballardini
University of Bologna

L'interprétation a gagné en visibilité au cours du XXe siècle grâce à deux événements historiques couramment mentionnés dans les *Interpreting Studies* : la Conférence de paix de Paris (1919), où les interprètes consécutivistes jouent un rôle fondamental, et le procès de Nuremberg (1945–1946), où l'interprétation simultanée s'impose à l'échelle internationale. Ces deux événements donneront en effet à cette profession un prestige sans précédent. Au lendemain de la Seconde Guerre mondiale, avec la naissance des écoles pour traducteurs et interprètes, la recherche sur l'interprétation prendra son essor : consacrée essentiellement à l'interprétation de conférences, elle négligera toutefois, pendant longtemps, des modalités d'interprétation différentes, considérées à tort comme « mineures », bien que plus anciennes et plus répandues. Depuis quelques années, un nombre croissant de travaux s'attache à reconstruire l'histoire d'une pratique langagière qui s'échelonne sur plusieurs millénaires. Initialement centrées sur l'Occident, voire sur l'Europe, de plus en plus de recherches dépassent désormais ce cadre originel. Le présent article examine ce tournant épistémologique dans l'historiographie de l'interprétation, les problèmes méthodologiques qu'il implique, ses enjeux et ses perspectives.

Mots clés : horizon de projection disciplinaire, prédiction, prévision, accommodation en linguistique, Congrès international de linguistes (1928–1939)

1. Introduction

L'interprétation, que nous entendons ici dans le sens de traduction orale par opposition à la traduction écrite, a gagné en visibilité et en prestige au cours du XXe siècle. Et cela grâce à deux événements internationaux de portée historique que l'on mentionne habituellement dans les *Interpreting Studies*.

https://doi.org/10.1075/sihols.133.06bal

Le premier est la Conférence de paix de Paris (1919) où, au lendemain de la Grande Guerre, un nouvel ordre mondial entre les États vainqueurs et les États vaincus fut négocié, portant à la disparition de trois Empires et à la naissance de nouveaux États et d'organismes internationaux, entre autres la Société des Nations et l'Organisation Internationale du Travail. Plusieurs interprètes participèrent aux pourparlers ; ils étaient pour la plupart diplomates, universitaires, hommes de lettres, militaires bilingues ou polyglottes, et on les définira a posteriori "interprètes consécutivistes".

Le deuxième moment fondateur que l'on évoque couramment dans l'histoire de l'interprétation moderne est le procès de Nuremberg (1945–46), qui a porté à l'attention internationale la technique de l'interprétation simultanée.

Loin d'être des acteurs de second plan, les interprètes ont joué dans ces deux circonstances un rôle capital, acquérant sur le terrain ces lettres de noblesse qui allaient garantir à l'interprétation un statut et une réputation supérieurs à tout autre mode de traduction orale.

Cette double consécration historique a entraîné une reconnaissance sociale et économique conséquente. Elle a eu aussi pour corollaire la mise en place *ex novo* d'une formation universitaire spécifique et professionnelle, parallèle à celle des traducteurs, soucieuse de répondre aux besoins des services linguistiques des organisations internationales nées durant l'entre-deux-guerres et, surtout, au lendemain de la deuxième guerre mondiale. Ainsi, après l'expérience pionnière de l'Institut de formation d'interprètes en Etudes linguistiques et Economiques de Mannheim, fondé en 1930 par le philologue suisse Charles Glauser et rattaché en 1933 à l'Université de Heidelberg, l'Ecole d'Interprètes de Genève, qui voit le jour en 1941 grâce à Antoine Velleman, devient le modèle à suivre en Europe et ailleurs.

A partir des années 1950, une activité réfléchie de description et de théorisation de l'interprétation s'est frayée un chemin dans le monde académique en tant que discipline autonome. Axée sur l'interprétation de conférence, choix largement légitimé par le cadre historico-politique international, elle a contribué à affermir une profession nouvelle, distincte des autres formes de médiation interlinguistique et interculturelle. Mais elle a longtemps laissé dans l'ombre des modes d'interprétation considérés à tort comme mineurs, voire inférieurs, bien qu'incomparablement plus anciens et géographiquement plus répandus.

Depuis une trentaine d'années, de nombreuses études ont permis d'aller au-delà de ce cadre originel, dépassant une vision centrée principalement sur l'interprétation de conférence et découvrant des champs de recherche jusque-là inexplorés. C'est dans cette ouverture vers l'Autre interprétation, *outside the booth* et *outside the conference hall* que vient se greffer une réflexion féconde sur l'*Histoire de l'interprétation* ou, si l'on veut, sur les *interprètes dans l'Histoire*.

2. D'une historiographie accessoire au renouveau des *Interpreting studies*

Le volet historiographique des études sur l'interprétation est donc relativement récent. En 1995, Gile constatait en effet dans ses *Regards sur la recherche en interprétation de conférence* que "les textes historiques représentent une démarche quelque peu isolée dans la recherche sur l'interprétation. Ils constituent un système fermé et n'interagissent guère avec d'autres types de textes" (1995: 27). Jusqu'aux années 1990, les rares apports étaient relégués la plupart des fois dans les marges historiographiques d'ouvrages consacrés à la traduction écrite. Dans le meilleur des cas, ils prenaient l'ampleur d'un chapitre à part, parfois introductif, puisqu'il faut bien reconnaître que la parole précède l'écriture. Les interprètes et les traducteurs partageaient en l'occurrence des origines communes et ancestrales (Mounin 1963, Delisle & Woodsworth 1995), amalgame que l'on retrouve d'ailleurs dans des essais historiographiques plus récents (Ballard 2013).

Les chercheurs-interprètes qui s'attachent à donner des assises historiques à leur propre activité et savoir-faire ne sont pas nombreux en ces temps-là. Cependant ils font autorité et exerceront une influence durable dans les études sur l'interprétation : Herbert (1952), Thieme *et al.* (1956), Hermann (1956/2002), Glässer (1956), Cary (1956), Van Hoof (1962), Gofmann (1963), pour ne citer que les plus éminents. Falbo (2004) observe avec acuité que ces amorces d'historiographie avaient surtout pour but de fournir une toile de fond historique à des "manuels" de pédagogie de l'interprétation de conférence, pour étayer une formation relative à une activité au statut social et professionnel encore fragile. En effet, dans les années 1950–1960, il fallait affirmer un ancrage plusieurs fois millénaire de l'interprétariat, pratique langagière largement ignorée par l'historiographie, et revendiquer sa reconnaissance sur le plan professionnel et académique. A bien des égards, ces premières explorations du passé fonctionnaient un peu comme une réserve d'antécédents dans laquelle puiser pour soutenir des revendications actuelles. Une démarche qui rejoint les projets d'historicisation de bien d'autres types d'activités humaines, de professions, d'arts et métiers, d'artisanat.

Au départ, cet intérêt pour l'histoire présente donc un caractère accessoire et, surtout, fonctionnel. Mais bientôt ce sont les origines de l'interprétation simultanée notamment qui retiennent l'attention des chercheurs (Roditi 1982, D. and M. Bowen 1985, Skuncke 1989, Gaiba 1998). C'est là que survient, nous semble-t-il, un changement de cap important, non seulement sur le plan historiographique mais aussi pour les *Interpreting Studies*. Et cela pour deux raisons, du moins telle est l'hypothèse que nous formulons.

La première raison est liée au fait d'avoir choisi le procès de Nuremberg, donc l'interprétation au tribunal, comme lieu et date de naissance de l'interprétation simultanée – "Tout a commencé à Nuremberg" selon Skuncke (1989) – plutôt que les expériences, artisanales et bien moins connues, menées entre les deux guerres mondiales à Genève (1927), Moscou (1928), Berlin (1930), Leningrad (1935), au Parlement belge (1936) (Gofman 1963, Černov 1978 et 1992, Ŝvejcer 1999, Chernov S. 2016). Ce recadrage épistémologique a rapidement débouché sur une pléthore de travaux consacrés entièrement à la didactique de l'interprétation en milieu judiciaire (Berk-Seligson 1990, Dueñas Gonzáles, Vásquez and Mikkelson 1991, De Jongh 1992, Edwards 1995, Collins and Morris 1996). Avec, toujours, quelques pages introductives d'encadrement historique.

Or l'interprétation au procès pénal, à toutes ses étapes, non seulement aux débats en salle d'audience, suppose des formes d'interactions verbales et non verbales, interlinguistiques et interculturelles, qui relèvent davantage de l'interprétation de dialogue, ou de modes hybrides de médiation orale et écrite, que de l'interprétation de conférence à proprement parler. Cette caractéristique a conduit progressivement les chercheurs à s'intéresser à des pratiques de médiation linguistique et culturelle qui diffèrent de la consécutive et de la simultanée et qui étaient considérées jusque-là, de manière plus ou moins voilée, comme un sous-genre de l'interprétation, une sorte de "demi-sœur" ou de "Cendrillon", une "second rate form of interpreting which is not worthy of specific attention in terms of status, training, remuneration and research" (Gentile 1997:117).

Deuxième raison : la fonction d'interprète au service de la justice existe, en tout cas pour ce qui est du Vieux Continent et de ses territoires colonisés, depuis de nombreux siècles. Ce qui donne d'emblée à l'interprétation une tout autre envergure historique et géographique.

Cette "sortie de la salle de conférence" et "de la cabine du simultanéiste" a ouvert la voie à la recherche sur le monde composite de l'interprétation de dialogue, de liaison, communautaire, de service public, en langue des signes, pour les médias, humanitaire, en zone de guerre, etc. Devenue aujourd'hui le courant principal des *Interpreting Studies,* cette réflexion implique en quelque sorte un retour aux sources, aspect qui nous intéresse de près. On observe ainsi une tension heuristique vers d'autres perspectives spatiales et temporelles, d'autres chronologies et d'autres cartographies de l'interprétariat. Le tout dans l'esprit de ce *tournant culturel* invoqué par beaucoup (Cronin 2002), qui encourage de nouvelles façons d'enquêter le lien entre l'histoire et l'interprétation.

3. Une lecture foncièrement occidentocentrique

Vingt ans après Gile, Baigorri-Jalón exprime une satisfaction mesurée lorsqu'il observe le nombre croissant d'études historiographiques sur l'interprétation : "While still a relatively small area or work in interpreting studies, the volume of historical research on interpreting has increased considerably in recent times" (2015: 184). Cet essor s'inscrit essentiellement dans la tradition historiographique occidentale. C'est-à-dire que sur le plan épistémologique et méthodologique on y adopte les périodisations issues du modèle d'évolution linéaire et mesurable de matrice européenne et qui prennent comme repère spatial un planisphère, "un théâtre du monde", au centre duquel se trouve l'Europe. La recherche a donc recours ici à un outillage et à des catégories historiographiques bien établis. La plupart des chercheurs s'en tiennent pour des raisons de praticité méthodologique, aux scansions canoniques du passé, subséquentes à l'avènement de l'écriture (histoire de l'Antiquité, histoire du Moyen-âge, histoire moderne et contemporaine), appliquées à des espaces géographiques pertinents (à savoir que l'on se garde d'inventer une "Amérique médiévale" ou une "Antiquité australienne"). C'est à partir de ce système spatio-temporel bien campé que l'investigation historique sur l'interprétation se ramifie ensuite en zoomant sur des micro-contextes hétérogènes et aux frontières souvent perméables. Etablir clairement le cadre géographique et chronologique d'une recherche historique est évidemment nécessaire pour circonscrire l'objet que l'on souhaite analyser. Loin d'être une simple question de quantité et de qualité des données accessibles, la périodisation et la spatialisation rendent en effet observable le chaos des sources. Mais c'est aussi et surtout le choix d'un regard sur l'Histoire, qui est dans ce cas foncièrement occidental.

On comprend bien que dans un premier temps cette recherche naissante s'oriente d'abord vers les axes thématiques où il est possible de s'appuyer sur des sources d'un accès apparemment plus simple. Tenter de dresser ici l'inventaire de toutes les pistes de recherche qui ont été suivies jusqu'à présent dans ce domaine dépasserait de loin le cadre de cet article. Pour une synthèse, nous renvoyons, entre autres, aux essais remarquables de Van Hoof (1962, 1991, 1996), M. and D. Bowen, Kaufmann, Kurz (1995), Baigorri-Jalón (2000), Alonso-Araguás (2008), Alonso-Araguás and Baigorri-Jalón (2021).

De plus en plus nombreuses, ces enquêtes ont le mérite de mettre en lumière la présence des interprètes, et des langues et cultures en contact, dans des milieux très disparates (militaires, religieux, diplomatiques, institutionnels, administratifs-juridiques, commercial). Certains sujets sont abordés de manière plus fréquente que d'autres, ce qui favorise aussi les débats entre chercheurs.

Dans ce contexte, qui évolue très rapidement, une démarche historiographique semble particulièrement appréciée car elle peut être appliquée à l'étude des périodes les plus variées : la prosopographie. Le récent ouvrage de Baigorri-Jalón (2019), *Lenguas entre dos fuegos. Intérpretes en la Guerra Civil española. 1936–1939*, constitue à ce titre un parangon du genre, tout à fait exemplaire sur le plan méthodologique. A travers un immense travail de dépouillement des archives, l'auteur non seulement reconstruit des "vies sans histoire", pour citer Balliu (2008), mais il nous fait découvrir en même temps des versants peu connus de la Guerre d'Espagne.

Un autre champ d'intérêt privilégié ces dernières années est celui de l'histoire des interprètes organisés ou institutionnalisés, comme c'est le cas, par exemple, de l'Association Internationale des Interprètes de conférence (Keiser 1999, 2004), des interprètes aux Nations Unies (Baigorri 2004) ou encore des interprètes encadrés dans les administrations coloniales, dont la présence est relativement bien documentée dans les archives relatives aux colonies hispano-américaines, françaises, anglaises et autres. Il est évident que les thèmes se chevauchent parfois et s'enchevêtrent les uns dans les autres. Et il est tout aussi clair que les catégorisations et la diversité des termes et des concepts utilisés de nos jours dans les études d'interprétation pour désigner et différencier les multiples formes d'interprétation peuvent être difficiles à conjuguer au passé. Même la distinction entre traducteur et interprète devient une abstraction purement académique et perd tout son sens quand on l'applique à des temporalités et des horizons lointains. Cela dit, ce qui importe c'est que depuis quelques années, on commence à mieux connaitre la place dans l'histoire de *l'interpres*, de *l'hermēneus*, du *maistre latinier, du peregrini sermonis peritus*, du *truchement, meturdgeman, drugeman, turdjuman ou dragoman*, de *l'alfaqueque*, des *giovani di lingua* et des *Jeunes de langue*, des *fixeurs, courtiers-interprètes, interprètes de conférence*, de *dialogue*, de *liaison*, *communautaires, judiciaires*, et ainsi de suite.

4. Réflexions et itinéraires méthodologiques

Cette production scientifique foisonnante appelle quelques remarques méthodologiques. Sur ce plan, on soulignera d'emblée que la toute première difficulté est liée au simple constat qu'il existe un lien indéniable entre l'apparition du concept même d'histoire et l'usage de l'écriture.

Déjà Andronikof (1968: 9) observait dans une *Introduction* érudite et stimulante à *L'interprète dans les conférences internationales* de Seleskovitch (1968) qu'"il est naturel qu'aucun nom d'interprète n'ait marqué l'histoire, puisqu'il ne fait que parler et sa matière première comme son produit fini sont oraux, donc évanescents". Près de 50 ans plus tard, Takeda et Baigorri-Jalón confirment cette difficulté dans leur *New Insight in the History of Interpreting* : "Granted, compared to translation, which handles written texts, there are much fewer records related to interpreting and interpreting activities due to the ephemerality of speech and the generally subaltern status of interpreters as agents in historical events" (2016: VIII). Il ne fait guère de doute que l'oral est condamné à une existence éphémère tant qu'il n'est pas fixé sur un support. Pourtant, "le dicton classique *verba volant scripta manent* qui est aujourd'hui compris comme une sorte de louange à la permanence, à la fixité immuable et donc rassurante de l'écrit par rapport à un oral fugitif, infiniment changeant et par conséquent peu fiable, signifiait jadis exactement le contraire. Il avait été forgé à la louange de la parole qui a des ailes et peut voler par contraste avec le mot écrit, silencieux et inerte sur la page, mort" (Galazzi 2001: 3–4). Or s'il est vrai qu'il n'appartient pas aux interprètes, en règle générale, d'être sous les feux de la rampe mais d'œuvrer plutôt dans les coulisses, on constate avec étonnement qu'une partie non négligeable de la narration historique, notamment événementielle, ne fait pas grand cas de la question linguistique dans l'histoire. Comme si le thème du pouvoir de la langue, et de la langue du pouvoir, était un aspect non axiologique, non pertinent pour les historiens. Comme si la langue n'avait jamais représenté un enjeu identitaire important, voire un *casus belli* dans l'histoire.

L'essence volatile du discours oral et l'invisibilité de l'interprète font pressentir l'énorme difficulté de l'historien de l'interprétation, si l'on considère que "dès le jour où des communautés de langues différentes durent entrer en contact les unes avec les autres – et cela avant même l'invention de l'écriture – il leur fallut, pour se comprendre, faire appel à des intermédiaires" (Van Hoof 1996: 9).

Cette pénurie de données observables, surtout pour ce qui est des périodes lointaines, détermine non seulement le choix des méthodologies à adopter, mais encore l'objet même de l'analyse : à la différence du domaine de la traduction, dès lors qu'il est impossible d'examiner le "produit" de l'interprétation, c'est sur l'interprète en tant qu' "agent" et sur la "fonction" de l'interprétation que se concentrent les recherches relatives aux périodes historiques qui précèdent le XXe siècle. Il s'ensuit que les sources dont on dispose pour essayer de reconstruire l'histoire de l'interprétation sont essentiellement écrites, primaires et secondaires, tandis que les documents non écrits, par exemple iconographiques, restent rares. Les méthodologies appliquées à cette très large période – quatre millénaires – sont donc classiques et apparemment bien rodées. Il en est ainsi également pour les premières recherches consacrées à l'histoire de l'interprétation, réalisées dans des secteurs scientifiques étrangers à l'interprétariat, telles les études orientales (Gehman 1914a, 1914b) ou l'archéologie (Gardiner 1915) – ce que Baigorri-Jalón (2015: 184) qualifie de proto-historiographie de l'interprétation –, travaux longtemps peu remarqués par la communauté des interprètes-chercheurs, hormis les plus attentifs.

Pour ce qui est de l'interprétation contemporaine, les chercheurs peuvent compter en revanche sur un éventail bien plus riche de moyens pour analyser une plus grande quantité et variété qualitative de données. On s'appuie sur les nouvelles technologies, on a accès à des sources écrites et orales, des archives, des actes et des documents déclassifiés, des mémoires, du matériel iconographique, photographique, phonographique, cinématographique et audiovisuel, on peut consulter également des correspondances, des revues et des journaux, des chroniques, des manuscrits, des enregistrements et des entretiens avec des témoins directs ou indirects.

C'est dire toute l'ampleur du sujet et du champ d'investigation. L'historien de l'interprétation évolue en effet dans un cadre épistémologique particulièrement complexe, difficile à appréhender, au carrefour de nombreuses disciplines. Alors que le temps présent voue trop souvent le monde de la recherche au cloisonnement et à des formes de polarisation concurrentielle des débats, il serait souhaitable, au contraire, d'œuvrer de concert. Loin de nier les apports individuels, les approches du groupe Histoire de l'AIIC, du groupe HISTAL de l'Université de Montréal ou encore, pour la partie historiographique de ses projets de recherche, du groupe Alfaqueque de l'Université de Salamanque sont en ce sens des exemples féconds de travail collectif qui méritent d'être retenus.

Par ailleurs, ne conviendrait-il pas d'encourager, ici aussi, le dialogue interdisciplinaire, la confrontation scientifique de perspectives différentes et complémentaires (histoire, anthropologie, sociologie, *cultural studies*, linguistique, philologie, droit, etc...) ? Une telle démarche permettrait sans doute de se mettre à l'abri de l'a priori conceptuel, du regard uniquement endogène, celui des praticiens interprètes, dont l'identité professionnelle risque parfois d'inhiber le regard critique. Elle pourrait favoriser les visions décalées, en fonction de contrepoids, évitant ainsi de projeter sur le passé des instances associées au présent.

Ces considérations nous conduisent à souligner d'autres aspects problématiques qui pèsent sur la recherche en question. Pour des raisons d'espace, nous nous limiterons à en citer trois, à titre d'exemple, sans aucune prétention d'exhaustivité.

Figure de proue de la recherche en histoire de l'interprétation, Baigorri-Jalón, historien et géographe de formation avant de suivre une brillante carrière d'interprète de conférence à l'ONU, n'hésite pas à affirmer que les interprètes ne sont pas formés aux méthodes historiographiques (2015: 184). Or, que l'on souhaite travailler sur des sujets circonscrits, par exemple sur des micro-études de cas, sur la micro-histoire ou, à rebours, sur des coordonnées spatio-temporelles plus amples, il importe de choisir un regard et des méthodologies propres aux historiens, autrement dit, il faut "écrire l'histoire comme les historiens de profession" (Delisle 1997–1998: 33).

Cette carence est parfois très visible dans le traitement des sources intrinsèquement complexes – c'est le deuxième exemple qu'il nous paraît important de mentionner – comme les *mémoires*, à savoir ces écrits "qui visent à perpétuer la présence de ces témoins silencieux" que sont les interprètes, selon l'expression de Balliu (2008: 21). Effectivement, les mémoires sont le reflet d'une perception subjective, et les omissions ou les distorsions, intentionnelles ou non, inhérentes à tout témoignage, devraient être abordées avec les précautions méthodologiques propres aux historiens. Songeons par exemple aux difficultés que peuvent poser à l'historien les écrits autobiographiques, par ailleurs d'un intérêt certain, d'Eugen Dollmann (1963), interprète de Hitler et de Mussolini, ou les *Carnets d'une interprète de guerre* de Elena Rževskaja (2005), ou encore les *Carnets* de Pavel Palažčenko (2020), interprète de Gorbačev et de Ševarnadze.

Enfin, citons un troisième écueil difficile à éviter, en particulier dans le secteur de l'interprétation en milieu politique-diplomatique, militaire et judiciaire. Avec la création d'associations professionnelles et l'élaboration conséquente de codes éthiques, l'impératif déontologique du respect du secret professionnel peut représenter pour les historiens de l'interprétation contemporaine une pierre d'achoppement souvent difficile à surmonter. D'une part, le précepte de la confidentialité, que l'on demande aux interprètes de respecter sans faille, a indéniablement contribué à protéger la réputation de l'ensemble des interprètes (Thiéry 1985, 2008) ; d'autre part, et contrairement à d'autres catégories professionnelles tenues à cette même obligation, il tend à condamner les interprètes à ce silence et à cette invisibilité dont la recherche historique voudrait justement les sortir.

5. En guise de conclusion

A l'heure où l'on s'interroge sur le devenir de l'interprétation, révolutionnée comme tant d'autres activités par des innovations technologiques qui pourraient rendre obsolète le clivage entre la traduction et l'interprétation fondé sur le critère de la communication orale ou écrite (Salevsky 2018: 185), nous estimons que la recherche sur l'histoire de l'interprétation trouve sa raison d'être non seulement dans le cadre des sciences du langage et, en l'espèce, des *Interpreting Studies*, mais aussi des études historiques en général. Ce que Van Hoof affirme à propos de l'histoire de la traduction vaut également pour l'interprétation : "Étudier l'histoire de la traduction équivaut en quelque sorte à reprendre l'histoire du monde, l'histoire des civilisations, mais par le biais de la traduction" (1986: 5). Ainsi, précisément parce que l'interprète est un intermédiaire, un *entre-deux*, s'attacher à reconstruire son histoire pourrait être l'occasion de nuancer et de multiplier les points de vue sur l'Histoire elle-même.

Aider à renouveler l'échelle historiographique habituelle, explorer au-delà des frontières de l'Occident, changer de clefs de lectures, encore trop occidentalo-centrées, voire carrément eurocentriques car confortées par l'idée d'un continuum généalogique avec l'Antiquité et héritières des rapports de force historiquement établis, des relations asymétriques entre dominants et dominés, véritable reflet de la vision du "vainqueur": c'est ce changement que la recherche historique sur l'interprétation pourrait favoriser. On se souviendra à ce propos de l'enseignement de Tzvetan Todorov (1982), qui laisse entendre dans son essai *La conquête de l'Amérique. La question de l'autre* (où l'auteur mentionne par ailleurs le célèbre cas de la Malinche, esclave, maîtresse et interprète de Hernan Cortèz) que, dès lors que l'on parle de civilisations *pré-colombiennes*, du fait même de l'emploi du nom de Christophe Colomb, on colle une étiquette européenne à une réalité qui ne l'est pas, on impose aux vaincus le récit des vainqueurs. Songeons également aux *Croisades vues par les Arabes* d'Amin Maalouf (1983), ou à *La vision des vaincus* de l'historien et anthropologue Nathan Wachtel (1971), œuvre capitale qui permet de renouveler notre regard, notre rapport à l'autre, et l'image que nous projetons sur l'Histoire.

Or on constate parfois que l'historiographie de l'interprétation n'est pas toujours à l'abri de cette mainmise sur l'histoire, ce *Theft of History*, selon le titre du célèbre ouvrage de l'anthropologue Jack Goody (2006) dénonçant la narration d'un passé que l'Occident, fort de sa suprématie politique et économique, impose au monde.

Beaucoup reste à faire, car le champ de recherche est ici, évidemment, immense. En ce sens, les enquêtes micro-historiques et les études de cas sur l'interprétation en Asie, en Chine ou au Japon, ou ailleurs (Torikai 2009, Takeda 2010, Lung and Li 2005, Lung 2011, Falbo & Riccardi 2016) vont dans la direction souhaitée, qui consiste à ouvrir la réflexion à des territoires et des temporalités souvent méconnus des chercheurs occidentaux. En s'émancipant du Grand Récit calibré essentiellement sur le méridien de Greenwich, expression que l'on emprunte aux travaux éclairants du géohistorien Christian Grataloup (2011), en dépassant un découpage spatio-temporel communément admis, elles ont le mérite de nous conduire vers des pistes inexplorées, d'éclairer des scènes historiques et géographiques qui n'ont rien de périphérique, de dévoiler les interrelations, les interactions, les points de rencontre, les interfaces, les connexions, entre les cultures et les langues que le travail d'interprète implique. Ces enquêtes sont menées non pas pour récuser ou remplacer les connaissances acquises ni pour en diminuer l'importance historiographique, mais, au contraire, pour les enrichir et les compléter. Car comme l'écrit l'historien français Paul Veyne (1971: 271), que nous citons pour conclure “l’histoire ne progresse pas, elle s’élargit ; ce qui signifie qu’elle ne perd pas en arrière le terrain qu’elle conquiert en avant”.

Bibliographie

Alonso-Araguás, Icíar. 2008. “Historia, historiografia e interpretación. Propuestas para una historia de la mediación lingüística oral”. *La traducción del futuro: mediación lingüístca y cultural en el siglo XXI* dir. par Luis Pegenaute, Janet De Cesaris, Mercè Tricás & Elisenda Bernal, 429–440. Barcelona: PPU/AIETI.

Alonso-Araguás, Icíar & Jesús Baigorri-Jalón. 2021. “Interpretación: historia y profesión”. *Interpretare da e verso l’italiano. Didattica e innovazione per la formazione dell’interprete* dir. par Mariachiara Russo, 459–475. Bologna: Bononia University Press.

Andronikof, Costantin. 1968. “Introduction”. *L’interprète dans les conférences internationales. Problèmes de langage et de communication* dir. par Danica Seleskovitch, 1–20. Paris: Minard Lettres modernes.

Baigorri-Jalón, Jesús. 2000. *La interpretación de conferencias: el nacimiento de una profesión. De París a Nuremberg.* Granada: Comares.

Baigorri-Jalón, Jesús. 2004. *Interpreters at the United Nations: A History.* Salamanca: Ediciones Universidad de Salamanca.

Baigorri-Jalón, Jesús. 2015. “History”. *Routledge Encyclopedia of Interpreting Studies* dir. par Franz Pöchhacker, 183–186. London & New York: Routledge.

Baigorri-Jalón, Jesús. 2019. *Lenguas entre dos fuegos. Intérpretes en la Guerra Civil española. 1936–1939.* Granada : Editorial Comares.

Ballard, Michel. 2013. *Histoire de la traduction. Repères historiques et culturels.* Bruxelles: De Boeck.

Balliu, Christian. 2008. “L’interprète : une vie sans histoire”. *Interprète de la République* dir. par Christopher Thiéry, 15–21. Bruxelles: Les éditions du Hazard.

Berk-Seligson, Susan. 1990. *The Bilingual Courtroom: Court Interpreters in the Judicial Process.* Chicago: University of Chicago Press.

doi Bowen, Margareta, David Bowen, Francine Kaufmann & Ingrid Kurz. 1995. “Interpreters and the making of history”. *Les traducteurs dans l’histoire* dir. par Jean Delisle, Judith Woodsworth, 245–279. Ottawa : Les Presses de l’Université d’Ottawa.

Cary, Edmond. 1956. *La traduction dans le monde moderne.* Genève: Georg & Co.

Černov, Gelij V. 1978. *Teorija i praktika sinchronnogo perevoda* [Théorie et pratique de l’interprétation simultanée]. Moskva: Meždunarodnye otnošenija.

Chernov, Gelij V. 1992. “Conference Interpretation in the USSR: History, Theory, New Frontiers”, *Meta* 37:1. 149–162.

doi Chernov, Sergei. 2016. “At the Dawn of Simultaneous Interpreting in the USSR. Filling some gaps in the history”. *New Insights in the History of Interpreting* dir. par Takeda, Kayoko & Jesús Baigorri-Jalón, 135–165. Amsterdam & Philadelphia: John Benjamins.

Collins Joan and Ruth Morris. 1996. *Interpreters and the Legal Process.* Winchester: Waterside Press.

Cronin, Michael. 2002. "The Empire Talks Back: Orality, Heteronomy and the Cultural Turn in Interpretation Studies". *Translation and Power* dir. par Maria Tymoczko & Edwin Gentzler, 45–62. Amherst & Boston: University of Massachusetts Press.

De Jongh, Elena M. 1992. *An Introduction to Court Interpreting. Theory and Practice.* New York: University Press of America.

Delisle, Jean, Judith Woodsworth, dir. 1995. *Les traducteurs dans l'histoire.* Ottawa: Les Presses de l'Université d'Ottawa.

Delisle, Jean. 1997–1998. "Réflexions sur l'historiographie de la traduction et ses exigences scientifiques". *Equivalences* 26:2/27:1. 21–43.

Dolmann, Eugen. 1963. *Dolmetscher der Diktatoren.* Bayreuth: Hestia.

Edwards, Alicia B. 1995. *The Practice of Court Interpreting.* Amsterdam & Philadelphia: John Benjamins.

Falbo, Caterina. 2004. *La ricerca in interpretazione.* Milano: FrancoAngeli.

Falbo, Caterina & Alessandra Riccardi, dir. 2016. *Interpreting and Interpreters throughout History. Interpreter's Newsletter* 21. Trieste: EUT.

Gaiba, Francesca. 1998. *The Origins of Simultaneous Interpretation: The Nuremberg Trial.* Ottawa: University of Ottawa Press.

Galazzi Enrica. 2001. "Oral imaginaire et imaginaire de l'oral". In *Oralité dans la parole et dans l'écriture. Oralità nella parola e nella scrittura. Analyses linguistiques, valeurs symboliques, enjeux professionnels* dir. par Mariagrazia Margarito, Enrica Galazzi & Monique Lebhar Politi, 3–4. Torino: Edizioni Libreria Cortina.

Gardiner, Alan H. 1915. "The Egyptian Word for Dragoman". *Proceedings of the Society of Biblical Archeology* 37:117–125.

Gehman, Henry S. 1914a. The Interpreters of Foreign Languages among the Ancients: A Study Based on Greek and Latin Sources. PhD dissertation. Philadelphia: Lancaster Intelligencer Printing Co.

Gehman, Henry S. 1914b. "The Use of Interpreters by the Ten Thousand and by Alexander". *The Classical Weekly* 8:2. 9–14.

Gentile, Adolfo. 1997. "Community Interpreting or Not? Practices, Standards and Accreditation". *The Critical Link: Interpreters in the Community* dir. par Silvana E. Carr, Roda P. Roberts, Aideen Dufour & Dini Steyn, 109–118. Amsterdam & Philadelphia: John Benjamins.

Gile, Daniel. 1995. *Regards sur la recherche en interprétation de conférence.* Lille: Presses Universitaires de Lille.

Glässer, Edgar. 1956. "Dolmetschen im Mittelalter". *Beiträge zur Geschichte des Dolmetschens* dir. par Thieme et al., 61–79. München: Isar.

Gofman, Evgenij A. 1963. "K istorii ustnogo perevoda" [A propos de l'histoire de l'interprétation]. *Tetradi perevodčika* 1: 20–26.

Gonzáles Dueñas Roseann, Victoria F. Vásquez & Holly Mikkelson. 1991. *Fundamentals of Court Interpretation.* Durham, North Carolina: Carolina Academic Press.

Goody, Jack. 2006. *The Theft of History.* Cambridge: Cambridge University Press.

Grataloup, Christian. 2011. *Faut-il penser autrement l'histoire du monde?* Paris: Armand Colin.

Herbert, Jean. 1952. *Manuel de l'interprète. Comment on devient interprète de conférences.* Genève : Librairie de l'Université, Georg & Co.

Hermann, Alfred. 2002 [1956]. "Interpreting in Antiquity". *The Interpreting Studies Reader* dir. par Franz Pöchhacker & Miriam Shlesinger, 15–22. London and New York: Routledge.

Keiser, Walter. 1999. "L'histoire de l'Association Internationale des Interprètes de conférence." *History of Interpreting* dir. par Ingrid Kurz & Margareta Bowen. Special Issue Interpreting 4:1.81–95.

Keiser, Walter. 2004. "L'interprétation de conférence en tant que profession et les précurseurs de l'Association Internationale des Interprètes de Conférence (AIIC) 1918–1953". *Meta* 49: 3.576–608.

Lung, Rachel. 2011. *Interpreters in Early Imperial China.* Amsterdam & Philadelphia: John Benjamins.

Lung, Rachel & Donghui Li. 2005. "Interpreters as Historians in China." *Meta* 50:3.997–1009.

Maalouf, Amin. 1983. *Les croisades vues par les Arabes. La barbarie franque en Terre sainte.* Paris: Jean-Claude Lattès.

Mounin Georges. 1963. *Les problèmes théoriques de la traduction.* Paris: Gallimard.

Palažčenko, Pavel R. 2020. *Professija i vremja. Zapiski perevodčika-diplomata* [*La profession et le temps. Carnets d'un interprète*]. Moskva: Novaja gazeta.

Roditi, Edouard. 1982. *Interpreting. Its History in a Nutshell.* Washington D.C.: Georgetown University.

Rževskaja, Elena M. 2005. *Zapiski voennogo perevodčika* [*Carnets d'une l'interprète de guerre*]. Moskva: Knižnij klub.

Salevsky, Heidemarie. 2018. "The Origins of Interpreting in the Old Testament and the *Meturgeman* in the Synagogue". *The Bible Translator* 69: 2.184–198.

Seleskovitch, Danica. 1968. *L'interprète dans les conférences internationales. Problèmes de langage et de communication.* Paris: Lettres Modernes Minard.

Skuncke, Marie-France. 1989. "Tout a commencé à Nuremberg". *Parallèles* 11.5–8.

Švejcer, Aleksandr. D. 1999. "At the Dawn of Simultaneous Interpretation in Russia". *Interpreting* 4:1.23–28.

Takeda, Kayoko. 2010. *Interpreting the Tokyo War Crimes Tribunal. A sociopolitical analysis.* Ottawa: University of Ottawa Press.

Takeda, Kayoko & Jesús Baigorri-Jalón, dir. 2016. *New Insights in the History of Interpreting.* Amsterdam & Philadelphia: John Benjamins.

Thieme, Karl, Alfred Hermann & Edgar Glässer, dir. 1956. *Beiträge zur Geschichte des Dolmetschens.* München: Isar.

Thiéry, Christopher. 1985. "La responsabilité de l'interprète de conférence professionnel ou pourquoi nous ne pouvons pas écrire nos mémoires". *Meta* 30:1.78–81.

Todorov, Tzvetan. 1982. *La conquête de l'Amérique. La question de l'autre.* Paris: Le Seuil.

Torikai, Kumiko. 2009. *Voices of the Invisible Presence: Diplomatic Interpreters in Post-World War II in Japan.* Amsterdam & Philadelphia: John Benjamins.

Van Hoof, Henri. 1962. *Théorie et pratique de l'interprétation. Avec application particulière à l'anglais et au français.* München: Max Hueber Verlag.

Van Hoof, Henri. 1986. *Petite histoire de la traduction en Occident.* Louvain-la-Neuve: Cabay.

Van Hoof, Henri. 1991. *Histoire de la traduction en Occident.* Paris / Louvain-La-Neuve: Duculot.

Van Hoof, Henri. 1996. "De l'identité des interprètes au cours des siècles". *Hieronymus Complutensis* 3.9–20.

Veyne, Paul. 1971. *Comment on écrit l'histoire. Essai d'épistémologie.* Paris: Le Seuil.

Wachtel, Nathan. 1971. *La vision des vaincus: les Indiens du Pérou devant la Conquête espagnole*, 1530–1570. Paris: Gallimard.

Abstract

Interpretation gained visibility in the 20th century thanks to two major historic events: the Paris Peace Conference (1919), in which consecutive interpreters played a crucial role, and the Nuremberg Trials (1945–1946), in which simultaneous interpretation gained international recognition. These key events helped to give the profession unprecedented prestige. The emergence of schools for translators and interpreters after World War II fostered the development of Interpreting Studies along with Translation Studies. Essentially conference interpreting centered, these studies have unfortunately neglected for a long time other forms of interpreting, wrongly regarded as lower-ranking forms, although older and more widespread. Today, an increasing number of studies aim to reconstruct the global history of this millennia-old language practice. Initially West-centered, if not Europe-centered, currently more and more works go beyond this original framework. The present article examines this epistemological shift in the historiography of interpreting, the methodological problems it implies, its challenges and perspectives.

Keywords: interpreting, history, historiography, methodology

CHAPTER 7

"Computational linguistics" as the horizon of projection of early machine translation

Jacqueline Léon
HTL UMR7596, CNRS, Université Paris Cité

In my paper, I will discuss the articulation between the horizon of projection (the anticipation of the evolution of a field of knowledge) and the horizon of retrospection (its background) in the special case of early machine translation. Because its horizon of retrospection (World War II sciences and technologies, information theory and mathematical logic) did not include linguistics, the horizon of projection of machine translation could not be high quality machine translation, but formal and computational linguistics. The horizon of computational linguistics thus projected was piloted and installed by institutions, funded and evaluated by state agencies, with conclusions and recommendations stated by expert reports, illustrating a new form of relationship between institution and sciences.

Keywords: machine translation, computational linguistics, horizon of retrospection, horizon of projection

1. Introduction

This text was presented as part of the workshop "Horizons of Projection – the Future of Linguistic Knowledge: a Historical perspective" initially proposed by our late colleague and friend Valérie Raby who passed away in December 2019, Jean-Marie Fournier and Christian Puech. All three had worked on the notion of horizon of retrospection (see Puech and Raby eds. 2006 and 2011). The project to explore horizons of projection was a "natural" continuation of that work. In the presentation text of the workshop, they define horizons de projection "as the anticipation of the evolution of a field of knowledge, a discipline, a theory or a school of thought".

https://doi.org/10.1075/sihols.133.07leo

Sylvain Auroux, who introduced the notion of horizon of retrospection in 1987, associated it with horizon of projection in his text "L'histoire des sciences du langage et le paradoxe historiographique" published in 1995:

> [...] every act of knowledge is a historical reality; [...] Because it is limited, the act of knowledge possesses by definition a temporal thickness, a horizon of retrospection, as well as a horizon of projection. Knowledge (or the instances that implement it) does not destroy its past, as is often mistakenly believed; it organizes it, chooses it, forgets it, imagines it or idealizes it, just as it anticipates its future by dreaming it at the same time as it builds it. Without memory and without project, there is simply no knowledge.
> (Auroux 1995: 49. All quotes from Auroux have been translated into English by the present author)

In his 2006 article "Modes d'historicisation", he says:

> In general, the historian must try not to resort to teleology, i.e. to explain the past by the future. He must use the causal explanation that goes from the past to the future; he can of course use the virtual future of the "research program", insofar as this is a cause of the production of knowledge. (Auroux 2006: 106)

In my paper, I will discuss the articulation between horizon of projection and horizon of retrospection in the special case of early machine translation. I would like to show how, because of its horizon of retrospection, the horizon of projection of machine translation could not be high quality machine translation, but formal and computational linguistics.

It is worth recalling that machine translation (MT below) had a rapid and dazzling start. In its original plan, as outlined by Warren Weaver in his Memorandum *Translation* in 1949 (Weaver [1949] 1955), MT was to overcome the lack of human translators by producing mass translations of scientific and technical texts from Russian into English. After, the Memorandum was sent to about 100 prominent people, MT centers were created at American universities, funded by the NSF, the Department of Defense, and the CIA.

However, contrary to the premature announcements made by some researchers to the media and the public, the results were poor and disappointing. The weak capacities of the computers, limited in memory and speed, were of course to blame, but also the linguistic difficulties which had not been identified nor measured.

As a result, MT as a publicly funded technology was soon subject to evaluation. Yehoshua Bar-Hillel, commissioned by the NSF, produced a highly critical report in 1960, followed by the creation of the Automatic Language Processing Advisory Committee (ALPAC), commissioned by the Academy of Sciences. The ALPAC report, published in 1966, recommended the end of funding for MT centers in the

United States. Research was also stopped in most countries that had undertaken experiments. On the other hand, the ALPAC report recommended the development of "Computational linguistics".

After defining MT's horizon of retrospection and showing how it included its horizon of projection from the start, I will describe the steps in the process of MT's erasure in favor of computational linguistics.

2. The horizon of retrospection of MT

MT did not start from scratch. It had its own horizon of retrospection, viz., the first mathematization of language and the military technologies of the post -World War II military-industrial complex. Both Warren Weaver and Yehoshua Bar-Hillel helped establishing the new horizon, which, it should be noted, did not include linguistics.

2.1 MT as a cold war technology and an application of information theory

Warren Weaver (1894–1978), who first came up with the idea of MT, was a mathematician.[1] During World War II, he was a member of the very powerful U.S. Office of Scientific Research and Development, which was the very center of the military-science complex. After the war, he returned to his position at the Rockefeller Foundation to organize and fund research in the United States and Europe. In addition, he was one of the founding members of the RAND Corporation created in 1945–46. In this context, his conception of machine translation is part of the war sciences characterized by an interpenetration between science and engineering. For him, MT is an application of information theory at the intersection of engineering and basic science.[2]

As one of the founders of RAND, Weaver was a proponent of improving operations research. RAND aimed to develop "rational life", according to which technical and human systems (transportation systems, the army, companies) are coordinated units, which can be optimized according to common objectives and criteria. Rational life implies the elimination of human work through the generalization of automation. According to the principles of cybernetics, this automation consists in erasing the frontier between man and machine through algorithmization.

1. Note that other pioneers of MT, such as the Russian Trojanskij, had the idea of MT as early as the 1930s, well before the appearance of the first computers (Léon 2021).

2. In 1949, he wrote the introduction of *The Mathematical Theory of Communication*, gathering Shannon's work on information theory (Shannon & Weaver 1949).

Specifically, with respect to translation, Weaver considered that languages have invariants that make translation possible, and of these invariants, statistical invariants are the most significant for MT. In *Mathematical theory of communication*, he indicates that MT should use the statistical and probabilistic methods (especially Markov chains) used in cryptography.

Weaver is aware of the linguistic difficulties of automating translation, but he dismisses them by considering that scientific texts are less difficult than literary ones. Moreover, he considers that a rough translation, even one containing errors, should be sufficient for the use of scientists.

However, Weaver remained a facilitator and did not undertake any MT experiments himself. Thanks to him, MT received funding from the Rockefeller Foundation, including funding for a storage memory developed by Andrew Booth at Birkbeck College in London (Booth 1975), and a grant through which Yehoshua Bar-Hillel was recruited by the RLE (Research Laboratory of Electronics) at MIT in 1951 as the first MT researcher. He also funded the first MT conference held at MIT in 1952.

2.2 Yehoshua Bar-Hillel and the computationalization of linguistics

Yehoshua Bar-Hillel (1915–1975) was an Israeli mathematician, logician and philosopher of science. His horizon of retrospection is that of the first mathematization of language resulting from the work of the logicians of the 1930s, at the intersection of formal languages, mathematical logic, algorithms and syntactic analysis.

As an assiduous disciple of Rudolf Carnap and his logical syntax, he thought about a universal system of syntactic categories and developed the first categorial grammar that would serve as a formal framework for what he called an operational syntax for MT (Bar-Hillel 1953c).

The horizon of retrospection of MT, which includes the war sciences and the first mathematization of language, does not include linguistics.[3] Morphology, left aside, is replaced by engineers with a linguistics for the machine, namely a simplified morphology adapted to electronic dictionaries.

For Bar-Hillel (1953a), the work of American structuralist linguists is incompatible with automatic processing. The machine represents an inescapable challenge for these linguists who exclude meaning, whereas to translate is precisely to transmit meaning.[4] The linguists targeted by Bar-Hillel were the Neo-bloomfieldian

3. This does not mean that linguists are absent from the process: at the first colloquium organized in 1952 by Bar-Hillel at MIT, there were, among the 18 participants, 4 academic linguists specialized in languages, against, it is true, 9 mathematicians and computer scientists.

descriptivist linguists who described Amerindian languages according to inductive and empirical methods of phonological and morphological analysis.

Besides, structural linguists worked synthetically, not analytically, as required by a syntactic analysis necessary for MT.[5] What an "operational syntax" could do, on the other hand, was to analyze a sentence into its immediate constituents and determine its syntactic function.

Z.S. Harris, from whom Bar-Hillel borrowed transformational grammar for his operational syntax, was not counted by Bar-Hillel among structuralists. He was one of the founders of algebraic linguistics, along with Hockett, Hjelmslev and Uldall. In Chapter 14 "Four lectures on algebraic linguistics and machine translation" of his book *Language and Information* published in 1964, Bar-Hillel places Chomsky's hierarchy of syntactic structures (Chomsky 1956) in the lineage of algebraic linguistics, of Harris in particular, and of the logicians Carnap and Ajdukiewicz, of Emil Post for the recursive functions and of Haskell Curry for the combinatory logic. He praises Chomsky's model of natural languages for its rigor and testability. For him, algebraic linguistics and automata theory combine in a complementary way to form 'theoretical linguistics':

> It seems that a major change in the peaceful but uninspiring coexistence of structural linguistics and syntax-oriented logicians came along when the idea of *mechanizing the determination of syntactic structure* began to take hold of the imagination of various authors. As a final surprise, it has recently turned out that these two disciplines, automata theory and algebraic linguistics, exhibit extremely close relationships which at times amount to practical identity.
>
> (Bar-Hillel 1964: 187)

This idea of mechanizing the determination of syntactic structure, of the close relationship between algebraic linguistics and automata theory was of course perfectly illustrated by his own operational syntax. It initiated the computationalization of linguistics.

4. "[...] their thesis that language can be exhaustively described in non-referential terms undergoes here an *experimentum crucis*. If, in a translation program, some step has to be taken which directly or indirectly depends upon the machine's ability to understand the text on which it operates, then the machine will simply be unable to make this step, and the whole operation will come to a full stop. (I have in mind present day machines that do not possess a semantic organ. The situation will change in the not too distant future)" (Bar-Hillel 1953a: 217).

5. "The structural linguist provides, in general, a description from which the linguistic forms of the treated language can be synthesized, but he does not provide a method by which any given sentence, presented as a sequence of certain discrete elements, can be analyzed into its constituents and their syntactic function determined" (Bar-Hillel 1953a: 218).

3. From MT to computational linguistics

We will now examine the steps by which the horizon of projection of MT was constituted as computational linguistics.

3.1 Stage 1: The 1952 conference

In its conclusions, the conference organized redundancy by Bar-Hillel in 1952 at MIT and financed by the Rockefeller Foundation, considered that a fully automated high quality translation (FAHQT) was impossible, not only because of the limits of the machine, but also for theoretical reasons that Bar-Hillel would develop in Appendix III to his 1960 report (see below).

At first, Bar-Hillel evoked the idea of learning machines capable of understanding texts. But for reasons of computing capacity, this idea was ruled out. "A fully automatic and fully accurate translation will require a trillion-bit storage or a machine capable of learning. Otherwise, human assistance will be necessary or a less accurate result will be tolerated" (Bar-Hillel 1953b: 2). In 1964, he returned to this idea (in the fourth lecture on algebraic linguistics and machine translation entitled "Why machines won't learn to translate well") where he reflected on the possibilities offered by artificial intelligence (in particular by Rosenblatt's Perceptron), but again, he rejected it (Bar-Hillel 1964: 212).[6]

Automating translation is, for Bar-Hillel, about producing a "machine-aided translation", with a pre-editor and, more importantly, a human post-editor capable of resolving semantic ambiguities and smoothing the results.

At the end of the conference, the participants agreed to proceed in two steps where linguistic operations and machine hardware and software configurations (storage memory and programming) are closely associated.

First, according to the proposal of Andrew D. Booth of Birkbeck College, the aim was also to develop a storage memory to store an automatic dictionary. The first step was to build an operational automatic dictionary, i.e. a dictionary of forms without lemmatization (tokens) and therefore without morphological analysis. Secondly, according to Bar-Hillel's wishes, it was necessary to undertake an operational syntactic analysis providing the syntactic structure of a sentence in the form of immediate constituents, with the prospect of its being programmed for the machine. The actual grammatical problems were postponed.

6. As the ancestor of neural networks, Frank Rosenblatt's Perceptron combined photoelectric cells and cables to recognize letters of the alphabet.

3.2 Stage 2: The power of MIT

The first MT conference at MIT included 6 MIT members among the 18 participants, including the director of the Digital Computer Laboratory (Jay W. Forrester), the two successive directors of the Research Laboratory of Electronics, Jerome B. Wiesner and Victor Yngve; finally, the director of the Department of Modern Languages, W.N Locke. At the end of the conference, MIT and the Department of Defense were the most willing to finance the project once it takes concrete form. In comparison, IBM was much more cautious.

The role of Victor Yngve (1920–2012), director of the RLE from 1953 onwards, was decisive. In 1955, he hired four linguists to work on MT, financed by the NSF, including three students of Harris, among whom Noam Chomsky.[7] Chomsky, Joseph R. Applegate, Fred Lukoff, Robert Lees and G. Hubert Matthews worked on a project for a complete grammar of German. Yngve (1956) reports that Chomsky worked on grammatical theory. During this period, Yngve (1955, 1956) published several articles advocating the priority of syntactic analysis for MT and a bottom-up parsing strategy, arguing in particular for the difference in word order between languages. Above all, in 1958, he proposed a programming language called COMIT (Computer On Module Interconnect Technology) for processing strings of characters, adapted to the automatic processing of languages, in particular to MT. It was, he specified, a notation system easily usable by linguists so that they could do their own programming (Yngve 1958).

In other words, MIT was quickly at the forefront of MT with automatic syntactic analysis based on formal grammars (syntagmatic and then transformational grammars) as its priority area.

3.3 Stage 3: Bar-Hillel's Report 1960

Bar-Hillel, who had returned to Israel in 1953, came back to the United States in 1958, at the request of the NSF, to evaluate the MT groups.[8] The criticisms formulated in his report "The present Status of automatic translation of Languages" published in 1960, are very severe: weakness of the results, unreliability of the methods, few linguistic problems solved, exaggerated expectations of the public and the media caused by the abusive claims and announcements of some experimenters.

In addition, he presents theoretical arguments about the impossibility of fully automated high quality translation (FAHQT). To resolve semantic ambiguities,

7. Cf. *Journal of Machine Translation* (2–1 1955).

8. In 1958, there were ten MT centers in the USA and about ten others in Europe – seven centers in the USSR, two centers in Great Britain and one center in Italy (Hutchins 1986).

human translators rely on extra-linguistic commonsense knowledge. However, as things stand, there are no machines or programs that possess this knowledge or that can use it intelligently.

He advocates, as he did at the first colloquium in 1952, machine-aided translation, i.e., the intervention of a human post-editor to correct and smooth the translation produced by the machine, and the use of an operational syntax as the only valid method for MT.

He clearly shows his preference for the type of research carried out by MIT, of which he recalls that he was a member from 1951 to 1953. He criticizes the empirical and inductive methods based on corpora, and underlines the interest of formal grammars and syntactic analysis by indicating that they are strongly influenced by the recent work of 'Professor Noam Chomsky' whose conceptions are revolutionary.

In Appendix II of the report, devoted to linguistic obstacles to MT, he points out the shortcomings of the immediate constituent model (syntagmatic grammar) which he acknowledges having used in his operational syntax, but which performs poorly for MT. On the other hand, he praises the transformational model while pointing out that some theoretical difficulties, such as the theory of recursive functions, the theory of Post's canonical systems and the theory of finite automata, need to be solved before foreseeing its practical use in MT. He concludes by saying that sophisticated linguistic models are not useful for the preparation of practical MT programs. On the other hand, theoretical research in linguistics is essential and can be conducted independently without a practical purpose. This is the case, he says, with the research conducted at MIT.

It is clear that one of the aims of the report was to separate what he called theoretical linguistics, i.e. formal theories and grammars from MT, which he only saw as a practical activity. The report had a strong impact thanks to Bar-Hillel's fame and the strength of his arguments. It was followed in 1964 by the formation of the *Automatic Language Processing Advisory Committee* (ALPAC).

3.4 Stage 4: The ALPAC report (1966)

The assessment conducted by the ALPAC committee, commissioned by the National Academy of Sciences and the National Research Council, can probably be counted among the first systematic assessment in the scientific field. It was based on tests and experiments, in addition to consulting grey literature and hearing from key players (as Bar-Hillel had done). The ALPAC committee published its findings in 1966 in a report entitled "Language and Machines. Computers in Translation and Linguistics".

For the Committee, it was the high cost of MT in relation to the poor results that led them to recommend to stop the funding. Contrary to what was claimed, there was no shortage of human translators. Moreover, even computer-assisted translation with post-editing was ultimately too expensive compared to human translation.

The evaluation itself is accompanied by MT impact studies contained in several annexes. While the impact of MT on hardware is negligible, it is much more important on the software side, especially the development of computer programming languages. We have seen this with Victor Yngve's COMIT.

But the major impact is on linguistics (Appendix 19). Thanks to the computer, in particular with access to important data, computational linguistics or 'new linguistics', as ALPAC calls it, is experiencing an unprecedented and revolutionary boom, comparable to that of particle physics. Pierce, the Chairman of ALPAC, states in the report:

> The computer has opened up to linguists a host of challenges, partial insights, and potentialities. We believe these can be aptly compared with the challenges, problems, and insights of particle physics [...] the new linguistics presents an attractive as well as an extremely important challenge. (ALPAC, 1966: v)

The comparison of the rise of linguistics with that of physics was probably due to Charles F. Hockett who was initially a member of ALPAC for a short time. His article "The Human Revolution" published in 1964 in *Current Anthropology* is quoted in the report (Appendix 19, p. 121). Hockett (1964) refers to what he calls the "computer revolution" as the "third human revolution". After speech and tools, the computer is fundamentally changing the analysis of natural languages and the mathematisation of linguistics, just as it does for physics and the microscope for biology.

The ALPAC report also quotes Igor A. Mel'čuk, one of the Russian linguists who pioneered machine translation in the USSR, for whom computational linguistics became an indispensable technique for linguists: "computational linguistics is not a field of linguistics, a subspeciality for those who like computation; it is a technique inescapable for any linguist who honors his discipline" (Akhmanova, Mel'čuk, et al. 1963: 46 – quoted by ALPAC 1966: 121).

ALPAC's recommendations are clear. The committee recommends grants in two areas:

1. computational linguistics as part of linguistics: parsing; sentence generation, semantics, statistics, quantitative linguistics, including computer-aided and non-computer-aided translation experiments.

2. Automatic aids for translators, in the form of glossaries, dictionaries and specialised terminology banks.

This shows that what ALPAC called 'computational linguistics' in fact encompassed quite diverse fields, including experiments in machine translation (!!).

ALPAC points out that there are as yet no methods for dealing with large amounts of data and that there is a need to develop tools to help linguists verify and test theories and generalizations made from the data, including formal grammars.

Although Bar-Hillel was not a member of the ALPAC committee and had in fact been back in Israel for several years at the time of its creation (to continue his research in logic and philosophy of science as a professor at the Hebrew University of Jerusalem), it can be seen that his ideas profoundly influenced the conclusions and recommendations of the report.

Like Bar-Hillel, ALPAC recommends separating linguistics from machine translation and even empowering it by funding it independently as a science. Linguistics should be evaluated independently, by linguists, according to scientific criteria, and not according to its immediate or predictable contribution to practical translation. The commission dwells at length on the mistakes made by some of the pioneers of MT in limiting themselves to the practical aspects of MT, i.e. to produce translations in series, without reflection or theoretical perspectives.

It was a great fear of the Committee that linguistics would disappear with machine translation, like the baby with the bathwater. The report contains a letter from the Chairman of the "Committee on Science and Public Policy", Harvey Brooks, to Frederick Seitz, President of the National Academy of Science. The letter states that:

> John R. Pierce, the chairman, was asked to prepare a brief statement of the support needs for computational linguistics, as distinct from automatic language translation. This request was prompted by a fear that the committee report, read in isolation, might result in termination of research support for computational linguistics as well as in the recommended reduction of support aimed at relatively short-term goals in translation. (ALPAC 1966: v)

Like Bar-Hillel, ALPAC rejected Neo-bloomfieldian linguistics and advocated that computational linguistics should build on the advances proposed by Chomsky, disassociating computational linguistics from computers, which Chomsky did throughout his career.[9]

9. "Surely the most dramatic recent changes have been caused by Chomsky [...] and similar thinkers, and they have explicitly had little to do directly with computers [...]. The fundamental changes that they have brought to linguistics inhere rather in an altered view taken by linguistics

4. Conclusion

In conclusion, with the beginning of MT we encounter a particular case of articulation between the horizon of retrospection and the horizon of projection. It is because linguistics was not part of the retrospective horizon of MT that the horizon it projected could constitute a turning point, the computational turn of linguistics.

The horizon of linguistics thus projected was piloted and installed by institutions: funding by state agencies, evaluation by these same agencies, NSF or the Academy of Sciences, conclusions and recommendations by expert reports. This is probably one of the first cases of this type in the scientific field.

We are thus witnessing the emergence of the second mathematisation of language (the abstract algorithms of the first mathematisation are inscribed in the space and time of computer programming) which will have massive effects on the development of linguistics throughout the world from the 1960s.

The fact that the Chomskyan programme was thus projected as a new linguistics, which he himself called computational and dissociated from computers, was very much related to Bar-Hillel's intellectual domination of the field and to the institutional power of MIT.

References

Akhmanova Olga S., Mel'čuk Igor, A., Frumkina Revekka M. & Elena V. Paducheva. 1963. *Exact Methods in Linguistic Research.* Berkeley, University California Press.

ALPAC report. *Language and Machines. Computers in translation and linguistics. A report by the Automatic Language Processing Advisory Committee (ALPAC).* 1966. National Academy of Sciences, National Research Council.

Auroux, Sylvain. 1995. "L'histoire des sciences du langage et le paradoxe historiographique". *Le Gré des langues* 8.40–63.

doi Auroux, Sylvain. 2006. "Les modes d'historicisation". *Histoire Épistémologie Langage* 28.105–116.

doi Bar-Hillel, Yehoshua. 1953a. "Some linguistic problems connected with Machine Translation". *Philosophy of Science* 20.217–225.

Bar-Hillel, Yehoshua. 1953b. "Machine Translation". *Computers and Automation* 2:5.1–6

doi Bar-Hillel, Yehoshua. 1953c. "A Quasi-Arithmetic Notation for Syntactic Description". *Language* 29.47–58.

---

of the nature of science, of a scientific theory, and of the relation of empiricism to science" (ALPAC 1966: 122).

Bar-Hillel, Yehoshua. 1960. "The present Status of Automatic Translation of Languages". *Advances in Computers*, edited by F. C. Alt, vol I, 91–141. New York & London: Academic Press.

Bar-Hillel, Yehoshua. 1964. *Language and Information.* Addison-Wesley Publishing Company.

Booth, Andrew D. 1975. "Computers in the University of London 1945–62" *The Radio Electronic Engineer* 45–7.341–345.

Chomsky, Noam. 1956. "Three models for the description of language". *IRE (Institute of Radio Engineers) Transactions on Information Theory* IT-3. 113–124.

Hockett, Charles F. & Robert Ascher. 1964. "The Human Revolution". *Current Anthropology* 5.135–168.

Hutchins, William J. 1986. *Machine translation, past, present, future.* Chichester: Ellis Horwood Ltd.

Léon, Jacqueline. 2021. *Automating Linguistics.* Cham, Springer.

Puech, Christian & Valérie Raby, eds. 2006 & 2011. Histoire des idées linguistiques et horizons de rétrospection, *Histoire Epistémologie Langage* 28:1 & 28:2.

Shannon, Claude E. & Warren Weaver. 1949. *The Mathematical Theory of Communication*, Urbana-Champaign: Univ. of Illinois Press.

Weaver, Warren. 1955 [1949]. "Translation." *Machine Translation of Languages, 14 essays*, edited by William N. Locke & Andrew D. Booth, 15–23. Cambridge MA: MIT & New York: John Wiley.

Yngve, Victor H. 1955. "Syntax and the Problem of Multiple Meaning" *Machine Translation of Languages, 14 essays*, edited by William N. Locke & Andrew D. Booth, 208–226. Cambridge MA: MIT & New York: John Wiley.

Yngve, Victor H. 1956. "Mechanical Translation Research at MIT". *Machine Translation* 3:2.44–45.

Yngve, Victor H. 1958. "A programming language for Mechanical Translation". *Machine Translation* 5:1.25–42.

PART 2

Antiquity

CHAPTER 8

Declension and description

The ways of Sanskrit grammarians

Émilie Aussant
Université Sorbonne Nouvelle – EA 2120 GREI

This paper studies the different ways in which ancient Sanskrit grammarians presented nominal declensions. Based on twelve Sanskrit grammars (from Pāṇini's *Aṣṭādhyāyī* up to Bhaṭṭoji Dīkṣita's *Siddhāntakaumudī*) classified into three categories ("wholly generative" grammars, "partly generative" grammars and "pedagogical" grammars), it shows that though nominal paradigmatic sets were known from and used by various scholars – among whom grammarians – at a relatively early date, it is only with pedagogical grammars that they really enter the scene of grammatical description, i.e. as "official" grammatical or language teaching tools.

Keywords: nominal declensions, paradigmatic sets, pedagogical grammars, Sanskrit grammarians

1. Introduction

Sanskrit is – among its other properties – a highly inflected language. It is also one of the very few languages of the world which has given birth to a long – and deeply elaborate – tradition of endogenous description (*Vyākaraṇa* in Sanskrit), a tradition which is generally considered as starting in the 5th c. BC (with Pāṇini's *Aṣṭādhyāyī*) and ending in the 18th c. AD (with Nāgeśa Bhaṭṭa's works).

This paper aims to study the different ways in which Sanskrit grammarians presented nominal declensions, an essential component of both the Sanskrit language and the descriptive apparatus of Sanskrit grammarians.

By "nominal declensions", I mean the set of forms a nominal item – i.e. a noun, an adjective or a pronoun – can take depending on its syntactic functions within a sentence. Word-classes were identified quite early in Ancient India. The oral transmission of Vedic hymns led to the elaboration of sophisticated parsing methods and, on the basis of recurring morpho-phonological features, to

https://doi.org/10.1075/sihols.133.08aus

the identification and the classification of segments terminating with endings (Cardona 2014: 91–92).

The most ancient formal distinction between nouns and verbs we are acquainted with goes back to Pāṇini, the author of the *Aṣṭādhyāyī* (hereafter A), the founding text of the Sanskrit grammatical tradition. Pāṇini classifies finite words (*pada*s) into two groups: *sub-anta-pada*s "words ending in *sUP* (i.e. nominal endings)" and *tiṅ-anta-pada*s "words ending in *tiṄ* (i.e. verbal endings)", *sUP* being the acronym of the nominal endings list – to which I will come back later – and *tiṄ* the acronym of the verbal endings list.

This being said, does Pāṇini account for the set of forms nominal items can take? And, if he does, how does he proceed? How did grammarians who succeeded him proceed? Do we have lists of rules for declining nouns? Paradigmatic sets? If yes, how many sets? Presented in which order? These are some of the main questions to which this paper tries to provide answers. It is organised into four parts: Part 1 gives a brief presentation of the corpus studied, Part 2 is devoted to the presentation of nominal declensions in wholly and partly generative grammars, Part 3 to the presentation of nominal declensions in pedagogical grammars and Part 4 is intended as a concluding thought on the emergence of paradigmatic sets in Sanskrit grammars.

2. The corpus

The study is based on twelve grammars of Sanskrit, all written in Sanskrit. The list is provided in Table 1.

Table 1.

Aṣṭādhyāyī	5th c. BC	Cat. 1
Kātantra	5th c. AD?	Cat. 2
Cāndravyākaraṇa	5th c. AD	Cat. 2
Jainendravyākaraṇa	5th–7th AD?	Cat. 1
Śākaṭāyanavyākaraṇa	9th c. AD	Cat. 2
Rūpāvatāra	10th–12th c. AD?	Cat. 3
Sarasvatīkaṇṭhābharaṇa	1042	Cat. 2
Siddhahemacandra	10th–12th c. AD	Cat. 2
Mugdhabodha	13th c. AD	Cat. 2
Prakriyākaumudī	14th–15th c. AD	Cat. 3
Prakriyāsarvasva	1616	Cat. 3
Siddhāntakaumudī	16th–17th c. AD	Cat. 3

These twelve grammars can be subdivided into three categories, according to the way they organize, formulate and illustrate the grammatical rules:

a. The first category (Cat. 1) brings together "wholly generative" grammars: (1) they are not organized in topical sections, (2) their rules, which aim to generate finite words, are formulated in a very concise way and follow a number of metarules, (3) they do not provide examples (these are generally given in glosses);
b. The second category (Cat. 2) includes grammars which consist in generative strings organized in topical sections: their rules, which aim to generate finite words, which are formulated in a very concise way and which follow a number of metarules, are grouped together in topical sections. The topical sections recurrently (if not systematically) present are: technical terms, phonetics, nouns and verbs. These grammars do not provide examples either;
c. The third category (Cat. 3) is comprised of grammars which consist in pedagogical and detailed instructions organized in topical sections: as manuals, they explain, in a very pedagogic way, grammatical procedures making it possible to derive finite words from A to Z. They are organized in topical sections and subsections, and provide examples.

Texts which came down to us suggest that there is a historical continuity between the three categories: the most ancient grammar, the *Aṣṭādhyāyī* of Pāṇini, on which nearly all of the other grammars are more or less based, is wholly generative; and grammars of the third category were still composed at a late date, as is the case for the *Siddhāntakaumudī*. But it is not at all impossible that pedagogical tools (like oral explanatory glosses) were used at a very early date. The fact is that there is no ancient trace of such tools.

As I am going to show, the most drastic changes, in the presentation of nominal declensions, appear with grammars of the third category. Let us first see how things are going in "wholly" and "partly generative" grammars.

3. Presentation of nominal declensions in wholly and partly generative grammars

The best example of a wholly generative grammar is without a doubt Pāṇini's *Aṣṭādhyāyī*. On a practical level, this grammar provides guidelines for forming finite words – the *padas* – by means of affixes. These affixes (*pratyaya*) are directly introduced (under meaning conditions and cooccurrence conditions) in some of the four thousand Pāṇinian rules, unlike most of the bases with which they combine and which are either verbal roots (*dhātu*) or nominal bases (*prāti-*

padika). Verbal and nominal bases constitute the two main formal starting points of the derivational process which occurs throughout Pāṇinian rules. A crucial point for our topic, is that the very first step, in the Pāṇinian derivational system, is a weak semantic level, closely related to syntax: nouns and verbs are not derived apart from the utterance of which they are a constituent (cf. Cardona 1997: 136–185). This explains, I think, the way in which nominal inflection is presented in wholly and partly generative grammars of Sanskrit.

In Pāṇini's grammar, several groups of rules, located in different parts of the work, are involved in the derivation of inflected nouns:

a. The first group of rules, which goes from A 1.4.23 up to A 1.4.55, introduces the syntactic-semantic values (the *kārakas*) the nominal endings can convey. One of the characteristics of Pāṇini's approach is that he clearly distinguishes both the syntactic-semantic values and the linguistic forms which convey them. As an example of a rule belonging to this first group, one can quote the *sūtra* A 1.4.49 *kartur īpsitatamaṃ karma* "[The technical term] *karman* ['object', designates] what the agent most desires [to reach through his action]";[1]
b. The second group of rules, which goes from A 2.3.1 to A 2.3.73, stipulates which ending can be used to express which syntactic-semantic value: e.g. A 2.3.2 *karmaṇi dvitīyā* "The second [case (i.e. the accusative) is used to express] the object (*karmaṇi*)". It is in this group of rules that the names of the seven cases are given: *prathamā* "first" (A 2.3.46) which corresponds to what we call "nominative case", *dvitīyā* "second" = our "accusative" (A 2.3.2), *tṛtīyā* "third" = our "instrumental" (A 2.3.6), *caturthī* "fourth" = our "dative" (A 2.3.13), *pañcamī* "fifth" = our "ablative" (A 2.3.28), *ṣaṣṭhī* "sixth" = our "genitive" (A 2.3.50) and *saptamī* "seventh" = our "locative" (A 2.3.36). Note that numerical indices were frequently used in the field of ritual to denote various things (formulas, ceremonial tools, specific times); this procedure of naming nominal cases, hence, is not at all special within the context of ancient India (cf. Pinault 1989: 328).[2]
c. The third group of rules consists in two rules A 4.1.1 and 4.1.2. Rule A 4.1.1 states the forms which the nominal endings are added to: *Ṅy-āP-prātipadikāt* "After [a word ending in] *Ṅī* or *āP* (i.e. after a feminine word) and after a nominal stem" and rule A 4.1.2 enumerates the list of nominal endings which can

1. Adapted translation of Katre (1989).

2. Note these two exceptions: the *Jainendravyākaraṇa*, from the seven phonemes of the word *vibhakti* ("division"), creates the terms *vā* for *prathamā*, ***ip*** for *dvitīyā*, ***bhā*** for *tṛtīyā*, ***ap*** for *caturthī*, ***kā*** for *pañcamī*, ***tā*** for *ṣaṣṭhī* and ***īp*** for *saptamī*; the *Mugdhabodha* uses ***prī*** for *prathamā*, ***dvī*** for *dvitīyā*, ***trī*** for *tṛtīyā*, ***cī*** for *caturthī*, ***pī*** for *pañcamī*, ***ṣī*** for *ṣaṣṭhī* and ***ptī*** for *saptamī*.

be added to these forms: *sU-au-Jas-am-auṬ-Śas-Ṭā-bhyām-bhis-Ṅe-bhyām-bhyas-ṄasI-bhyām-bhyas-Ṅas-os-ām-Ṅi-os-suP*.[3] The 21 items that make up the list are not given randomly.[4] There are seven triplets, as shown in Table 2:

Table 2.

sU-au-Jas	sg.-dual-pl. endings of the 1st case
am-auṬ-Śas	sg.-dual-pl. endings of the 2nd case
Ṭā-bhyām-bhis	sg.-dual-pl. endings of the 3rd case
Ṅe-bhyām-bhyas	sg.-dual-pl. endings of the 4th case
ṄasI-bhyām-bhyas	sg.-dual-pl. endings of the 5th case
Ṅas-os-ām	sg.-dual-pl. endings of the 6th case
Ṅi-os-suP	sg.-dual-pl. endings of the 7th case

If we look at the first triplet, *sU-au-Jas*, we have *sU*, the singular ending of the 1st case, *au*, the dual ending of the 1st case, and *Jas*, the plural ending of the first case. And so on and so forth. Capital letters correspond to metalinguistic markers used for various purposes I will not explain here.

d. All the morpho-phonological phenomena linked to or generated by the addition of the various endings to the nominal forms – that is to say, the inflexion process as such from a Greco-Latin point of view – are treated in a huge group of rules (going from A 6.1.1 up to A 8.4.68) dealing with all kinds of substitution and/or junction processes. Some of these rules concern nominal stems ending in a specific phoneme, like A 7.1.9 ***aTo*** *bhisa ais* "*ais* replaces *bhis* (i.e. the plural ending of the third case) **after [a stem ending in]** ***a***" (*deva+bhis* = *devais* "by/with the Gods"), while others concern various nominal stems, like A 6.1.102 *prathamayoḥ pūrvasavarṇaḥ* "[A long vowel, homophonous to the final vowel of **a stem**,[5] replaces this final vowel and the initial vowel of the ending] of the first and the second cases", which accounts for the forms *agni+au* = *agnī* "two fires", *vāyu+au* = *vāyū* "two winds", *vṛkṣa+as* = *vṛkṣās* "trees".

3. In order to facilitate the reading of the list, sandhi rules are not applied. Note that *suP* designates the locative plural ending (*su* + *P*, a letter, conventionally transcribed as an upper-case letter in Western works, which is added for metalinguistic purpose). *sUP* is an abbreviation made up of *sU* (which designates the nominative singular ending, given at the very beginning of the list in A 4.1.2) and *P*, the metalinguistic marker which closes the said list; *sU...P* designates the whole list of nominal endings. In the following footnote, *sUPaḥ* is the genitive singular of *sUP*.

4. Cf. A 1.4.103 *sUPaḥ* "[The triplets of endings' series denoted] by *sUP* [taken one by one, are respectively designated by *ekavacana* 'singular', *dvivacana* 'dual' and *bahuvacana* 'plural']."

5. *prātipadikāt* "nominal stem" (mentioned in A 4.1.1) must be tacitly understood in A 6.1.102.

So we have only one abstract nominal paradigm, represented by the complete endings list, and from this initial abstract paradigm, a long series of rules teaches how to inflect all nominal stems. Pāṇini does not resort to different paradigmatic sets, then. As I said previously, within his perspective, finite forms are considered as *sentential units* and are generated as such. Finite forms – hence, inflected nouns – are therefore thought of within *syntagmatic* strings (as if the grammar user were taking the sentence *devadatta odanaṃ pacati* "Devadatta cooks rice" and asks himself how to proceed to form each unit of *this* sentence). It would simply make no sense to deal with paradigmatic sets within such a framework.

"Partly generative" grammars also operate with generative rules (Pāṇinian rules in most cases) but tend to bring together rules related to the same topic.

In the *Cāndravyākaraṇa* (hereafter C) for instance, the list of nominal endings (C 2.1.1) – the same as in Pāṇini's grammar – is followed by a group of rules (C 2.1.2–2.1.42) accounting for morpho-phonological substitution and/or junction phenomena specific to nominal declensions. Thus, C 2.1.2 is nothing more than A 7.1.9 *aTo bhisa ais* "*ais* replaces *bhis* (i.e. the plural ending of the third case) after [a stem ending in] *a*" (note however that not all rules for substitution/junction phenomena are given here: some – related to stems ending in *-i*, *-u*, *-ṛ* or consonants – are located in Sections 5 and 6 of the *Cāndravyākaraṇa*).

Succeeding immediately this group of rules (i.e. C 2.1.2–2.1.42), one finds (up to C 2.1.98) *sūtras* stipulating the syntactic-semantic values nominal endings can convey: C 2.1.43 *kriyā-āpye dvitīyā* corresponds to A 2.3.2 *karmaṇi dvitīyā* "The second [case (i.e. the accusative) is used to express] the object". So the *Cāndravyākaraṇa* puts, in one and the same section – the first *pāda* of the second *adhyāya* – the various rules dealing with nominal declensions. And the other partly generative grammars do the same.

The organization of generative rules according to topics certainly gives more visibility to the nominal inflexion thematic and is much more "learner friendly". In substance however, it does not entail any deep change in the wholly generative (Pāṇinian) system: the syntagmatic perspective is still there, and furthermore, paradigmatic sets do not arise in partly generative grammars either.

4. Presentation of nominal declensions in pedagogical grammars

As mentioned earlier, the most drastic changes, in the presentation of nominal declensions, appear in grammars of the third category.

The topical arrangement of these works is generally very clearly structured. For instance in the *Rūpāvatāra*, which dates back to the 10th–12th centuries AD, and which, as far as we know, is the most ancient pedagogical manual based on

Pāṇinian rules which has come down to us, the section dealing with nominal declensions runs as follows:[6]

- *aJanta-puṃliṅga-prakaraṇam* | "Chapter on masculine [nominal stems] ending in vowels"
  followed by the grammatical procedure for the declension of masculine stems ending in *-a*, *-ā*, *-i*, *-ī*, *-u*, *-ū*, *-ṛ*, *-ḷ*, *-e*, *-o*, *-ai* and *-au*.
- *atha_aJanta-strīliṅga-prakaraṇam* | "Now, the chapter on feminine [nominal stems] ending in vowels"
  followed by the grammatical procedure for the declension of feminine stems ending in *-ā*, *-i*, *-ī*, *-u*, *-ū*, *-ṛ*, *-ai* and *-au*.
- *atha_aJanta-napuṃsakaliṅga-prātipadikāni* | "Now, neuter nominal stems ending in vowels"
  followed by the grammatical procedure for the declension of neuter stems ending in *-a*, *-ā*, *-i*, *-ī*, *-u*, *-ū*.
- *haLanta-puṃliṅga-prakaraṇam* | "Chapter on masculine [nominal stems] ending in consonants"
  followed by the grammatical procedure for the declension of masculine stems ending in *-h*, *-v* and *-r* (*yaÑ*), *-m* and *-n* (*ñaM*), *-dh*, *-j* and *-d* (*jhaŚ*), *-th*, *-c*, *-t* and *-p* (*khaY*), *-ś*, *-ṣ* and *-s* (*śaR*).
- *atha haLanta-strīliṅga-prātipadikāni* | "Now, [the chapter on] feminine nominal stems ending in consonants"
  followed by the grammatical procedure for the declension of feminine stems ending in *-h*, *-v*, *-r*, *-m*, *-n*, *-bh*, *-dh*, *-j*, *-d*, *-c*, *-t*, *-p*, *-ś*, *-ṣ* and *-s*.
- *atha haLanta-napuṃsakaliṅga-prātipadikāni* | "Now, [the chapter on] neuter nominal stems ending in consonants"
  followed by the grammatical procedure for the declension of neuter stems ending in *-h*, *-v*, *-r*, *-m*, *-n*, *-j*, *-d*, *-c*, *-t*, *-p*, *-ṣ* and *-s*.
- *iti liṅgaviśiṣṭā haLantāḥ parisamāptāḥ* | "These were all [the nominal stems] ending in consonant [and] distinguished by gender"
- *atha haLanteṣv aliṅga-prakaraṇam* | "Now, the chapter on genderless [nominal stems] ending in consonant"
- *iti vibhakty-avatāraḥ* | "This was the introduction [of nominal] endings"

As is obvious, the division into different subsections appears clearly. We note moreover that:

6. Cf. Rangacharya's edition (1916–1927).

a. nominal stems are *classified*
b. *stem ending* associated with *stem gender* are used as criteria for nominal stems' classification
c. the subclassification of vocalic and consonantal stem endings is made according to the order of Pāṇini's sound catalog (*akṣarasamāmnāya*): *a, i, u, ṛ, ḷ, e, o, ai, au, h, (y), v, r, (l), (ñ), m, (ṅ), (ṇ), n, (jh), (bh), (gh), (ḍh), dh, j, (b), (g), (ḍ), d, (kh), (ph), (ch), (ṭh), th, c, (ṭ), t, (k), p, ś, ṣ, s.*

This classification of nominal stems, which is explicitly stated in the *Rūpāvatāra*[7] at the beginning of the chapter on masculine stems ending in vowels, is not the only significant innovation.

The text provides the detailed grammatical procedure to form the entire paradigm of *vṛkṣa-* ("tree"), a masculine stem ending in short *-a*. Step by step, the formation of the nominative singular, dual and plural, then the formation of the accusative singular, dual and plural, and so on up to the locative case, are explained (as well as the syntactic-semantic values of the cases) and relevant Pāṇinian rules are quoted in support. Once the grammatical procedure to form the entire paradigm of *vṛkṣa-* is over, a brief stanza gives again the whole paradigm.[8] Same thing with *kavi-* ("poet"),[9] a masculine stem ending in short *-i*, and so on, up to *adas-* ("that"), a neuter pronoun ending in *-s*. So we clearly have a presentation of nominal declensions according to *paradigmatic sets*.

---

7. *sU au Jas iti prathamāḥ, am auṬ Śas iti dvitīyāḥ, Ṭā bhyāṃ bhis iti tṛtīyāḥ, Ṅe bhyāṃ bhyas iti caturthī, ṄasI bhyāṃ bhyas iti pañcamī, Ṅas os ām iti ṣaṣṭhī, Ṅi os sup iti saptamī | etāḥ sapta-vibhaktayaḥ prātipadikāt pare bhavanti | dvividhaṃ prātipadikam ajantaṃ halantaṃ ca | tat punaḥ trividhaṃ puṃliṅgaṃ strīliṅgaṃ napuṃsakaliṅgaṃ ceti | tatra ajanteṣu prātipadikeṣu puṃliṅgeṣu prathamam akārāntāt vṛkṣa-śabdāt sapta-vibhaktayaḥ pare yojyante | tat kathaṃ?* [...] "*sU au Jas* [are the endings of] the first [case], *am auṬ Śas* [the one of] the second [case], *Ṭā bhyām bhis* [the one of] the third [case], *Ṅe bhyām bhyas* [the one of] fourth [case], *ṄasI bhyām bhyas* [the one of] the fifth [case], *Ṅas os ām* [the one of] the sixth [case], *Ṅi os suP* [the one of] the seventh [case]. These seven endings come after nominal stems. Nominal stems are of two kinds: those which end in a vowel and those which end with a consonant. [Nominal stems] are also of three kinds: masculine, feminine and neuter. In the case of masculine stems with a vocalic ending, the seven endings are first added to the word *vṛkṣa-* ("tree") which ends in *-a*. How? [...]"

8. ***vṛkṣas*** *tiṣṭhati kānane kusumitā* ***vṛkṣaṃ*** *latā saṃśritā* ***vṛkṣeṇa****_abhihato gajo nipatito* ***vṛkṣāya*** *deyaṃ jalam |* ***vṛkṣād*** *ānaya mañjarīm abhinavāṃ* ***vṛkṣasya*** *śākhonnatā* ***vṛkṣe*** *nīḍam idam kṛtaṃ śakuninā he* ***vṛkṣa*** *kiṃ kampase ||* (p. 36).

9. Except that there is no "conclusive stanza" in that case (as well as in the following).

Moreover, these paradigmatic sets are generally not limited to the declension of only one stem. One observes that a first paradigm, considered as the most representative, is explained in its entirety. Then follows the explanation of some other paradigms which are more or less distinct from the most representative one. A good example is provided by the paradigm set of masculine stems ending in short *-i*:

a. first, the grammatical procedure to form the entire paradigm of *kavi-* ("poet" – the most representative stem) is given, together with the Pāṇinian relevant rules;
b. the grammatical procedure ends with the following indication: *evam agni-giri-hari-ravi-maṇi-prabhṛtayaḥ* "the same [procedure] applies to *agni-* ("fire"), *giri-* "mountain"), *hari-* ("horse"), *ravi-* ("sun"), *maṇi-* ("jewel"), etc.";
c. then the text says: *sakhi-śabdasya tu bhedaḥ* "But the word *sakhi-* ("friend") is different". And the forms of *sakhi-* which do not follow the *kavi-* paradigm are explained;
d. after that, one observes the same thing with *pati-* ("husband"): the special forms are explained and – without much comment – the whole paradigm is given, in the running text, in list form: [Nom.] *patiḥ, patī, patayaḥ* | [Voc.] *he pate, he patī, he patayaḥ* | [Acc.] *patim, patī, patīn* | [Instr.] *patyā, patibhyām, patibhiḥ* | [Dat.] *patye, patibhyām, patibhyaḥ* | [Abl.] *patyuḥ, patibhyām, patibhyaḥ* | [Gen.] *patyuḥ, patyoḥ, patīnām* | [Loc.] *patyau, patyoḥ, patiṣu* |
e. then the text goes on: *dvi-śabdasya bhedaḥ* "The word *dvi-* ('two') is different" and the special forms are explained;
f. again: *tri-śabdasya bhedaḥ* "The word *tri-* ('three') is different" and the special forms are explained;
g. two last words are given, including *kati-* (interrogative pronoun "how much"); the special forms are explained and the text states: *anyatra kavi-śabdavat* "elsewhere (i.e. for the other cases), [the declension of *kati-* proceeds] as in the case of the word *kavi-*."

This last mention obviously shows that pedagogical manuals function with an initial paradigm which serves as a basis for the other members of the set; the explanation is limited to what distinguishes the other members of the set from the initial paradigm, and only to that.[10]

10. Note that, in its principle, this way of explaining facts is not an innovation specific to pedagogical grammars. It is one of the characteristic features of the "scholastic spirit" of ancient India, which can be observed particularly in ritual and grammar (not only Sanskrit grammar).

In a later stage pedagogical grammars will follow the same presentation of nominal declensions, with an almost identical number and order of paradigmatic sets. Some texts are nevertheless more complete than others in that they quote all the Pāṇinian rules. This is the case of the *Siddhāntakaumudī*, in particular.

5. About the emergence of paradigmatic sets in Sanskrit grammars

Data presented so far tend to demonstrate that the emergence of nominal paradigmatic sets lies in pedagogical grammars. I am still convinced of that. Two arguments can nevertheless be put forward to show the reverse, in other words, that pedagogical grammars did not bring anything new. Let us consider briefly these arguments.

The first argument is that we do find early traces of paradigmatic sets. Evidence comes both from outside and inside the grammatical field:

a. In the ritual sphere, to begin with, a domain which grammar is largely rooted in (cf. Renou 1941–42), some invocations are used for ritual purposes which contain the name of divinities inflected in all cases. A good illustration is provided by Yāska, in his *Nirukta* (a work providing an elucidation of the meaning of difficult Vedic words, the goal being to attempt to find out how a word comes to mean what it does), on p.132 (cf. Sarup's edition: 1998):

> ***índro** divá índra īśe pṛthivyā́ḥ* | (nominative case)
> ***índram** íd gāthíno bṛhát* | (accusative case)
> ***índreṇa**_eté tṛ́tsavo véviṣāṇāḥ* | (instrumental case)
> ***índrāya** sā́ma gāyata* | (dative case)
> *na_**índrād** ṛté pavate dhā́ma kíṃ caná* | (ablative case)
> ***índrasya** nú vīryā́ṇi prá vocam* | (genitive case)
> ***indre** kāmā ayaṃsata* |[11] *iti* | (locative case)
> "Indra rules heaven, Indra the earth.
> The chanters [praise] very much Indra alone.
> These Tṛtsus being active with Indra.
> Chant the sāma-stanzas for the sake of Indra.
> Without Indra, no place whatsoever is pure.
> I will indeed proclaim the heroic exploits of Indra.
> Our desires rest on Indra."[12]

11. The quotation is untraced.
12. Sarup's translation (1998: 113).

These seven *mantras*, which are mainly verses extracted from Ṛgvedic hymns, begin with the name *indra* inflected in a different case and they are recited together, *as a set*. The initial intent was certainly not grammatical: using the name *indra* in all its inflected forms was, first of all, a way to exalt the divinity in all its aspects and then, to make the invocation more efficient (cf. Pinault 1989: 325). But the fact is that these series of *mantras* give, at a very ancient date, complete paradigms.[13] The brief stanza which gives the whole paradigm of *vṛkṣa-* in the *Rūpāvatāra* can be seen as a late echo of these series of *mantras*.[14]

b. Another evidence, though perhaps less direct, is the idea of a representative nominal stem (*nāyaka*), which one finds for instance in the *Agnipurāṇa*, a theological text whose earliest layers date back to the 7th c. AD. There, the term *śraddhā-* ("faith") is used to denote feminine stems ending in *-ā*, the term *nadī-* ("river") denotes feminine stems ending in *-ī* or *-ū*, and the term *agni* ("fire") denotes masculine stems ending in *-i* or *-u* (cf. Chatterji 1964: 62).
c. Finally, in the grammatical sphere, the evidence comes from glosses (*vṛtti*), which are generally transmitted along with wholly and partly generative grammars. In the case of Pāṇini's grammar, the most ancient complete gloss that came down to us – the *Kāśikāvṛtti* (KV) – dates back to the 7th c. AD, so it would have been composed long after the text it comments on. But, as I mentioned earlier, we suspect that oral glossing accompanies Pāṇini's text right from the beginning. In the case of Candra's grammar – the partly generative grammar I dealt with previously –, the gloss edited by Liebich (1966 [1918]) would have been composed by the author of the grammar himself[15] and then, probably transmitted along with the text right from the beginning. And the fact is that, in their commentary on the rule which provides the list of nominal endings, these glosses give complete nominal paradigms: *kumārī-* ("young girl", as a *Ṅy-anta-pada* "word ending in suffix *Ṅī*", cf. A 4.1.1 on page 121), *khaṭvā* ("couch", as an *āP-anta-pada* "word ending in suffix *āP*", cf. A 4.1.1 on page 121) and *dṛṣad-* ("rock", as a *prātipadika* "nominal stem", cf. A 4.1.1 on page 121) in the KV, *dṛṣad-* in the *Candravṛtti*.

So nominal paradigmatic sets were known from and used by various scholars – among whom grammarians – at a relatively early date.

13. The play on the various inflected forms of the name of a God is observed in Poetics as well (cf. Filliozat 1988: 90).

14. This kind of stanza is still used in modern Sanskrit manuals (cf. K.L.V. Sastry & L. Anantharama Sastri: 2000).

15. On this complicated issue see, among others, Timalsina (2022).

The second argument is that classes of nominal stems based on stem ending and on stem gender are already present in Pāṇini's grammar though not taught explicitly. Indeed, rules such as A 7.1.9 ***aTo** bhisa ais* "*ais* replaces *bhis* (i.e. the plural ending of the third case) after [**a stem ending in**] ***a***" and A 6.1.111 ***ṛTa** uT* "[A single substitute vowel] short *u* replaces [both **the stem-final**] **short vowel *ṛ*** [and the following initial short *a* of the 5th and 6th case endings in continuous utterance]" presuppose that some nominal stems end in *-a*, some other in *-ṛ*, and that the grammatical operations they are subjected to are not the same. Same thing with gender: A 7.1.72 ***napuṃsakasya** jhaL-aCaḥ* "[The increment *n* is added after the last vowel] of **a neuter** [**stem** ending in] a non-nasal consonant or a vowel [before the strong *sUP* triplets]" implies that some grammatical operations are specific to neuter nominal stems.

To the first argument, one could reply that, indeed, paradigmatic sets were known and used at an early date. But they really enter the scene of grammatical description – that is to say as "official" *grammatical* or *language teaching tools* – with pedagogical grammars.

To the second argument, one could reply that, with the exception of feminine stems ending in *-ā* (*āP*), in *-ī* (*Nī*) or in *-ū* (*nadī*),[16] it's quite obvious that classes of nominal stems based on *both* the stem ending *and* the gender are not operative classes within Pāṇini's generative system. One cannot simply reduce variations in grammatical description to a mere matter of "arrangement", as already stated by Scharfe in his volume on Sanskrit grammatical literature (1977: 175): "Because so much in grammar is formal, it is not a meaningful critique of these works [i.e. pedagogical grammars] to say that 'they differ only in the arrangement of the material.'"

If one is sensitive to this idea, one must concede that nominal paradigmatic sets in Sanskrit pedagogical grammars do constitute a grammatical innovation.

Abbreviations

A: *Aṣṭādhyāyī*
C: *Cāndravyākaraṇa*
KV: *Kāśikāvṛtti*

16. Note that *nadī-* covers feminine stems ending in *-ī* or in *-ū* (cf. A 1.4.3).

References

Cardona, George. 1997 [1988]. *Pāṇini. His work and its traditions, volume I: Background and Introduction*, 2nd revised and completed edition. Delhi: Motilal Banarsidass.

Cardona, George. 2014. "Segmentation of Vedic texts: *padapāṭhas*". *Bulletin d'Études Indiennes* 32 (Proceedings of "The Indian Traditions of Language Studies", Workshop, *ICHoLS XI*, Potsdam), edited by É. Aussant & J.-L. Chevillard, 87–100. Paris: Association Française pour les Études Indiennes.

Chatterji, Kshitish Chandra. 1964 [1948]. *Technical Terms and Technique of Sanskrit Grammar.* Calcutta: Sanskrit Book Depot.

Filliozat, Pierre-Sylvain. 1988. *Grammaire sanskrite pāṇinéenne.* Paris: Picard.

Katre, Sumitra M., ed. 1989. *Aṣṭādhyāyī of Pāṇini.* Roman Transliteration and English Translation. Delhi: Motilal Banarsidass.

K.L.V. Sastry, Vidyasagar & Anantharama Sastri, L. 2000. *Śabdamañjarī. Enlarged Edition with a most interesting Chapter on Samasa, Foot-Notes and Glossary.* Kalpathi / Palghat: R.S. Vadhyar & Sons.

Liebich, Bruno, ed. 1966 [1918]. *Candra-vṛtti, der original Kommentar Candragomin's zu seinem grammatischen Sūtra.* Abhandlungen für die Kunde des Morgenlandes 14. Nendeln: Kraus Reprint.

Pinault, Georges-Jean. 1989. ""Travaux à partir du corpus védique". *Histoire des idées linguistiques Tome 1 (La naissance des métalangages en Orient et en Occident")*, edited by S. Auroux, 303–330. Liège: Mardaga.

Rangacharya, Rao Bahadur M., ed. 1916–29. *The Rūpāvatāra of Dharmakīrti. Edited with Additions and Emendations for the Use of College Students.* Madras: G.A. Natesan and Co.

Renou, Louis. 1941–42. "Les connexions entre le rituel et la grammaire en sanskrit". *Journal asiatique* 233.105–165.

Sarup, Lakshman, ed. 1998 [1920–27]. *The Nighaṇṭu and the Nirukta.* Edited and translated. Delhi: Motilal Banarsidass.

Scharfe, Hartmut. 1977. *Grammatical Literature.* Wiesbaden: Otto Harrassowitz (A History of Indian Literature).

Timalsina, Ramhari, ed. 2022. *The Sumatipañjikā: A Commentary On Cāndravyākaraṇavṛtti 1.1 and 1.4.* Pondicherry: Institut Français de Pondichéry / École française d'Extrême-Orient (Collection Indologie n°153).

CHAPTER 9

Constituent-order in Sanskrit Bahuvrīhi compounds

The role of the qualifier[1]

Maria Piera Candotti & Tiziana Pontillo
Università di Pisa | Università di Cagliari

Modern and ancient interpreters contrast karmadhārayas, made up of two co-referential constituents, i.e. a qualifier and a qualificand, with bahuvrīhis, in an attempt to understand "where" the "adjective" occurs. They concentrate on the fact that, unlike in karmadhārayas, in bahuvrīhis the qualifier unexpectedly occupies the right-hand slot. Pāṇini's compounding rules are indeed targeted on singling out the non-head of the compounds which is attributed the first place by default, mirroring the natural order of the alternating syntagm. In particular cases some different principles govern their constituent-order: one of them, illustrated in *Aṣṭādhyāyi* 2.2.35, is based on the concept of *viśeṣaṇa* which shares several features with the modern notion of qualifier. The present inquiry aims at showing how in Pāṇini's system the concept of *upasarjana* as the constituent whose syntax is frozen is kept separated from that of qualifier, with the consequent re-appraisal of his role within the history of linguistics.

Keywords: Sanskrit Bahuvrīhi, head in compounds, word-order in compounds, Pāṇini, qualifier-qualificand relation

1. Constituent order and its relevance in compounding

The peculiar condition of Vedic and Sanskrit compounds, caught midway between morphological and syntactic processes, has long been the subject of heated discussion. And indeed, the issue is still far from being settled. Suffice it to recall how two important recent articles devoted to Bahuvrīhi compounds

1. All translations are by the authors, unless explicitly stated otherwise. This paper is the result of joint research discussed and shared by the authors: for the sake of academic requirements, §§ 1; 3; 3.1 are attributed to M.P. Candotti, §§ 2; 3.2; 4 to T. Pontillo.

https://doi.org/10.1075/sihols.133.09can

arrive at opposing solutions. Gillon (2008) mainly focuses on the quite productive classical Sanskrit possessive Bahuvrīhi compound and proposes a morphological solution by applying a phonetically null suffix to a pre-existing endocentric compound,[2] an approach which he erroneously attributes at least in part to Pāṇini.[3] Lowe, on the other hand, in the very first lines of his article states that (2015: 72) "the major rules of compounding in Sanskrit can be most appropriately characterised in syntactic, not morphological, terms: that is, as syntactic phrases rather than as complex words". We have already had occasion in Candotti & Pontillo 2019 and Candotti & Pontillo 2022 to show that Pāṇini's solution, when correctly interpreted, basically establishes a frozen syntactic relation between one of the constituents of the Bahuvrīhi and the denotatum of the whole compound. Thus the focus of his description, at least as far as Bahuvrīhi compounds are concerned, is mainly syntactic.

Here we continue our reflection on the syntactic dimension of the Bahuvrīhi compounds in Pāṇinian description and its reception in the Western sphere, turning our attention to another particularly significant feature, namely how constituent order is treated in Pāṇini's grammar and the specificities of Bahuvrīhis in this respect. To use Hock's (2015: 4) words, it is well-known that "Sanskrit (like other early Indo-European languages) exhibits a remarkable degree of free word order – not just free phrase order." The question is still open as to whether we may consider Vedic and Sanskrit as having a basic (even if not binding) SOV order[4] or whether it is more fruitful to resort to a linear order without syntactic value, following the path once traced by Staal (1967) with the concept of the 'wild tree', i.e. a tree without linear order within the syntagm.[5] The first hypothesis is undoubtedly the one with the longest tradition in modern and contemporary linguistic studies, even though it is not without uncertainties. According to Delbrück (1878: 27; see also Hock 2014) the predicate-initial order would have been a marked order while Speyer (1896: 10) on the contrary specifies that "if the predicate be a noun it is put before the subject". On the other hand, Staal 1967 (rediscussed in Gillon & Shaer 2005: 466) shows how all the possible configurations of a sentence NPsubject + V-NPobject are attested, the only exception being "sentences with an overt copula of predication, in which the subject NP never follows the VP".

2. e.g. *sama-citta-* 'even mind' → *sama-citta-* + Ø 'even-mind-ed' (Gillon 2008: 2).

3. See also Kiparsky (1982: 139): "Exocentric compounds [...] must [...] be assigned zero derivational suffixes since they otherwise would share the properties of their heads, i.e. be endocentric."

4. Hock (2015) and bibliography quoted there.

5. Gillon and Shaer (2005) adopt and modify Staal's (1967) notion of "Wild Trees", i.e. trees without phrase-internal linear ordering.

Staal (1967: 36) considered his approach as being quite similar to that of traditional grammarians who never regulated word order, since they were convinced "not that such rules are beyond the scope of grammar, but that there are no such rules, since word order [...] is free". But perhaps this statement goes too far. As we will show below, one can glean indirect information about how Pāṇini interprets the order of the constituents within the syntagm precisely because he uses the syntagm as an implicit starting point (and explicit touchstone) for the construction of the compounds themselves.

On the other hand, the earliest post-Pāṇinian grammarians were already definitely aware of the fact that a stricter ordering of the constituents is certainly one of the most important identifying elements for distinguishing a compound from its corresponding syntagm. The following table summarises the possible phenomena concerning compounds that can be traced back either to the presence of several words in a syntactic relation (a sort of variant of the matching syntagm) or to the morphological creation of a new nominal base that may be subject to further morphological processes of derivation (see following table).

It is clear even from a cursory glance that there is a shift from a more syntactic status in the use of Vedic compounds to a greater rigidity that is typical of classical compounds. However, whatever the case, the element of strongest distinction with respect to the syntagm lies precisely in the fixed order of the constituents.

Syntagm	Morph
1. phonosyntactic rules proper to the word boundary applied to the internal constituents;	1. a single set of endings;
2. double *vṛddhi* / double accent e.g. *daivamānuṣaka* 'concerning gods and men'; *índrāsómā* (only Vedic);	2. a single accent e.g. *ahorātrám* "day-and night" = one day
3. syntactic relation of the subordinate constituent with an external element, e.g. *devadattasya gurukulam* 'the house/family of Devadatta's teacher'[6];	3. possibility of compound affixation, e.g. *bahu-khaṭvá-ka-/bahu-khaṭvá-* 'in which there are many beds'
4. maintenance of endings of the first constituent, e.g. *dūrādāgata-* 'come from afar' (productive only in Vedic?);	4. fixed order of constituents
5. tmesis (only Vedic Dvandvas) e.g. *arcan dyā́vā námobhiḥ pṛthiví́* 'They should venerate Heaven with salutations and Earth.'[7]	

6. Possibility discarded as incorrect by post-Pāṇinian grammatical tradition.

7. While discussing Insler 1998, Kiparsky (2010: 8–9) proposes an interesting interpretation of such cases.

As regards the internal order of the Bahuvrīhi, we have already hinted at the fact that modern scholars have often relied on a conversion principle that started from underlying compounds and thus indirectly accounted for the order of the constituents in the Bahuvrīhi as well.[8] Most interpreters in fact contrast Karmadhārayas that are made up of two co-referential constituents, i.e. a qualifier and a qualificand, with Bahuvrīhis, in an attempt to understand "where" the qualifier – be it an "adjective" or a "noun" – occurs (e.g. Bopp 1827: 318–320; Wackernagel 1957: 302–304).[9] Apart from the perplexities that may emerge with this model, it is certainly not the descriptive model proposed by Pāṇini who used a different way to account for constituent order in both endocentric and exocentric compounds.

2. Bahuvrīhi in Pāṇini's description

In Pāṇini's grammar, the teaching of how a Bahuvrīhi compound is formed comes almost at the end of the entire section on compounding. The general compounding rule is

(1)

A 2.1.4	[*sup* 2]	*saha*	*supā*
	nominal ending (technical term) NOM.M.SG	with-PREP	nominal ending (technical term) INS.M.SG

It teaches to form a compound by combining two nominal inflected nouns called *sup* with each other. This string made up of two inflected nouns is the source-phrase[10] of the compound or, from a different perspective, it represents the constituent-analysis of the compound, called *vigraha* in the traditional indigenous grammar.

Furthermore, this string is to be considered an alternative option available to express the same sense conveyed by the matching compound. More precisely, this string is the least recommended choice in most compounding rules (A 2.1.18–

8. One of the most influential statements in this regard goes back to Brugmann (1906: 75) who describes Bahuvrīhis as substantives transformed into adjectives, i.e. determinative compounds used in an exocentric manner.

9. Tribulato (2015: 117) also pointed out the difficulty in getting rid of any internal analysis of constituents whatsoever, with special reference to ancient Greek compounds with a verb as first constituent (e.g. φερεοίκος "carrying one's own home"). She observes that, although this class of compounds should be considered as exocentric, i.e. headless, the first constituent "is a sort of *determinatum* and thus a sort of *semantic head*".

10. As for the relation between the compound and the source-phrase, we rely on A 2.1.1, interpreted according to Pontillo 2013: 111–118.

2.2.9) – at least in line with Kiparsky's (1979:3) and Radicchi's (1988: 56–58) overall interpretation of the phenomenon – probably due to its lack of synthesis and syntactic effectiveness. In fact, *vā* which commonly expresses the "preferable option" throughout the *Asṭhādhyāyī* – thus translated as 'preferably' – is part of rule A 2.1.18 and has to be continued in the following compounding rules up to A 2.2.9. On the other hand, the "marginal option" signified by means of *vibhāṣā* 'marginally' is valid from A 2.1.11 to 2.1.17.

After the general compounding rule A 2.1.4, the whole chapter A 2.1 is devoted to the formation of

a. the small category of compounds used in an indeclinable status, i.e., the so-called Avyayībhāvas (A 2.1.5–2.1.21);
b. the broad category of the endocentric compounds called Tatpuruṣas (A 2.1.22–2.2.22), which also includes those whose members are coreferential with each other, i.e. the Karmadhārayas (A 2.1.49–72);
c. and the compounds whose first constituent is a numeral, i.e. the Dvigus (A 2.1.49–52).

Rules A 2.2.23–24 are the two main/general rules which teach to form a Bahuvrīhi compound.

(2)

A 2.2.23	*śeso*	*bahuvrīhih*	[*samāsaḥ* 2.1.3]
	remainder-M.SG.	Bahuvrīhi (technical term)-M.SG	compound-N.M.SG
	"The remainder is the Bahuvrīhi [compound]."		

(3)

A 2.2.24	*anekam*	*anyapadārthe*
	not-NEG=one-N.SG	other-inflected.word-meaning-LOC.M.SG
	"Two or more inflected words [preferably combine] in the meaning of another inflected word (i.e., the meaning of an inflected word different from the constituents)."	

As clearly explained by Joshi and Roodbergen (1995:255), *śesa* 'remainder' is a device Pāṇini always used to refer to something "other than what has been stated in a particular section."[12] The Bahuvrīhi is consequently the "residual [category]" in the section A 2.1.4–2.2.38, i.e., a compound whose formation rules have not been captured by the other rules in that given section.[13]

12. See also Sharma (2010:1) and Cardona (2013:104).

13. Indeed, as noticed by Kobayashi (2021:217), such a "reminder" is not necessarily something "marginal": it "can in effect overlap with *utsarga* 'general rule'".

Scholars have mostly concentrated on the constraint *anyapadārthe* "in the meaning of another word". This probably even inspired the use of the label "exocentric" which became the universally preferred term for this typology of compounds (Sadovski 2002: 352).[14] Nonetheless, the term *artha* at the end of *anyapadārthe* hardly matches the modern syntactic and semantic notion of "head", and thus it is better to refrain from any kind of hurried overlapping between A 2.2.24 and some widespread definition of "exocentric compound" in contemporary linguistics.[15]

In Candotti & Pontillo 2019 and in Candotti & Pontillo 2022 respectively we tried to show the limits of the postulation of a phonetically null suffix and the drawbacks of the analysis of the Bahuvrīhi based on the head. However, what is most important here is the fact that Pāṇini's definition of the Bahuvrīhi, just like that of all the other compounds, is not based on its head, but rather on the so-called *upasarjana*, which can roughly be conceived of as the "non-head" constituent of the compound. Another pair of rules teach how the *upasarjana* can be singled out. The first rule simply teaches a metalinguistic device by which Pāṇini indicates which the *upasarjana* constituent is:

(4)

A 1.2.43	*prathamānirdiṣṭaṃ*	*samāsa*	*upasarjanam*
	first-stated-NOM.N.SG	compound-LOC.M.SG	*upasarjana* (technical term)-N.SG

"What is stated in the nominative in a compound-[rule] is called *upasarjana*."

Therefore, the nominative of *anekam* in rule A 2.2.24 teaches that all the surface-constituents of the Bahuvrīhi compound constitute the *upasarjana*, and we shall see below what the syntactic consequences of this analysis are. Before focusing on this special case of *upasarjana*, it is important to become familiar with this notion in easier examples. For instance, in the following rule, the *upasarjana* is the word expressed in the nominative case i.e., the noun *tṛtīyā* 'the third ending/instrumental case' in the source phrase.

14. In the context of more recent research focused on a kind of conversion from underlying endocentric compounds, exocentricity is no longer considered as an inherent property of the compound nor as a prime for analysis, but rather as something which "may arise from use in context" (Lundquist & Yates 2018: 2120). See also Scalise & Bisetto (2009: 45) who present a list of compounds used with both an endocentric and exocentric meaning.

15. See e.g. Lindner 2011: 24–25; Štekauer, Valera & Körtvélyessy 2012: 80.

(5)

A 2.1.30	*tṛtīyā*	*tatkṛtārthena*	*guṇavacanena*	[*vā* 2.1.18]
	third-NOM.F.SG	this-made-meaning-INS.N.SG	quality-expression-INS.N.SG	preferably-ADV.

"[An inflected noun ending with] the third ending (i.e. inflected in the instrumental case) combines with [an inflected word] which denotes a quality, whose meaning is determined by this (i.e by the noun ending with) the third ending."

For example, *śaṅkulā-khaṇḍa-* combines a noun inflected in the instrumental case (*śaṅkulā-* 'scissors') with *khaṇḍa-* 'split into pieces'. The matching source-phrase is *śaṅkulayā khaṇḍaḥ* "split into pieces by scissors".

If Pāṇini had contented himself with this single rule for the definition of the *upasarjana* (A 1.2.43), there would have been problems in some rules such as A 2.2.18 (*ku-gati-prādayaḥ*),[16] because what is stated in the nominative case, namely a series of indeclinable words are in fact non-*upasarjana*, i.e. they play the role of what is commonly called "head". A classical example of a compound formed in accordance with this rule is *niṣkauśāmbi-*, which denotes "someone who has departed (*niṣ-*[*krāntaḥ*]) from the town named Kauśāmbī". The indeclinable *nis-* (included in the *prādi*-list) combines with the ablative form *kauśāmbyāḥ* "from Kauśāmbī". It is clear that the non-head is the latter constituent, but the nominative is used in the phrasing of rule A 2.2.18 to indicate *nis-*, which is instead the head of the compound. Rule A 1.2.44 solves the problem, by teaching that the *upasarjana* is recognisable even when it is not stated in the nominative in the grammar, precisely because it is *ekavibhakti*, i.e. it can adopt one ending only, regardless of its position.

(6)

A 1.2.44	*ekavibhakti*	*ca*	*apūrvanipāte*
	one-ending-NOM.N.SG	and-CONJ.	not-first-place-LOC.N.SG.

"And what has one single ending, even when it is not in the first place."

Now, let us see how the *ekavibhakti* criterion in rule A 1.2.44 works in complying with the need of singling out the *upasarjana* of our compound. Let us imagine that we have to embed our compound in several sentences with different syntactic functions: whatever case ending is applied to the compound, the ablative *kauśāmbyāḥ* remains unchanged in its source-phrase, i.e., it will always have "one single

16. A 2.2.18 *ku-gati-prādayaḥ* [*saha supā* 2.1.4] [*tatpuruṣaḥ* 2.1.22] [*nityam* 2.2.17] "The indeclinable word] *ku-* and the units termed *gati* or included in the list beginning with *pra-* [compulsorily combine with an inflected word, to form a tatpuruṣa compound]."

ending" and the other member is inflected in exactly the same way as the whole matching compound.

(7)

niṣkrāntaḥ gone out-PTCP.NOM.M.SG	*kauśāmbyāḥ* Kauśāmbī-ABL.F.SG from Kauśāmbī	→ *niṣkauśāmbiḥ* gone out of-Kauśāmbī-NOM.M.SG
niṣkrāntam gone out-PTCP.ACC.M.SG		→ *niṣkauśāmbyam* gone out of-Kauśāmbī-ACC.M.SG
niṣkrāntena gone out-PTCP.INS.M.SG		→ *niṣkauśāmbinā* gone out of-Kauśāmbī-INS.M.SG. [...]

Indeed, this feature of the *upasarjana* is verifiable in any compound explained in the compounding section preceding the Bahuvrīhi rules (A 2.1.5–2.2.22), regardless of the word-order. In this case the *upasarjana* is the constituent that is linked to the other constituent by means of a frozen syntactic relationship even though it is not the right-hand constituent.

(8)

puruṣaḥ man-NOM.M.SG	*rājñaḥ* king-GEN. M. SG	→ *rājapuruṣaḥ* (*lit.* king's man =) royal officer-NOM.M.SG
puruṣam man-ACC.M.SG		→ *rājapuruṣam* royal officer-ACC.M.SG
puruṣena man-.INS.M.SG		→ *rājapuruṣeṇa* royal officer-INS.M.SG. [...]

Nonetheless, the Bahuvrīhi is a type of compound whose constituent order cannot be predicted on the basis of the *upasarjana* criterion. Since all the surface-constituents in the Bahuvrīhi constitute the *upasarjana*, they are all inflected in a frozen case in the source-phrase. Consequently, the surface-constituents do not change, despite the specific case ending which is applied to the resultant compound when it is used in a sentence. Let us analyse the following classical Sanskrit compound.

(9)

siṁharṣabhasya gatiḥ lion-bull-NOM.M.SG gait-NOM.F.SG	*asya* that-GEN.M.SG	→ *siṁharṣabhagatiḥ* one whose gait is that of a bull-like lion-NOM.M.SG
		→ *siṁharṣabhagatim* one whose gait is that of a bull-like lion-ACC.M.SG
		→ *siṁharṣabhagatinā* one whose gait is that of a bull-like lion-INS.M.SG. [...]

There is no change in either of the two surface-constituents of the compound or in the relation between this phrase and the denotatum, while the resultant compound is inflected in different cases in accordance with the syntax of the sentence in which it is embedded.

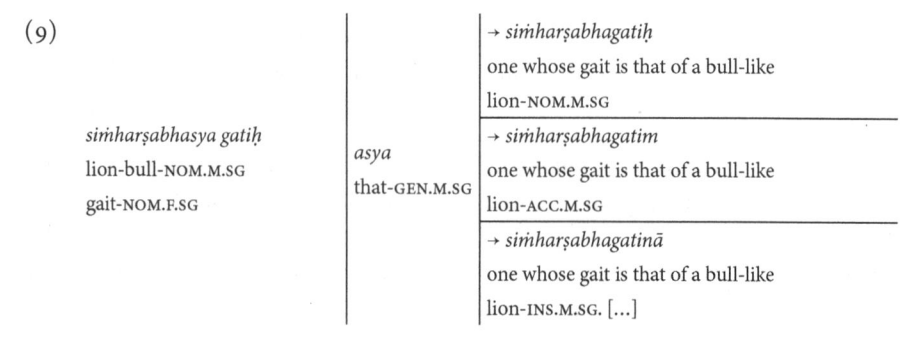

3. Bahuvrīhi constituent-order as a special case

The default constituent order is recalled by the following rule:

(10)

A 2.2.30	*upasarjanaṃ*	*pūrvam*
	upasarjana (technical term)-NOM.N.SG.	first-NOM.N.SG.
	"A constituent termed *upasarjana* is placed first in a compound"	

But this was already indirectly taught by the metalinguistic structure of A 2.1.4, where the noun inflected in the nominative case – which overlaps with the *upasarjana* constituent, with the exceptions dealt with in §2 – is quoted first in each rule.

As an exception to this very general rule, A 2.2.31 teaches a list of compounds headed by the compound *rājadanta*, where the *upasarjana* is always supposed to be the second constituent. In the remaining rules up to the end of chapter 2.2, Pāṇini deals with the types of compounds for which the *upasarjana* criterion does not work in assigning the internal order of constituents. The rules in this last section must cover the total amount of relevant cases since otherwise it would be impossible to decide on the position of individual members.

Rules A 2.2.32–34 and rules A 2.2.35–37 are respectively devoted to the constituent order in Dvandva and Bahuvrīhi compounds, whose members all belong to the same syntactic level, so that A 2.2.30 cannot help us to predict the constituent order of the Bahuvrīhi, even if we resort to A 1.2.44. In particular, the general casuistry regarding Bahuvrīhi-compounds is exhausted in the three types identified as being relevant by rules A 2.2.35–37: constituents in the function of *viśeṣaṇa*, those in the locative case (2.2.35) and constituents represented by nominal forms of the verb (2.2.36–37).[17] We will concentrate on the first and second type:[18]

17. A 2.2.38 is an exception as it governs a specific typology of Karmadhārayas, whose *upasarjana* is "preferably" (i.e. not always) placed first.

18. A 2.2.36 [*pūrvam* 30] *niṣṭhā* [*bahuvrīhau* 35] "In a Bahuvrīhi the constituent which is a participle ending with *-ta* and *–tavat* is the first constituent."; A 2.2.37 *vāhitāgnyādiṣu* [*pūrvam* 30] [*niṣṭhā* 36] "In the compounds of the group beginning with *āhitāgni-* the constituent which is a participle ending with *-ta* and *–tavat* is preferably the first constituent." A.M. Borghero and T. Pontillo recently studied the third type, presenting their results during the 18th World Sanskrit Conference, Canberra, 9th–13th January 2023 (Special Panel: *Uncovering Sanskrit syntax*),

(11)

A 2.2.35	[*pūrvam* 30]	*saptamīviśeṣaṇe*	*bahuvrīhau*
	first-NOM.N.SG	seventh-qualifier-NOM.N.DU	Bahuvrīhi (technical term-LOC.M.SG

"In a Bahuvrīhi a constituent ending with a seventh case ending (i.e. nouns inflected in the locative case) or which plays the role of a qualifier is placed first."

As for the qualifier (*viśeṣaṇa*), the stock examples in the commentarial literature (see e.g. M and KV ad A 2.2.35), are *citragu-* "the one whose cows are bright (*citra-*)"; *śabalagu-* "the one whose cows are mottled", whereas as regards cases with the locative in the first constituent, we find *kaṇṭhe-kāla-* "black on the neck/ throat" = as an epithet of Śiva, and *urasi-loman-* "hairy-chested".

3.1 *viśeṣaṇa* constituents in the Bahuvrīhi

The second part of the rule thus assigns the first position to the constituent that performs the function of *viśeṣaṇa*. This notion in Pāṇini's grammar stands for what in modern terms we would call the "determinant/qualifier", i.e. the element that helps to identify, to specify, the denotation of another term. While it is true that this function is often performed by that lexical class that answers to the name of adjectives, it is equally important to emphasise that there is no perfect overlap between these two classes.[19] The role of determinant can also be played by a noun in relation to an adjective as in the case of *śastriśyama-* "knife-black". A determinant is not a lexical (or even semantic) class but a function that is constructed in relation to something else (sometimes referred to as *viśeṣya* "determinand/qualified"). This term is seldom used in grammar but it is one that has a certain relevance since, in addition to our rule, it is also employed in a rule of broad scope that applies to Karmadhāraya compounds:

19. This is also indirectly proven here by rule A 1.2.52 in which two types of qualifiers (*viśeṣaṇa*) are distinguished: qualifiers that do not signify a class (more like adjectives) and qualifiers that do. The example *godau ramaṇīyau* lit. "The pleasant 'Two Godas'" (proper n. of a village) belongs to the first case, *godau grāmaḥ* "The village 'The two Godas'", to the second one.

(12)

A 2.1.57	*viśeṣaṇam*	*viśeṣyeṇa*	*bahulam*
	qualifier-NOM.N.SG	qualificandINS.N.SG	variously-ADV.

"A qualifier [inflected word] combines under various conditions with a qualified [inflected word]."[20]

e.g. *nīlam utpalam*→*nīlotpala* "blue water lily".

The rule teaches that it is the constituent that performs the function of qualifier (expressed in the nominative, thus *upasarjana*) that can be compounded with a following element that is identified with it (*viśeṣya*, expressed in the instrumental). The phrasing of the rule itself gives us the order of the constituents which sees the subordinate member, expressed in the nominative, placed on the left, in a position that replicates the order of the corresponding syntagm: *nīlam utpalam*. Although this is a very productive way of forming both Karmadhāraya and Bahuvrīhi compounds, Pāṇini cannot rely on 2.1.57 for the constituent order of Bahuvrīhi since, as we have already seen, it does not proceed by derivation from endocentric compounds. He must therefore explicitly choose an *upasarjana* with a qualifying function from the constituents that make up the Bahuvrīhi, in order to assign it the first position by means of A 2.2.35.

3.2 Locative constituents in the Bahuvrīhi

Now, let us reflect on the first part of rule A 2.2.35, which uses a morphosyntactic category ("locative ending") instead of a semantic one ("qualifier"). Both the commentarial examples quoted above, i.e. *kaṇṭhe-kāla-* and *urasi-loman* are compounds that violate the principle which teaches the zero-replacement of the nominal endings of the individual inflected words that are combined in compounds. This principle is taught as follows:

20. Following Kiparsky's (1979: 206) suggestion, we consider that *bahulam* indicates the fact that the rule adds further kinds of restrictions to the relevant provisions. Some of these concern the order of members or the specific member that can occur in a given context and are spelt out in the subsequent rules up to A 2.1.72.

(13)

A 2.4.71	[*luk* 58]	*supo*	*dhātuprātipadikayoḥ*
	zero-replacement (technical term)-NOM.M.SG.	nominal ending (technical term) GEN.M.SG	verbal base-nominal stem-LOC.N.DU.

"A case-ending which occurs as a part of a verbal base or of a nominal stem is zero-replaced[21] (whatever the nominal stem is)."

In other words, just as happens in the well-known type of Latin compound *terraemotus* (instead of **terramotus*), the first constituents of both *kaṇṭhe-kāla*-and *urasi-loman*, are inflected in the locative case instead of occurring in their thematic status, as might be expected according to A 2.4.71 (**kaṇṭha-kāla*; **uro-loman*).[22]

The function of the locative is here quite different to that of the qualifier and must therefore be explicitly singled out: *kaṇṭhe-* in *kaṇṭhekāla-* does not specify the quality of blackness as much as, for example, one of Siva's qualities who is said to be "black (only) on his neck", just as *uraśiloman* is someone who is "hairy (only) on his chest".

On the other hand, one could also wonder whether Pāṇini deliberately ignored the use of the type with a possible locative as second member, such as *gaḍu-kaṇṭha-* and *gaḍu-śiras-* "with an excrescence on the neck/head", which are the two examples that Patañjali explains while commenting on the following Vt.:

(14)

Vt. 3 *ad* A 2.2.35	*saptamyāḥ*	*pūrvanipāte*	*gaḍvādibhyaḥ*	*paravacanam*
	seventh-GEN.F.SG	first-place-LOC.N.SG	excrescence-beginning-ABL.N.PL	second (place)-mention-NOM.N.SG.

"After the nominal bases of the list beginning with *gaḍu*, the second place should be stated for the constituent inflected in the locative case."

In fact, both Whitney (1889: 507) and Wackernagel (1957: 279) recorded a specific typology of Bahuvrīhis with a right-hand member conveying a part of the body, plausibly interpreted as a locative. This type is highly productive for example in the *Ṛgveda*:

- *mádhujihva-* "honey-tongued" ṚV 1.44.6;
- *ghṛtápṛṣṭha-* "butter-backed" ṚV 5.37.1;
- *maṇi-grīva* "with an amulet around his neck" ṚV 1.122.14.

21. We dealt with Pāṇini's zero-typology at ICHOLS 2008. See Candotti & Pontillo 2014: 68–80.

22. This class of exceptions is dealt with in A 6.3.1–24.

One of the most productive combinations uses *hasta-* 'hand' as the second constituent. See e.g.:

- *vájrahasta-* "having a thunderbolt in hand" ṚV 8.24.24;
- *khā́dihasta-* "ring-handed" ṚV 5.58.2;
- *grā́vahasta-* "holding the Soma-stones in his hands" ṚV 1.15.7
- *híranyahasta-* "golden-handed" ṚV 1.35.10;
- *gṛtáhasta-* "whose hands are buttered" ṚV 7.16.8;
- *ákravihasta-* "whose hands are bloodless" ṚV 5.62.6.

Patañjali's commentary partially records such use while commenting on the following Vt. on A 2.2.36.

(15)

Vt. 4 *ad*	*praharaṇārthebhyaś*	*ca*
A 2.2.36	weapon-meaning-ABL.N.PL.	and-CONJ
	"[A mention of the second place for the past participles (Vt. 1)] [should be made] after constituents conveying weapons."	

Along with the two examples that he quotes as relevant to this Vt., namely *asyudyataḥ, musalodyataḥ* "having a raised sword/club", Patañjali also inserts the two examples *asipaṇi-*, *daṇḍapaṇi-* "having a sword/stick in his hand". Indeed, he explicitly extends Kātyāyana's additional statement (14), which was limited to past participles, to the case of nouns inflected in the locative.[23]

Nevertheless, since one can exclude the fact that Pāṇini in turn did not know these compounds, it is clear that he analysed them in a different manner. In the ancient grammarian's analysis, the member inflected in the locative case in the source-phrase is not an *upasarjana*. Bopp attempted (1827: 320 fn. 3) to re-align the discussed irregularity with the common constituent-order (with a qualifier placed first) by interpreting e.g. *śūlahasta-* not as "having the spear in his hand", but as "spear-handed", an explanation which was also endorsed by Wackernagel (1957: 279).[24] Thus, what is often expressed by a locative, i.e. a part of the body, might have indeed been used as a qualificand. As a consequence, the possessive meaning of the whole compound mainly points to a part of the body which is characterised by a given attribute, e.g. a weapon, so that this weapon plays the role of a qualifier with respect to the part of the body. In brief, these *Ṛgvedic* examples are to be considered under the domain of the criterion teaching the *viśeṣaṇa-* as

23. *praharaṇārthebhyaś ca pare niṣṭhāsaptamyau bhavata iti vaktavyam* "It must be taught that a past participle and the locative ending are placed in the second position after constituents conveying weapons."

24. "Bopp vielleicht mit Recht: Hinterglied gibt Hauptgegenstand, Vorderglied modifizierend."

the mandatory left-hand member in a Bahuvrīhi, while only certain specific locatives that express some sort of restrictive complement need a special mention in the phrasing of rule A 2.2.35. This seems to give a reasonable explanation as to why Pāṇini formulated this rule by using s*aptamī-viśeṣaṇe* "a locative case or a qualifier is placed first".

4. Conclusion

If we return to the opening question, we can now say that Pāṇini's assumed syntactic approach to compounding is also confirmed for constituent order. The main rule is based on singling out the non-head among the constituents of the compound (4) which is attributed the first place (10) following an order which almost mirrors the natural order of the alternating syntagm.

Some different principles only apply to Dvandvas and Bahuvrīhis; in particular the latter finds its main tool in the concept of *viśeṣaṇa* which shares several features with the modern notion of qualifier.

References

Bopp, Franz. 1827. *Ausführliches Lehrgebäude der Sanskrita Sprache*. Berlin: Dümmler.

Brugmann, Karl. 1905–1906. *Grundriß der Indogermanischen Sprachen*. Berlin: De Gruyter.

Candotti, Maria Piera & Tiziana Pontillo. 2014, "Pāṇini's zero morphs as allomorphs in the complexity of linguistic context". *Proceedings of the Workshop "The Indian Traditions of Language Studies", XI ICHOLS 2008*, edited by Jean-Luc Chevillard & Emilie Aussant, *Bulletin d'Etudes Indiennes* 32.55–85.

Candotti, Maria Piera & Tiziana Pontillo. 2019. "Lexical subordination in derivation and compounding". *Studi e Saggi Linguistici* 58:2.155–175.

Candotti, Maria Piera & Tiziana Pontillo. 2022. "Dispensing with ellipsis in the analysis of Sanskrit bahuvrīhi: Resurfacing, testing and assessing Pāṇini's model". *Proceedings of Special theme Session 1 in 35th South Asian Languages Analysis Roundtable: Ellipsis in South Asian Languages*) edited by Emily Manetta. *Journal of South Asian Linguistics* 12:1.1–22.

Cardona, George. 2013. "Pāṇini and Pāṇinīyas on *śeṣa* relations". *Indological research: different standpoints* edited by P.C. Muraleemadhavan, 99–146. Delhi: New Bharatiya.

Delbrück, Berthold. 1878. *Die altindische Wortfolge aus dem Çatapathabrāhmana dargestellt*. Halle: Verlag der Buchhandlung des Weisenhauses.

doi Gillon, Brendan. 2008. "Exocentric Compounds in Classical Sanskrit". *First International Sanskrit Computational Linguistics Symposium*, Oct 2007, Rocquencourt, France, edited by Gérard Huet & Amba Kulkarni. http://hal.inria.fr/SANSKRIT/fr/. <inria-00202860>.

Gillon, Brendan & Benjamin Shaer. 2005. "Classical Sanskrit, 'Wild Trees', and the Properties of Free Word Order Languages". *Universal Grammar in the Reconstruction of Ancient Languages* edited by Katalin É. Kiss, 457–493. Berlin / Boston: De Gruyter Mouton.

Hock, Hans Heinrich. 2015. "Some Issues in Sanskrit Syntax". *Selected Papers Presented at the Seminar on Sanskrit Syntax and Discourse Structures, 13–15 June 2013, Université Paris Diderot*, with an updated and revised bibliography by Hans Henrich Hock, Peter M. Scharf, 1–52. Providence: The Sanskrit Library.

Insler, Stanley. 1998. "*mitrā́várunā* or *mitrā́ várunā* ?". *Mír Curad: Studies in Honor of Calvert Watkins* edited by Jay Jasanoff, H. Craig Melchert & Lisi Olivier, 283–290. Innsbruck: Institut für Sprachwissenschaft der Universität Innsbruck.

Joshi, S. D. & J. A. F. Roodbergen. 1995. *The Aṣṭādhyāyī of Pāṇini with Translation and Explanatory Notes, Vol. IV (1.4.1–1.4.110)*. New Delhi: Sahitya Akademi.

Kiparsky, Paul. 1979. *Pāṇini as a Variationist.* Pune: Poona University Press / Cambridge: MIT Press.

Kiparsky, Paul. 1982. "From Cyclic Phonology to Lexical Phonology". *The Structure of Phonological Representation*, Vol. 1 edited by H. van der Hulst and N. Smith, 131–175. Dordrecht: Foris.

Kiparsky, Paul. 2010. "Dvandvas, Blocking, and the Associative: the bumpy ride from phrase to word". *Language* 86:2.302–331.

Kobayashi, Masato 2021. "Pāṇini's Definition of the Bahuvrīhi as *śeṣa* 'Remainder'". *Śabdānugama. Indian Linguistic Studies in Honor of George Cardona. Volume I Vyākaraṇa and Śabdabodha* edited by in Peter M. Scharf, 217–236. Providence: The Sanskrit Library.

Lindner, Thomas. 2011. *Komposition (Indogermanische Grammatik 4,1)*. Heidelberg: Winter 2011.

Lowe, John J. 2015. "The Syntax of Sanskrit Compounds". *Language* 91:3. 71–114.

Lundquist, Jesse & Anthony D. Yates. 2018. "The Morphology of Proto-Indo-European". *Handbook of Comparative and Historical Indo-European Linguistics* edited by Jared Klein, Brian Joseph & Matthias Fritz (in cooperation with Mark Wenthe) Vol. 3, 2079–2195. Berlin: de Gruyter.

Pontillo, Tiziana 2013. "'Where the Sense is Intended although the Corresponding Speech Unit is not Employed': the *ekaśeṣa* case". *Vyākaraṇa Across the Ages. Proceedings of the 15th World Sanskrit Conference, Delhi 5–10 January 2012 (Vol. II: Vyākaraṇa Session* edited by George Cardona, 107–143. New Delhi: D.K. Printworld.

Radicchi, Anna. 1985–1988. *La teoria pāṇiniana dei samāsa secondo l'interpretazione delle scuole grammaticali indiane dal quinto all'ottavo secolo d.C.* 2 Volumes. Firenze: Elite.

Sadovski, Velizar. 2002. "Dvandva, Tatpuruṣa and Bahuvrīhi. On the Vedic sources for the names of the compound types in Pāṇini's grammar". *Transactions of the Philological Society* 100:3. 351–402.

Sharma, Rama Nath. 2010. "Rule Interaction, Blocking and Derivation in Pāṇini". *Sanskrit Computational Linguistics, 4th International Symposium, New Delhi, India, December 10–12, 2010 (Lecture Notes in Artificial Intelligence 6455)* edited by Girish Nath Jha, 1–20. Berlin, Heidelberg: Springer.

Staal, Johan Frederik. 1967. *Word order in Sanskrit and Universal Grammar. (Foundations of Language, supplementary series, 5)* Dordrecht: Reidel.

Štekauer, Pavol, Salvador Valera & Livia Körtvélyessy. 2012. *Word Formation in the World's Languages. A Typological Survey.* Cambridge: Cambridge University Press.

Tribulato, Olga. 2015. *Ancient Greek Verb-initial Compounds: Their diachronic development within the Greek compound system.* Berlin / Boston: Walter de Gruyter.

Wackernagel, Jakob. 1957. *Altindische Grammatik II/1. Nominalsuffixe, hrsg. von Albert Debrunner.* Göttingen: Vandenhoeck und Ruprecht.

CHAPTER 10

The internal order of Sanskrit compounds

A dialogue between Pāṇini and generative grammar

Davide Mocci
Università degli Studi di Cagliari

In this study I show that the internal order of Sanskrit Noun-Noun endocentric compounds cannot be captured by means of the notion 'head', defined in semantic or morphological terms (§§1–2). Next, I outline the strategy devised by the Indian grammarian Pāṇini (4th century B.C.) to handle the internal order of Sanskrit compounds (§3). Finally, I argue that the notion relevant for determining the internal order of Noun-Noun endocentric compounds in Sanskrit can be identified by combining Pāṇini's intuitions with the formalism developed within generative grammar (§4). In this way, this study provides an additional example of how useful the history of linguistics (specifically, the study of Pāṇini's grammar) may be for solving a problem in contemporary linguistics (specifically, the puzzle as to how the internal order of a certain class of compounds is determined).

Keywords: embedded constituent, head, metaphorical compounds, *upasarjana*

1. Heads and the internal order of compounds

In accordance with Guevara & Scalise (2009: 107), a compound is a lexical category Z such that: i. Z is the output of combining a lexical category X with another lexical category Y; ii. some implicit grammatical relation *r* holds between X and Y in Z, in the sense that *r* is not spelled out by any morpheme.[1] Formally: $[X\ r\ Y]_Z$.

The order in which the two lexical categories X and Y are arranged within the compound Z (i.e., the internal order of Z) is not random. Consider, e.g., the following compounds.

1. Lexical categories are those lexical items that name things of the extra-linguistic world. Here I take lexical categories to be nouns, verbs, adjectives, and prepositions. By 'grammatical relation', I mean a subordinative, attributive, or coordinative relation (Scalise & Vogel 2010: 6–7).

https://doi.org/10.1075/sihols.133.10moc

(1) $[_Z [_X \text{study}]\text{-}[_Y \text{room}]]$

(2) $[_Z [_X \text{tiger}]\text{-}[_Y \text{man}]]$

(3) $[_Z [_X \text{sala}] [_Y \text{studio}]]$
lit. room study (= "study-room") (Italian)

(4) $[_Z [_X \text{uomo}] [_Y \text{tigre}]]$
lit. man tiger (= "tiger-man", i.e., mighty man) (Italian)

The English compounds in (1)–(2) are synonymous with the Italian compounds in (3)–(4), respectively; however, the internal order of (1)–(2) is the mirror image of the internal order of (3)–(4). To explain the mirror image order of (1)–(2) with respect to (3)–(4), linguists ordinarily have recourse to the notion 'head'. Consider how.

At least three kinds of heads are identified in compounding: categorial, morphological, and semantic head (Scalise & Fábregas 2010). For the sake of simplicity, I will confine my attention to the semantic head here, noting however that the three kinds of heads coincide in the examples considered in this study (but see § 2 below). A compound-member X qualifies as the (semantic) head of a compound Z when X is a hyperonym of the compound as a whole (Scalise & Fábregas 2010: 111; Laurie Bauer 2017: 64). Therefore, *room* is the head of *study-room* (1) because *room* is a hyperonym of *study-room*; likewise, *sala* is the head of *sala studio* (3) because *sala* is a hyperonym of *sala studio*. (1) and (3) are referred to as endocentric compounds, because one of their internal members coincides with the compound head. Reasoning along the same lines, we can classify *tiger-man* (2) and *uomo tigre* (4) as endocentric compounds headed by *man* and *uomo*, respectively. Since the compound-members featuring in each of the compounds in (1)–(4) are nouns, we may label (1)–(4) as "Noun-Noun endocentric compounds".

At this point, a linearization parameter comes into play. This parameter is endowed with two values, namely left and right (Guevara & Scalise 2009: 114): if the value 'left' is chosen for a language, that language will display left-headed compounds (i.e., compounds in which the head is allocated to the left-hand slot of the compound itself); conversely, if the value 'right' is chosen, that language will display right-headed compounds. Specifically, English (Germanic) compounds are said to be right-headed, whereas Italian (Romance) compounds are said to be left-headed (see, among many others, Booij 2009: § 3; Masini & Scalise 2012: 81–82).[2] In

2. To be precise, the right-headedness of English endocentric compounds as well as the left-headedness of Italian endocentric compounds should be confined to productively formed compounds (see Grandi 2006: 44 n. 19; Masini & Scalise 2012: 81). The compounds in (1)–(4) are all productively formed, in the intuitive sense that they are not listed in a native speaker's mental lexicon.

this way, we can exploit the notion of head, combined with the linearization parameter, to determine the internal order of compounds (1)–(4): the internal order of *study-room* (1) and *tiger-man* (2) can be traced back to the right-headedness of English compounds; conversely, the internal order of *sala studio* (3) and *uomo tigre* (4) is traceable to the left-headedness of Italian compounds.

All in all, the notion of head, coupled with a linearization parameter, makes it possible to account for the internal order of Noun-Noun endocentric compounds in English and Italian. Thus, I conclude that the notion relevant for determining the internal order of Noun-Noun endocentric compounds in English and Italian is the notion of head.

2. Compounding in Sanskrit

The question now is whether the notion of head is also relevant for determining the internal order of Noun-Noun endocentric compounds in Sanskrit.

putrá- "son" is a hyperonym – and hence, the head – of *rāja-putrá-* "king's son" in (5), while *śaphá-* "hoof" is a hyperonym – hence, the head – of *aśva-śaphá-* "horse's hoof" in (6).

(5) *R̥gveda* 10.40.3c-d[3] (Sanskrit)
$[_{\text{Noun}}$ $[_{\text{Noun}}$ rāja]-$[_{\text{Noun}}$ putrá]-]
lit. [[king.M]-[son.M]-]M (= "king's son")

(6) *Śatapathabrāhmaṇa* 13.3.4.4[4] (Sanskrit)
$[_{\text{Noun}}$ $[_{\text{Noun}}$ aśva]-$[_{\text{Noun}}$ śaphá]-]
lit. [[horse.M]-[hoof.M]-]M (= "horse's hoof")

Thus, (5) and (6) suggest that Sanskrit Noun-Noun endocentric compounds are right-headed. Put another way, the linearization parameter is specified for the value 'right' in Sanskrit.

Let us now consider the Noun-Noun endocentric compounds in (7)–(9): *áśva-* "horse" is the head (qua hyperonym) of *aśva-vr̥ṣá-* "horse that is a bull"; *cakra-* "discus" is the head (qua hyperonym) of *cakra-padma-* "discus that is a lotus"; finally *mukha-* "face" is the head (qua hyperonym) of *mukha-padma-* "face

3. *kásya dhvasrā́ bhavathaḥ kásya vā narā/ rājaputréva sávanā́va gachathaḥ//* "For whom do you become occulted, or for whom do you descend to his soma-pressings like kings' sons, o men?" (tr. Jamison & Brereton 2014).

4. *aśvaśaphéna dvitī́yām ā́hutiṃ juhoti paśávo vā ékaśaphā rudráḥ sviṣṭakŕ̥t* "The second oblation he offers on a horse-hoof; for the one-hoofed (animals) are cattle, and the Sviṣṭakr̥t is Rudra". (tr. Eggeling 1882–1900).

that is a lotus".[5] For convenience, I shall refer to the compounds in (7)–(9) as metaphorical compounds, insofar as they involve a metaphor: one of the two compound-members serves as the benchmark or metaphor vehicle (e.g., *vṛ́ṣan-* "bull" in (7)), and the remaining compound-member serves as the corresponding subject of comparison or metaphor topic (e.g., *áśva-* in (7)).[6]

(7) *Śatapathabrāhmaṇa* 14.4.2.7–8 (= *Bṛhadāraṇyaka-Upaniṣad* 1.4.4)[7] (Sanskrit)
[$_{Noun}$ [$_{Noun}$ aśva]-[$_{Noun}$ vṛṣá]-]
lit. [[horse.M]-[bull.M]-]M (= "horse that is a bull", i.e., male horse)

(8) *Mahābhārata* 6.55.89[8] (Sanskrit)
[$_{Noun}$ [$_{Noun}$ cakra]-[$_{Noun}$ padma]-]
lit. [[discus.N]-[lotus.N]-]N (= "discus that is a lotus", i.e., beautiful discus)

(9) *Rāmāyana* Su. 7.35[9] (Sanskrit)
[$_{Noun}$ [$_{Noun}$ mukha]-[$_{Noun}$ padma]-]
[[face.N]-[lotus.N]-]N (= "face that is a lotus", i.e., beautiful face)

---

5. Comparable to (7)–(9) is *puruṣa-vyāghra-* (lit. man-tiger). According to Brigitte Bauer (2017: 313, 359–360), *puruṣa-vyāghra-* is – to use the terminology of Arcodia, Grandi & Wälchli (2010) – a hyperonymic coordinative compound on a par with English *singer-actor*: much as *singer* and *actor* are both hyperonyms of *singer-actor*, in the same way *puruṣa-* "man" and *vyāghra-* "tiger" would both be hyperonyms of *puruṣa-vyāghra-*. However, Brigitte Bauer's analysis of *puruṣa-vyāghra-* is incompatible with the information provided by Pāṇini about this compound, as discussed by Mocci & Pontillo (2019: 32–33). Brigitte Bauer's analysis cannot be applied to the compounds in (7)–(9) either: in the textual passages quoted, only one of the compound-members (e.g., *áśva-*) is a hyperonym of the compound as a whole (e.g., *aśva-vṛṣá-*).

6. The Indian grammatical tradition addressed the question of whether compounds like (7)–(9) involve a simile or a metaphor. For on overview of this discussion, see Candotti & Pontillo (2017); Mocci & Pontillo (2019: 15–16).

7. *sā gáur ábhavat/ vṛṣabhá ítaras tā́ṃ sám evā̀bhavat táto gā́vo 'jāyanta// vā́ḍavétarā́bhavat/ aśvavṛṣá ítaro gardabhī́tarā gardabhá ítaras tā́ṃ sám evā́bhavat táta ékaśapham ajāyata//* "So she became a cow. But he became a bull and again copulated with her. From their union cattle were born. Then she became a mare, and he a stallion; she became a female donkey, and he, a male donkey. And again he copulated with her, and from their union one-hoofed animals were born." (tr. Olivelle 1998).

8. *sudarśanaṃ cāsya rarāja śaures tac cakrapadmaṃ subhujorunālam/ yathādipadmaṃ taruṇārkavarṇaṃ rarāja nārāyaṇanābhijātam//* "And his good-looking [weapon] looked like Śauri's lotus of a discus – whose wide stalk [Śauri's] beautiful arm is – just as it looked like the original lotus, which sprang from Nārāyaṇa's navel and whose color is that of the sun just risen."

9. *imāni mukhapadmāni niyataṃ mattaṣaṭpadāḥ/ ambujānīva phullāni prārthayanti punaḥ punaḥ //* "Surely intoxicated bees must repeatedly seek out these lotuslike faces as if they were blooming lotuses sprung from the waters." (tr. Goldman & Sutherland Goldman 1996).

The data in (7)–(9) suggest that Sanskrit Noun-Noun endocentric compounds are left-headed. But the data in (5)–(6) led us to the opposite conclusion, namely that Sanskrit Noun-Noun endocentric compounds are right-headed. We have thus run into a contradiction: Sanskrit Noun-Noun endocentric compounds are both left-headed and right-headed.

In order to avoid this contradiction, one may consider the left-headedness of metaphorical compounds like (7)–(9) as representing an unproductive compound type, namely a type which would have ceased to be productive at the stage when right-headed compounds like (5)–(6) were formed. However, this explanation is untenable insofar as metaphorical compounds like (7)–(9) are not by any means unproductive in Sanskrit.

A second possibility to avoid the contradiction in question is to appeal to the notion 'morphological head': the morphological head of a compound is the unit whose grammatical gender and inflectional class coincide with the grammatical gender and inflectional class of the compound as a whole (Scalise & Fábregas 2010: 124). For instance, *candra-* is the morphological head of *mukha-candra-* (10), because the compound *mukha-candra-* has the same grammatical gender (masculine) and inflectional class (thematic declension) as *candra-* (*mukha-* being instead a neuter noun). Note that, in the case of (10), the morphological head does not coincide with the semantic head: the semantic head of *mukha-candra-* is *mukha-* and not *candra-*, because *mukha-* "face" is a hyperonym of *mukha-candra-* "face that is a moon".

(10) *Kāvyādarśa* 2.91[10] (Sanskrit)
[$_{\text{Noun}}$ [$_{\text{Noun}}$ mukha]-[$_{\text{Noun}}$ candra]-]
lit. [[face.N]-[moon.M]-]M (= "face that is a moon", i.e., shining face)

It may then be suggested that the notion relevant for determining the internal order of Sanskrit Noun-Noun endocentric compounds is the notion of morphological head: all Noun-Noun endocentric compounds are right-headed in Sanskrit, in the sense that the morphological head is allocated to the right-hand slot in this class of compounds. This solution, which may work for determining the internal order of (10), cannot be extended to the compounds in (5)–(9): since the gender and inflectional class of the compound as a whole (e.g., *cakra-padma-*) coincides with the gender and inflectional class of both compound-members (e.g., of both *cakra-* and *padma-*) in (5)–(9), it is impossible to identify one single

10. *mukhacandrasya candratvam ittham anyopatāpinaḥ/ na te sundari saṃvādīty etad ākṣeparūpakam//* "'Unto thy face-moon that thus torments another, O beautiful one, the character of moon is not accordant'. – This is Negatived Metaphor." (tr. Belvalkar 1924). See Candotti & Pontillo (2019: 29–30) for an analysis of *mukha-candra-*.

compound-member as the morphological head to be allocated to the right-hand slot of the compound in (5)–(9).

All in all, the notion of head is not relevant for determining the internal order of Sanskrit Noun-Noun endocentric compounds: when considered in regard to compounds (5)–(9), the notion of semantic head yields a contradiction, while the notion of morphological head is simply inapplicable. What is, then, the notion relevant for determining the internal order of Sanskrit Noun-Noun endocentric compounds? In the next section, we shall see Pāṇini's answer to this question.

3. The upasarjana in Pāṇini's model of compounding[11]

Pāṇini came from the ancient province of Gandhāra, in modern-day Pakistan, and was active in the 4th century B.C. His grammar is known as the *Aṣṭādhyāyī* "the eight-chapter [work]" ("A" for short), consisting of approximately 4000 *sūtras*, i.e., rules written in the form of aphorisms (see Cardona 1997 for a general overview). A section of this grammar, namely A(ṣṭādhyāyī) 2.1–2.2, is devoted specifically to compounding, while other rules from other sections of the grammar provide ancillary information and definitions regarding compounds and compound-members. In what follows, I will briefly examine Pāṇini's model of compounding, focusing on the *Aṣṭādhyāyī* rules which teach how to determine the internal order of Noun-Noun endocentric compounds.

To begin with, according to rules A 1.2.46, 2.1.4, and 2.4.71, compound-members are inflected words of a special sort:[12] like run-of-the-mill inflected words, they are endowed with a case ending, but – unlike in run-of-the-mill inflected words – such a case ending is silent (technically, it is zero-replaced).[13] For example, in Pāṇini's model of compounding, the compound *aśva-śaphá-* "horse's hoof" is to be represented as "*aśva-Ø*^{GEN} *śapha-Ø*^{NOM}", which only differs from *áśva-sya śaphá-ḥ* (i.e., a combination of run-of-the-mill inflected words) in that the genitive and nominative endings attached to *áśva-sya śaphá-ḥ* are overt, while the genitive and nominative endings attached to "*aśva-Ø*^{GEN} *śapha-Ø*^{NOM}" are silent.

11. The present section is a summary of Mocci (2023: 283–294).

12. The reading of A 1.2.46, 2.1.4, and 2.4.71 advocated for here is based on Cardona (1997: 21–23, 186, 207); Kiparsky (2009: 67, 81–82); Candotti & Pontillo (2019: 31). Interestingly, Lowe (2015) also proposed – twenty-four centuries after Pāṇini – that the members of Sanskrit compounds are words, rather than sub-word units.

13. On the notion 'zero' in Pāṇini, see among others Pontillo (2003a: 139–140); Candotti & Pontillo (2013); Kiparsky (2009: 80).

Consider now the notion of *upasarjana*. Pāṇini introduces this notion in A 1.2.43:

> A 1.2.43: *prathamānirdiṣṭaṃ samāsa upasarjanam*
> "What is mentioned in the nominative in a compound(-rule) goes under the rubric *upasarjana*."

The content of this rule is best understood when considered in combination with compound-rules such as A 2.2.8:

> A 2.2.8: *ṣaṣṭhī* [*samāsaḥ* 2.1.3] [*saha supā* 2.1.4] [*vā* 2.1.18] [*tatpuruṣaḥ* 2.1.22].
> "a noun inflected in the genitive preferably combines with a nominal inflected word to form a *tatpuruṣa* compound."

Rule A 2.2.8 teaches to form, e.g., *aśva-śaphá-* (6) from the combination of run-of-the-mill inflected words *áśvasya śapháḥ* "horse's hoof" (this combination technically constitutes a Noun Phrase, or NP for short). Consider how. *ṣaṣṭhī* "noun inflected in the genitive" is mentioned in the nominative in A 2.2.8, which is a compound-rule; by A 1.2.43, a form X that is mentioned in the nominative in a compound-rule (including all those forms that fall under the scope of X) gets the designation *upasarjana*; *áśvasya*, being inflected in the genitive, falls under the scope of *ṣaṣṭhī*; accordingly, *áśvasya* gets the designation *upasarjana* in the NP *áśvasya śapháḥ*.

By means of A 1.2.43, one may form a set of the elements which count as *upasarjana* within the *Aṣṭādhyāyī*. However, A 1.2.43 does not tell us what features the elements inserted in such a set (call it the '*upasarjana* set') share; that is, A 1.2.43 does not provide us with a linguistic criterion which justifies the membership of those elements to the *upasarjana* set. Such a criterion is indeed offered by Pāṇini in A 1.2.44: the *upasarjana* is the *ekavibhakti* element, i.e., the element which has one single (*eka-*) case ending (*vibhakti-*).

> A 1.2.44: *ekavibhakti cāpūrvanipāte* [*upasarjanam* 1.2.43]
> "And what has one single case ending also goes under the rubric *upasarjana*, even when it does not occupy the left-hand slot [of a compound]."

To understand what it means for a certain element to have one single case ending, consider again the NP *áśvasya śapháḥ* "horse's hoof". When this NP fulfils different syntactic functions, the case ending of *śaphá-* "horse" changes, whereas the case ending of *áśva-* "horse" remains unchanged. Thus, *śaphá-* is inflected in the ablative in (11a), where the NP *áśvasya śapháḥ* fulfils the function of circumstantial complement of place, but is inflected in the accusative in (11b), where the NP *áśvasya śapháḥ* fulfils the function of direct object; on the other hand, *áśva-* remains inflected in the genitive in both (11a) and (11b).

(11a) *Ṛgveda* 1.117.6 (Sanskrit)
śaphā́d áśvasya śatám [...] *kumbhā́n asiñcatam mádhūnām.*
hoof.ABL horse.GEN hundred pots.ACC pour.IND.IMPF.2DU honey.GEN
"You two poured a hundred pots of honey from the horse's hoof."

(11b) (Invented example) (Sanskrit)
aśvasya śapham paśyāmi.
horse.GEN hoof.ACC see.IND.PRS.1SG
"I see a horse's hoof."

The meaning of "having one single case ending" (*ekavibhakti*) should be transparent at this point: *áśva-* has one single case ending in (11), in the sense that the case ending of *áśva-*, unlike that of *śaphá-*, remains unchanged in these sentences. Insofar as it has one single case ending, *áśva-* gets the designation *upasarjana* in the NP *áśvasya śapháḥ* in compliance with A 1.2.44. In this way, A 1.2.43 and 1.2.44 conspire to identify *áśvasya* as *upasarjana* in the NP *áśvasya śapháḥ*.

Thus, A 1.2.44 provides a linguistic criterion whereby certain elements (e.g., *áśva-*) and not others (e.g., *śaphá-*) are included in the *upasarjana* set: all the elements of the *upasarjana* set share a specific feature, namely that their case ending remains unchanged when the syntactic function fulfilled by the NP to which they belong changes.[14] A specification is needed at this point. Recall that the compound *aśva-śaphá-* is represented as the NP "*aśva-Ø*^{GEN} *śapha-Ø*^{NOM}" (where both *aśva-Ø*^{GEN} and *śapha-Ø*^{NOM} are nominal inflected words) in Pāṇini's model of compounding. Since *aśva-śaphá-* (= "*aśva-Ø*^{GEN} *śapha-Ø*^{NOM}") is identical to *áśvasya śapháḥ*, except for the phonological realization of the case endings, any designation assigned to *áśvasya* in *áśvasya śapháḥ* also applies to *áśva-* (= *aśva-Ø*^{GEN}) in *aśva-śaphá-*. Accordingly, the designation *upasarjana* which was assigned to *áśvasya* (i.e., to a run-of-the-mill inflected word) on the grounds of A 1.2.43–44 also applies to *aśva-* (i.e., to a compound-member) in Pāṇini's model of compounding.

Going back to the wording of A 1.2.44, this also contains the segment *cāpūrvanipāte* "even when [what has one single case ending] does not occupy the left-hand slot of a compound". As pointed out by Candotti & Pontillo (2019: 24), this segment acknowledges that there are exceptions to the general rule A 2.2.30 regulating the position of the *upasarjana* inside compounds. Here I will abstract away from such exceptions, focusing instead on A 2.2.30.

14. My presentation of A 1.2.43–44 is based on work by Tiziana Pontillo and Maria Piera Candotti (see Pontillo 2003b; Candotti & Pontillo 2019: 22–24; Pontillo 2021: 505–509). Given constraints of space, I am omitting many details concerning A 1.2.43–44 here (but see Mocci 2023 and the works quoted in this footnote).

A 2.2.30: *upasarjanaṃ pūrvam*
"A constituent termed *upasarjana* occupies the left-hand slot [in a compound]."

According to this rule, the canonical position occupied by the *upasarjana* is the left-hand slot of Sanskrit compounds. Thus, since *aśva-Ø*^{GEN} is the *upasarjana* in the compound formed from *aśva-Ø*^{GEN} and *śapha-Ø*^{NOM}, *áśva-* (= *aśva-Ø*^{GEN}) is allocated to the left-hand slot of such a compound. Hence: *aśva-śaphá-* (= "*aśva-Ø*^{GEN} *śapha-Ø*^{NOM}").

All in all, the notion that, according to Pāṇini, is relevant for determining the internal order of Sanskrit Noun-Noun endocentric compounds is *upasarjana*, indicating the element X whose case ending remains unchanged when the grammatical function of the phrase to which X belongs changes.

4. A geometrical approach

Some complications arise when Pāṇini's *upasarjana*-based account of the internal order of Noun-Noun endocentric compounds is extended to metaphorical compounds like (7)–(9). Thus, Pāṇini designates the metaphor topic of metaphorical compounds like (7)–(9) as *upasarjana* in A 2.1.56:[15] for instance, *áśva-* gets the designation *upasarjana* in *aśva-vṛṣá-* (7). Qua *upasarjana*, the metaphor topic is allocated to the left-hand slot of the compound in compliance with A 2.2.30 (see §3 above). This apparently captures the internal order of metaphorical compounds like (7)–(9), where the metaphor topic (e.g., *áśva-*) systematically occupies the left-hand slot of the metaphorical compound (e.g., *aśva-vṛṣá-*). However, the problem with this account is that it is very difficult to prove that the metaphor topic satisfies the definition of *upasarjana* as *ekavibhakti* in (7)–(9), i.e., it is very difficult to prove that the case ending of, e.g., *áśva-* as occurring in *aśva-vṛṣá-* remains unchanged when the grammatical function of the phrase which *áśva-* belongs to changes (see Mocci & Pontillo 2019 for discussion).[16]

Rather than abandoning Pāṇini's *upasarjana*-based account of the internal order of (7)–(9), here I adopt a slightly revised version thereof which naturally captures the internal order of Noun-Noun endocentric compounds, including

15. My interpretation of this rule follows Mocci & Pontillo (2019).

16. To the best of my knowledge, the present problem has not been discussed by commentators of Pāṇini's grammar. The lack of such a discussion may be traced back to the fact that, before Pontillo's (2003b) innovative study, A 1.2.44's definition of *upasarjana* as *ekavibhakti* was confined to compounds like *niṣ-kauśāmbi-* "(one) who is out of the city termed *Kauśāmbī*", so needed not be satisfied in metaphorical compounds (see especially Pontillo 2003b: 30). I am thankful to an anonymous reviewer for drawing my attention to this point.

metaphorical compounds. Firstly, I make the following observation: given a phrase P made up of two nominal inflected words X and Y, if the case ending of X does not change when the grammatical function of P changes, it is typically the case that X is embedded with respect to Y in P. Such an observation suggests defining the *upasarjana* not in terms of changeability of case ending, but rather in terms of embedding: the *upasarjana* is the element – X or Y – which is embedded in P.

Secondly, I take the phrase corresponding to *aśva-vṛṣá-* to be *vṛ́ṣā áśvaḥ* (lit. bull.NOM horse.NOM) "horse that is a bull", in which *áśva-* agrees in case with *vṛ́ṣan-* (much as *urbs* agrees in case with *Roma* in the Latin type *urbs Roma* "the city of Rome" – see Brigitte Bauer 2017).[17]

Thirdly, elaborating on Mocci & Pontillo (2019: 29–32), I take the structure of *vṛ́ṣā áśvaḥ* to be equivalent to the structure assigned in the generative tradition to the Italian phrase *gioiello di donna* "jewel of a woman" (see (12)).[18] That is, *vṛ́ṣā áśvaḥ* has the structure in (13), which only differs from (12) in that X° is silent in (13).

(12)

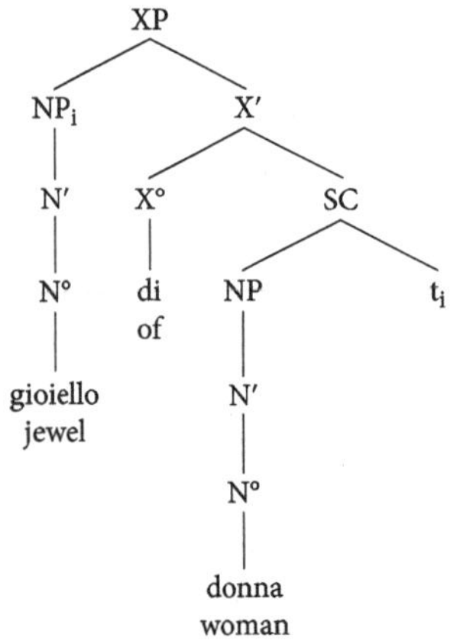

17. Evidence for the correspondence between *aśva-vṛṣá-* and *vṛ́ṣā áśvaḥ* comes from the following passages. *Ṛgveda* 7.69.1ab: *ā́ vām rátho ródasī badbadhānó/ hiraṇyáyo vṛ́ṣabhir yātv áśvaiḥ/* "Let your golden chariot, ever pressing upon the two world-halves, journey here with those bulls, your horses." (tr. Jamison & Brereton 2014). *Ṛgveda* 1.164.34cd: *pṛchā́mi tvā vṛ́ṣṇo áśvasya rétaḥ/ pṛchā́mi vācáḥ paramáṃ vyòma//* "I ask you about the seed of the bull(-like) horse. I ask about the highest heaven of speech." (tr. Jamison & Brereton 2014). According to Speijer (1886: 164), the phrase corresponding to *aśva-vṛṣá-* should rather be *vṛ́ṣā áśvasya* (lit. bull.NOM horse.GEN) "that bull of a horse" (or "horse that is a bull"), with *áśvasya* a genitive of equivalence. I cannot adopt Speijer's proposal because *áśvasya vṛ́ṣā* is never attested in Sanskrit in the meaning of "that bull of a horse".

18. The representation in (12) is based on Kayne (1994: 106); Moro (2000: 52–53); den Dikken (2006: 161–246).

(13)

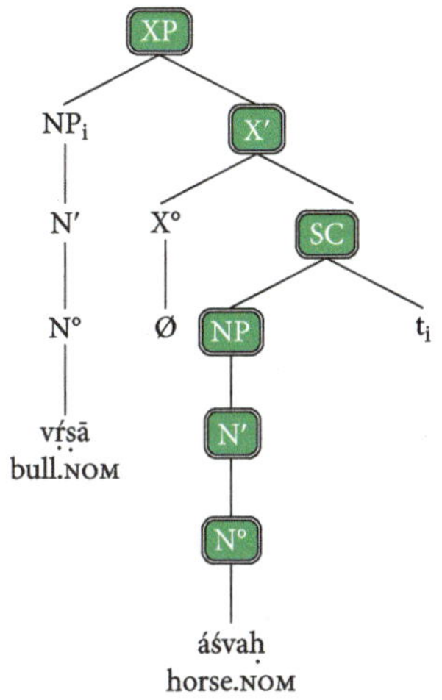

Fourthly, I define the notion 'embedded' in purely geometrical (qua configurational) terms: *áśvaḥ* is embedded with respect to *vṛ́ṣā* in (13), insofar as the number of nodes which dominate *áśvaḥ* within XP (emphasized in green) is greater than the number of nodes dominating *vṛ́ṣā* within XP. Thus, *áśvaḥ* is the *upasarjana* in the phrase *vṛ́ṣā áśvaḥ*, in the sense that it is the embedded constituent in this phrase. By virtue of the correspondence between the compound *aśva-vṛṣá-* and the phrase *vṛ́ṣā áśvaḥ*, the compound-member *áśva-* is also designated as *upasarjana* in *aśva-vṛṣá-*.

Lastly, following Pāṇini's rule A 2.2.30, I take the left-hand slot of Sanskrit Noun-Noun endocentric compounds to be occupied by the *upasarjana*, i.e., by the embedded constituent. Thus, *áśva-* is allocated to the left-hand slot of *aśva-vṛṣá-*, as desired. The internal order of the other metaphorical compounds (*cakra-padma-* and *mukha-padma-*) can be explained along exactly the same lines, by designating the metaphor topic (i.e., *cakra-* and *mukha-*, respectively) as 'embedded constituent' or *upasarjana*. Most importantly, the notion of *upasarjana* also permits capturing the internal order of non-metaphorical Noun-Noun endocentric compounds such as *rāja-putrá-* (5) and *aśva-śaphá-* (6). For instance, *áśva-* is the *upasarjana* of *aśva-śaphá-* because *áśvasya* is the embedded constituent (in the sense specified above) in the phrase marker for *áśvasya śapháḥ*, given in (14).[19] Qua *upasarjana*, *áśva-* is allocated to the left-hand slot of *aśva-śaphá-*, as desired.

19. (14) parallels the phrase marker for such English NPs as *your book*, where *your* is a modifier of *book*.

(14)

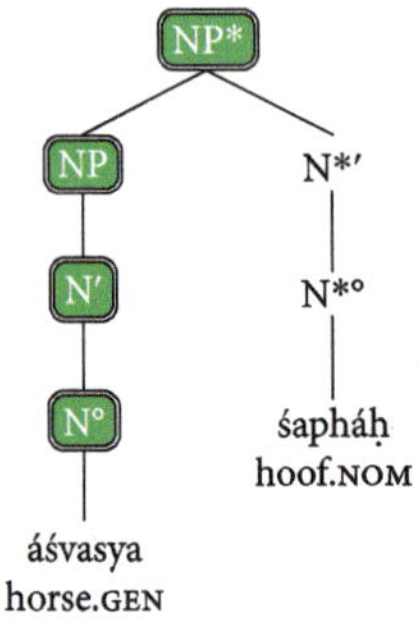

All in all, the notion relevant for determining the internal order of Sanskrit Noun-Noun endocentric compounds is the geometrically defined notion of 'embedded constituent'.[20] This notion springs from a translation of Pāṇini's notion of *upasarjana* into the formal apparatus of generative grammar.

5. Conclusion

In this study I have argued that the notion relevant for determining the internal order of Sanskrit Noun-Noun endocentric compounds is not the notion of head (defined in semantic or morphological terms), but rather the geometrically defined notion of 'embedded constituent'. Insofar as the latter notion is a translation of Pāṇini's notion of *upasarjana* into formal terms, the present study offers another example of the fact that the history of linguistics (in this case, the study of Pāṇini's grammar) provides valuable insights into contemporary linguistic problems such as the determination of the internal order of compounds. For other examples of this kind, see Graffi (this volume) and Lowe (2024).

Acknowledgments

My deepest gratitude goes to Matteo Greco, John Lowe, Andrea Moro, Tiziana Pontillo, an anonymous reviewer, and the audiences at ICHoLS XV and at the IUSS seminar "Elementi di sintassi sanscrita: il caso dei composti" (a.y. 2022–23) for stimulating discussion.

---

20. The view that geometrical notions can explain linguistic phenomena, such as the internal order of Sanskrit compounds, is clearly expressed in Moro (2016: 121); (2019).

References

Arcodia, Giorgio Francesco, Nicola Grandi & Bernhard Wälchli. 2010. "Coordination in Compounding". *Cross-Disciplinary Issues in Compounding* edited by S. Scalise & I. Vogel, 177–198. Amsterdam & Philadelphia: John Benjamins.

Bauer, Brigitte L.M. 2017. *Nominal Apposition in Indo-European: Its forms and functions, and its evolution in Latin-Romance.* Berlin & Boston: de Gruyter.

Bauer, Laurie. 2017. *Compounds and Compounding.* Cambridge: Cambridge University Press.

Belvalkar, S.K., translator. 1924. *Kāvyādarśa of Daṇḍin: Sanskrit text and English translation.* Poona: The Oriental Book-Supplying Agency.

Booij, Geert. 2009. "Compounding and Construction Morphology". *The Oxford Handbook of Compounding* edited by R. Lieber & P. Štekauer, 201–216. Oxford: Oxford University Press.

Candotti, Maria Piera & Tiziana Pontillo. 2013. "The Earlier Paninian Tradition on the Imperceptible Sign". *Signless Signification in Ancient India and Beyond* edited by T. Pontillo & M.P. Candotti, 99–153. London: Anthem Press.

Candotti, Maria Piera & Tiziana Pontillo. 2017. "Late Sanskrit Literary Theorists and the Role of Grammar in Focusing the Separateness of Metaphor and Simile". *Journal of Indian Philosophy* 45:2.349–380.

Candotti, Maria Piera & Tiziana Pontillo. 2019. "Lexical Subordination in Derivation and Compounding". *Studi e Saggi Linguistici* 57:2.11–43.

Cardona, George. 1997. *Pāṇini: His work and its tradition, vol. I: Background and Introduction.* Delhi: Motilal Banarsidass.

den Dikken, Marcel. 2006. *Relators and Linkers: The syntax of predication, predicate inversion, and copulas.* Cambridge, Mass.: MIT Press.

Eggeling, Julius, translator. 1882–1900. *The Satapatha-Brâhmana according to the Text of the Mâdhyandina School, books I-XIV.* Oxford: Clarendon Press.

Goldman, Robert P. & Sally J. Sutherland Goldman, translators. 1996. *The Rāmāyaṇa of Vālmīki: An epic of Ancient India, vol. V, Sundarakāṇḍa.* Princeton: Princeton University Press.

Graffi, Giorgio. This volume. "Can Linguistics and History of Linguistics Profit from each other?". History of Linguistics 2021. Selected papers from the 15th International Conference on the History of the Language Sciences (ICHoLS 15), Milan, 28 August–1 September edited by S. Raynaud, M.P. Tenchini, & E. Galazzi, 14–30. Amsterdam & Philadeplhia: John Benjamins.

Grandi, Nicola. 2006. "Considerazioni sulla definizione e la classificazione dei composti". *Annali online di Ferrara – Lettere* 1:1.31–52.

Guevara, Emiliano & Sergio Scalise. 2009. "Searching for Universals in Compounding". *Universals of Language Today* edited by S. Scalise, E. Magni, & A. Bisetto. *Studies in Natural Language and Linguistic Theory* 76.101–128.

Jamison, Stephanie W. & Joel P. Brereton, translators, 2014. *The Rigveda: The earliest religious poetry of India*, 3 vols. Oxford: Oxford University Press.

Kayne, Richard S. 1994. *The Antisymmetry of Syntax.* Cambridge, Mass.: MIT Press.

Kiparsky, Paul. 2009. "On the Architecture of Pāṇini's Grammar". *Sanskrit Computational Linguistics: Proceedings of the First and Second International Symposia, Rocquencourt, 29–31 October 2007, Providence, 15–17 May 2008* edited by G. Huet, A. Kulkarni, & P. Scharf. *Lecture Notes in Computer Science* 5402.33–94.

Lowe, John J. 2015. "The Syntax of Sanskrit Compounds". *Language* 91:3.71–114.

Lowe, John J. 2024. *Modern Linguistics in Ancient India*. Cambridge: Cambridge University Press.

Masini, Francesca & Sergio Scalise. 2012. "Italian Compounds". *Probus* 24.61–91.

Mocci, Davide. 2023. "Pāṇini and the non-Head (*upasarjana*) of Attributive Endocentric Compounds". *Bhasha: Journal of South Asian Linguistics, Philology and Grammatical Traditions* 2:2.279–316.

Mocci, Davide & Tiziana Pontillo. 2019. "Predication in *Aṣṭādhyāyī* 2.1.56: Syntactic analysis of a *karmadhāraya* compound". *Aevum* 93:1.3–38.

Moro, Andrea. 2000. *Dynamic Antisymmetry*. Cambridge, Mass.: MIT Press.

Moro, Andrea. 2016. *Impossible Languages*. Cambridge, Mass.: MIT Press.

Moro, Andrea. 2019. "The Geometry of Predication: A configurational derivation of the defining property of clause structure". *Philosophical Transactions of the Royal Society B* 375:1791.1–7.

Olivelle, Patrick. 1998. *The Early Upaniṣads: Annotated text and translation*. Oxford: Oxford University Press.

Pontillo, Tiziana. 2003a. "Morfi 'zeromorfi' in Pāṇini: un'introduzione alle regole specifiche di formazione con zero fonologico nella posizione di dati morfemi". *AIWN* 22.129–184.

Pontillo, Tiziana. 2003b. "La definizione di *upasarjana-* in Pāṇini". *Atti del Primo Incontro Genovese di Studi Vedici e Pāṇiniani, Genova, 16 July 2002* edited by R. Ronzitti & G. Borghi, 21–35. Recco: Le Mani.

Pontillo, Tiziana. 2021. "Did the Sanskrit Model Bring «True Enlightenment to European Scholars» when they Analysed and Classified the Bahuvrīhi Compounds?". *Studi Classici e Orientali* 67.497–514.

Scalise, Sergio & Antonietta Bisetto. 2009. "The Classification of Compounds". *The Oxford Handbook of Compounding* edited by R. Lieber & P. Štekauer, 34–53. Oxford: Oxford University Press.

Scalise, Sergio & Antonio Fábregas. 2010. "The Head in Compounding". *Cross-Disciplinary Issues in Compounding* edited by S. Scalise & I. Vogel, 109–126. Amsterdam & Philadelphia: John Benjamins.

Scalise, Sergio & Irene Vogel. 2010. "Why Compounding?". *Cross-Disciplinary Issues in Compounding* edited by S. Scalise & I. Vogel, 1–18. Amsterdam & Philadelphia: John Benjamins.

Speijer, Jacob Samuel. 1886. *Sanskrit Syntax*. Leiden: Brill.

PART 3

Sixteenth to twentieth century works

CHAPTER 11

How far are the horizons of descriptive linguistics?

Jean-Luc Chevillard
CNRS, Laboratoire HTL (UMR7597)

European missionaries engaged in the linguistic description of 16th–18th c. Tamil Nadu discussed two possible attitudes. Proença (1625–1666), who wrote in Portuguese, thought that the most important task was to concentrate on what is useful *pera a pratica* "for practical purposes" and wanted to master ordinary language, both (A) in its colloquial forms – including substandard and dialectal variants – and (B) in its more standardized form. Beschi (1680–1747), who wrote in Latin, thought he could become influential by mastering (C) *Centamiḻ*, the poetic "more elegant" dialect, cultivated for many centuries by traditional grammarians and poets of Tamil Nadu. This article evokes the strategies of Proença, Beschi and others, who navigated the components of Tamil "triglossia", in which both (A) and (C) can coexist with (B), but not simultaneously. Either (C) is ignored, being considered as "useless for practical purposes", or (A) is shunned, being considered as "barbaric".

Keywords: Tamil, diglossia, triglossia, Beschi, Proença, traditional language scholarship, language of poetry, ordinary language, standardized language, missionary grammars

https://doi.org/10.1075/sihols.133.11che

Chaque époque rêve la suivante
Michelet

Je suis belle, ô mortels! comme un rêve de pierre,
Et mon sein, où chacun s'est meurtri tour à tour,
Est fait pour inspirer au poète un amour
Eternel et muet ainsi que la matière.
Baudelaire

Parce qu'il est limité, l'acte de savoir possède par définition
une épaisseur temporelle, un horizon de rétrospection,
aussi bien qu'un horizon de projection.
Sylvain Auroux (1989: 13)

Calculemus
Leibniz

1. Accessibility of a forgotten ancient new world of linguistic descriptions

A forgotten corpus of linguistic descriptions, not composed in Modern English and dealing with many world languages as those languages existed several centuries ago, is in the process of slowly re-emerging, in front of our eyes, thanks to the concerted efforts of a number of historians of linguistics. This changing situation in the case of Tamil is exemplified by the six pairs, associating an author's name with an acronym or a title, which are visible inside Figure 1, and numbered, from ① to ⑥.

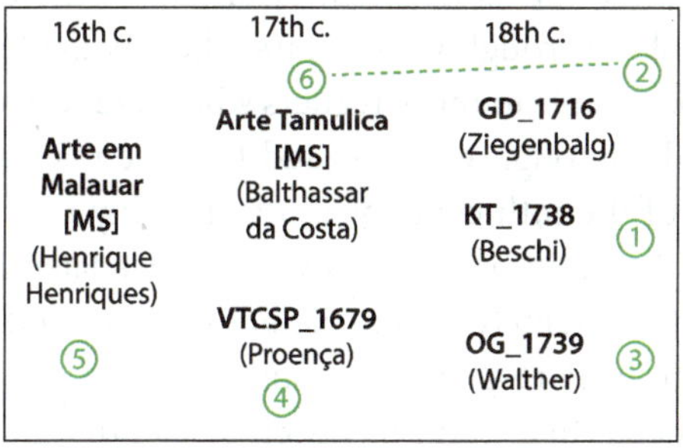

Figure 1. Foreign explorers of Tamil, in the 16th, 17th and 18th centuries, from most accessible to least accessible

The numbers which are on the sides of the six pairs attempt to rank, in a rough manner, with a bias towards our time, the **accessibility** of the corresponding texts for the interested readership during the time span separating the date of their composition from our present time. This means that the text ranked as last,

Table 1. Accessibility features of the six works appearing in Figure 1

Most to least accessible	①	②	③	④	⑤	⑥
Author	Beschi	Ziegenbalg	Walther	Proença	Henriques	Da Costa
Grammar or dictionary?	Gram.	Gram.	Gram.	Dic.	Gram.	Gram.
Metalanguage	Latin	Latin	Latin	Portuguese	Portuguese	Portuguese
Original printing or MS?	1738	1716	1739	1679	MS. (16th c.)	MS. (17th c.)
Known copies	several	several	several	one (Vatican)	one (Lisboa)	five
Subsequent reprinting	19th c.	1985	None	1966 Facsimilé		
Printing of original MS					Vermeer 1982	Muru 2022
English translation	Horst 1806 & 1831[2], superseded by Mahon 1848	Jeyaraj 2010	None	None	Hein & Rajam 2013	Muru 2022

i.e. ⑥, was made more easily accessible to its potential readers[1] only in 2022, both in the original Portuguese and as an English translation, thanks to Cristina Muru, after being inaccessible for roughly 300 years whereas the text ranked as ① has almost always been accessible to those readers who were reasonably informed and sufficiently motivated, although we must add that the majority of those readers, since the beginning of the 19th century, most probably read it in English translation rather that in the Latin original, as we shall see later. Regarding the other texts, among which two, namely ② and ③, are in Latin and the remaining two, namely ⑤ and ④, are in Portuguese, my ranking is of course highly subjective, being based on my belief that Latin has been a scientific *Lingua Franca* among scholars for a longer period than Portuguese, and also on the idea that a manuscript such as ⑤ was less susceptible to reach an audience than printed books

1. There were, of course, also readers in earlier periods, as attested for instance by the dotted line connecting ⑥ and ② inside Figure 1, which alludes to a probable case of plagiarism, of Da Costa's manuscript grammar by Ziegenbalg (1716), which is discussed in Jeyaraj (2010) and in Muru (2022).

such as ②, ③ and ④. I shall discuss in this presentation only a subset of the linguistic technical literature about Tamil which has been evoked inside the introductory section, including for instance the two works, to which the ranks given are ③ and ④. I shall also remark, seemingly contradicting myself, that those ranks might quickly become outdated, because the 20th century point of view is being ineluctably phased out, thanks to the pioneering works of Vermeer (1982), of Hein & Rajam (2013), of Jeyaraj (2010) and of Muru (2022), who have respectively made items ⑤, ② and ⑥ potentially as accessible today to modern linguists as Beschi's ① has been since the first half of the 19th century, thanks to his English translators (see Figure 4). On the other hand, a lot of efforts are still required if one wants the same to be true for the VTCSP_1679, alias ④, alias *Vocabulario Tamulico com a Significaçam Portugueza* (VTCSP), composed by Proença (1625–1666) and for the OG_1739, alias ③, composed by Walther (1699–1741), and this will be part of our focus here, because I have been engaged for now ten years in the preparation of an electronic edition of the first one (i.e. the VTCSP) and of an English translation of the second one.

2. There is more than one variety of Tamil

Before going more deeply into an exposition of the specificities and the difficulties of various texts, I must first of all provide the reader with more information concerning the situation of the Tamil linguistic universe, and especially with what I have called elsewhere[2] the Tamil Triglossia, expanding on the more familiar diglossia. That triglossia will occasionally be represented by the diagram 

, for which an expanded form – completed by a European analogy, for the sake of clarification – is provided inside Figure 2.

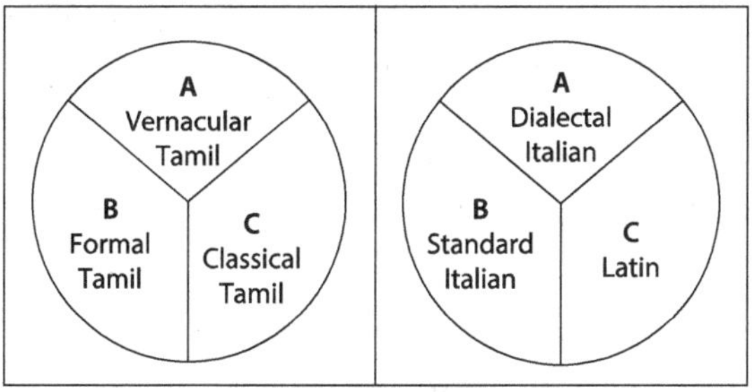

Figure 2. Comparing the linguistic situation of Tamil Nadu and the linguistic situation of Italyas two examples of "triglossia"

2. See Chevillard (2021).

Being aware of the existence of the Tamil triglossia is necessary indeed if one wants to understand the differences between what the three missionaries mentioned in Figure 3 ("Changing Horizons") were trying to do.

As already discussed elsewhere, by others and by me, the first grammatical description of Tamil made by a foreigner, which is the item referred to until now as ⑤, composed by Henrique Henriques (1520–1600), henceforth HH, in the 16th century, rediscovered in Lisboa by Thani Nayagam in the 20th century,[3] critically edited by Vermeer in 1982 and translated into English by Hein & Rajam (HOS, 2013), was primarily a description of a dialect of Tamil spoken on the "Fishery coast" (Costa de Pescaria), although it also incorporated forms taken from "the language of the educated" (Vermeer 1982: xx). To give a concrete example, HH makes the following two statements:

(1a) *Colliren que he por matar faz col e tãbẽ collu* "[The verb with citation form] *Colliren* 'I kill', which corresponds to *matar* 'to kill' becomes [in the imperative] *col* 'kill!' or *collu* 'kill!' " (Vermeer 1982: 82) [My translation]

(1b) *Nos verbos desta comjugaçaõ os que muito sabẽ os pronosiaõ muitas vezes cõ gui antes do Ren: coluguiren* "Regarding the verbs of this conjugation, those who know much (*os que muito sabẽ*) frequently utter them (*os pronosiaõ*) [i.e. the present forms] with a *gui* before *Ren*, as *coluguiren*."[4] (Vermeer 1982: 82) [My translation]

In these examples, the forms *colliren* "I kill" and *collu* "kill!" belong to one dialect of what I call the A-variety of Tamil (Vernacular Tamil), whereas the forms *coluguiren* "I kill" and *col* "kill!" are their counterparts in the B-variety of Tamil, i.e. "Formal Tamil", which was a standard used in formal speech occasions – see the use of *os pronosiaõ* "utter them" by HH – and also in writing. Concerning the special writing mode which we call Printing, I shall add that the B-variety is indeed the linguistic variety seen in another work composed by Henriques, namely the *Flos Sanctorum*, alias *aṭiyār varalāṟu* "life of the Saints", printed in 1586 on the Fishery Coast (Henriques 1967 [1586]). Also concerning writing and how it differs from ordinary speech, if we move in time up to the 18th century and now turn to Walther's *Observationes Grammaticae* (i.e. OG_1739 in Figure 1), we can see him declare in 1739:

3. See Thani Nayagam (1954).

4. *Colliren* "I kill" is the citation for one verb, which is also the model chosen by HH for the conjugation of a group of verbs (*5a comjugaçaõ, 1a maneira*). This explains the use of the plural "os", because what is said of *Colliren* is also true of the other verbs which are conjugated like it. It should also be noted that there is an inconsistency in the MS in the use of *Ren* and *ren,* in this sentence. Capital R and lower-case r are tentatively used for two distinct phonemes – written ற [ṟ] and ர [r] – but the scribe failed to maintain the distinction here.

(2) *Loquimur cum vulgo, ſed ſcribamus cum doctis* "we talk with the common people but with the learned we write" (Caput 3, §7, 13). (Walther, OG_1739, p.34)

and this will be familiar to everyone who has experienced the modern Tamil diglossia.

3. The Tamil linguistic hierarchy

Going beyond the ordinary diglossia, I shall now provide some explanations concerning the third level in what I have called the Triglossia and the central importance of level C, which I have referred to as "Classical Tamil" inside Figure 2, where I compare its role with the role of Latin in Europe.

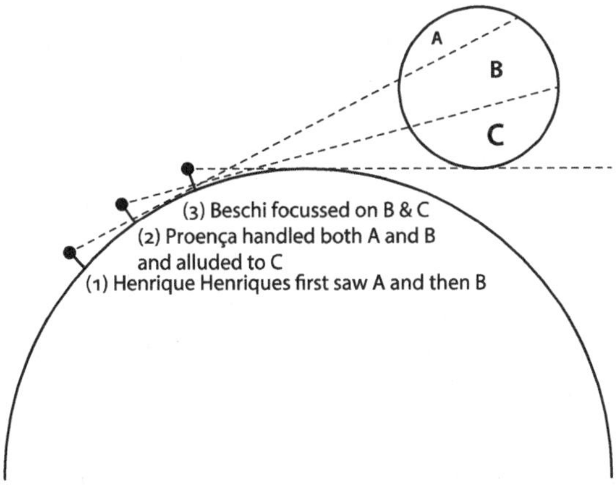

Figure 3. Changing Horizons. Three Jesuit missionaries progressively discover the Tamil triglossia, including Classical Tamil, in the course of two centuries

As a support for this statement, I shall provide the reader with an extract from the preface which appears inside a Paris BnF MS (indien 227) of Beschi's *Caturakarāti* "Quadruple dictionary", which is hand-written but has a title page dated 1732 which looks like a lithograph. In this passage, the 42-year old Constantius Joseph Beschi [1680–1711–1747][5] explains why it is extremely important to study Classical Tamil, which he refers to as the *elegantius idioma* "more elegant dialect".

5. The middle date is the date of his arrival in India.

(3a) *quâ ipsis utilitate futurum ſit, facile noverint // omnes, ſi paulisper animadverterint in his regionibus, // monumenta Deorum, Fabularum figmenta, scientiarũ // præcepta, Poëtarum carmina, astronomiæ calculos // medicinæ leges, musices, choreæq.e regulas, omnia deniq. // vel ipsa prima Grammaticæ rudimenta, elegantiori // hoc idiomate ab antiquis ſcripta fuisse*

(Beschi, *Caturakarāti*, 1732, Præfatio, BnF indien 227)

(3b) "and how useful it will be to them, everyone will easily know, if they have observed for a moment how in these regions the scriptures of the Gods, the fictions of their fables, the rules of science, the poems of the poets, the calculations of astronomy, the rules of medicine, the rules of music and dance, everything, and even the first rudiments of grammar, were written by the ancients in this more elegant register."

[translation excerpted from Trento & Chevillard (forthcoming)]

I must add to this, in order to give a more precise idea of Beschi's view of the world, that he had become so engrossed in his exploration of the Tamil linguistic universe that he wrote four distinct Tamil grammars, three in Latin and one in Tamil, in addition to his lexicographical efforts, some of which have just been evoked (See 3a and 3b). Among these grammars,

- the first grammar was written in Latin in 1728 and later printed in 1738 by the protestants in Tranquebar. It is mentioned here as KT_1738 in Figure 1, where the acronym KT stands for *Koṭun-Tamiḻ* "Rough Tamil" [lit. "Crooked Tamil"", in order to distinguish it from the second grammar, and a small citation appears in (7a) and (7b)].
- the second grammar contains a description of *Cen-Tamiḻ* "perfect Tamil" [litt. "Straight Tamil"].[6] Beschi wrote it shortly afterwards, its preface being dated 1730.[7] A small citation appears in (8a) and (8b).
- the third grammar is in Tamil and is called தொன்னூல் விளக்கம் [*toṉṉūl viḷakkam*], "Light/Lamp on the ancient treatises" (Beschi 1838).
- the fourth one, called *Clavis*, is a compendium, written in Latin, of all the five parts of traditional Tamil grammar (including poetical conventions, metrics and rethorical devices).[8]

6. "Perfect (or Straight) Tamil" and "Crooked Tamil" are my translations for *Centamiḻ* and *Koṭuntamiḻ*. The adjectives used by Beschi are "elegans" and "asperum". See KT_1738, p.4: "Ac ſi illud elegans Tamulicum idioma dicerent, hoc aſperum".

7. The MS of this grammar, written in Latin, was published as a book only in the 20th century, by Besse, in 1917, but an English translation, by Babington, had appeared in 1822.

8. The MS of Beschi's *Clavis* was published thanks to A.C. Burnell in 1876.

I must add that when Beschi made use of the terms *koṭuntamiḻ* and *centamiḻ*, in the titles of his 1728 and 1730 grammars (resp. Beschi 1738 and Beschi 1974 [1822]), in order to characterize these two varieties[9] in the preface of his KT_1738 book, he was not using ordinary terminology but borrowing two terms belonging to the poetical high language, i.e. to *Centamiḻ*.[10] If one looks for those terms inside Proença's VTCSP_1679, which is the oldest extant Tamil-Portuguese dictionary, one does not find them.[11] Among the terms which are found inside the VTCSP, one can mention:

(4) ***Koccai.*** Palaura, ruſtica, baixa. "Language which is low [and used by] rustic [people]" (VTCSP, entry 297_L_j)[12]

(5) ***Koccaiyaṉ.*** H. ruſtico, barbaro no falar "Man who is rustic and speaks in a barbaric manner". (VTCSP, entry 297_L_k)

What the wording of such entries from Proença's 17th c. VTCSP reflects, which will be taken to a higher level by Beschi in the 18th century, is the growing adoption, by missionaries, of the point of view of traditional Tamil scholars. Tamil grammarians categorize the language which they describe under two heads, which they call *Ceyyuḷ* "poetry [lit. (poetical) composition]" and *Vaḻakku* "(ordinary) usage". However, as stated in the last section of the *Tolkāppiyam*, the most ancient Classical Tamil grammatical treatise, probably dating back to the first half of the first millenium, not everyone's *vaḻakku* is fit to be called *vaḻakku*:

9. Those two terms, although they have stuck to the name of Beschi, in the course of history, because of the high visibility of book titles, were in fact **not** his preferred terms. See below (7a), (7b), (8a) and (8b) for more precision on Beschi's terminological preferences. One could also debate whether it was appropriate to make use of the expression *koṭun-tamiḻ* for referring to the B-variety, but that would take us too far. I shall simply say here that, before the missionary age, the terminological opposition between *cen-tamiḻ* and *koṭun-tamiḻ* has its roots in the attempted description of the regional variety of Tamil by traditional grammarians, concomitant with the codification of a poetical language, common to the users of all dialects, in a large area which encompasses both Tamil Nadu and modern Kerala. See Chevillard (2008).

10. The term *cen-tamiḻ* is as old as the *Tolkāppiyam* (1st half of 1st millenium). However, the oldest attestation of *koṭun-tamiḻ* seems to be found in the *Nūṟkaṭṭurai* (approx. "postface") to the *Cilappatikāram*, where it is paired with *centamiḻ*. *Koṭun-tamiḻ* is also found in medieval Tamil grammatical commentaries, as part of discussions on the concept of *ticai-c col* "regional word". See previous footnote.

11. They are, however, found inside Beschi's *Caturakarāti*, already presented.

12. The coordinate system which I use for identifying entries inside the VTCSP is explained in Chevillard (2021).

(6a) *vaḻakku* eṉappaṭuvatu* uyarntōr mēṟṟu* -ē // nikaḻcci avarkaṭṭu* ākalāṉa* (TP638i)[13]

(6b) "That which is to be called 'usage' (*vaḻakku*) rests on the Superior (i.e. learned) people, due to the fact that (significant) (language) events happen by them" [my translation]

We shall now turn to Beschi's 1728 preface to his first grammar, where he explains for the first time, the difference between the two language varieties which are the respective targets of this first grammar and of the second grammar which he was about to write, and would complete in 1730. Thus, he explains:

(7a) *Duplex in hâc regione Tamulicæ Linguæ idioma eſt: ſublimem dixerim unam, communem alteram. Aliqui non ſatis appoſité Poëticam vocant, quæ à communi recedit. Attamen, cùm eâ linguâ Tamulenſes non tam in his, quæ metro ligantur, quàm in cæteris omnibus, quæ ab antiquis hujus linguæ peritis ſolutâ quoque oratione conſcripta ſunt, uſos eſſe videamus, quod præcipuè in commentariis poëtarum patet: ea ſatiùs quam poëtica lingua, elegantior vel ſublimis vocabitur.* (Beschi 1728 [1738]: 3–4)

(7b) "In this region there are two dialects of the Tamul Language: I would call one the High, the other the Common. Some not very correctly call that which differs from the Common, the Poetical dialect. But since we see the Tamulians use that dialect, not so much in those writings which have the trammels of meter, as in all others which by the old authors skilled in this tongue are composed in prose also, which is especially to be seen in the commentaries of the poets, that dialect will be better named the more elegant, or high, than the poetic." (translation by Mahon, Beschi 1848: 2)

It could be interesting to determine whom the 38-year old Beschi is disagreeing with when he advocates the terminological use of "*elegantior vel ſublimis*", rather than "*poëtica lingua*". However, remaining focussed on our core topic, I shall now provide the reader with an extract from the 1730 grammar preface, where Beschi seems to have somehow changed his mind, because he declares:

(8a) *Cum vero quæ hoc idiomate scripsere Tamulenses fere omnia metro ligata sint, ne indecorum censeatis, quæso ; si vos ad profanos poetas adducere et ad poeseos studium advocare præsumo. Plura in D. Hieronymum acrius scripserint olim criminantes, quasi adductis a Poetarum codicibus exemplis, candorem Ecclesiæ ethnicorum sordibus pollueret, quibus eruditissime respondens D. Hieronymus, manifeste ostendit et apostolum Paulum passim in suis epistolis poetarum carmina adduxisse, et [...]* (Beschi 1917 [ms. 1730]: xi)

13. *Tolkāppiyam, Poruḷatikāram,* Cūttiram 638 (in the numbering of the *Iḷampūraṇam*). See Tolkāppiyam, Poruḷatikāram, Iḷampūraṇam, 2003.

(8b) "But since almost all the Tamil works in this dialect are in verse, I trust you will not deem it improper, if I venture to draw your attention to heathen poets, and to the study of poetry. In former times, St. Jerome was severely censured for having, by the introduction of examples from the poets, sullied the purity of the church with the pollution of the heathen. St Jerome, in his learned reply, demonstrates, that the apostle Paul repeatedly cites from the poets, in his epistles, and that [...]" (translation by Babington 1822, in Beschi 1974 [1822]: viii)

To wrap up our description of Beschi's activities in this field, I shall add that in addition to his composition of four grammars, enumerated earlier in this section, and to his compilation of dictionaries, multilingual and (Tamil) monolingual – see the *Caturakarāti* already mentioned in (3a) and (3b), modelled after the traditional poetical vocabularies used by traditional Tamil Scholars – he had also become himself a Tamil poet, known under the Tamil name of வீரமாமுனிவர் [vīramāmuṉivar][14] and had composed a long epic poem in Poetical Tamil, the *Tēmpāvaṇi*, in honour of Saint Joseph. This was the culminating point in a gradual change of horizon, visually represented in Figure 2, where the slow rising of C, i.e. of the Classical Tamil Sun is shown. That rising Sun shone on the stunning fact that a jesuit who had come from Italy to Tamil Nadu in order to be a missionary was himself converted to a form of devotion towards the high variety of the Tamil language and performed very significant தொண்டு [toṇṭu] "service" for it, becoming himself a Tamil Poet and having today his statue near the Marina beach in Chennai, all that happening "A. M. D. G."[15] of course.

4. From the age of AB to the age of BC, and back: "Calculemus!"

Having finished this short evocation of one of the paths which was followed by some of the early language explorers who lived in the 16th, 17th and 18th centuries, we shall now return to the 21st century and to the **accessibility problem** (for modern researchers) which we first discussed in the introductory section. Our new window of observation, for visualising the discontinuities and continuities in transmission, is represented by Figure 4, in which three of the items previously mentioned are represented with the addition of three elements which stand as elements in a chain between the past and the present.

14. For an overview of Beschi's career in South-India, see Ebeling & Trento (2018).

15. "Ad maiorem Dei gloriam".

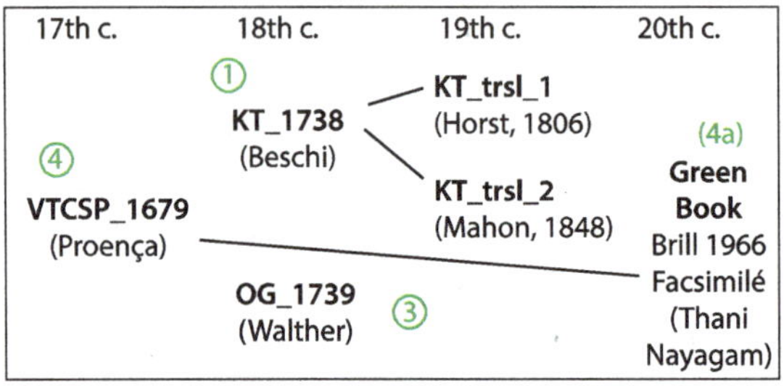

Figure 4. Crossing time, while exploring Tamil as a foreigner in the 17th, 18th and 19th centuries

Two of those items are 19th century translations of item ① from Latin into English, made respectively in 1806 and 1848, the latter one having been quoted in (7b). The third item, which appears in the diagram as **(4a)**, alias "Green Book",[16] is the 1966 facsimilé edition of the now familiar 1679 *Vocabulario* (or VTCSP). It contains an introductory part in Portuguese – for which the modern editor has provided an English translation. That introductory part is followed by 508 pages containing 16218 entries and we shall now evoke first the difficulties inherent in **moving in time**

- **from point** (4), in 1679, which is the moment when Proença's colleagues, probably as the result of a huge effort, printed a few copies of the posthumous VTCSP_1679, of which only a single one remains in existence today, in the Vatican Library,
- **to point (4a)** which is the time when Thani Nayagam published the 1966 facsimilé.

If we think of some of the possible reasons for gaps to occur in the transmission of collective knowledge, such as for example

- (a) when there is a change of scientific lingua franca and no translation is made
- (b) when a printed work has never been reprinted and very few copies are available
- (c) when a work has been transmitted only, or partly, as a MS
- (d) when a work is available but is not read, for various reasons (difficulty, absence of desire, absence of time, ...)

16. This refers to the well-known colour of many of the books published by Brill, including this one.

We can say that the printing in 1966 of the VTCSP facsimilé eliminates only the cause listed here as (b),[17] but leaves causes (a) and (d) unchallenged. Whoever wants to access the information contained in the 1966 facsimilé[18] encounters obstacles which are a combination of linguistic and logistic problems. At the level of the micro-structure, the modern reader must decode individual entries,[19] where Tamil words written following an archaic ambiguous spelling and 17th century Portuguese words which are not all found in Modern dictionaries are combined. At the level of the macro-structure, the reader is confronted with an incompletely lemmatized[20] "dictionary", where Tamil words are ordered in the Portuguese alphabetical order, which makes it difficult to find out whether a given Tamil word is contained in the VTCSP. More precisely, the VTCSP is a list of 16,218 Tamil word-forms (with explanations in Portuguese) which is ordered following the Portuguese alphabetical order, which we can represent by the sequence of eighteen letters "A, B, C, D, E, G, I, L, M, N, O, P, Q, R, S, T, V, X".[21] As a consequence, the 16,218 Tamil word-forms, printed in Tamil characters, are distributed between 18 larger sections, based on the initial letter of their virtual Portuguese transliteration. Those larger sections are further subdivided into 382 subsections, based on the letter, or the pair of letters, which follows the initial letter.[22] That means

17. To this can be added the fact that during the 3 centuries separating the two dates, 1679 and 1966, some authors complained that they were not able to locate a copy of the VTCSP_1679, although they tried because they had heard of its importance. We see for instance A.C. Burnell, in his 1880 catalogue of Portuguese sources pertaining to India, referring to this book and to its possible location, but declaring that the copy could not be found. Julien Vinson nevertheless explained in a 1910 article that he had successfully located the Vatican library copy of the VTCSP. This piece of information however did not reach S. Vaiyāpuri Piḷḷai, general editor of the Madras Tamil Lexicon (MTL), who declares in 1924 inside his introductory essay "History of Tamil Lexicography", on p. xxxvi inside the 1st volume of the MTL, that "no trace is found" of the VTCSP (Vaiyāpuri Piḷḷai 1982 [1924^1]).

18. I must mention that there was also a MS transmission of the VTCSP, but it would take us too far to discuss it in detail. See Gregory James (2000) and C. Muru (2010) for more information.

19. A typical entry in the VTCSP starts with a Tamil word-form followed by one or more Portuguese glosses, depending on the number of meanings which the explorer had managed to discover. Occasionally, Tamil sentences provided as examples are included in the entry, accompanied by Portuguese translations. There are also cross-references between some of the entries.

20. See Chevillard (2021).

21. Including variant forms for I and N, and taking into account the fact that lower case "u" is the counterpart of uppercase "V", the list of 18 can also be written as "A, B, C, D, E, G, I/Y/J, L, M, N/Nh, O, P, Q, R, S, T, U/V, X".

22. As an example, the largest section in the VTCSP is the Q section (or 13th section) and contains 2253 entries. It is subdivided into 44 subsections. Among these, the first 14 subsections all

that, in practice, the 1966 facsimilé of the VTCSP has remained a closed book for most modern readers, unless they have undergone a special training for reading the Tamil words, and are familiar with the Portuguese language, as it existed in the 17th century. Nevertheless, the VTCSP remains visible on the horizon, as a tantalizing possible target of research for linguists, and this is what Figure 5 is trying to suggest.

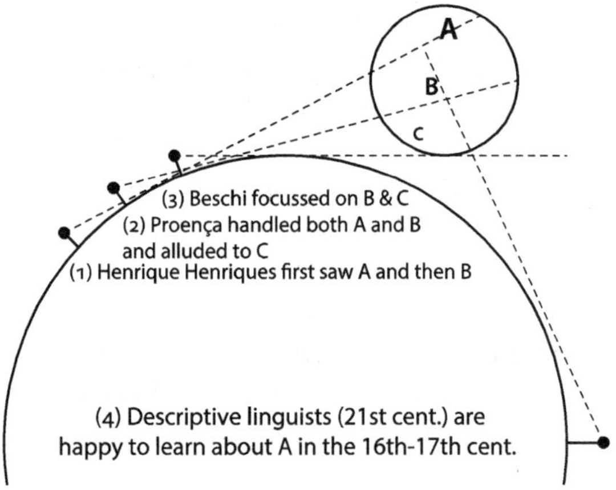

Figure 5. Doing field-work in ancient sources and rediscovering A, alias 17th century "Spoken Tamil"

One of its interesting features is that the opinions of Proença were quite different from those of Beschi, as far as poetical Tamil is concerned. This should become clear from the following quotation, to which our access has been greatly facilitated thanks to Thani Nayagam 1966 edition, and to his introduction and his translation of the preface (prepared jointly with another scholar). Taking a stand quite different from the one seen in the *Caturakarāti* preface, as shown in (3a) and (3b), the strongly worded preface of the VTCSP states that:

contain words starting with Q+A, the difference between them being the third letter. However, when the third letter is L, we are supposed to know that Tamil has "three types of L" (nowadays transliterated as l, ḷ and ḻ), and the same is true for R, of which there are "three types", nowadays transliterated as r, ṭ and ṟ. For more details, see Chevillard (2017). Given the fact that the standard phonemic inventory of Tamil consists of 12 vowels and 18 consonants, the mental exercise required for imagining where a Tamil word, apprehended through an unprecise transliteration, will be found inside the VTCSP is rather complex, unless one has gone through the whole text, which is now the case for me, after several years of efforts, although the final form which my electronic edition of the VTCSP will take is not yet completely decided.

(9a) ...Deixa- // =rey tambem as palauras poeticas (de que o vocabulario do P. Igna- // =cio Bruno eſtâ cheo) por que naõ ſeruem nada, pera â pratica, ov // profa. e dellas tem os poetas Tamuis ſeus vocabularios, â onde os // curioſos, que quizerem compor verſos, as podem ver...
(Proença, 1679, https://digi.vatlib.it/view/MSS_Borg.ind.12/17)

(9b) ... I shall leave out also poetic words (of which the vocabulary of Fr. Ignacio Bruno is full) because they are useless for practical purposes or for prose, and the Tamil poets have their own vocabularies for them, in which those who are interested and might wish to compose verses may find them...
(translation Edgar C. Knowlton & Xavier S. Thani Nayagam, Thani Nayagam 1966: 13)

A direct examination of the VTCSP shows that Proença made nevertheless a few exceptions to his stated principles, because several of his entries contain the mention *palaura de uerſo* ("word used in poetry").[23]

5. How far is the horizon of descriptive linguistics?

We have now reached the final section of this short presentation and it is now time to explain the title chosen, which is the contination of a conversation, started with Sylvain Auroux, about the two horizons,[24] and continued with Christian Puech and Valérie Raby, when HEL XXXIII-2, "Horizons de rétrospection", was under preparation (Puech & Raby 2011). I have always hesitated between two possible uses of the "horizon" metaphor, wondering whether the most important feature is to constantly tell ourselves that we do *not* know what lies behind the horizon, either because it has been forgotten or erased, or because we do not yet know what lies ahead. I was, at the time when the "Horizons de projection" workshop was planned engaged in a long-running task, which consisted in entering, in XML format, the content of the VTCSP, and I did not yet know how many entries it contained, although I now know that there are 16,218,[25] but am at the same time

23. See for instance the following entries: *peṇṭīr* (217_R_m) "Molher, honori- // =fice, hè palaura de uerso.", *pāṇi* (211_R_d) "Agoa, palaura de uerso.", and other similar ones.

24. That conversation is present in the choice of a title (South-Indian Horizons) for the Felicitation Volume in honour of François Gros which I have edited in 2004, with the collaboration of Eva Wilden as associate editor (Chevillard & Wilden 2004).

25. Although this kind of information appears simple, Thani Nayagam who published the facsimilé in 1966 wrote in his "Preface" (p.9) that "There are altogether 16,456 entries separate main entries against which meanings are given in Portuguese of Latin". The figure 16,456, which is too high by 238, is probaby the result of an estimation but has been repeated by several authors. Similarly, Vinson wrote in 1910 that the main body of the VTCSP consists of "247 feuil-

aware of the fact that most readers do not enjoy "drowning by numbers". Therefore, I shall in this brief conclusion simply call attention to the fact that much remains to be discovered inside the VTCSP, as it can progressively reveal itself to a larger audience, by being made readable, progressively overcoming the handicaps evoked in the previous section. Among the possible targets, I shall mention here

- The presence of many dialectal forms,[26] which the compilers of later dictionaries eliminated.
- The presence of many pairs of entries, linked by a cross-reference mechanism, one of them being the formal (B-variety) Tamil form and the other one being the spontaneous (A-variety) form, deprecated by later dictionaries, untill "Spoken Tamil" started to be reappreciated, in the 20th century, when descriptive linguists undertook to dethrone normative grammarians.
- The wealth of information on the morphology and the syntax of early modern Tamil.[27]
- The presence of many taboo terms, which are not found in any existing dictionary of Tamil, because of the statement found in the *Tolkāppiyam*: *avai-y-al kiḷavi maṟaittaṉar kiḷattal* (TC442c)[28] "expressions which do not belong in the assembly, should be uttered in a dissimulated manner". This probably explains why, when explaining many of the 96 such expressions found in the VTCSP, Proença switches from Portuguese to Latin,[29] also adding as a warning to the users of his *Vocabulario*, one label taken from the set {*modesté*, *modestissimé*, *turpe*, *turpissime*}.[30]

---

lets numérotés au recto" (Vinson 1910). This is however incorrect because there are in fact 254 "feuillets". The mistake is due to the fact that wrong folio numbers have been printed on most folios and that, as a consequence, only 16 folios are reliably numbered, on a total of 254. The last folio, which should have been numbered as 254, was numbered as 247.

26. See for instance entry 231_R_m: "*piṟā*. pomba, ou rola. *kāṭṭuppiṟā*. propriamente rola." The standard form would be *puṟā* "pigeon", as seen in the MTL. As per my XML-encoded data-basis, there are hundreds of such examples.

27. See for instance Chevillard (2021), which deals with a set of 298 entries, in which we see the earliest clear attestation of the use of vector verbs in compound verbal expressions in Tamil.

28. *Tolkāppiyam, Collatikāram, cūttiram* 442, as per the numbering in the *Cēṉāvaraiyam* (Tolkāppiyam, Collatikāram, Cēṉāvaraiyam, 2003).

29. Pupils in the Lycée Français de Pondichéry once told me, in 1982, that when they say: "nous parlons latin", it means in fact "nous disons des gros mots".

30. James (2007 and 2009) discusses some of the most extreme techniques, such as partial encryption, which are used in the VTCSP for dealing with some the topics labelled as "*turpissime*".

Regarding this last point, I shall offer as a final illustration (see Table 3), an extract from my listing of taboo expressions, hoping that it will be sufficiently intriguing for some readers, and entice them to embark in the exploration of that most beautiful language, the triglossic Tamil, following in the footsteps of their Portuguese and Italian predecessors, Proença and Beschi.

Table 3. Extract from the listing of Taboo words in the VTCSP

TABOO: @ ச ல த து வ # # ம (102_L_b)
Voeiro, cano // de agoa, item de orina, mo- // =destè.

TABOO: @ ச ல ம (101_R_p))
Agoa, item orina, mo- // destissimé.

TABOO: @ த # லி (369_L_k))
Verenda, mulieris vetu- // =læ, roindade itẽ C. q̃ naõ presta.

TABOO: @ த # ள (369_L_n) [also categorized as {BODY_PART | LITERARY}])
Hombro. {{@ த # ள @ ச –}} {{== ரு கி ற து}}. habère rem. com fæ- // =mina, modeste.

TABOO: @ ந # ணி (174_L_c))
Ceço, que ſae pera // fora a gente grande por doen- // =ça, item ſimilè in verendis fæ- // =minæ, item muito fraco e ma- // =gro.

TABOO: @ ந # ள ளி (174_L_a) [also categorized as {NOT_IN_MTL}])
Quòd. In medio pro- // =minet, verenda fæminæ tur- // =piſſime.

TABOO: @ ப # ச சு (237_R_p))
O traceiro; aliquantulum, modeſtè.

TABOO: @ ப # ட டி (243_L_n))
M. ruim, mo- // =deſtê, item apud. Br. ceſto.

TABOO: @ ப # த தி (244_L_e))
Testiculi, modeſtè.

TABOO: @ ப ண ணு ட ம பு (217_R_l))
verenda // mulieris modestè

TABOO: @ ப லு கி ற து (217_L_o) [also categorized as {V}{META}])
Cagar, fazer came- // =ra, turpe, ன @ ற ன. லு @ வ ன.

TABOO: @ ம # கி க கி ற து (135_R_d) [also categorized as {V | ALIAS}{SEX}])
Quòd. {{@ ப # கி க கி ற து}}. habere rem uenereã ou ter tentaçoens e eſtimulos, in re uenerea; aliquando ſolum, pati pollutionem, // aliquando perturbarse, vacilar.

Dedication

This article is dedicated to the memory of my late colleague and friend Valérie Raby, thanks to whom it was written.

Bibliography

Auroux, Sylvain. 1989. "Avant-propos". *Histoire des Idées linguistiques. Tome 1. La naissance des Métalangages en Orient et en Occident* edited by Sylvain Auroux. Liège/Bruxelles: Mardaga.

Babington, Benjamin. 1822. See Beschi (1974).

Beschi, C. J., 1732. *Caturakarāti*. Manuscrit BnF indien 227. Paris: Bibliothèque Nationale de France.

Beschi, Constantius Josephus. 1738 [ms. 1728]. *Grammatica Latino-Tamulica, ubi de Vulgari Tamulicæ Linguæ Idiomate கொடுந்தமிழ [KOṬUNTAMIḺ] dicto [...] [See translated title in following entries dated 1831 and 1848]*. Tranquebar: Typis Miſſionis Danicæ [Danish mission press].

Beschi, Constant Joseph. 1974 [1822]. *A Grammar of the High dialect of the Tamil Language, Called செந்தமிழ் [centamiḻ]* by Constant Joseph Beschi, translated from the original latin by Benjamin Guy Babington. Thanjavur, India: reprinted by The Tanjore Sarasvati Mahal Library.

Beschi, Constantius Josephus. 1831^2 [1806^1]. *A Grammar of the Common Dialect of the Tamulian Language, Called Koṭuntamiḻ.* [translated by Christopher Henry Horst]. Madras: Vepery Mission Press.

Beschi, 1838, *[Vīramāmuṉivar tiruvāymalarn taruḷicceyta vaintilakkaṇat] Toṉṉūl Viḷakkam [mūlamum uraiyum]*. Putuvai (Pondicherry). (IFP Library "TA GRAM 41", Pondichéry).

Beschi, C. J. 1848. *A Grammar of the Common Dialect of the Tamul Language, Called கொடுந்தமிழ் [KOṬUNTAMIḺ], Composed for the Use of the Missionaries of the Society of Jesus, by, Missionary of the Said Society in the district of Madura*. Translated from the original Latin by George Wiliam Mahon. Madras, Vepery: Christian Knowledge Society's Press.

Beschi, C. J. 1876. *Clavis Humaniorum Literarum Sublimioris Tamulici Idiomatis. Auctore R. P. Constantio Josepho Beschio Societatis Jesu, in Madurensi Regno Missionario*. Tranquebar, India: Printed for A. Burnell by the Evangelical Lutheran Mission Press.

Beschi, C. J. 1917 [ms. 1730]. *A Grammar of High Tamil, Latin text Published for the first time by L. Besse, s.j., with the English Translation by B.G. Babington, M.C.S.*, 2nd ed. [*Grammatica Latino-Tamulica, ubi de elegantiori linguæ tamulicæ dialecto செந்தமிழ் [centamiḻ] dicto [...]*. Trichinopoly, India: St. Joseph Industrial School Press.

Besse, L. 1917. see Beschi (1917).

Burnell, Arthur Coke. 1880. *A Tentative List of Books and Some Mss. Relating to the History of the Portuguese in India Proper*. Mangalore: Printed at the Basel mission press.

Chevillard, Jean-Luc. 2008. "The Concept of *ticai-c-col* in Tamil Grammatical Literature and the Regional Diversity of Tamil Classical Literature". *Streams of Language: Dialects in Tamil* edited by M. Kannan, 21–50. Pondicherry, India: French Institute of Pondicherry. (https://shs.hal.science/halshs-00442188v1)

doi Chevillard, Jean-Luc. 2017. "How Tamil was Described Once Again: Towards an XML-encoding of the Grammatici Tamulici". *Histoire Epistémologie Langage* 39:2.103–127.

doi Chevillard, Jean-Luc. 2021. "From Grammar to Dictionary. The early challenge of lemmatizing Tamil verbal forms, through categories used for Latin and Portuguese". *Journal of Portuguese Linguistics*, 20. (https://jpl.letras.ulisboa.pt/article/id/5689/).

Chevillard, Jean-Luc, 2021. "The use of vector verbs in early modern Tamil". *Trends in South Asian Linguistics* edited by Ghanshyam Sharma and John J. Lowe, 367.261–290.

Chevillard, Jean-Luc & Eva Wilden, ed. 2004. *South-Indian Horizons. Felicitation volume for François Gros on the occasion of his 70th birthday*. Pondicherry: Institut Français de Pondichéry & École Française d'Extrême-Orient. [https://books.openedition.org/ifp/7481.]

Ebeling, Sascha & Margherita Trento. 2018. "From Jesuit Missionary to Tamil Pulavar. Costanzo Gioseffo Beschi SJ (1680–1747), the 'Great Heroic Sage'". *L'Inde et l'Italie* edited by Tiziana Leucci, Claude Markovits & Marie Fourcade, 53–89. Paris : Éditions de l'École des hautes études en sciences sociales. (https://books.openedition.org/editionsehess/23276)

Hein, Jeanne & V. S. Rajam. 2013. *The Earliest Missionary Grammar of Tamil. Fr. Henriques' Arte da Lingua Malabar: Translation, history and analysis*. Harvard Oriental Series (v. 76). Cambridge, Mass.: Harvard University Press.

Henriques, Henrique. 1967 [1586]. *Aṇṭir̲īkku aṭikaḷār iyar̲r̲iya Flos Sanctorum en̲r̲a aṭiyār varalār̲u*. [*The Flos Sanctorum composed by the Venerable Henriques, also called History of the Saints*]. Edited by Ca. Irācamāṇikkam. Tūttukkuṭi (India): Tamil̲ Ilakkiyak Kal̲akam. [The original 1586 book is freely accessible online on the Vatican Library web site: https://digi.vatlib.it/view/MSS_Vat.ind.24]

Horst, Christopher Henry, 1831^2 [1806]. See Beschi (1831^2 [1806])

James, Gregory. 2000. *Colporul. A History of Tamil Dictionaries*. Cre-A, Chennai.

James, Gregory. 2007. "The Manuscript and Printed Versions of Antão de Proença's Vocabulario tamulico (1679)". no:kku, 1.

James, Gregory, 2009. "Aspects of the Structure of Entries in the Earliest Missionary Dictionary of Tamil". *Missionary Linguistics IV: Lexicography. Selected papers from the Fifth International Conference on Missionary Linguistics, Mérida, Yucatán, 14–17 March 2007*. (= Studies in the History of the Language Sciences, 114) edited by Otto Zwartjes, R. Arzápalo & T. Smith-Stark, 273–301. Amsterdam: John Benjamins.

Jeyaraj, Daniel. 2010. *Tamil Language for Europeans: Ziegenbalg's Grammatica Damulica (1716)*. Translated from Latin and Tamil, annotated and commented by Daniel Jeyaraj Wiesbaden: Harrassowitz Verlag.

Mahon, G. 1848. See Beschi (1848).

Muru, Cristina. 2010. *Missionari Portoghesi in India nei secoli XVI e XVII. Studio comparato di alcuni manoscritti*. Viterbo, Italy: Sette Città.

Muru, Cristina. 2022. *The Linguistic and Historical Contribution of the Arte Tamulica by Baltasar da Costa, S.J. (c. 1610–1673)*. Annotated and commented Portuguese transcription and English translation from Portuguese and Tamil by Cristina Muru. Centro de Estudos em Letras / Universidade de Trás-os-Montes e Alto Douro, 25, LINGUÍSTICA, 978-989-704-496-0. [https://hal.science/hal-03878660]

Proença, Antam (de). 1679. *Vocabulario Tamulico com a Significaçam Portugueza (VTCSP)*. [See Thani Nayagam 1966]. [The original is available online on the Vatican Library web site at https://digi.vatlib.it/view/MSS_Borg.ind.12]

Puech Christian & Valérie Raby. 2011. "Présentation. Formes et enjeux de la rétrospection". *Histoire Épistémologie Langage* XXXIII:2.5–14.

Thani Nayagam, Xavier S. 1954. "Tamil Manuscripts in European Libraries". *Tamil Culture* 3.219–228.

Thani Nayagam, Xavier S. 1966. *Antaõ de Proença's Tamil-Portuguese Dictionary A.D. 1679*, [University of Malaya, Kuala Lumpur]. Leiden, Netherlands: E.J. Brill.

Tolkāppiyam, Poruḷatikāram, Iḷampūraṇam. 2003. *Patippāciriyar T.i. Vē. Kōpālaiyar* (2 vol.). Chennai, India: Tamiḻ maṇ patippakam.

Tolkāppiyam, Collatikāram, Cēṉāvaraiyam. 2003. *Patippāciriyar T.i. Vē. Kōpālaiyar*. Chennai, India: Tamiḻ maṇ patippakam.

Trento, Margherita & Jean-Luc Chevillard. (Forthcoming). *"Fishing for Words with Beschi in Tamil Traditional Poetical Vocabularies", TST volume [final outcome of the ANR-DFG project "Texts Surrounding Texts" (TST)]* edited by Eva Wilden & Emmanuel Francis.

Vaiyāpuri Piḷḷai, S. 1982 [1924[1]]. "History of Tamil Lexicography". *Madras Tamil Lexicon (MTL)*, Vol. 1., xxv–xliv. Madras: University of Madras.

Vermeer, Hans J. 1982. *The First European Tamil Grammar. A critical edition*. [English version by Angelika Morath]. Heidelberg: Julius Groos Verlag.

Vinson, Julien. 1910. "Le premier vocabulaire tamoul imprimé". *Revue de Linguistique et de Philologie Comparée* 43.74–82.

VTCSP (= Vocabulario Tamulico com a Significaçam Portugueza). See: Proença 1679.

Walther, Christoph Theodosius. 1739. *Observationes Grammaticae, quibus Linguae Tamulicae idioma Vulgare [...]*, [*Grammatical Observations Pertaining to the Ordinary Variety of Tamil*]. Tranquebar: Typis Miſſionis Regiæ [Royal mission press].

Ziegenbalg, Bartholomäus. 1716. *Grammatica Damulica*. [Tamil grammar]. Halae Saxonum (Halle): Orphanotrophei [Orphanage]

CHAPTER 12

The relevance of B. Delbrück's work on Indo-European syntax (a century after his death)

Massimo Vai
Università degli Studi di Milano

Delbrück's work on Indo-European syntax, particularly his contribution to the analysis of Vedic syntax, is still a useful tool for those wanting to deal with the study of Old Indian and Indo-European comparative syntax. Indeed, it is methodologically comparable with the recent analyses of the left periphery of the sentence. In fact, the notions of basic order of the major constituents of the sentence and of marked order are already present in Delbrück's 1878 work, together with formal considerations that relate the variation of the order of constituents to the interface between the syntax and information structure of the sentence.

Keywords: B. Delbrück, Neogrammarians, PIE syntax, Vedic syntax, Left periphery syntax

1. On PIE word order: Delbrück vs. Braune

In the 3rd volume of *Vergleichende Syntax* (Delbrück 1900) some considerations already present in Delbrück (1878) were comparatively extended to the whole Indo-European family known in the nineteenth century and projected into the reconstruction of the syntax of the *Ursprache.*

Some of his general observations on syntax are particularly useful in order to understand the theoretical assumptions contained in his work.

Delbrück (1900: 38):

> At the beginning of an investigation into word order, the question naturally arises as to whether there was a fixed word order at all in the languages under consideration here, or whether the order of the words resulted in each individual case from the processes of consciousness, i.e. whether the word order was completely free. Observation teaches that the latter was not the case. Rather, it can be shown

https://doi.org/10.1075/sihols.133.12vai

> that in the individual languages a certain type of word order was handed down from one generation to the next one. (my translation: henceforth m.t.)[1]

On the contrary, Braune (1894: 50) had a completely different position:

> I consider it indubitable that the proto-Germanic verbal position was a free one, i.e. the verb could be at the beginning, in the middle or at the end of either the main clause or the subordinate clause, depending on how sooner or later it appeared in the consciousness of the speaker (m.t.).[2]

Delbrück (1907: 66), on the other hand, argues that the order of the constituents of the sentence cannot be free, because the speaker's mind does not contain just lexical elements, but also types of morphological and syntactic forms, which are part of the most stable component of the language:

> Braune presupposes a freedom of the individual in relation to tradition, which does not exist now and should not have existed in the past. As is well known, in the memory of the individual there are not just words and forms, but types of word formation, inflection and sentence formation that belong to the most solid stock. In particular, the types of word order that we now have in our language consciousness are, so to speak, indestructible (m.t.).[3]

Moreover, Delbrück (1878: 77): "If the order of the words were completely free, there would have to be a greater variety than is actually available" (m.t.).[4]

---

1. "Am Anfang einer Untersuchung über Wortstellung erhebt sich naturgemäss die Frage, ob in den hier in Betracht kommenden Sprachen überhaupt eine feste Wortfolge vorhanden gewesen ist, oder ob die Reihenfolge der Wörter sich in jedem einzelnen Falle aus den Bewusstseinsvorgängen ergab, d. h. ob die Wortstellung vollkommen frei war. Die Beobachtung lehrt, dass das Letztere nicht der Fall war. Es lässt sich vielmehr zeigen, dass in den Einzelsprachen ein gewisser Wortstellungstypus von einer Generation zur anderen überliefert wurde".

2. "Ich halte es für unzweifelhaft, dass die urgermanische Verbalstellung eine freie war, d. h. das Verbum konnte sowohl im Hauptsatze als im Nebensatze ganz beliebig am Anfang, in der Mitte und am Schluss stehen, je nachdem es im Bewusstsein des Sprechenden früher oder später in die Erscheinung trat".

3. "Braune setzt eine freiheit des einzelnen gegenüber der überlieferung voraus, die jetzt nicht vorhanden ist und früher auch nicht vorhanden gewesen sein dürfte. in dem gedächtnis des einzelnen sind ja, wie bekannt, nicht etwa bloß wörter und formen, sondern es sind wortbildungs-, flexions- und satzbildungstypen vorhanden, welche zu dem festesten bestande gehören. namentlich sind die wortstellungstypen, die wir jetzt in unserm sprachbewustsein haben, sozusagen unzerstörbar".

4. "Wäre die Ordnung der Wörter vollkommen frei gewesen, so müsste sich eine grössere Mannichfaltigkeit zeigen, als thatsächlich vorhanden ist".

2. Non-configurational languages

Since the 1980s, the study of some Australian languages has again awakened the debate on word order, already well present at the end of the 19th century – e.g., in Delbrück's controversy with Braune (1894) -, but revisited in the form of a parameter of configurationality: languages without constituents exist and hence, the possibility of organising structures made up of several words in such languages is therefore questionable. Kenneth Hale (1983) introduced the notion of *configurationality* and the partition between configurational and non-configurational languages: in Warlpiri there seems to be absolute freedom of placement of words, with the only restriction being the placement of the auxiliary (mandatory in finite sentences) in the second position (according to a kind of Wackernagel's law). Sometimes a nominal expression may appear non-adjacent to another, although both refer to the same nominal element, e.g. Hale (1983: 6):

(1) **wawirri** **yalumpu** kapi-rna panti-rni.
kangaroo that AUX spear NONPAST
(2) **wawirri** kapi-rna panti-rni **yalumpu**
kangaroo AUX spear NONPAST that
"I will spear that kangaroo".

On the basis of the assumption that what precedes the auxiliary must be one (and only one) constituent, Hale & Laughren & Simpson (1995: 1434) believe that the ungrammaticality of sentences like the following depends on the fact that what precedes the auxiliary, i.e. the complex complement + verb (*wawirri nya-nyi*), cannot be interpreted as a single constituent:

(3) *wawirri nya-nyi ka-rna
kangaroo see-NPST IMPF-1ss
(4) *nya-nyi wawirri ka-rna
see-NPST kangaroo IMPF-1ss
"I see a kangaroo".

Since in Warlpiri it is not possible to identify a constituent formed by a single verb with its argument, Hale & Laughren & Simpson (1995: 1435) conclude that the syntactic structure of the sentence in Warlpiri must be flat, e.g. without a VP: in other words, it can be said to be a non-configurational language.

3. Configurationality and Indo-European

Based on observations of morphological and syntactic typology, Meillet-Vendryes (1924: 519) supported the idea of free word order in the reconstructed IE sentence: since each word would have had an inherent case, therefore connected to a specific argument role, there would have been no need for government through an order-based relation. However they add (Meillet-Vendryes 1924: 520):

> Cependant on y voit apparaître déjà les germes d'une transformation. Le principe de cette transformation est que les mots tendent à s'unir en groupes définis, dans lesquels la forme de l'un est commandée par un autre. Au type d'apposition d'éléments autonomes se substitue peu à peu un type nouveau, caractérisé par la «rection».

Thus, according to them a progressive tendency towards the grammaticalisation of a more rigid word order came to be observed in all the Indo-European languages. According to some exponents of this line of research, Old Indo-Aryan did not behave any differently from Warlpiri, and the birth of the formation of a grammar organised in phrases would only have been accomplished with the formation of Neo-Indo-Aryan, as a form of grammaticalisation. So, e.g. according to Reinöhl (2016: 51):

> Vedic Sanskrit shows non-configurationality to a far-reaching degree, even greater than Warlpiri in certain respects. By contrast, Hindi, in the same way as other New Indo-Aryan languages, has developed postpositional phrases, but still allows for free constituent order and null arguments, so that it is best characterized as being low-level configurational.

Thus, these observations have favoured a vision of ancient Indo-European languages as being characterised by features typical of non-configurational languages, accompanied however by a path that leads towards an ever-increasing configurationality that characterises the diachronic development towards modern Indo-European languages. The non-configurational properties that characterised the ancient Indo-European languages can be summarised through Devine & Stephens' (2000: 142, ff.) analysis for ancient Greek, which they believe is

> reminiscent of, though not necessarily identical to, features of non-configurational languages [...] historical residue of a much earlier stage when the syntax had a more pronounced non-configurational character than it has in the classical period [...] many of the same features are found in Vedic.

However, at least for ancient Indo-European languages, there is another way to explain the presence of features that recall those typical of non-configurational languages. For this purpose, one needs to go back to some of Delbrück's observations on Indo-European syntax.

4. The opposition between 'traditionelle' and 'occasionelle Wortstellung'

Delbrück (1878: 13) presents the fundamental opposition between *traditionelle* and *occasionelle Wortstellung*:

> There is a traditional word order that is best recognised in the plain narrative. It is almost identical to the one we know from Latin. The subject begins the sentence, the verb closes it, the dative, accusative, etc. are placed in the middle, but in such a way that the accusative is immediately before the verb. The adjective comes before its substantive, as does the genitive. The participle comes after its noun, as does the apposition. The preposition comes after the case (m.t.).[5]

To use more recent terminology,[6] for Delbrück, Vedic prose presents the basic order S(IO)OV. Delbrück (1900: 38) contrasts the "occasional" (i.e. marked) order with the "traditional" (or "habitual", i.e. unmarked) order:

> The habitual sequence can be deviated from, if a term in the sentence needs to be emphasised, if the connection to another sentence requires a shift, or for whatever other reason. I call this deviant position the occasional one (m.t.).[7]

It is important to note that even the *occasionelle Wortstellung* is not the outcome in every single case of a free extemporaneous decision made by the speaker: what regulates the relationship between the *traditionelle Wortstellung* and the *occasionelle Wortstellung* is not the result of a free choice. The connection between the

5. "Es giebt eine traditionelle Wortstellung, die sich am besten in der ruhigen Erzählung erkennen lässt. Sie ist mit derjenigen so gut wie identisch, die wir aus dem Lateinischen kennen. Das Subject beginnt den Satz, das Verbum schliesst ihn, der Dativ, Accusativ u. s. w. werden in die Mitte genommen, jedoch so, dass der Accusativ unmittelbar vor dem Verbum steht. Das Adjectivum steht vor seinem Substantivum, ebenso der Genitiv. Das Participium steht nach seinem Substantivum, ebenso die Apposition. Die Praeposition steht nach dem Casus".It should be noted that *ruhige Erzählung* is compared to *bewegtere Erzählung* a few lines later.

6. See e.g. McCone (1997: 363).

7. "Von der habituellen Folge kann abgewichen werden, wenn ein Begriff im Satze besonders hervorgehoben werden soll, wenn die Anknüpfung an einen anderen Satz eine Verschiebung erfordert, oder aus was sonst für Gründen. Ich nenne diese abweichende Stellung die okkasionelle".

two orders is in fact governed by a law (Delbrück: *Grundesetz*), that he mentions several times in his works from at least 1878 onwards: "*Jeder Satztheil, der dem Sinne nach stärker betont sein soll, rückt nach vorn*" (Delbrück 1878: 13).[8]

Moreover, Delbrück (1900: 38):

> The occasional position of the words does not always result from a free momentary decision made by the speaker but can be influenced by tradition. Thus, as a basic law of occasional word order that runs through all Indo-European languages, it can be established that the word to be emphasised moves forward (m.t.).[9]

Also Delbrück (1888: 16):

> In addition to the traditional word order, there is an occasional one, whose most important basic law is the following: The more important a word appears to the speaker, the more decisively it strives towards the beginning of the sentence. Or, since the importance of the word is indicated by the stress: the more a word is distinguished by the tone, the more it moves forward (m.t.).[10]

The idea of this law comes to Delbrück from the observation of Vedic verb syntax: if the verb is to be highlighted as the salient element of the sentence, it goes to the beginning of the sentence and maintains its original accent (Delbrück 1900: 81):

> This can be observed particularly well for the verb in Old Indic, where the verb, when it is to be emphasised as important, comes to the head of the sentence and retains its original accent (m.t.).[11]

8. "Any part of the sentence that needs more emphasis is moved forward" (m.t.).

9. "Auch die okkasionelle Stellung der Wörter geht nicht in jedem einzelnen Falle aus einem freien Augenblicksentschluss des Sprechenden hervor, sondern kann unter der Einwirkung der Überlieferung stehen. So lässt sich als ein durch alle indogermanischen Sprachen durchgehendes Grundgesetz der okkasionellen Wortstellung das aufstellen, dass das hervorzuhebende Wort nach vorne rückt".

10. "Neben der traditionellen Wortstellung giebt es occasionelle, deren hauptsachlichstes Grundgesetz das folgende ist: Je wichtiger ein Wort dem Redenden erscheint, umso entschiedener strebt es dem Anfang des Satzes zu. Oder da man die Wichtigkeit des Wortes durch die Betonung zu erkennen giebt: je mehr ein Wort durch den Ton ausgezeichnet wird, um so mehr rückt es nach vorn".

11. "Das lässt sich für das Verbum besonders gut im Altindischen beobachten, wo das Verbum, wenn es als wichtig hervorgehoben werden soll, an die Spitze des Satzes tritt und seinen ursprünglichen Accent behält".

5. Examples of traditional and occasional order

Traditionelle Stellung, see e.g. Delbrück (1878: 25):

(5) ŚB 1.8.2.8
cʰándāṃsi yuktā́ni devébʰyo yajñáṃ vahanti
harnessed-NOM metres-NOM gods-DAT sacrifice-ACC carry-3PL
"the metres, being harnessed, convey the sacrifice to the gods".

In the *occasionelle Stellung*, the verb can occupy the first position and is accented (1888: 36), thus we have:

(6a) devā́ ásurān **ajayan** (*traditionelle Stellung*)
(6b) **ájayan** devā́ ásurān (*occasionelle Stellung*)
"the gods overcame the Asuras"

e.g.:

(7) ŚB 1.2.4.9
Té ha devā́ ūcuḥ jáyāmo vā
dem-NOM.PL PTCL gods-nom say-PRF.3PL win-IND.1PL PTCL
ásurāṃs tátas tv_èvá naḥ púnar upóttiṣṭʰanti
asura-ACC.PL then PTCL PTCL us again PREV_PREV-rise-PRS.IND.3PL
"The gods then said 'We do, no doubt, vanquish the Asuras, but nevertheless they afterwards harass us again'".

If the verb is accompanied by a preverb, Delbrück (1888: 45) specifies that: "The preposition in these cases takes the place which, if the verb were simple, the verb itself would take" (m.t.),[12] e.g.:

(8) TS 2.2.2.4
yám ávareṣāṃ vídʰyanti jī́vati sá
REL-ACC.SG near-GEN.PL pierce-3PL live-3SG he
yám páreṣām prá sá mīyate
REL-ACC.SG foe-GEN.PL PREV he die-3SG
"whomsoever of those near (him) they pierce, he lives; whomsoever of the foe [they pierce], he dies".

In this case, *jī́vati sá* parallels *prá sá mīyate*.

12. "Die Praeposition nimmt in diesen Fällen diejenige Stelle ein, welche, wenn das Verbum einfach wäre, dieses selbst einnehmen wurde".

Other similar examples are *párā evá bʰavati* and *bʰávaty evá*:

(9) ŚB 2.5.1.2
tā́ asya párā evá babʰūvus
DEM-NOM.PL his PREV PTCL pass-PRF3PL
"these (second) creatures of him also passed away".

(10) ŚB 2.5.1.1
tā́ asya prajā́ḥ sr̥ṣṭā́ḥ párābabʰūvus
DEM-NOM his offsprings-NOM emit-PST.PTCP.NOM PREV-pass-PFR3PL
"The living beings created by him passed away".

(11) TS 2.1.5.5
sá evái_nam bʰū́tiṃ gamayati bʰávaty evá
he PTCL him prosperity-ACC go-CAUS.3SG prosper-3SG PTCL
"Verily he causes him to attain prosperity; he prospers.".

Delbrück (1888: 45) also adds:

> However, a verb together with a preposition can also be advanced occasionally[13] [...] This happens when the concept expressed by the preposition and the verb is particularly clearly felt as something unified (m.t.).[14]

In these cases, when the compound verb is found at the beginning of the sentence, the preverb is accented and is graphically separated from the simple verb which is unstressed:

(12) ŚB 1.2.5.3
ví bʰajante ha vā́ imām ásurāḥ pr̥tʰivīḿ
PREV divide-MID3PL PTCL PTCL this-ACC Asuras-NOM earth-ACC
"The Asuras are actually dividing this earth"

13. "Es kann aber auch ein Verbum sammt Praeposition occasionell vorgeschoben werden".

14. "Dies geschieht, wenn der durch die Praeposition und das Verbum ausgedrückte Begriff besonders deutlich als etwas Einheitliches empfunden wird".According to McCone (1997: 373), this seems to suggest that at a certain stage of PIE, after the separation of Anatolian, the first preverb alone stood for the verbal expression as a whole for purposes of topicalisation. In other words, *far from reflecting the preverb's autonomy in relation to the verb at a late stage of the parent language, this type of tmesis testifies to a semantic and grammatical fusion comparable with that observed in Modern German* (my emphasis).

(13) ŚB 4.1.5.7
sáṃ jānītām me grā́ma íti
PREV be-harmonious-IMP3SG my clan QUOT
tásya ha táta evá grā́maḥ
of-him PTCL since-then PTCL clan
"'Let there be peace again in my clan'. Since then there was peace again in his clan".

According to Delbrück (1878: 18), in this case *sáṃ jānītām* is at the beginning of the sentence because it emphasises the meaning, as it expresses Śaryāta's prayer, but the unmarked order is found in the next sentence (1878: 21).

Delbrück (1878: 26) deals with the marked position of the case: "As soon as a case receives a stronger emphasis on meaning, it moves forward" (m.t.).[15] For example the topicalisation of the objects can be found:

(14) ŚB 1.1.1.7
máno ha vái devā́ manuṣyàsy_ā́ jānanti
mind-ACC PTCL PTCL gods-NOM man-GEN PREV know-3PL
"For assuredly, (he argued,) the gods see through the mind of man".

According to Delbrück, the unmarked order would be *devā́ manuṣyàsya mánas ā́ jānanti*, however "nun wird mánas an die Spitze [*scil.* des Satzes] geschoben", the remainder remains unchanged, hence the attested order.

Other examples of topicalisation:

(15) ŚB 11.6.2.5 (Delbrück 1878: 28)
brāhmaṇā́ vaí vayáṃ smo, rājanyàbandhur asaú. yády
brahmins-NOM PTCL we-NOM are-1PL prince-friend-NOM that-NOM that-ACC
O S V
amúṃ vayáṃ jáyema kám ajaiṣm_éti brūyāma
we-NOM won-OP1PL whom-ACC won-AOR1PL_QUOT say-OTT1PL if
S O V O S
átha yády asā́v asmā́n jáyed brāhmaṇā́n rājanyàbandhur
PTCL if that-NOM us-ACC won-OTT3SG brahmins-ACC prince-friend-NOM
V
ajaiṣīd íti no brūyuḥ
won-AOR3SG QUOT us-CL say-OTT3PL.
"We are Brahmins, and he is a layman: if we were to vanquish him, «whom should we have vanquished?» we would say. But if he were to vanquish us, people would say of us that «a layman had vanquished Brahmanas!".

15. "Sobald ein Casus eine stärkere Sinnbetonung erhält, rückt er nach vorn".

In *yády amúṃ vayáṃ jáyema*, the object *amúṃ* placed before the subject indicates a marked position; in the next sentence *yády asā́v asmā́n jáyed*, the arguments maintain the same reciprocal position, but in the latter case, *asáu* is in the nominative. The position of *amúṃ/asáu* in both sentences may indicate that these terms are the theme (or the focus?: "if HE were to vanquish us ...").

We might think that *brāhmaṇān* should be interpreted as the theme of the latter sentence; in this case the translation could be: "The Brahmins have been defeated by a *rājanyàbandhur*!". According to Reinöhl (2016: 33–34), this example shows the freedom of placement of S, O, V and that the adjacency of O and V in Vedic can be broken. In her opinion this proves that the existence of a VP in Vedic could be questioned. However, according to Hale's observations, it seems that there *cannot* be a VP in a non-configurational language like Warlpiri, which constitutes a much stronger assumption than the generally very frequent possibility that parts of a phrase could be subject to movement, e.g. due to focus reasons, as Reinöhl also observes.

6. Looking for a VP in Sanskrit

So far, it has been observed that the lack of a VP is one of the features that characterise non-configurational languages. Can a VP be identified in Vedic? We can try to look for a VP by means of some constituency tests.

Ellipsis Criterion (only constituents can be omitted):

(16) RV 8.48.14
mā́ no nidrā́ī́śata *mó_tá jálpiḥ*
NEG us sleep master-INJ3SG NEG_or mumbling
"Let sleep not master us, nor mumbling".

Here *mā́ utá jálpiḥ* implies *naḥ ī́śata*, and therefore, by the criterion of ellipsis, O+V form a constituent.

One can also add something like the *substitution test*:

(17) ŚB 1.7.2.2
sá yád evá yájeta, téna devébhya r̥ṇáṃ jāyate
sá inasmuch PTCL sacrifice-OTT3SG therefore gods-DAT debt is-born-3SG
tád dhy èbhya etát karóti yád enān yájate yád ebhyo
hence PTCL to-them this does when to-them sacrifice when to-them
juhóti
make-offerings-3SG
"For, inasmuch as he is bound to sacrifice, for that reason he is born as (owing) a debt to the gods: hence when he sacrifices to them, when he makes offerings to them, he does this (in discharge of his debt) to them".

In this case *etát+karóti* seems to be a generic substitute[16] for *enān yájate* and *ebhyo juhóti.*

It would thus seem that a VP can be identified in Vedic: in this case, unlike non-configurational languages, Vedic seems to show typical features of configurationality.

7. Clitics in Delbrück (1878)

Other important observations by Delbrück that show the relevance of his work for Indo-European syntax concern the placement of clitics and the initial position of the verb in the sentence.

He makes an interesting observation about the placement of clitics (1878: 47–48), more than ten years before Wackernagel (1892):

> Enclitic words move to the beginning of the sentence as much as possible [...] The enclitic is attracted to the most stressed word, which is the first in the sentence, as if by a magnet (m.t.).[17]

8. Verb-initial sentences due to textual cohesion

Delbrück (1878: 22) proposed that the anteposition of the verb is connected to the relationship between two sentences, e.g.:

(18) ŚB 3.8.2.1.
yadā prā́ha sáṃjñaptaḥ paśur iti
when PREV_announce-3SG quieted victim-NOM QUOT
átʰā_dʰvaryúr āha néṣṭaḥ pátnīm udā́nayéty *ud*
then_*adhvaryu*-NOM says néṣṭr̥-VOC lady-ACC PREV_PREV-lead-IPV2SG PREV
ā́ *nayati* néṣṭā pátnīm pānnéjanam bíbʰratīm
PREV lead-3SG néṣṭr̥-NOM lady-ACC foot-vessel-ACC bear-PTC-ACC.F
"When he (the slaughterer) announces: 'The victim has been quieted!' the Adhvaryu says: 'Neshtar, lead the lady up!' The Neshtar leads the (sacrificer's) wife up bearing a vessel of water for washing the feet".

---

16. Of course, only if you accept the fact that sequences like *doing so/it/that* can be a substitute for a VP.

17. "Enklitische Wörter rücken möglichst an den Anfang des Satzes [...] Die Enklitika wird von dem am stärksten betonten Worte, und das ist das erste im Satze, wie von einem Magnet angezogen".

Dressler (1969: 3; 22) claimed to identify a *Textsyntaktische Regel* in this type of verb preposition. Such a rule was common to other Indo-European languages and dated back to a period in which real subordinates were still not present in the protolanguage.[18] These cases of V1 seem to be comparable with some cases of Verb First (V1) described by Sigurðsson (1990) for Icelandic and observed in a comparative key by Luraghi (1995). Old Icelandic and Modern Icelandic present V1 in contexts of so-called narrative inversion: the main function of V1 is to signal some type of connection with the previous discourse.[19]

9. Reception of Delbrück's work in recent years

In the proceedings of the conference held in the 1990s on Delbrück and Indo-European syntax (*Coloquio de la indogermanische Gesellschaft*, Madrid 1994) some particularly relevant considerations emerged in the contributions by Stephanie Jamison and Thomas Krisch.[20] According to Jamison (1997: 246–247), Delbrück's syntactic explanations in Delbrück (1888) and in Delbrück (1900) in the comparison between Rgveda poetry and Vedic prose, are essentially synchronic and derivational in nature, just like the relationship between deep and surface structure in transformational grammar. Krisch (1997: 301) is even more explicit in commenting on Delbrück's *Occasionelle Wortstellung* (Delbrück 1900: 83):

> The verb was at the end of the independent declarative sentence and was weakly stressed. If it was particularly important, it went to the top of the sentence and was heavily emphasized (m.t.).[21]

Krisch notes that Delbrück assumes a basic position, expresses the deviation of the initial position of the verb from the final position with a movement metaphor (*kommt*) and the indicated conditions are set for deviations from this position

18. "Bedeutet dies, daß die zweiteilige idg. Regel auf eine Zeit hinweist, in der es noch keine Nebensätze (im engeren Sinn) gegeben hat? Dies wäre immerhin denkbar [...] Wenn in einer Hauptsatzfolge, die textsyntaktisch als Hypotaxe zu interpretieren wäre, indem z.B. der Erstsatz konzessiven Sinn, der Zweitsatz eine anaphorische Anfangsstellung hätte, so wäre, bei der historischen Umwandlung des ersten Hauptsatzes in einen Nebensatz, die Anfangsstellung im (zweiten) Hauptsatz erhalten geblieben".

19. Bernstein (1897: 31) called this phenomenon *Rhetorical Inversion*.

20. Lehmann (1993: 189 ff.) constitutes another fundamental contribution to the study of Delbrück's work on IE syntax.

21. "Das Verbum stand im unabhängigen Aussagesatz am Ende und war schwachbetont. War es besonders wichtig, so kam es an die Spitze des Satzes und wurde stark betont".

(*besonders wichtig*). The idea of a basic position or basic structure is represented by both syntactic typology and generative grammar. The metaphor of movement was and is particularly well-known in generative grammar.

10. The *Occasionelle Wortstellung* as a historical explanation

The concept expressed as *Grundgesetz of the Occasionelle Wortstellung* is also interpreted as a historical explanation by Delbrück (1900,73–74), who explains the unmarked order VSO of Insular Celtic as follows:

> We may assume similar states of affairs in Proto-Celtic, and it can be assumed that the consistent preposition of the verb only developed in Insular Celtic, apparently out of the habit of using the verb in the narrative to seek a connection to what came before, like we found it in Nordic (m.t.).[22]

Similar conditions can be hypothesised for Proto-Celtic, and the continuous preposition of the verb is assumed to have first developed in Insular Celtic, and evidently from the habit of looking for a connection to what precedes through the verb in narrative contexts, as happened in Norse. The conditions existing in the older stage of Celtic have recently been confirmed by Celtiberian inscriptions which show an SOV order.

Delbrück (1900: 61–68) compares the order in Old Norse with its initial verb (often introduced by coordinating conjunctions such as *ok* and *þa*) with what he defines as *Modifizierte Anfangsstellung* with *verba dicendi* which frequently occur in Vedic prose dialogues. The latter have an anaphoric pronoun or a particle at the beginning of the sentence, followed by a verb of saying in the past tense, and then by the subject, i.e. the type:[23]

(19) Brhad-Aranyaka-Upanisad 2.4
sá ha_uvāca Yā́jñavalkyaḥ
he PTCL_said-3SG Yājñavalkya-NOM
"Yājñavalkya said (in replay)".

In any case, the *basic law of the occasional word order* appears to be itself a law operating in synchrony and to go beyond the exclusively Indo-European sphere.

---

22. "Wir dürfen für das Urkeltische ähnliche Zustände voraussetzen, und es ist anzunehmen, dass die durchgängige Voranstellung des Verbums sich erst im Inselkeltischen entwickelt hat, und zwar offenbar aus der Gewohnheit, durch das Verbum in der Erzählung den Anschluss an das Vorhergehende zu suchen, etwa wir es im Nordischen gefunden haben".

23. This type falls under sentences equipped with *Schleppe*, cf. further on.

It is a law that connects the sentence's syntax and information structure and resembles the theories proposed by the Cartographic Program (see e.g. Rizzi 2004). Moreover, as we have seen, it should be noted that Delbrück himself also uses this law to explain syntactic change.

11. Amplified sentences

There are other cases in which the structure of the Vedic sentence seems to contradict the *traditionelle Stellung.* Delbrück (1878) deals with them in a dedicated section: *Der Satz hat eine Schleppe.* Delbrück (1878: 51):

> A sentence can be given a train (*Schleppe*) either for reasons that lie in the sentence itself or through the influence of the following sentence [...] namely 1) a weakly stressed noun falls to the end of the sentence, 2) a supplementary noun term adds something new. (m.t.)[24]

Other cases, corresponding to sentences with *Schleppe* in Delbrück's analysis, are reinterpreted by Gonda (1959: 7) within the category indicated as *amplified sentences*, i.e.:

> they are from their beginning until the verb complete in themselves and all the words following the verb may be left out without mutilating the sentence; sometimes the words following the verb are thrown into relief, or their position is conditioned by rhythmical motives.

In other words, according to the theory of amplified sentences, if a sentence does not end with a verbal entry, this means that something has been "added" to the right, provided, however, that the valences of the verb have all already been saturated. More recently, McCone (1997: 372), on the basis of Hale (1987), suggests that amplifications can occur "sometimes as a strategy for avoiding unduly long phrases before the verb and otherwise perhaps to provide a secondary topic or focus". This analysis can explain those cases in which the unstressed verb does not appear as the last element of the sentence, e.g.:

24. "Ein Satz kann eine Schleppe erhalten entweder aus Gründen, die im Satze selber liegen, oder durch die Einwirkung des folgenden Satzes [...] nämlich 1) ein schwach betontes Nomen sinkt an das Ende des Satzes, 2) ein ergänzender Nominalbegriff bringt etwas Neues hinzu".

(20) RV 1.1.1a
agním īḷe puróhitaṃ
Agni-ACC invoke-1SG foremost-placed-ACC
yajñásya devám ṛtvíjam
sacrifice-GEN god-ACC priest-ACC
"Agni do I invoke – the one placed to the fore, god and priest of the sacrifice".

In this case, from the point of view of the saturation of the arguments of the predicate, the sentence *agním īḷe* is already complete: the successive characterisations of the god are added after the verb which is regularly placed in the final position.

12. *Occasionelle Stellung* and Left Periphery[25]

In the cases considered above, it is often difficult to determine whether the topicalised element is of the thematised or focused type. According to Keydana (2011: 111–112)

> Vedic has a discourse functional slot (henceforth Df-slot) to the left of [Spec, CP]. This slot is usually filled with only one word [...] This makes it nearly impossible to determine the discourse functions of constituents in Vedic verse. Still, some examples with reasonably clear patterns can be found. They show that the Df-slot hosts topics and foci alike [...] with a filled Df-slot and a Wh-word in [Spec, CP]

The clearest cases in the ṚgVeda are those in which Topic elements precede interrogative pronouns. According to Rizzi (1997: 325), in main questions, such pronouns compete with focused phrases for the Spec of Focus, as Keydana also noticed, e.g.:

(21) RV 6.27.1b
índraḥ kím asya sakhyé cakāra
Indra-NOM what of-it fellowship-LOC made-PRF3SG
"What did Indra create in the fellowship of it?"

(22) RV 8.64.9
ukthé ká u svid ántamaḥ
recitation-LOC who PTCL PTCL closest-NOM
"Who at the recitation is closest (to you)?".

In some cases, it seems that in Vedic prose, unlike the ṚgVeda, the presence of an even more complex left periphery is recognisable starting from the syntactic

25. For this terminology, I refer to the studies that began with Rizzi (1997).

structure. This is typically found e.g. in cases (here taken from Œrtel 1926) where the prefixed element is resumed by an anaphoric pronoun, e.g.:

(23) ŚB 4.4.5.1 (Œrtel 1926:36)
áthaitác chárīraṃ **tásmin** ná ráso 'sti
PTCL that body it-LOC NEG sap is
"Now that body, there is no sap in it".

The pronominal resumption indicates that the element is functionally thematised. In Benincà (2001:43) it can correspond to the cases of *Hanging Topic* or *Left Dislocation*. In the classical languages, the Hanging Topic typically corresponds to the *Nominativus Pendens*.

The following is another particularly interesting example, with a phrase in accusative case resumed by a pronoun in the same case, therefore a case of left dislocation:

(24) TB 3.2.8.2. (Œrtel 1926:75)
ā́pa óṣadhīḥ paśū́n tā́n evá asmā ekadhā́ saṁsṛ̥́jya
waters-ACC plants-ACC cattle-ACC tá-ACC PTCL him-DAT together uniting
mádhumataḥ karoti
sweet-ACC.PL makes-3SG
"The waters, plants, (and) cattle, – uniting these together he makes (them) sweet for him" (Œrtel's translation).

Someone recently (e.g. Lühr 2017) has attempted to analyse the pragmatic value of some particles that behave like syntactic clitics (with or without an accent): this would make it possible to determine the informative function of the element highlighted by the single particle and could be a way forward for further research. If, as since Grassmann/Kozianka (1996:301, 6),[26] *evá* seems to function as a focusing particle, this could be a case of co-occurrence of Topic-Focus in the left periphery, as demonstrated by Rizzi (1997).

Furthermore, if we admit that an entire CP can be thematised and found in SpecTopP, we would have cases, also in RV, like:

26. "*evá* hebt das hervorgehende Wort hervor, so dass von dem dadurch ausgedrückten oder angedeuteten Begriff in vollem oder vorzüglichem Maße die Aussage gilt".

(25) RV 1.1.4
ágne yáṃ yajñám adhvaráṃ viśvátaḥ paribhū́r
Agni-VOC REL-ACC sacrifice-ACC rite-ACC from-all-side surrounding-NOM
ási sá íd devéṣu gachati
are-2SG that PTCL gods-LOC go-3SG
"O Agni, the sacrifice and rite that you surround on every side – it alone goes among the gods".

Lühr 2017: 286 ascribes *id* to the category of focusing particles, so the following could be a representation of the left periphery of the latter sentence according to the Cartographic Program (see for instance Benincà & Munaro 2010: 3–15):

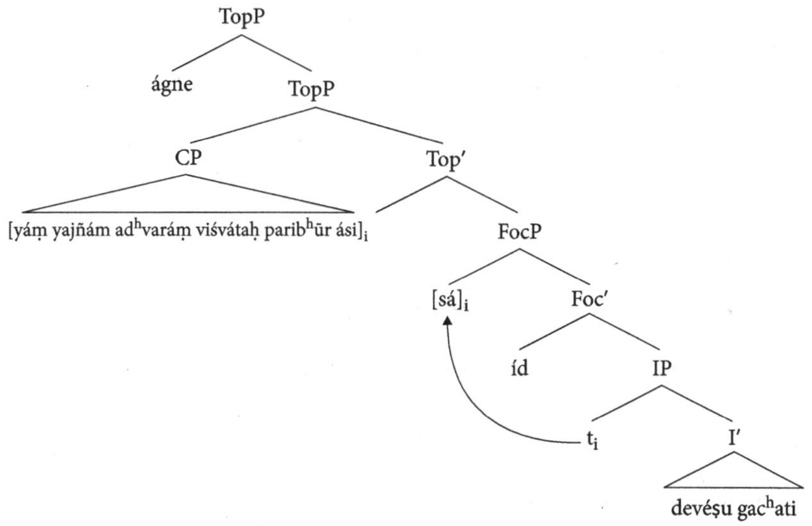

Figure 1.

13. Conclusions

A century after his death, Delbrück still represents one of the greatest syntacticists in the history of linguistics. In particular, Delbrück's law of *Occasionelle Wortstellung* represents one of the major results of Neogrammarian linguistic research in the field of syntax: through the definition of a basic order of the constituents of the sentence in Vedic – subsequently extended to Proto-Indo-European – and a movement rule correlated to the informative value of the constituents, it constitutes a fundamental moment of research in syntax that is still valid today, even outside the scope of Indo-European syntax.

References

Benincà, Paola 2001. "The Position of Topic and Focus in the Left Periphery". *Current Studies in Italian Syntax Offered to Lorenzo Renzi* edited by Guglielmo Cinque & Giampaolo Salvi, 39–64. Amsterdam: Elsevier-North Holland Academic Graphics.

Benincà, Paola & Nicola Munaro, eds. 2010. *Mapping the Left Periphery. The cartography of syntactic structures*, Vol. 5. Oxford & New York: Oxford University Press.

Bernstein, Ludwig. 1897. *The Order of Words in Old Norse Prose.* New York: Knickerbocker Press.

Braune, Wilhelm. 1894. "Zur Lehre von der deutschen Wortstellung". *Forschungen zur deutschen Philologie. Festgabe für Rudolf Hildebrand zum 13. März 1894*, 34–51. Leipzig: Verlag von Veit und Comp.

Delbrück, Berthold. 1878. *Die altindische Wortfolge aus dem Çatapathabrāhmaṇa dargestellt.* Halle: Verlag der Buchhandlung des Weisenhauses.

Delbrück, Berthold. 1900. *Vergleichende Syntax der indogermanischen Sprachen*, vol. III. Strassburg: Karl J. Trübner.

Delbrück, Berthold. 1907. "Die wortstellung im Beowulf von John Ries". *Anzeiger für deutsches Altertum und deutsche Literatur* XXXI.65–76.

Devine, Andrew M. & Laurence D. Stephens. 2000. *Discontinuous Syntax. Hyperbaton in Greek.* Oxford & New York: Oxford University Press.

Dressler, Wolfgang. 1969. "Eine textsyntaktische Regel der idg. Wortstellung". *Zeitschrift für vergleichende Sprachforschung* 83.1–25.

Gonda, Jan. 1959. "On Amplified Sentences and Similar Structures in the Veda". *Four Studies in the Language of the Veda*, 7–69. 's-Gravenhage: Mouton & Co..

Graßmann, Hermann. 1996. *Wörterbuch zum Rig-Veda. 6.*, [*überarbeitete und ergänzte Auflage von Maria Kozianka*]. Wiesbaden: Harrassowitz Verlag.

Hale, Kenneth. 1983. "Warlpiri and the Grammar of Non-Configurational Languages". *Natural Language & Linguistic Theory* 1.5–47.

Hale, Kenneth, Mary Laughren, & Jane Simpson. 1995. "Warlpiri". *Syntax. Ein internationales Handbuch zeitgenössischer Forschung. An International Handbook of Contemporary Research* vol. II edited by Joachim Jacobs, Armin von Stechov, Wolfgang Sternefeld & Theo Vennemann, 1430–1451. Berlin & New York: de Gruyter.

Hale, Mark. 1987. *Studies in the Comparative Syntax of the Oldest Indo-Iranian Languages.* Cambridge, Mass.: Harvard University Dissertation.

Jamison, Stephanie W. 1997. "Delbrück, Vedic Textual Genres, and Syntactic Change". *Berthold Delbrück y la sintaxis indoeuropea hoy. Actas del Coloquio de la Indogermanische Gesellschaft. Madrid, 21–24 de septiembre de 1994* edited by Emilio Crespo & José Luis García Ramón, 239–251. Madrid & Wiesbaden: Ediciones De La UAM–Wiesbaden: Dr. Ludwig Reichert Verlag.

Keydana, Götz. 2011. "Wackernagel in the Language of the Rigveda. A Reassessment". *Historische Sprachforschung / Historical Linguistics.* 124.106–133.

Krisch, Thomas. 1997. "B. Delbrücks Arbeiten zur Wortstellung aus heutiger Sicht". *Berthold Delbrück y la sintaxis indoeuropea hoy. Actas del Coloquio de la Indogermanische Gesellschaft. Madrid, 21–24 de septiembre de 1994* edited by Emilio Crespo & José Luis García Ramón, 283–309. Madrid & Wiesbaden: Ediciones De La UAM–Wiesbaden: Dr. Ludwig Reichert Verlag.

Lehmann, Winfred P. (1993). *Theoretical Bases of Indo-European Linguistics.* Routledge: London & New York.

Lühr, Rosemarie. 2017. *Stressed and Unstressed Particles in Old Indic. Discourse particles* edited by Klaus von Heusinger, Gereon Müller, Ingo Plag, Beatrice Primus, Elisabeth Stark & Richard Wiese, 281–303. Berlin & Boston: De Gruyter.

McCone, Kim. 1997. "Delbrück's Model of PIE Word Order and the Celtic Evidence". *Berthold Delbrück y la sintaxis indoeuropea hoy. Actas del Coloquio de la Indogermanische Gesellschaft. Madrid, 21–24 de septiembre de 1994* edited by Emilio Crespo & José Luis García Ramón, 363–396. Madrid & Wiesbaden: Ediciones De La UAM–Wiesbaden: Dr. Ludwig Reichert Verlag.

Meillet, Antoine & Joseph Vendryes. 1924. *Traité de grammaire comparée des langue classiques.* Paris: Honoré Champion.

Œrtel, Hans. 1926. *The Syntax of Cases in the Narrative and Descriptive Prose of the Brāhmaṇas. The disjunct use of cases.* Heidelberg: Carl Winter Universitätsbuchhandlung.

doi Reinöhl, Uta. 2016. *Grammaticalization and the Rise of Configurationality in Indo-Aryan.* Oxford & New York: Oxford University Press.

doi Rizzi, Luigi. 1997. "The Fine Structure of the Left Periphery". *Elements of Grammar* edited by Liliane Haegeman, 281–337. Dordrecht: Kluwer.

doi Rizzi, Luigi. 2004. *The Structure of CP and IP. The cartography of syntactic structures, Volume 2.* Oxford & New York: Oxford University Press.

doi Wackernagel, Jacob. 1892. "Über ein Gesetz der indogermanischen Wortstellung". *Indogermanische Forschungen* 1.333–436.

CHAPTER 13

Three documents bearing on the foundation of the Linguistic Society of America in the age of scientific racism

Margaret Thomas
Boston College

The centennial of the Linguistic Society of America invites reflection on how the organization has arrived at its current activist stance, which prioritizes social-justice issues and anti-racist initiatives within the discipline of linguistics. This article highlights the inward-looking nature of the foundation of the LSA in 1924, offset against the so-called scientific racism that imbued early twentieth-century American public discourse. I examine three short texts produced at the outset of the institutionalization of the LSA, all (co-)authored by Leonard Bloomfield, that communicate the centripetal social dynamics of the foundation of the society and its insistence on the scientific nature of the study of language – together lending a particular complexion to the group within the sociocultural world of early twentieth-century America.

Keywords: Foundation of the Linguistic Society of America, racism in linguistics, scientific racism, Leonard Bloomfield

1. Introduction

The Linguistic Society of America, the largest professional organization of linguists in the United States, was first initiated 100 years ago, in December 1924. The centennial of this group is a opportune moment in which to reflect on what the Society has, versus has not, accomplished on the behalf of language scholarship. It is also an invitation to consider whether the LSA has contributed to building a more equitable and inclusive society, within which the study of language is carried out with all due respect for the full scope of variation and intricacy in all forms of human linguistic expression. That ambitious and urgent goal informs many of the present-day activities of the Society, which, in twenty-first century terms, aspire to prioritize diversity, equity, and inclusion (Linguistic Society of

https://doi.org/10.1075/sihols.133.13tho

America 2019; Charity Hudley et al. 2018; Charity Hudley, Mallinson, & Bucholtz 2020). This article looks back to the origins of the LSA by the light of twenty-first century priorities, to try to characterize the social and intellectual climate out of which the Society first emerged. That climate was one where discrimination thrived openly – discrimination against (among others) immigrants, Jews, and people of African and of Native American descent. The purpose in reflecting on this material is to increase our understanding of the context of the foundation of the LSA, and of the origins of a professional organization which has evolved to arrive at its current activist stance.

2. Three texts that document the foundation of the LSA

A convenient starting point would be three key texts in the history of the LSA, all either written or co-written by Leonard Bloomfield (1887–1949). Bloomfield was perhaps the most prominent American structuralist linguist from the 1920s through the 1940s. He worked on Algonquian and on Indo-European comparative linguistics, with additional publications on Tagalog. His self-described "mechanistic", "non-animistic and non-teleological" (Bloomfield 1944: 52, 55) orientation aimed to depict the distribution of linguistic units in a language without relying on ill-defined mental notions like "thought, concept, image, feeling, act of will" (Bloomfield 1933: 132), or on categories and terminology presumed to be relevant to all languages. In addition to Bloomfield's intellectual role in shaping a distinctively American style of structuralism, he participated in the institutionalization of linguistics as a discipline in the early decades of the twentieth century in the United States.[1] In particular, Bloomfield generated three texts that document efforts to promote a professional society of linguists.

2.1 The recruitment letter

The first key text is a letter typed on the stationary of Bloomfield's German Department of the Ohio State University, dated 18 January 1924, and co-signed by Bloomfield, George Melville Bolling (1871–1963) and Edgar Howard Sturtevant (1875–1952). We do not know the full set of people to whom copies of this letter

1. Falk (2002) suggests that Bloomfield's role in the founding of the LSA may have been exaggerated. She points out that in the first decade of the Society Bloomfield's colleagues George M. Bolling and Edward H. Sturtevant both participated more actively than he did in organizational and committee work. However, no one disputes Bloomfield's authorship, or at least co-authorship, of the three documents examined below.

were sent.[2] Its importance was brought to light by Swiggers (1994), who discovered a copy of it in the Franz Boas archives held at the library of the American Philosophical Society in Philadelphia (B/B 61, Boas–Bloomfield correspondence, Folder #1). The purpose of Bloomfield, Bolling, and Sturtevant's letter was evidently to recruit language scholars to join the authors in calling for the establishment of a Linguistic Society of America. Referring to themselves with the third person, as "the undersigned", Bloomfield, Bolling, and Sturtevant assert that "the study of the linguistic sciences is at present greatly neglected in this country", and that founding a professional society would be a first step toward "an improvement in the general condition of linguistic studies" (Swiggers 1994: 303). They do not elaborate on the nature of that "general condition" which the founding of a professional society would redress. Rather, they sketch out something of the character of the proposed organization: that it would eventually publish its own journal; that it would meet biennially in consort with established scholarly societies to which many linguists already belonged; and that its establishment would bolster (in unspecified ways) not just the study of language but "all humanistic studies" (Swiggers 1994: 303). The letter closes by inviting addressees – characterized as "a few men who have been most conspicuous for the publication of linguistic work" (Swiggers 1994: 303) – to indicate whether they would join the authors in publicly supporting the establishment of such an organization, and if not, to communicate why they do not support its establishment.

The Boas archives also include a copy of Boas's response to the letter. Addressed exclusively to Bloomfield, it is dated 21 January 1924, a short three days later. Boas expressed unreserved support for the initiative, and offered to "cooperate with [Bloomfield, Bolling, and Sturtevant] in every way" (Swiggers 1994: 302). He included the postal address of his student Edward Sapir, which Bloomfield had requested in a note accompanying the recruitment letter. Boas suggested that the same appeal be circulated to Pliny Earl Goddard of the American Museum of Natural History, Alfred L. Kroeber of the University of California at Berkeley, and John R. Swanton of the Bureau of American Ethnology (Swiggers 1994: 302–3). Sapir, Goddard, Kroeber, and Swanton all went on to support the early LSA.

Bloomfield, Bolling, and Sturtevant's January 1924 recruitment letter may count as the first entry in the archives of the history of the LSA. Its content can be best appreciated when offset against the second and third of the three key documents.

2. Dallaire (1984: 12) lists a letter from Bloomfield to Edward Sapir dated 18 January 1924, which turns out to be the identical text.

2.2 "The call"

The second document is a text that came to be known as "the Call" ("Call" 1925). This document, again produced on Bloomfield's typewriter (Joos 1986:3) and dated 15 November 1924, spells out the benefits of establishing a professional society of linguists. It articulates multiple warrants for the creation of a professional society, including that it would allow linguists to meet, to exchange ideas, and to "represent the interests of our studies". Furthermore, a professional society would enhance the public standing of linguistics among the sciences, because although the hospitality of other learned societies to linguists was appreciated, for language scholars to meet only under the aegis of professional organizations of philologists, Classicists, anthropologists, or literary scholars "divides us into groups across whose boundaries there is little acquaintance" (p.6). The Call goes on to assert that in the absence of an association of linguists "No one can tell how much encouragement and inspiration is thereby lost" (p.6).

Moreover, the Call takes a step forward in inviting readers to attend an organizational meeting to be held at 10:00 AM on 28 December 1924, at New York City's American Museum of Natural History. Recipients of the letter interested in either joining the society or attending the meeting are asked to notify the organizing committee, comprised of Bloomfield, Bolling, and Sturtevant. The Call is co-signed by 28 scholars based in the United States, plus Edward Sapir, then affiliated with the Victoria Memorial Museum in Ottawa. Presumably, these 29 scholars comprise the population who responded positively to the January 1924 recruitment letter.

Aside from its newsworthy content in announcing the December organizational meeting (and the promise that that meeting would also include presentation of scientific papers), the Call has a bolder and less circumspect tone than the January recruitment letter, as if the response to that letter had strengthened the authors' confidence in their initiative. What else stands out is a shift away from the cooler, reserved, third-person plural rhetorical posture of the January letter ("the undersigned...*they* point to the fact that...*They* believe that...*They* are writing therefore..."; italics added) to the more urgent, personalized, first-person plural rhetoric of the Call ("[forming a society would] enable *us* to meet *each other*, give *us* the opportunity for the exchange of ideas, and represent the interests of *our* studies"; italics added). It is as though the Call itself, in advance of the actual foundation of the LSA, anticipated the successful tightening of bonds among linguists to the point where the organizers presupposed that they could speak on the behalf of the group, from within the group itself. The argument they made was essentially to increase the centripetal forces acting on the group: "the present state of things has many disadvantages. The most serious, perhaps, is the fact that we do not meet" (p.6).

2.3 Bloomfield (1925): "Why a linguistic society?"

The third document is a short essay written by Bloomfield, published in the first five pages of the first issue of the Society's journal *Language* (Bloomfield 1925), immediately preceding a reproduction of the Call. Bloomfield's title poses the question "Why a linguistic society?" The essay motivated the foundation of the LSA, on two bases. The first basis echoes, and amplifies, the content of the recruitment letter and the Call: that forming a Society would build professional and personal solidarity among American linguists, offsetting their geographical dispersal. Appropriating the diction of the Call, Bloomfield made this case with reference to language scholars exclusively in the first-person plural, repeatedly using the pronouns "we", "us", "our", and "ourselves" as if the group were an inherently closed, inward-looking, intellectual community with secure boundaries. He used the expression "students of language" freely, but to Bloomfield that term referred to professional language scholars, not neophytes entering the discipline. Nowhere, in fact, did he advert to an oncoming generation of linguists, or to the role of a professional society in attracting newcomers or integrating outliers into the field.

Bloomfield's second motivation for founding the Society was to ensure the establishment of linguistics as "a *science* of language" (1925: 1; emphasis added). The identification of linguistics as a science was present in the earlier two texts, in that the recruitment letter adverted to "linguistic science" and the Call to "our science". But both those texts presupposed the identification of linguistics with science, rather than asserted it. In the 1925 essay, Bloomfield repeatedly identified linguistics as a science, making this assertion a theme of his text. He uses the word "science" and its morphological derivatives 25 times in four and a half pages, at essentially the same rate as he uses the word "language(s)" (27 times). Bloomfield points out where linguistics resembles mathematics, and then physics (p. 2); he claims that linguistics avoids some of the weaknesses of economics and of "the historical sciences" (p. 3); and he specifically denies that linguistics is a branch of philology or literary studies (p. 4). Moreover, he takes failure to recognize the scientific nature of linguistics as responsible for "desperate hardship" (p. 4) in the professional experiences of at least one linguist, and for school teachers' ignorance of the relationships of speech to writing, and of languages to dialects (p. 5).

Bloomfield was by no means the first to identify linguistics as a science (see Goldsmith & Laks 2019: 8–16), although his insistence on the point stands out. But what did it mean to be a "science" in 1924? Moreover, what did it mean to establish the LSA as a kind of club that would strengthen the social and professional bonds among Bloomfield's "we", depicted as an encapsulated group of language scientists submerged in a culture of uncomprehending outsiders? These two questions probe into Bloomfield's two main warrants for establishing the LSA. Both may help us understand the nature of the LSA in its foundation years, the starting point for an institution that now takes for granted its responsibility to serve as an agent of diversity, equity, and inclusion in language scholarship. We will examine these two questions separately.

3. A professional society for "us" linguists

Bloomfield represents the community of linguists as something like a private club which, in 1924, lacked a place to meet. The "clubbiness" of the group hinted at in the Call, and made more explicit in "Why a linguistic society?" is not an accident of Bloomfield's diction. It can be read between the lines, and is sometimes made conspicuous, in other texts by Bloomfield (e.g., Bloomfield 1946); in literature produced by second-generation insiders who narrate the accomplishments of the group (Marckwardt 1964; Hall 1975; Haugen et al. 1975; Joos 1986); and in accounts by historians of linguistics (Hymes & Fought 1981; Murray 1991).

3.1 The inward-looking nature of the early LSA in a context of external threats

Insularity, clubbiness, or even elitism in a professional society may be off-putting to outsiders, but it may also be a rational response when a group faces external threats. Many such threats were in the air in mid 1920s America. For some linguists, those threats went beyond the general difficulties of pursuing an academic career in the runup to the Great Depression. For example, a number of the founders and early Presidents of the LSA were either first- or second-generation immigrants to the U.S. That means they, or their families, were new arrivals near the peak of the anti-immigrant fervor that had been building since the late 1800s. In 1924, the same year that the LSA was founded, U.S. President Calvin Coolidge signed into law the Johnson-Reed Act, culminating forty years of immigration restriction legislation. The Johnson-Reed Act extended and tightened quotas imposed on immigrants to the United States. The quotas were ostensibly based on the immigrants' countries of origin, but had no plausible rationale other than race and ethnicity. Among the 29 signatories to the Call, all were apparently white males; four were born to Jewish families; 11 were either first- or second-generation Americans.[3] Of those whose families had recently immigrated

3. Leonard Bloomfield, his uncle Maurice Bloomfield, Franz Boas, and Edward Sapir identified as Jews, and all served as Presidents of the LSA. Maurice Bloomfield, Boas, and Sapir were first-

to the U.S., the preponderance had arrived from northern Europe. Although the Johnson-Reed Act favored northern European immigrants over immigrants from southern Europe, Africa, or Asia, as a policy with broad popular support it undercut the stability and status of all non-native-born residents. In addition to anti-Semitism, there was also the well-attested fact that anti-German prejudice swept the nation during the years surrounding World War I. Eduard Prokosch, for example – signer of the Call and LSA President in 1930, an ethnically German first-generation immigrant from Austria – was dismissed from his position on the faculty of the University of Texas in 1919 on unproven suspicion of disloyalty to the United States (Nicholas 1972).

The 1920s was also an active decade for the Galton Society, an exclusive New York-based association dedicated to promoting eugenics. Galton Society members had access to tremendous wealth and political and intellectual authority. Membership was by invitation only. The group's purpose was to address what they viewed as the on-going deterioration of American racial stock by, for example, promoting selective immigration restrictions and enforced sterilization of peoples they considered unfit, thereby turning around (by law if necessary) what they considered to be a catastrophic erosion of America's white Anglo-Saxon gene pool.

A charter member of the Galton Society was the prominent eugenicist Henry Fairfield Osborn (1857–1935) (Selden 1999). Osborn served as President of American Museum of Natural History from 1908 to 1933. He co-founded the American Eugenics Society in 1922, and hosted the Second International Eugenics Congress on the premises of the museum in 1921. Delegates to that Congress likely walked the same halls, and may have sat in the same auditorium, where in December 1924 the first meeting of what became the LSA was convened. We do not have a record of whether Osborn personally approved of the use of the museum facilities for the organizational meeting of the LSA, plausibly in response to a request by Boas's former student Pliny Earl Goddard, who was employed as a curator at the museum. But Osborn's path crossed that of the nascent LSA, at least passively, because the proceedings of the December 1924 meeting include the text of a letter of thanks addressed to the museum President and Trustees on the behalf of the Society, thanking them for their hospitality in having provided meeting rooms for the group ("Proceedings" 1925: 12).

---

generation immigrants; Leonard Bloomfield was second-generation. Other signatories of the Call who immigrated to the U.S. include Hermann Collitz, Paul Haupt, Hans C. G. von Jagemann, Walter Petersen, and Edward Prokosch; second-generation immigrants included Aurelio Espinosa and Alfred L. Kroeber.

3.2 Racism and the early LSA

In these ways, the LSA first emerged into an environment saturated with racist ideologies and public policies that presupposed race-based discrimination, although neither racial discrimination nor its eradication was among the explicit concerns of the LSA. Little awareness of those issues disturbed the complacent, inward-looking, allegiances of the group.[4] American linguists may have sought professional and personal solidarity in the LSA as they weathered an uninviting anti-immigrant, pro-eugenicist, climate; they may also have been agents, not merely patients, of racism. For example, Bloomfield's co-signer of the recruitment letter and the Call George M. Bolling was the son of a decorated Confederate Army officer (Krick 2003: 77), and the brother of a member of the Daughters of the American Revolution, during a period when this group stanchly excluded Black women (National Society 1914: 180).[5] Bolling served as LSA President in 1932, when the so-called "Jim Crow laws" in his ancestral state of Virginia restricted African Americans' opportunities to vote, travel, own property, start businesses, borrow money, attend schools, and to feel confident that their fellow citizens would respect their civil rights.[6]

On the other hand, at least one early participant in the LSA descended from a family that had taken a public stance against the subjugation of African Americans. Roland G. Kent, signatory of the Call, LSA Treasurer from 1924 to 1942, and President in 1941, was born into a family of Quaker abolitionists going back three generations. Kent's father, Lindley Coates Kent (1844–1916) was an officer in the 109th Regiment of the U.S. Colored Infantry during the Civil War ("Military Order" 1916). His distant relatives had participated in the Underground Railroad and in founding the American Anti-Slavery Society (Snodgrass 2008).

Linguists involved in forming the LSA may also have included those who neither were themselves subjected to discriminatory treatment on racial grounds, nor either consciously subjected others to it, or worked to eliminate such treatment. Nevertheless, since institutional racism affects all parties, none of us is naive. In

4. It is also salient that the early LSA solicited financial support from foundations and philanthropists, without evincing any scruples about how potential benefactors had amassed their fortunes.

5. Bolling's sister, Rebecca Bolling Littlejohn, and her daughter Charlotte Townsend Littlejohn, both became Foundation Member of the LSA, apparently as 'a gesture of family support for Professor George Bolling, Rebecca Bolling Littlejohn's brother' (Falk 1994: 464).

6. Among the scholars involved in setting up the LSA, none identified as African American. In fact, it would not be until 2015 that a Black linguist, John Rickford, would be elected to serve as President of the Society. Yuen Ren Chao, a naturalized U.S. citizen born in China, was LSA President in 1945.

particular, racism surrounded the context of one of American structuralists' trademark achievements, the analysis and recording of threatened Native American languages. Many early LSA members focused on American indigenous languages, carrying out extensive on-site linguistic fieldwork. They gathered data directly from tribal members, sometimes for years, sometimes forming long-lasting personal relationships with their local contacts. Through these interactions, linguists could observe the operation and the fallout of racism at close hand. The extent to which they resisted racialization of Native Americans, or participated in it, remains to be investigated.[7]

Whether or not those who collaborated to create the Society, or those who helped fund it, were otherwise involved in the various manifestations of racism, the institutionalization of the LSA within a culture permeated with scientific racism is significant. If racism is, in the words of Barkan (1992: xi), "a universal affliction", the null hypothesis would be for American linguistics to be equally as afflicted as any other field of study in the relevant period, and for the LSA to be neither more nor less infused with racism than any other professional society. However, there are reasons to anticipate *more* influence of racist ideology on American linguistics than on other fields.

One reason to expect a strong presence of racism on the development of American linguistics is that the tension between studying how languages resemble each other versus how they differ shadows the debate about whether humans are united as a species, or comprise a collection of inherently disjoint or immiscible groups. The long-running debate between monogenesis and polygenesis predated the foundation of the LSA, but was still alive in the 1920s (Gossett 1963/1997; Stocking 1968), and was still playing out in the study of language.

A second reason resides in the relationship of linguistics to philology. Abberley writes that nineteenth-century philologists often "blurred" (2011: 45; see also Messling 2016) language and race together: the fact that Indo-European languages formed a linguistic family with no discernable connection to, say, Chinese, provides a tempting model on which to assert that speakers of Indo-European languages form an independent "racial" group. In the educations of some of the founders of the LSA, philology in this sense was the received version of what it meant to study language. Bloomfield, among other members of the early LSA, turned sharply away from philology. But for others, it remained their approach

7. Among early supporters of the LSA, Franz Boas is best known for having repeatedly taken a public stance against racial discrimination (Lewis 2001; Whitfield 2010). That reputation that has been recently problematized (Anderson 2019; Bernasconi 2019), especially with respect to Boas's professional and personal relationships with Native Americans (Blackhawk & Wilner 2018).

and central interest, so that the entanglement of race with language persisted in the backdrop to the institutionalization of linguistics in the United States.

4. A society to promote the science of language

To understand the development of the LSA, then, we need to sort out how the newly-institutionalized academic discipline either amplified, cooperated with, acquiesced to, ignored, or undercut the pervasive racism of the day. What else we need to grasp is that – remarkably from the perspective of the twenty-first century – early 1900s Jim Crow laws, immigration restriction initiatives, eugenicist social engineering, and disregard for the autonomy of Native peoples were then considered to be based on incontestable scientific evidence. The so-called "scientific racism" of the late 1800s into the early 1900s had been worked out by biologists, natural historians, anthropologists, and scholars of medicine (Stepan 1982). They claimed to have proven, on scientific grounds, that humans could be sorted into racial groups whose immutable characteristics made them variously eligible to assume positions of authority and to enjoy social and educational privileges. Political, legal, social and religious leaders, and academics (themselves almost uniformly identified with the most favored racial class) accepted these self-serving claims at face value. They then imposed a racially-stratified society on a generally cooperative white-dominant public, which, for the most part, found those views congenial. As Stepan and Gilman (1991) have pointed out, to oppose this tableau would be to oppose the authoritative conclusions of science, which was the most culturally powerful mode of discourse, held up as "an apolitical, nontheological, universal, empirical, and uniquely objective…form of knowledge" (1991: 77).

Where did linguists, either individually or in their incorporation into an inward-looking group, stand with respect to these very consequential matters? In particular, what did it mean to insist, as Bloomfield did, on the "scientific" character of linguistics in an age of scientific racism? We have seen that in his 1925 essay, Bloomfield repeatedly identified linguistics as a science. But his warrant for that identification seems oddly superficial: he noted that the collection of linguistic data requires close observation and "highly specialized equipment" (p. 4); he pointed out that the findings of the science of language sometimes run counter to common sense (p. 1). Curiously, these traits are also shared with scientific racism, which likewise entails close observation, specialized equipment, and sometimes produced unexpected results. But where scientific racism failed was in the circularity of its logical structure: the bulk of scientific racist research started out with a value-laden proposition to be proved (e.g., "Group X is inferior to Group Y") and then construed scientific data – whatever they were – as consistent with that conclusion (Gould 1981/1996; Tucker 1994).

Bloomfield's science of language did not, in the manner of scientific racism, exploit data to confirm a researcher's prejudices. However, his notion of science also seems inadequate, but for a different reason. Bloomfield did not root the scientific nature of linguistics in its capacity to extend empirical observations into predictions that go beyond attested facts. This may not be surprising, granted Bloomfield's well-known adherence to behaviorism, which limits scientific inquiry to what can be observed and experienced. Bloomfield's "science of language" as articulated in these three documents seminal to the foundation of the LSA was definitely not the science of scientific racism. But neither Bloomfield nor scientific racism took possession of the full set of tools a scientific mindset makes available, which would include cycles of observation, inference-making, hypothesis-testing, and prediction, carried out in such a way as to admit creativity and imagination while scrupulously resisting any predetermined outcome.

5. Conclusion

Close examination of these three short texts provides a glimpse into the foundation of the LSA. We see evidence here of an initiative to draw American linguists more tightly together, and to insist on the scientific nature of their shared profession, in a context where at least some linguists faced external hostility. That evidence must, of course, be tested against a wider collection of texts, data, memoirs, and records of events, to get a full sense of the tenor of the early Linguistic Society of America.

References

doi Abberley, Will. 2011. "Race and Species Essentialism in Nineteenth-Century Philology". *Critical Quarterly* 53:4.45–60.

Anderson, Mark. 2019. *From Boas to Black Power*. Stanford, Calif.: Stanford University.

Barkan, Elazar. 1992. *The Retreat from Scientific Racism: Changing concepts of race in Britain and the United States between the World Wars*. Cambridge: Cambridge University.

doi Bernasconi, Robert. 2019. "A Most Dangerous Myth". *Angelaki* 24:2.92–103.

Blackhawk, Ned & Isaiah Lorado Wilner, eds. 2018. *Indigenous Visions: Rediscovering the world of Franz Boas*. New Haven, Conn.: Yale University.

Bloomfield, Leonard. 1925. "Why a Linguistic Society?" *Language* 1:1.1–5.

Bloomfield, Leonard. 1933. *Language*. New York: Henry Holt.

Bloomfield, Leonard. 1944. "Secondary and Tertiary Responses to Language". *Language* 20:2.45–55.

Bloomfield, Leonard. 1946. "Twenty-One Years of the Linguistic Society". *Language* 22:1.1–3.

"Call for the Organizational Meeting". 1925. *Language* 1:1.6–7.

Charity Hudley, Anne H., Christine Mallinson, Mary Bucholtz, Nelson Flores, Nicole Holliday, Elaine Chun & Arthur Spears. 2018. "Linguistics and Race: An interdisciplinary approach towards an LSA statement on race". *Proceedings of the Linguistic Society of America Salt Lake City, Utah, January 5–8, 2018* edited by Patrick Farrell, 3:8.1–14.

Charity Hudley, Anne H., Christine Mallinson & Mary Bucholtz. 2020. "Toward Racial Justice in Linguistics: Interdisciplinary insights into theorizing race in the discipline and diversifying the profession". *Language* 96:4.e200–e235; with commentaries and response by the authors, e236–e319.

Dallaire, Louise. 1984. *Edward Sapir's Correspondence: An alphabetical and chronological inventory, 1910–1925*. Ottawa: National Museums of Canada.

Falk, Julia. 2002. [Letter to the Editor]. *Language* 78:4.viii.

Goldsmith, John A. & Bernard Laks. 2019. *Battle in the Mind Fields*. Chicago: University of Chicago.

Gossett, Thomas. 1997. *Race: The history of an idea in America* (New ed.). New York: Oxford University. Original work published 1963.

Gould, Stephen Jay. 1981. *The Mismeasure of Man*. New York: W. W. Norton. Revised ed. 1996

Hall, Robert A. Jr. 1975. *Stormy Petrel in Linguistics*. Ithaca, New York: Spoken Language Services.

Haugen Einar, Martin Joos, J Milton Cowan, Archibald A. Hill, Thomas A. Sebeok, & Arthur S. Abramson. 1975, March. "Golden Reminiscences". *LSA Bulletin* 64.25–39.

Hymes, Dell & John Fought. 1981. *American Structuralism*. The Hague: Mouton.

Joos, Martin. 1986. *Notes on the Development of the Linguistic Society of America*. Ithaca, New York: Linguistica.

Krick, Robert E. L. 2003. *Staff Officers in Gray: A biographical register of the staff officers in the army of Northern Virginia*. Chapel Hill, North Carolina: University of North Carolina.

Lewis, Herbert S. 2001. "The Passion of Franz Boas". *American Anthropologist* 103:2.447–467.

Linguistic Society of America. 2019. *"LSA Statement on Race"*. Approved by the LSA Executive Committee May 2019. https://www.linguisticsociety.org/content/lsa-statement-race

Marckwardt, Albert H. 1964. "Opportunity and obligation". *Language* 30:4.26–37.

Messling, Markus. 2016. "Text and Determination: On racism in 19th century European philology". *Philological Encounters* 1:1–4.79–104.

Military Order of the Loyal Legion of the United States. 1916. "In Memoriam Lindley Coates Kent Major 109th U.S. Colored Troops". *Commandery of the State of Pennsylvania* 8.839. Philadelphia, Pennsylvania.

Murray, Stephen O. 1991. "The First Quarter Century of the Linguistic Society of America, 1924–1949". *Historiographia Linguistica* 18:1.1–48.

National Society of the Daughters of the American Revolution. 1914. *Lineage Book Vol. XXXIX* edited by Sarah Hall Johnston. Harrisburg, Pennsylvania: Telegraph Printing.

Nicholas, William E. 1972. "World War I and Academic Dissent in Texas". *Arizona and the West* 14:3.215–230.

"Proceedings of the Linguistic Society of America at the Organizational Meeting in New York, December 28, 1924". 1925. *Language* 1:1.8–13.

Selden, Steven. 1999. *Inheriting Shame: The story of eugenics and racism in America.* New York: Teachers College.

doi Snodgrass, Mary Ellen. 2008. *The Underground Railroad: An encyclopedia of people, places, and operations.* London: Taylor and Francis.

doi Stepan, Nancy. 1982. *The Idea of Race in Science: Great Britain 1800–1960.* London: Macmillan.

Stepan, Nancy Leys & Sander L. Gilman. 1991. "'Appropriating the Idioms of Science': The rejection of scientific racism". *Perspectives on Hegemony and Resistance* edited by Dominick LaCapra, 72–103. Ithaca, New York: Cornell University.

Stocking, George W., Jr. 1968. *Race, Culture, and Evolution: Essays in the history of anthropology.* New York: The Free Press.

doi Swiggers, Pierre. 1994. "'The Study of the Linguistic Sciences is at Present Greatly Neglected in this Country': The Linguistic Society of America in the making". *Orbis* 37.299–304.

Tucker, William H. 1994. *The Science and Politics of Racial Research.* Urbana, Ill.: University of Illinois.

doi Whitfield, Stephen J. 2010. "Franz Boas: The anthropologist as public intellectual". *Society* 47.430–438.

CHAPTER 14

Archival resources for the study of the historiography of American linguistics

Frederick J. Newmeyer
University of Washington | University of British Columbia | Simon Fraser University

The first part of this paper describes the content of several archives containing letters, documents, etc. which have relevance to the history of American linguistics, particularly from the 1940s to the 1980s. The second part shows how material from these archives has already helped to solve debates about linguistic historiography.

Keywords: archival resources for linguistics, Noam Chomsky, Charles Hockett, Roman Jakobson, Martin Joos, Linguistic Society of America

1. Introduction

This paper has two goals.[1] One is to describe the archives that exist for the study of the history of American linguistics from roughly the 1920s to the 1960s, that is, the period where structural linguistics was dominant (i.e. just before the advent of generative grammar). The other is to give a few examples of how material in these archives bears on debates in the historiography of linguistics. Section 2 presents the archives available to the researcher, while Section 3 indicates how some material in these archives is relevant to linguistic historiography. Section 4 is a brief conclusion.

2. Archives for the study of American linguistic historiography

A good place to start is at the extensive archive of the Linguistic Society of America (LSA) at the University of Missouri in Columbia, Missouri. It contains letters to and from the LSA, committee reports, (some) minutes from the LSA Executive

1. For a much more detailed account of the material in this paper, see Newmeyer (2022).

https://doi.org/10.1075/sihols.133.14new

Committee meetings, and editorial correspondence pertaining to the journal *Language*. There is very little material from before 1940 (even though the LSA was founded in 1924) and contains only sporadic material from later than the 1980s, given the ever more frequent use of (generally unsaved) email messages.

It is commonly agreed that the three pioneers of American linguistics in the early years of the twentieth century were Franz Boas (1848–1952), Edward Sapir (1884–1939), and Leonard Bloomfield (1887–1949). For Boas, there is a collection of letters and notes at the American Philosophical Society in (APS) Philadelphia. For Sapir, there is less. He worked in Ottawa, Canada between 1910 and 1925; his letters from that time are preserved at the National Museum there. Unfortunately, there is not much available after 1925, though his correspondence with A. L. Kroeber from 1905 to 1925 is available as a pdf. Material on Bloomfield is even harder to find. Some of his Amerindian notes are at the APS, but no other central location contains his correspondence, which appears to have been lost.

Now let us turn to some of the major figures in American linguistics. For Martin Joos (1907–1978), there is an extraordinary collection at the APS. It contains everything that one might wish to know pertaining to his editing of *Readings in Linguistics*, which was published in 1957, and about his defeat at the hands of Dwight Bolinger for the LSA Presidency in 1970. For Bernard Bloch (1907–1965), most of his letters are at the Yale University Library in New Haven, Connecticut. They contain lots of juicy interchanges with other leading figures in US linguistics, from Boas to Chomsky. Dwight Bolinger (1907–1992) was one of the leading critics of both structuralist and generativist approaches and was the first important American 'functional linguist'. Hundreds of his letters are stored at the Stanford University library, in Palo Alto, California. As for Roman Jakobson (1896–1982), the MIT library in Cambridge, Massachusetts contains dozens of his letters, dating from his arrival in the US in 1942 up to his correspondence the 1960s. Of special interest are his exchanges with Bloomfield, Harris, and Chomsky. Thomas Sebeok (1920–2011) was a Prague School-influenced linguist, and a major administrator of the LSA in the 1950s and 1960s. Hundreds of his letters fill dozens of cartons at the Indiana University library in Bloomington, Indiana. These letters complement beautifully the holdings in the LSA archives. Archibald Hill (1902–1992) was Secretary-Treasurer of the LSA in the 1950s. He left some letters to the University of Texas library, but unfortunately they are from only the 1970s and 1980s. Finding material from Charles Hockett (1916–2000) is not simple. He left many of his papers to the Smithsonian Institution in Washington, DC. They contain mainly field notes and correspondence related to his publications. Fortunately, most of the other archives I consulted are full of letters from Hockett. As far as Kenneth Pike (1912–2000) is concerned, copious letters of his are said to be preserved in the SIL International (Summer Institute of Linguistics) library in

Dallas, Texas. I have not had a chance to go there to inspect them, however. What about Noam Chomsky, who was born in 1928? He is leaving all of his correspondence to the MIT library. However, it will not be made available until five years after his death. Fortunately, all of his correspondence with Mouton Publishers is on file in Leiden, Netherlands as part of the Cornelis van Schooneveld collection and is available to the public.

3. The archives and debates about American linguistic historiography

As noted above, archival material can be used to help resolve debates about American linguistic historiography. We turn now to five examples.

3.1 Noam Chomsky and the publication of LSLT

Let us begin with the question of whether Chomsky tried to get *The Logical Structure of Linguistic Theory* (his 1955 manuscript) published. He has claimed on several occasions that it was rejected by MIT Press and that he did not submit it anywhere else (see for example Chomsky 1975: 3). That claim appears to be false. The following letter from Chomsky is on file at the van Schooneveld archive:

> Dear Cornelius,
> I was very pleased to hear that you would be interested in publishing my long manuscript. The situation with respect to it is as follows. I have a tentative agreement with North Holland to publish it, if it meets their length requirements (i.e., if it is shortened significantly), I don't feel ready to make a definite commitment as yet, since I am still not satisfied with the present form of the manuscript, and I feel that the exposition can be very much improved in places. I hope to spend most of the year reworking it, and, with luck, I may be finished in the spring. As I say, I don't feel that I can say anything more definite until I am a little clearer as to the final form of the manuscript. Perhaps I may contact you then, if you will still be interested. Sorry I missed you when you were here. Thanks for sending the review.
> Sincerely,
> Noam (Chomsky to van Schooneveld, 12 September 1957)

In other words, not one, but two publishers were interested in publishing Chomsky's manuscript.

3.2 Jakobson's welcome to the United States

Let us turn now to a frequently-heard claim, namely that the principal figures of American structuralism were opposed to Roman Jakobson's entry into the United States and wanted him to be sent back to Europe. To a significant degree, this claim is false, as the following quotes reveal:

> Boas to Bloomfield: 'I am very much disgusted but it seems quite impossible to find any position for Roman Jakobson.' (28 September 1942; Boas Archive)

> Zellig Harris to Jakobson: 'It is with great regret that I have to tell you that our plans for you here at the University [of Pennsylvania] have apparently come to nothing.' (2 August 1942; Jakobson Archive)

> Bloomfield to Jakobson: 'It is painful to have to tell you about the situation here [at Yale]; There is no possibility here of an appointment in Slavic languages.'
> (28 March 1944; Jakobson Archive)

Nevertheless, other American linguists of the period were fiercely anti-Jakobson. One of these was Charles Hockett, who wrote to Morris Halle on 22 February 1989, attempting to explain his shocking behaviour, where he and his colleagues played a little 'joke' on Jakobson:

> In after-hour bar sessions and evening get-togethers of our group, the resentment [against Jakobson and other émigré scholars] came to be concretized, some time early in 1943, in the form of a two-dollar bill club. Each 'member' had a two-dollar bill, on which all 'members' signed their names; the avowed 'purpose' was to pay for Jakobson's return to Europe on the first available cattle boat. I should not really have to add that all of this was intended purely for internal consumption. It was a metaphor designed as a basis for communion and mutual commiseration. Anyone in the group would have stood aghast at the notion of really delivering anyone into the clutches of the Nazis. That was so obvious to all of us that it never had to be said. I will not name 'members' of the club other than myself (most of the others are dead by now). [...] To the best of my belief, neither our 165 Broadway group nor anyone of those in or close to it was at any time in any position either to promote Jakobson's search for a decent academic appointment in this country or to stand in the way of such an appointment.
> (Hockett to Morris Halle, 22 February 1989; Sebeok Archive)

Thomas Sebeok was cc'ed on Hockett's letter to Halle. In a reply to Hockett, after dismissing the latter's outrage at various interpretations of forty-five-year-old events in the field, Sebeok concluded his letter by writing: 'Where was your moral indignation when you, in the uniform of the U. S. Army, signed John Kepke's notorious "two-dollar bill"?' (Sebeok to Hockett, 3 March 1989; Sebeok Archive).

3.3 Joos's *Readings in linguistics*

Our third example of how archival information can help inform historiographic research revolves around Martin Joos's book *Readings in Linguistics: The Development of Descriptive Linguistics in America since 1925* (Joos 1957). Joos's volume is the best-selling anthology in the history of American linguistics, and quite possibly world linguistics as well. It collected all of the major papers of American structuralism, in particular the extreme positivist wing, which included Bernard Bloch, Zellig Harris, and Charles Hockett. Most of all, it became famous for Joos's wildly empiricist Introduction to the book and comments in a similar vein after most of the chapters. The Joos and other archives document every step of the process by which the chapters in the *Readings* were chosen. At the beginning of the process, Joos intended the volume to be genuinely representative of the American descriptive linguistics of the epoch. However, archival material reveals that the prospective contents became narrower and narrower as Joos prepared the book. Those not in the hyper-positivist ingroup were almost completely shut out from the final version. Hockett ended up having seven of his articles published, while Kenneth Pike, who departed from the positivist mainstream in many ways, had none. Linguists not in the post-Bloomfieldian in group were outraged. As Pike wrote to Hockett years later:

> If I read you correctly, and I may not, your assertion is that times have changed radically, and that in the former generation all points of view found ready access to *Language*. This is false. Bloch, for example, rejected my *Intonation of American English*, even though in my presence Bloomfield urged him to publish it. Bloch rejected my *Tone Languages*. He also rejected my "Grammatical Prerequisites" – one item which was of some interest to the transformational grammarians. [...] [I]n the last generation you were on the 'inside' of the climate, and did not feel the freeze. Nor was it just one person – one editor – involved. Martin Joos in his preliminary letter suggesting persons whose materials should be enclosed in his 'readings' to describe 'the development of descriptive linguistics in America since 1925' listed a couple of my articles. Every one was rejected from the published version – because, he told me, people in the discipline objected. Yet in that very volume you have *seven* of your articles reprinted. This historical perspective is indeed hard on you – but it ought not be allowed to blind you. [...]
>
> (Pike to Hockett, 30 November 1982; LSA Archive)

3.4 The contested LSA presidential election of 1970

Our next archival-supported example also involves Martin Joos. The biggest crisis in the history of the LSA took place in 1970. The LSA's constitution allows for the 'official' candidate for an LSA office to be challenged. Dwight Bolinger in that year became the first challenger for the office of President. Bolinger defeated Joos easily. Everything that one might want to know about the challenged election is in the Bolinger Archive, the Joos Archive, and the LSA Archive. Why then was there a challenge and why did Bolinger win? What we learn from the archives is that the conflict had little to do with debates in the field per se, as both Joos and Bolinger were quite anti-generative. And it had little to do directly with a 'generation gap'. Joos and Bolinger were born the same year. Two factors led to Bolinger's victory. First, Joos by 1970 was viewed by many members as too mentally unstable to take on the presidency:

> There is considerable, even enthusiastic, approval of your candidacy for the Vice-Presidency of the LSA along the West Coast among the 'independent voters'. You certainly can count on MY vote! And I hope you not follow any pressure brought to bear on you (and designed to make you withdraw from the race) to influence your judgment. We need a <u>sound</u> Vice-President in 1971 and an equally sound President in 1972 – rather than a living corpse or a mummy! [...].
>
> (Yakov Malkiel to Bolinger, 3 November 1970; Bolinger Archive)

Secondly, Joos was viewed as a symbol of how linguistics used to be done. The archives show that both generative grammarians and Labovian variationists voted en masse for Bolinger, even though Bolinger was neither a generative grammarian or a variationist. A majority of LSA members took an 'anybody but Joos' position.

3.5 Charles Hockett's attempt to resign from the LSA

Our last example of the archives at work centres on Charles Hockett. No American structuralist took the advent of generative grammar harder than he did. Like many of his generation, he felt that the LSA had come under the control of Chomskyan linguists and wrote to Martin Joos on 26 June 1972: 'For about two years I have been tempted to resign my membership in the LSA, not to save money (since I am a life member) but just to avoid cluttering my shelves with absolute junk' (Joos Archive). A decade later he attempted to make good on his temptation, as we see in this letter to LSA Secretary-Treasurer Victoria Fromkin:

> Dear Victoria,
> I have read your letter of 9 November about the Fund for the Future of Linguistics. The problem of my proper comportment as a former president of the LSA has disturbed me for some time. I have finally been forced to the unhappy conclusion that my only appropriate action is to resign from the Society. This is my official letter of resignation.
> You are entitled to an explanation, as is Bill Bright [the editor of *Language*] and as are my fellow former presidents. They will therefore receive copies of this communication. [...] If the Society were today what is was at the beginning, I would joyfully work through it to insure the future of our branch of science. But even when I was president, two decades ago, things were changing, and now they have altered beyond recognition.

Hockett ended his letter by pointing to the inability of his best students from the 1970s to find employment in the field, obliquely blaming this circumstance on the idea that Chomskyan linguists now controlled the job market:

> [...] I find it extremely disheartening that my three best students, all trained during the 1970s [...] have had to turn to other activities to make a living. The academic positions they should be holding were already filled or controlled by third- and fourth-raters ignorant of our long tradition, individuals who could not reach up to tie the shoestrings of our giant predecessors to say nothing of climbing onto their shoulders, but who hewed to the party line and could neither tolerate nor understand brilliance shining from a different source. These top-quality students of mine were perhaps my most crucial contribution to the Future of Linguistics. It is not my responsibility if, for totally extraneous reasons, their contribution will never bear fruit. [...]
> Perhaps you can see from the foregoing that, from my point of view, the invitation in your letter is, in effect, a request that I lend moral and financial support to policies and practices directly antithetical to my own scientific and ethical principles. [...] Even my continued membership in the Society would constitute a degree of endorsement I would consider improper; hence my resignation.
> With great regret,
> Charles F. Hockett (Hockett to Fromkin, 15 November 1982, with cc's to past LSA presidents; Linguistic Society of America Archive)

Fromkin was terribly upset by Hockett's decision:

> Dear Charles,
> Your letter of November 15, 1982, made me more unhappy than any single event since my election as Secretary-Treasurer of the LSA. I think I once mentioned to you that your textbook was my introduction to linguistics, in my first course taught by Harry Hoijer. That book and that course changed my life [...]. I cannot of course argue with your perception of the present situation in our field, although I do not see it as you do. In fact, I see more 'eclecticism' today than when

> I entered the discipline, and greater breadth of subject matter, and more competition of theories. The leadership of the Society as represented by its officers and executive committee members during my tenure as Secretary-Treasurer would, I think, support this view.
> I have read Bill Bright's letter to you since he kindly sent me a copy. It seems to me he has stated the case for Language much better than I could. I would, however, suggest that Bill, as editor of the journal, has been meticulous in his struggle to publish what is good no matter what the theoretical background of the writer. [...]
> When I first read your letter I was going to simply write to you to say I was sorry you had reached a decision to resign from the Society. [...] whatever its weaknesses, it cannot be strengthened if the critics among us leave us to continue without them.
> Sincerely,
> Victoria A. Fromkin
> (Fromkin to Hockett, 30 November 1982; Linguistic Society of America Archive)

The LSA Archive contains several more messages to Hockett from leading LSA members, urging him to reconsider his decision.

In an aerogramme dated 7 January 1983, Hockett told his former student Robert Ladd that 'I have resigned my membership in the LSA because of its dreadful domination by TG fanatics'. What he must have not known at that moment was that LSA Associate Secretary John Hammer had just sent him the following letter:

> Dear Professor Hockett,
> [...] Your decision to resign from the LSA unfortunately presents certain administrative problems. [...] You have been a Life Member since 1952 [...] The LSA Constitution provides no mechanism for one to terminate one's life membership.
> (Hammer to Hockett, 4 January 1983; Linguistic Society of America Archive)

And, indeed, every LSA membership register from then on listed Hockett as a member. What is more, Hockett published four items in *Language* after his resignation attempt: two obituaries and three book reviews.

4. Conclusion

We have had a look at the major archives available for the study of American linguistic archives and how the material in these archives sheds light on ongoing debate about events in the history of American linguistics.

References

Chomsky, Noam. 1975. *The Logical Structure of Linguistic Theory*. Chicago: University of Chicago Press.

Joos, Martin, ed. 1957. *Readings in Linguistics: The Development of Descriptive Linguistics in America since 1925*. Washington: American Council of Learned Societies.

doi Newmeyer, Frederick J. 2022. *American Linguistics in Transition: From Post-Bloomfieldian Structuralism to Generative Grammar*. Oxford: Oxford University Press.

CHAPTER 15

Courses in general linguistics by Roman Jakobson at the École Libre des Hautes Études

Pierre-Yves Testenoire
Sorbonne Université

This paper focuses on Roman Jakobson's general linguistics lectures in New York during World War II. These courses, that Claude Lévi-Strauss attended, have played a major role in the spreading of post-war "generalized structuralism". However, they only came to be known by the later testimonies of the two scholars and partial editions from the 1970s and 1980s. Therefore, this study aims at showing that taking into account unpublished sources can bring something new to our knowledge of these teachings.

After the description of the institutional context of the École Libre des Hautes Études that housed this teaching, the list of Roman Jakobson's general linguistics classes is retraced and put in perspective with the unpublished notes that have been kept in his archives. Taking into account the preparatory manuscripts of these classes sheds light on the logic that governs Jakobson's teaching at the École Libre, conceived as a critical reinterpretation of the *Course in General Linguistics*.

Keywords: Roman Jakobson, Claude Lévi-Strauss, structuralism, École Libre des Hautes Études, archives, Ferdinand de Saussure

1. Introduction

Scholars from different backgrounds, driven on the roads of exile, met at the École Libre des Hautes Études (lit. 'Free School for Advanced Studies') in New York from 1942 to 1945. This step marks a milestone in the constitution of the post-war generalized structuralism. The teachings of Roman Jakobson (1896–1982) and their reception by Claude Lévi-Strauss (1908–2009) play a crucial role in this moment of "crystallization of structuralism" (Loyer et Maniglier 2018). However, the content of these courses is only known through the testimony of the protago-

https://doi.org/10.1075/sihols.133.15tes

nists and through two texts that were later revised, namely "Six lectures on Sound and Meaning" (1942), whose revised version has been published in 1976, and the paper entitled "La théorie saussurienne en retrospection" (lit. "The Saussurean Theory in retrospection") published posthumously in 1984. The objective of this paper is to further describe the content of these lectures relying on unpublished sources in addition to the selected and retrospectively reedited documents.

After focusing on the institutional context of the École Libre, the syllabus of the classes and seminars Roman Jakobson taught at the École Libre will be retraced from its archives as well as from the Roman Jakobson Papers kept at the Massachusetts Institute of Technology (MIT). Jakobson's handwritten notes will shed light on the logic governing his teachings. In New York, they are characterized by a structured program based on the rereading of the *Course in General Linguistics* and a reinterpretation of three of its dualities.

2. The institutional context: L'École Libre des Hautes Études

The École Libre des Hautes Études is a unique institution in the academic landscape of the United States insofar as it is a French language advanced education institution managed by Belgian and French scholars on American soil. Its very existence from 1942 to 1946 is linked to the exceptional circumstances fostered by the war. Created during the Autumn of 1941, the École Libre opened on February 14th, 1942, in the premises of the New School for Social Research, thanks to the Rockefeller Foundation financial support.[1]

In the 1930s, the Rockefeller Foundation had funded an exile and installation program for German scholars who were persecuted by Nazism. After the French debacle, a similar operation is repeated, the *Emergency Program for European Scholars*. It consists in the creation of about one hundred grants intended for threatened European scholars. The foundation relies on a New York progressive institution, the New School for Social Research. Its director, Alvin Johnson (1874–1971), is coordinating the rescue operation and is committed to creating chairs for the exiled. Between the Summer of 1940 and the winter of 1941, about 50 European scholars, among which 30 French ones, thus receive an invitation to teach at the New School and arrive in the United States. The idea of creating a French speaking institution emerges during the Autumn of 1941 among these

1. About the history of the École Libre des Hautes Études see Rutkoff & Scott (1983), Zolberg & Callamard (1998), Chaubet & Loyer (2000), Duranton-Crabol (2000), Loyer (2007 [2005]), as well as Testenoire (2022), a part of which has been reedited in this paper.

teachers assigned to the New School. Alvin Johnson is seduced by the idea and imposes it on the Rockefeller Foundation.[2]

The École Libre is really devised by its proponents as the importation of a Franco-Belgian university on American soil. Beside the fundings from the Rockefeller Foundation, it receives grants from the National French Committee and the Belgian government, which has found refuge in London. It is also supported by the Polish, Czechoslovakian, and Dutch governments in exile. The diplomas delivered by the École Libre are recognized by the French National Committee as "full French titles" (Decree of February 9th, 1942). Its teachings and its publications are done exclusively in French. Finally, the School benefits from a total independence even though it is housed in the New School premises. It is managed by French and Belgian scholars, who have a budget of their own and who determine the content of the teachings as well as the modalities of its pedagogical organization.

"First university of Free France",[3] the École Libre is also an instrument of Gaullist policy. It plays the role of a soft power for the general public in New York but also for the American administration, hostile to de Gaulle. It is an integral part of the strategy developed by Free France to discredit Vichy, recognized by the State Department until November 1942, and to gain legitimacy with the Roosevelt administration. The politic dimension of the school can be noticed as soon as the day of inauguration since a message from de Gaulle is read out. It can also be perceived through the composition of the executive board as several members, among which Alexandre Koyré (1892–1964) and Raoul Aglion (1904–2004), have been sent from London to defend the interests of Free France. The publications of the school reflect this political orientation, especially its journal *Renaissance* with its pronounced Gaullist undertone.[4]

The hybrid nature of the institution – both scientific and political – generates internal tensions. The proponents of an academic neutrality, guaranteed by the director of the school, Jacques Maritain, face those who openly support Gaullism, foremost among them Koyré and Lévi-Strauss who take turns as Secretary-General. The tension aggravates from 1943 on along with the perspective of an end to the war. Some teachers wish to extend the school over time, sometimes applying for naturalization in the US, whereas Gaullists consider that the school mission is ending with the war. The French government fulfils the latters' demand by

2. About the detailed circumstances of the creation of the École Libre, see Zolberg & Callamard (1998: 928–938).

3. *Renaissance* 2–3 (1944–1945: 2).

4. The *Renaissance* Journal has known two deliveries – a first in 1943 and a double issue for 1944 and 1945 published in 1945.

cutting subsidies in 1946. The École Libre thus loses its autonomy from the New School and survives but a few years as a French language school, far from its primary mission.

The École Libre is emulating the functioning of three French higher education institutions.

> In accordance with the tradition of the Collège de France, the École des Hautes Études in Paris and the former European universities, so fortunately taken over by the universities of the New World, it [the École Libre] wanted to open its doors to everyone who wants to take part in an undertaking whose essential object is to help maintain, in the intellectual sphere, the values defended by the United Nations – from which Fighting France is inseparable. ("Avertissement", *Renaissance* 1(1), January-March 1943: 7) [Translation]

The École Libre borrows a number of features which are distinctive of the three institutions. The link with the École Pratique des Hautes Études does not only rely on the institutional designation of the school.[5] The École Libre borrows from its Parisian model several aspects concerning its pedagogical and administrative management, such as the organization of seminars or the fact that the teachers, just as in the EPHE, are not required to have the country citizenship. As the University of Paris, the École Libre is organized into three departments (Literature, Law, and Sciences), even though the Science department, less developed than the other ones will only become a full department from 1942–43 on. The school also takes up the distinction between non-public classes intended for enrolled students and open classes, free, open to all. Moreover, it creates academic institutions and associated study centres (such as the Institute of Oriental and Slavic Philology and History, the Institute for Comparative Law Studies, etc.) inspired, for example, by the Phonetics Institute associated with the Sorbonne. Finally, along with the Collège de France, the École Libre shares a mission of popularization of French science and culture. As few students have registered to pass diplomas recognized as "full French titles" by the French National Committee, this role in the diffusion of science to the general educated public becomes the school primary mission. The École Libre met a rapid success, proportional to the evolution of the student population. The number of students jumped from 300 at the opening of the school to a thousand after a few months.[6]

5. The designation as a "school" soon prevails as the title of "university" was rejected both by the American authorities and by the scholars of the École Libre. The adjective "libre" [free] presents the advantage linked to its polysemy, as Zolberg & Callamard (1998: 928–933) point out. Besides its affiliation to the "France Libre" [Free France], it refers to Catholic teaching for the French and to the "free inquiry" principle of the Free University of Brussels for the Belgians.

3. Jakobson's teachings at the École Libre

Roman Jakobson arrives in New York on June 4th, 1941. He and his wife left Sweden where they had fled Nazi invasions. Jakobson is offered to teach linguistics at the École Libre upon its creation. During the first year he is the only linguistics teacher. The following years, other linguistics classes from the college of literature aggregate to his own, namely Giuliano Bonfante (1904–2005) in comparative linguistics, Wolf Leslau (1906–2006) on semitic languages, Henri Muller (1879–1959) on the history of the French language and André Spire (1868–1966) on versification.[7]

In the 1943 edition of the *Who's Who*, Jakobson is mentioned as "Professor of General Linguistics and Czechoslovakian Philology" at the École Libre. His teachings correspond to the designation as the classes he is teaching can be grouped into three categories:

1. General linguistics classes in the College of Literature;
2. Slavic linguistics and philology classes in the Institute of Oriental and Slavic Philology and History;
3. Classes and seminars in collaboration.

The present paper focuses on general linguistics classes. Different sources kept either in the New School Institutional Collections or in Jakobson's private archives provide information on the linguist's activities at the École Libre. Among these sources, three kinds of documents can be identified.

1. The documents published by the New School (its semi-annual *Curricula* and the *New School Bulletin* which draws up the weekly list of conferences and events organized within the institution);
2. The official documents edited by the École Libre, such as the *Annual Booklets* and the monthly "courses lists" providing a detailed schedule of the lectures;
3. The grey literature kept in Jakobson's private archives (courses lists, curriculum vitae, reports, and research projects, etc.).

6. Regarding the number of students during the first year, the journal of the school provides the following figures: February 1942, 326; March 1942, 790; April 1942, 850; May 1942, 928; first term 1943, 851 ("Chronique de l'École Libre des Hautes Études" [Chronicle of the École libre des Hautes Études], *Renaissance* 1:1, January-March 1943: 168).

7. For more details on these teachings and on the process of recognition of linguistics as an official discipline at the École Libre, see Testenoire (2022).

Relying on these sources, the list of Jakobson's general linguistics lectures in the Literature Department of the École Libre can be retraced. He gives two courses each semester, a public one, and a closed one:

> May-June 1942: On Sound and Meaning (Public lecture).
> May-June 1942: General Linguistics (Bachelor lecture. Non-public lecture).
> 1942–1943, 1st term: Phonology (Non-public lecture).
> 1942–1943, 1st term: Changes in Language (Public lecture).
> 1942–1943, 2nd term: Phonology (Non-public lecture).
> 1942–1943, 2nd term: The Affinity and the Kinship of Languages (Public lecture).
> 1943–1944, 1st term: General Linguistics (Non-public lecture).
> 1943–1944, 1st term: The Russian Language, Mirror, and Culture Vehicle (Public lecture).
> 1943–1944, 2nd term: General Linguistics (Bachelor lecture. Non-public lecture).
> 1944–1945, 1st term: Language disorders (Public lecture).
> 1944–1945, 1st term: Grammatical Structure of the Russian Language Compared with the French and the English Languages (Bachelor lecture).
> 1944–1945, 1st term: The Russian Revolution seen by a linguist (Public lecture).
> 1944–1945, 2nd term: Grammatical Structure of the Russian Language Compared with the French and the English Languages (Bachelor lecture).
> 1944–1945, 2nd term: Poetic Rhythm. Issues in General and comparative linguistics (Public lecture).
> 1945–1946, 1st term: Structure of the Verb in Russian, French and English: Contrastive Analysis (Public lecture).
> 1945–1946, 2nd term: Structure of the Verb in Russian, French and English: Contrastive Analysis (Public lecture).
> 1946–1947, 1st term: On Sound and Meaning. Introduction to General Linguistics (Public lecture).
> 1946–1947, 2nd term: The contribution of French linguistics to World Science (Public lecture).
> 1947–1948: Infant Language (Public lecture).
> 1947–1948: Language disorders (Public lecture). [Translation]

To these regular lectures, must be added several courses in general linguistics given with Lévi-Strauss, which both scholars evoked retrospectively with much emphasis.[8]

Lectures and seminars, sometimes bearing on interdisciplinary themes, are set up in associated research institutions, at an early stage of the school's existence, that is during its first years. For two years (1942–44), the Byzantinist Henri

8. See Jacob *et al.* (2018 [1968]); Lévi-Strauss (2018 [1971]), (1976), (1985); Lévi-Strauss & Eribon (1990 [1988]: 61–65); Jakobson (1972: 33 ff.), (1972–1974), (2018 [1985]); Georgin & Georgin (1978: 17).

Grégoire (1881–1964) thus organizes an interdisciplinary seminar on the Russian Epic poem *The Tale of Igor's Campaign* at the Institute of Oriental and Slavic Philology and History. It gathers philologists (Henri Grégoire, Waclaw Lednicki 1891–1967), linguists (Roman Jakobson), philosophers (Alexandre Koyré) and historians (Marc Szeftel (1902–1985) and George Vernadsky (1887–1973). This collaboration led to the publication of a critical edition of this poem (Grégoire, Jakobson & Szeftel 1948).[9] Classes, seminars, or lecture series involving Jakobson are organized every year at the Institute of Oriental and Slavic Philology and History. Jakobson and Lévi-Strauss base their common courses on this model. Their collaboration takes the form of teachings on three occasions only. In the Autumn of 1942, both scholars create "an ethnography and linguistics department" within the Institute of Sociology where a series of lectures is organized for only one year:

> 1942–43: "The Place of Primitive Peoples in the Post-War World" (R. Jakobson & C. Lévi-Strauss).[10]

Their collaboration resumes in 1945 at the College of Literature where they organize two seminars along with Raymond de Saussure, the linguist's son, Professor in psychology at the École Libre.[11]

> 1945–46, 1st term: Structure of the Popular Institutions (Language, culture, folklore). (R. Jakobson & C. Lévi-Strauss)
> 1945–46, 2nd term: Principles of Structural Analysis. (R. Jakobson, C. Lévi-Strauss, & R. de Saussure)

These two common seminars are the only teachings Lévi-Strauss maintained for the last year he spent at the school. He resigns his functions as Secretary-General

9. *The Tale of Igor's Campaign* is a Russian epic poem, known through a manuscript discovered in the 18th century. Its authenticity was contested as soon as the 19th century and later again by André Mazon in an important study (Mazon 1940). This argument was refuted by the 1948 critical edition that was published in the proceedings of the École Libre seminar. On this discussion, see Bossuat (1948), Roudet (2011), as well as Jakobson and Benveniste's correspondence (Laplantine & Testenoire 2021: 146–149).

10. For the detailed syllabus of this class, see Testenoire (2022: 171). The addressed issues echo the political ones that worry Lévi-Strauss and that he develops in his work at that time, particularly in "The Theory of Power in a Primitive Society" and in "The Foreign Policy of a Primitive Society" (Lévi-Strauss 2019 [1944] and [1949]). See also Vincent Debaene's foreword to the edition of these texts, particularly Lévi-Strauss (2019: 36–43).

11. On the relationship between Jakobson and Raymond de Saussure, see the edition of their correspondence (Jakobson & Saussure 2018).

on December 3rd, 1945, in a general climate of hostility.[12] The introduction of the notion of "structure" coincides with its growing importance in the titles of Jakobson's courses: "Grammatical Structure of the Russian Language Compared with the French and the English Languages" (1944–45), "Structure of the Verb in Russian, French and English: Contrastive Analysis" (1945–46). It also coincides with the publication of the first issue of the *Word* Journal, in which Lévi-Strauss's papers "Structural Analysis in Linguistics and Anthropology" as well as Cassirer's "Structuralism in Modern Linguistics" take the shape of a manifesto. The 1945–46 common seminars are the outcome of informal collaborations between Jakobson and Lévi-Strauss who used to attend each other's classes from 1942 on and to extend the discussions in a "nearby bistro" after the sessions.[13]

4. The contribution of Roman Jakobson's archives

Roman Jakobson's archives are housed in the Department of Distinctive Collections of the Library of the Massachusetts Institute of Technology in Cambridge. The records are considerable as the four cubic metres of documents are currently distributed into 137 listed and monitored archive boxes. To these must be added about fifteen boxes, collected more recently, and not catalogued yet.[14] The stored documents comprise a variety of items such as manuscripts, typescripts, prints, press clippings, passports, photographs, film reels, etc. They cover a timespan from the 1880s to the mid-1980s. They encompass the linguist's whole life even though the American period of Jakobson's life is better documented due to the destruction of part of his archives when he fled from Czechoslovakia.[15]

12. On Lévi-Strauss's role in the closure of the École Libre and the circumstances surrounding his departure, see Mehlman (2005 [2000]: 223–229).

13. See Lévi-Strauss (2018 [1971]: 399), Jakobson (1972–1974), Sebeok (1977: 414). The correspondence between the two scholars (Jakobson & Lévi-Strauss 2018, completed by Testenoire 2019) is a testimony to the extension of this intellectual collaboration, even after Lévi-Strauss came back in France.

14. The catalogue of these holdings is available at: https://archivesspace.mit.edu/repositories/2/resources/633. For a general presentation of these archives, see D'Ottavi (2018).

15. In the foreword to the edition of Trubetzkoy's letters, Jakobson explains the circumstances surrounding the large destruction of his pre-war archives: "When, warned by the urgent call of a well-informed friend, I abandoned Brno on the eve of March 15, 1939, my archives were hastily reduced to sixteen pailfuls of ashes, but the bundle of Trubetzkoyana, together with a slender part of my own drafts and notes, were squeezed into a capacious Czech briefcase and wandered with me." (Trubetzkoy 1975: vi)

The New York years (1941–49) are represented by official documents, grey literature, correspondence, and manuscripts of sometimes unpublished works, among which can be identified several notes of courses given at the École Libre. Among the latter, can be recognized five preserved general linguistics classes which were taught at the Literature Faculty:

- *Le son et le sens des mots* ["On Sound and Meaning"] (May-June 1942)[16]
- *Linguistique générale* ["General Linguistics"] (May-June 1942)[17]
- *Phonologie* ["Phonology"] (October-December 1942)[18]
- *Les Changements de la langue* ["Changes in Language"] (January 1943)[19]
- *L'Affinité et la parenté des langues* ["The Affinity and the Kinship of Languages"] (May 1943)[20]

It is no coincidence that the preserved notes match the classes Jakobson mentions in the 1976 edition of the "Six lectures on Sound and Meaning":

> L'École Libre des Hautes Études (the Free School of Advanced Studies) was founded in New York at the beginning of 1942 by French and Belgian scientists in exile. It immediately offered a Professorship in General Linguistics to Roman Jakobson, who inaugurated the first term with six lectures 'On Sound and Meaning', together with a course on the linguistics of Ferdinand de Saussure. There followed, during the 1942–3 academic year, two courses devoted respectively to 'Changes in Language' and to 'The Affinity and the Kinship of Languages', not to mention fifteen lectures given each semester on 'Phonology'.
> These courses were followed by certain of the School's Professors – Henri Gregoire, Jacques Hadamard and Claude Levi-Strauss – and by linguists such as J. Mattoso Camara, Paul L. Garvin, Charles F. Hockett, Henry M. Hoenigswald and Thomas A. Sebeok. Roman Jakobson gave at the same time, at the institute of Oriental and Slavic Philology and History, attached to the School, a course on 'Czech Poetry of the 9th to the 15th Centuries'. (Jakobson 1978 [1976]: ix)

The foreword also explains the reason why only the notes from the first years of the École Libre have been preserved: "Because he was not then used to delivering lectures in French Jakobson prepared a draft of his 'Six Lectures on Sound and Meaning' and used this draft as the basis for a more informal oral presentation." *(ibid).* In an interview with *Le Monde*, Jakobson insists on the exceptional nature, "almost unique" for him of this practice:

---

16. Roman Jakobson Papers, MC 72, Box 24, Folders 27–30.
17. Roman Jakobson Papers, MC 72, Box 28, Folders 129–133.
18. Roman Jakobson Papers, MC 72, Box 11, Folders 35–36.
19. Roman Jakobson Papers, MC 72, Box 32, folder 10–12.
20. Roman Jakobson Papers, MC 72, Box 32, folder 13–14.

> If this text is available, it is because I was quite embarrassed at that time that I was not used anymore to delivering lectures in French. Thus, something almost unique in my life happened. Instead of simply delivering my lecture, I have written down my speech for the first time. (Jakobson 1976a: 24)

Therefore, breaking away with his working habits, he prepared almost complete drafts for his two 1942 lectures. In 1943, the situation has already evolved. To the fully drafted first pages of the lecture on "Changes in Language" progressively succeed course notes made up of scattered comments. Finally, during the following term, Jakobson seems confident enough to deliver the whole lecture "The Affinity and the Kinship of Languages" (May 1943) in French, according to his habit, with but the support of a few brief notes from which he reconstructs his speech.

The exceptional circumstances and the necessity to teach in French explain that the 1942 lectures have been entirely drafted as well as preserved. Jakobson did not keep all his course notes. However, he made an exception for the 1942–43 notes precisely because the drafts could be used for a further publication. The idea to publish the École Libre's classes arises quite soon. It can be traced back to the 1960s when Jakobson reworks several notes. The "Six lectures on Sound and Meaning" published by the Éditions de Minuit in 1976 is the only publication that comes to fruition during Jakobson's lifetime. Jakobson also reworks his course notes on "General Linguistics" under the new title "The Saussurean theory in retrospection" but fails to publish it. After his death Linda Waugh publishes the first part of this lecture, which is entirely penned, leaving aside the "rather incomplete and sketchy notes" of the second part "about the linguistic sign" (Waugh in Jakobson 1984: 157).

To sum up, besides the course notes on "Sound and Meaning" whose publication was assured by Jakobson himself, his archives give an access to four more general linguistics lectures which have been preserved, namely "General Linguistics" (May-June 1942) from which only one part was published posthumously by Linda Waugh, as well as "Phonology" (October-December 1942), "Changes in Language" (January 1943) and "The Affinity and the Kinship of Languages" (May 1943), which constitute entirely new material. We are currently preparing a critical edition of these four lectures.

5. A *Course in general linguistics* critical reading programme

It seems Jakobson was totally free concerning his teaching syllabus at the École Libre. However, one is bound to remark, on the one hand, the retrospective logic that emanates from his general linguistics courses and, on the second hand, the central place devoted to Saussure and his *Course in General Linguistics.* The syllabus follows a coherent progression. Each lecture, far from repeating one another, relies on the previous one to tackle a different issue in general linguistics.

In this structured syllabus, Saussure is given a central position, so much so that the first classes at the École Libre can be considered as a series of classes devoted to the critical rereading of the *Course in General Linguistics.* Jakobson offers a critical examination of the three main Saussurean dualities tackled one after the other:

- "On Sound and Meaning" (1942) explores the *significant/signifié* relationship.
- "General Linguistics" (1942) is a detailed discussion of the *langue/parole* dichotomy.
- "Changes in Language" (1943) is devoted to the *synchronie/diachronie* distinction.

In each of these classes, Jakobson describes and more importantly criticizes these three main dualities in accordance with the ideas developed by the Prague Linguistic Circle. In the three classes, his discussion is conducted in three steps.

Jakobson starts by presenting the problematic of his class, or as he calls it the "positivist" or "atomist" doxa of the linguists of the end of the 19th century. He develops the sound/meaning relationship in the first class, the question of the freedom of the subject in the language in the second class, and the question of linguistic changes in the third one. In a second step, he presents the Saussurean dualities (*signifiant/signifié*; *langue/parole*; *synchronie/diachronie*) that he analyses as "oppositions" or "antinomies". He introduces them as important dichotomies that have helped clarify the way problems are addressed but these are steps he describes as still borrowed from the "Neogrammarians' positivism". These judgements meet around the definition of the object of linguistics:

> *Tout en combattant la prédominance de l'historicisme dans la linguistique orthodoxe du XIXe siècle de Saussure succombe dans ce cas (comme dans certains autres) à la tradition combattue.*[21]

21. "While fighting the prevalence of historicism in the orthodox 19th century linguistics, Saussure yields in this case (as in some others) to the tradition he fights." ("General Linguistics": Roman Jakobson Papers, MC 72, Box 28, Folder 129, p. 15).

They concern the definition of *parole*:

> *En définissant la parole de cette façon, Saussure se trouve dans l'impasse de la pensée rigoureusement individualiste dénotant la fin du siècle, mais d'autre part le maître lui-même s'écarte à maintes reprises de ce principe fondamental emprunté à la tradition néogrammairienne.*[22]

They also converge on the concept of synchrony:

> *Comme nous l'avons souligné tout à l'heure, le Cours de Saussure se trouve situé à la limite de deux époques. En parlant de la linguistique de son temps, il nous dit que depuis qu'elle existe, « elle s'est absorbée toute entière dans la diachronie ». Et c'est également la linguistique diachronique qui pendant des longues dizaines d'années a absorbé les recherches de Saussure. C'est bien caractéristique qu'en jetant au commencement de son cours un coup d'œil sur l'histoire de la linguistique, Saussure répète encore l'opinion traditionnelle.*[23]

Finally, a last step is devoted to the overcoming of these "antinomies" by a synthesis movement. Jakobson analyses the Saussurean dualities as the accumulation of improperly assimilated oppositions. The langue/parole pair would imply the social/individual and potential value/actual value oppositions. The synchronie/diachronie pair would cover the simultaneity/successivity and static/dynamic oppositions. Jakobson aims at subverting the pairing of these oppositions by asserting the social aspect of the parole and by defending the idea of a "dynamic synchrony". The outcome he reaches is presented as a radical break with what he poses as the traditional approach. This is made evident by the last sentence taken from the notes of the "Changes in Language" lecture devoted to linguistic changes: "*Vous voyez que dans ce point essentiel comme dans tant d'autres l'attitude des recherches actuelles est carrément opposée à celle de la linguistique classique.*[24]"

22. "In defining the *parole* in such a way, Saussure finds himself in the dead end of the rigorously individualist thought correlated with the practises of the end of the century. On the other hand, the master himself distances himself on several occasions from this fundamental principle borrowed from the neogrammarian tradition."("General Linguistics": Roman Jakobson Papers, MC 72, Box 28, Folder 130, p. 49–50).

23. "As we have pointed out earlier, Saussure's *Course* is situated at the limit of two eras. Talking about the linguistics of his time, he tells us that since it exists "it totally sank in the diachrony". And it is also diachronical linguistics that has swallowed Saussure's research for many long decades. And it is really typical that Saussure, starting his lecture, had a look at the history of linguistics, repeating again the traditional approach."("Changes in Language": Roman Jakobson Papers, MC 72, Box 32, Folder 10, p. 10).

24. "You can see that on that essential point as on many others, the position of the current research is outright opposed to the classical linguistics one." ("Changes in Language": Roman Jakobson Papers, MC 72, Box 32, Folder 12, p. 120).

In Jakobson's demonstration, the *Course in General Linguistics* is clearly a step within a dialectical movement, a transitory moment of linguistic thought.

With the fourth lecture "The Affinity and the Kinship of Languages" (May 1943) Jakobson departs from the critical study of the *Course in General Linguistics* for a discussion of comparative grammar methods. Jakobson tackles questions linked to what he calls "the study of the kinship of languages" and makes a plea for the consideration of languages "affinities", in keeping with his work during the inter-war period dealing with the "Sprachbund" (lit. "language federation").[25]

Whereas the first two lectures were partially known, the lectures entitled "Phonology", "Changes in Language" and "The Affinity and the Kinship of Languages" were never published. Yet, these last two lectures entirely deal with the question of languages through time, which is one of the main topics studied by the Prague Linguistic Circle. They contradict the still circulating idea, that structural linguistics would be a negation of history or diachrony. Among the lectures Lévi-Strauss attended, at least two of them directly concern the questions of linguistic changes. The summary of the arguments of each lecture suffices to illustrate how careful Jakobson was when he developed this course, which was organized as a preparatory class to the major questions of general linguistics. The ideas presented in each class are not new, they take up elements developed in Jakobson's inter-war work. Joseph (1989) showed that the lectures on "On Sound and Meaning" refer to the content of the talk "Zur Struktur des Phonems" given at the Copenhagen Linguistic Circle on May 25th, 1939. The issues discussed in "Changes in Language" had already been addressed in former works (Jakobson 1928a, 1928b, 1929, and 1931a). The situation is similar for "The Affinity and the Kinship of Languages" which follows the structure of the paper "On the Theory of Phonological Affinities between Languages" presented during the Fourth International Congress of Linguists in Copenhagen (Jakobson 1938). It refers to even older works (Jakobson 1931b, 1931c, and 1931d). The course notes not only develop ideas that are handled more synthetically in scientific papers, but they shed a new light on them. The arguments are exemplified by more numerous illustrations, more straightforward formulation, and more striking metaphors than in the published texts. The course notes are especially richer with bibliographical references than Jakobson's publications. They are a privileged access to the sources of his work.

25. On Jakobson's perspective on this notion, see Schaller (1997), Sériot (1999) and Tchougounnikov (2006).

6. Conclusions

In conclusion, the question remains: why did Jakobson devote his early lectures at the École Libre to a critical analysis of the *Course in General Linguistics*? If Saussure was obviously a very important reference for Jakobson since the beginning of the 1920s, the latter had never devoted a whole class or text to the analysis of the principles of the *Course in General Linguistics*. Why did he do so when he arrived in New York in 1942? Julia Falk (1995) claimed that Jakobson had decided to devote his class to Saussure because his treatment of infant language, then his current concern, was not well received in the United States. The idea that it would amount to a "more or less by default" choice (Falk 1995: 348) is contradicted by the coherence of the syllabus of the classes at the École Libre.

A first factor that can account for this choice lies in the target audience of the lectures. At the École Libre, Jakobson is delivering his lectures in French, and they are intended for French speakers. This can explain his choice to present what he considered as the most important linguistic work published in French in the last 30 years. It was even more relevant if it was unknown to his audience.

Moreover, choosing the *Course in General Linguistics* is embedded into a legitimation strategy. In his writings and interviews, Jakobson insists a lot on the title of his chair at the École Libre, namely "General Linguistics". The title is clearly rare. In all the universities where he had been teaching so far, the titles of his positions had been more specific such as "Russian Philology and Old Czech Literature" in Brno, Scandinavia or "Czechoslovak Studies" at Columbia University (New York City). There is obviously a desire from Jakobson to position his general linguistics teachings as a mirror to Saussure's general linguistics classes. To analyse Saussure's *Course* – and to throw some of it back in the past – allows Jakobson to rise to his level and to turn his own lectures in equally important inaugural classes. In a performative perspective, it is also a way to record the overcoming of the phase of transition embodied by the *Course*, position he tries to defend through his own lessons.

Within this strategy, the polemic dimension of the argumentation developed in his courses must also be highlighted. The whole interpretation of the *Course in General Linguistics* developed by Jakobson stands indeed in opposition with Charles Bally's and Albert Sechehaye's. In his teachings at the École Libre, Jakobson constantly criticizes Bally's and Sechehaye's Saussurism, in particular on the questions of the "sign", the "parole", and of the "affectivity", themes on which the Genevans put a great emphasis. This criticism, generally implicit, is in line with Jakobson's desire to enforce his own critical interpretation of the *Course* against what he calls the Genevans' "orthodox" position. However, this polemic dimension has gone unnoticed by a listener like Lévi-Strauss who was not aware of the debates and therefore minimized the Jakobsonian intermediary in the presentation of Saussure's ideas.

Jakobson's general linguistics classes at the École Libre eventually present twofold interests, concerning Roman Jakobson's own life as well as the history of 20th century Saussurism. First, these courses correspond to a pivotal moment in Jakobson's biography. They form a transition between the end of his European era and the beginning of the American one. The context of the École Libre brings together The Old and the New World. On a theoretical point of view, the classes at the École Libre correspond for Jakobson to "the totality of his work in Europe in the 1920s and 1930s" (Jakobson 1976b: 471) and they show his adaptation to a new, largely hostile, academic context. In Jakobson's life, teaching in New York closes a first stage of confrontation with the Saussurean legacy. The second phase will be inaugurated in the mid-1960s with the discovery of Saussure's autograph texts. Jakobson's unpublished course notes also shed light on new references – such as Boas, Sapir, Hoijer, and Bloomfield – that appear alongside more classical references dating back to the Prague era – such as Saussure, Trubetzkoy, and Bühler. These new references reflect the change of direction of Jakobson's research in contact with the American context. Furthermore, the general linguistics classes at the École Libre are consistent with a key moment in the transmission of structural linguistics' achievements. Its reception by Lévi-Strauss paves the way for post-war generalized structuralism. This moment of transmission has largely been mystified retrospectively by both linguists, in several texts and interviews, which have had a lasting influence on the historiography. The description of what really has been transmitted at the École Libre des Hautes Études can be accessed through the content of these lessons, through the preserved course notes.

References

Archives

Massachusetts Institute of Technology, Institute Archives and Special Collections. *Roman Jakobson Papers*. MC 72.

Sources imprimées

1942–1947. *Livrets de l'École libre des hautes études.*

1943–1945. *Renaissance* 1–3.

Bossuat, Robert. 1948. "Compte rendu de *La Geste du prince Igor, épopée russe du XIIe siècle*". *Bibliothèque de l'École des Chartes* 107:1.123–124.

Cassirer, Ernst. 1945. "Structuralism in Modern Linguistics". *Word* 1:2.99–120.

Chaubet, François & Emmanuelle Loyer. 2000. "L'École libre des hautes études de New York : exil et résistance intellectuelle (1942–1946)". *Revue historique* 616.939–972.

Duranton-Crabol, Anne-Marie. 2000. "Les intellectuels français en exil aux États-Unis pendant la Seconde Guerre mondiale : aller et retour". *Matériaux pour l'histoire de notre temps* 60.41–47.

D'Ottavi, Giuseppe. 2018. "Les 'Roman Jakobson Papers' au Massachusetts Institute of Technology". *Genesis* 47.169–171.

Falk, Julia S. 1995. "Roman Jakobson and the History of Saussurean Concepts in North American Linguistics". *Historiographia Linguistica* 22:3.335–367.

Georgin, Robert & Rosine Georgin. 1978. "Entretien avec Roman Jakobson". *Jakobson. Cahiers Cistre* 5.11–26.

Grégoire, Henri, Roman Jakobson & Marc Szeftel, eds. 1948. *La geste du prince Igor, épopée russe du XIIe siècle.* New York & Bruxelles: Université libre de Bruxelles.

Jacob, François, Roman Jakobson, Claude Lévi-Strauss & Philippe Héritier. 2018 [1968]. "Vivre et parler". *Correspondance. 1942–1982, by Roman Jakobson & Claude Lévi-Strauss,* 363–384. Paris: Seuil. [*Les lettres françaises* 1221.3–7 ; 1222.4–5].

Jakobson, Roman. 1929. *Remarques sur l'évolution phonologique du russe comparée à celle des autres langues slaves. Travaux du Cercle linguistique de Prague* 2.5–118 [SW I: 7–116].

Jakobson, Roman. 1931a. "Prinzipien der historischen Phonologie". *Travaux du Cercle linguistique de Prague* 4.247–267.

Jakobson, Roman. 1931b. "Les unions phonologiques de langues". *Le Monde Slave* 1.371–378.

Jakobson, Roman. 1931c. "Über die phonologischen Sprachbünde". *Travaux du Cercle linguistique de Prague* 4.234–240 [SW I: 137–143].

Jakobson, Roman. 1931d. "O fonologičeskix jazykovyx sojuzax". *Evrazija v svete jazykoznanija,* 7–12. Prague: Izdanie Evrazikcev.

Jakobson, Roman. 1938. "Sur la théorie des affinités phonologiques entre langues". *Actes du IV Congrès International des Linguistes, Copenhague, 1936,* 48–58. Copenhague: Einar Munksgaard.

Jakobson, Roman. 1972. "Entretien avec Jean-Pierre Faye, Jean Paris et Jacques Roubaud". *Hypothèses. Trois entretiens et trois études sur la linguistique et la poétique,* Roman Jakobson, Morris Halle & Noam Chomsky, 33–49. Paris: Seghers.

Jakobson, Roman. 1928a. "O hlákoslovném zakonu a teleologickém hláskosloví". *Časopis pro moderní filologii* 14.183–184 [SW I: 1–2].

Jakobson, Roman. 1972–1974. *Archives du XXe siècle, entretiens avec J.-J. Marchand.* Paris: ORTF [transcription *in* Roman Jakobson Papers, Box 147].

Jakobson, Roman. 1976a. "Il reste beaucoup à faire…". *Le Monde,* October 9, 1976. 24.

Jakobson, Roman. 1976b. "Entretien avec Emmanuel Jacquart: autour de la poétique". *Critique* 348.461–472.

Jakobson, Roman. 1978 [1976]. *Six lectures on Sound and Meaning,* trans. by John Mepham. Cambridge Mass. & London: MIT Press.

Jakobson, Roman. 1984. "La théorie saussurienne en rétrospection". *Linguistics* 22:2.161–196.

Jakobson, Roman. 2018 [1985]. "Dear Claude, cher maître". *Correspondance. 1942–1982, by Roman Jakobson & Claude Lévi-Strauss*, 403–406. Paris: Seuil. [*On Signs: A Semiotic Reader* edited by Marshall Blonsky, 184–188. Baltimore: Hopkins University Press].

Jakobson, Roman & Claude Lévi-Strauss. 2018. *Correspondance. 1942–1982* edited by Emmanuelle Loyer & Patrice Maniglier. Paris: Seuil.

Jakobson, Roman & Raymond de Saussure. 2018. "Correspondance (1945–1968) au Massachussetts Institute of Technology" edited by Giuseppe D'Ottavi. *Cahiers Ferdinand de Saussure* 71.193–220.

Jakobson, Roman, Serge Karcevski & Nicolaï Troubetzkoy. 1928b. "Quelles sont les méthodes les mieux appropriées à un exposé complet et pratique de la phonologie d'une langue quelconque ?". *Premier Congrès International des Linguistes*, 36–38. Nijmegen: Richelle [SW I: 3–6].

doi Joseph, John E. 1989. "The genesis of Jakobson's 'Six lectures on sound and meaning'". *Historiographia Linguistica* 26:3.415–420.

doi Laplantine, Chloé & Pierre-Yves Testenoire. 2021. "La correspondance d'Émile Benveniste et Roman Jakobson", *Histoire Épistémologie Langage* 43:2.139–168.

doi Lévi-Strauss, Claude. 1945. "L'analyse structurale en linguistique et en anthropologie". *Word* 1:2.1–21.

Lévi-Strauss, Claude. 1976. "Préface". *Six leçons sur le son et le sens* by Roman Jakobson. 7–18. Paris: Minuit.

Lévi-Strauss, Claude. 1985. "Roman, mon ami". *Le Nouvel observateur*, February 1, 1985. 54–55.

Lévi-Strauss, Claude. 2018 [1971]. "Roman Jakobson: histoire d'une amitié". *Correspondance. 1942–1982, by Roman Jakobson et Claude Lévi-Strauss*. 397–401. Paris: Seuil. [*Le Monde*, October 16, 1971.20].

Lévi-Strauss, Claude. 2019 [1944]. "The Social and Psychological Aspects of Chieftainship in a Primitive Tribe: The Nambikuara of Northwestern Mato Grosso". *Anthropologie structurale zéro*, 173–194. Paris: Seuil. [*Transactions of the New York Academy of Sciences* 7:1.16–32].

Lévi-Strauss, Claude. 2019 [1949]. "La politique étrangère d'une société primitive". *Anthropologie structurale zéro*, 201–219. Paris: Seuil. [*Politique étrangère* 14:2.139–152].

Lévi-Strauss, Claude. 2019. *Anthropologie structurale zéro* edited by Vincent Debaene. Paris: Seuil.

Lévi-Strauss, Claude & Didier Eribon. 1990 [1988]. *De près et de loin*. Paris: Seuil.

Loyer, Emmanuelle. 2007 [2005]. *Paris à New York. Intellectuels et artistes français en exil (1940–1947)*. Paris: Hachette.

Loyer, Emmanuelle & Maniglier Patrice. 2018. "Préface. La critstallisation structuraliste". *Correspondance. 1942–1982 by Roman Jakobson & Claude Lévi-Strauss*, 9–50. Paris: Seuil.

Mazon, André. 1940. *Le Slovo d'Igor*. Paris: Droz.

Mehlman, Jeffrey. 2005 [2000]. *Émigrés à New York: les intellectuels français à Manhattan, 1940–1944*, trans. by Pierre-Emmanuel Dauzat. Paris: Albin Michel.

doi Roudet, Robert. 2011. "Mazon et le *Slovo d'Igor*". *Revue des Études Slaves* 82:1.55–67.

Rutkoff, Peter M. & William B. Scott 1983. "The French in New York: Resistance and Structure". *Social Research* 50:1. 185–214.

Schaller Helmut W. 1997. "Roman Jakobson's Conception of 'Sprachbund'". *Cahiers de l'ILSL* 9.19–204.

Sebeok, Thomas A. 1977. "Roman Jakobson's Teaching in America". *Roman Jakobson: Echoes of his Scholarship* edited by Daniel Armstrong & C. H. van Schooneveld, 411–420. Lisse: Peter de Ridder.

Sériot, Patrick. 1999. *Structure et totalité. Les origines intellectuelles du structuralisme en Europe centrale et orientale.* Paris: Presses Universitaires de France.

doi Tchougounnikov, Sergueï 2006. "De l''affinité élective' à la 'convergence'. Un exemple du substrat morphologique allemand du formalisme russe". *Revue germanique internationale* 3.127–141.

doi Testenoire, Pierre-Yves. 2019. "Compléments à la correspondance Jakobson – Lévi-Strauss". *Acta structuralica* 4: https://acta.structuralica.org/pub-229312.

doi Testenoire, Pierre-Yves. 2022. "Jakobson & Co. La linguistique à l'École Libre des Hautes Études". *La linguistique et ses formes historiques d'organisation et de production* edited by Didier Samain & Pierre-Yves Testenoire, 161–188. Paris. HEL Livres.

Troubetzkoy N. S. 1975. *N. S. Trubetskoy's Letters and Notes* edited by Roman Jakobson. The Hague – Paris: Mouton.

Zolberg, Aristide R. & Agnès Callamard. 1998. "The École Libre at the New School, 1941–1946". *Social Research* 65:4.921–951.

CHAPTER 16

Contribution de Agostino Gemelli (1878–1959) à l'analyse des variations phoniques du langage

Gemelli et l'analyse des variations phoniques du langage

Enrica Galazzi
Università Cattolica del Sacro Cuore Milan

Agostino Gemelli, médecin et psychologue, s'investit dans l'étude des variations phoniques par des moyens expérimentaux d'avant-garde qui lui ont permis une analyse pluri-paramétrique jusqu'alors inédite (Gemelli 1938 et 1939). Dans une approche holistique de l'homme qu'il souhaite fonder sur des données objectives mesurables, la langue n'est pas seulement un moyen de communication mais elle est également, à ses yeux de psychologue, « le miroir de l'âme et de l'attitude du locuteur ». Les résultats, publiés dans de nombreuses revues internationales furent présentés au IIIème Colloque international des Sciences Phonétiques (Gand 1938), ce qui lui valut un retentissement et une reconnaissance internationales. Une relecture des résultats obtenus permet de mesurer le rôle que le Laboratoire de l'Université Catholique de Milan a joué dans le progrès des recherches autour de la voix humaine, notamment dans le domaine de la phonostylistique naissante (Trojan 1948 ; Léon 1971 ; 1976 ; Fónagy 1977 ; 1982).

Mots clés : phonétique expérimentale, histoire de la phonétique, Agostino Gemelli, variations phonétiques

https://doi.org/10.1075/sihols.133.16gal

1. Introduction

Beaucoup a déjà été écrit sur la personnalité scientifique de Gemelli, passionné et tenace, boulimique de lecture, sur son extraordinaire force de travail et sur son profil exceptionnel de chercheur, son intuition précoce, ses multiples talents et sa foi inébranlable dans l'expérimentation.[1]

L'ensemble de ses activités scientifiques est un exemple de rigueur dans la recherche et d'humilité / stupeur face à la complexité du vivant qui paraît se dérober aux yeux des chercheurs.

De la fascination pour l'onde sonore découverte dans le laboratoire de Carl Stumpf à Berlin jusqu'à la création à Milan du laboratoire de phonétique le mieux équipé d'Europe dans les années 1920–1930, l'itinéraire de recherche de Gemelli suit deux chemins parallèles. Premièrement la quête obstinée d'appareils d'analyse de la voix de plus en plus perfectionnés (car il était constamment en état de veille technologique) dont témoignent la riche correspondance et ses visites dans les laboratoires et chez les constructeurs d'appareils scientifiques de différents pays, en particulier l'Allemagne, la France et les USA (Galazzi 2018b). Les deux volumes de 1934, *L'analisi elettroacustica del linguaggio*, en collaboration avec Giuseppina Pastori (1934a), richement illustrés, présentent une synthèse critique des méthodes d'analyse phonétique mises au point par les physiologistes, les psychologues, les linguistes, des méthodes qu'il n'aura de cesse d'améliorer tout au long de sa vie (Galazzi 2010a).

2. Agostino Gemelli: Le héraut des méthodes électroacoustiques d'analyse du langage

Grâce à l'analyse électroacoustique et à un engagement acharné, Gemelli comble les lacunes d'une phonétique à peine balbutiante en Italie, et passe de l'étude préliminaire de la nature acoustique des unités du langage (consonnes et voyelles) au timbre, au seuil de durée minimal pour la perception, pour aborder enfin le sujet qui l'avait le plus passionné et intrigué, à savoir les variations de l'onde sonore (et tout particulièrement les variations individuelles).

Dans les années 1930, la phonétique était avant tout articulatoire ; la priorité était donnée à l'étude physiologique de l'origine des sons (perspective génétique),

1. Le document vidéo "*Agostino Gemelli (1878–1959), psychologist and phonetician*" (2021, en anglais), élaboré par Enrica Galazzi et Savina Raynaud et présenté à l'ouverture du Colloque ICHoLS 2021, est accessible sur le site https://www.youtube.com/watch?v=xgtzbuXYgoo

cela étant dû aux limites des méthodes utilisées avant Gemelli qui, par son approche « objective », était en avance sur son temps.

Il écrivait que, entre 1931 et 1936, peu nombreux étaient ceux qui avaient utilisé les méthodes électroacoustiques car elles exigeaient des connaissances techniques approfondies et l'adaptation des appareils déjà existants en physique et dans la téléphonie, aux objectifs poursuivis (Gemelli 1937a). Il considérait que si, après Rousselot, la phonétique expérimentale n'avait pas donné les résultats espérés, c'est que ceux qui avaient pris la suite n'avaient pas une préparation suffisante aux niveaux psychophysiologique, physique, linguistique (Gemelli 1938b).

De par ses études de médecine, sa longue et patiente fréquentation des laboratoires d'histologie sous la direction rigoureuse du prix Nobel Camillo Golgi à Pavie et plus tard en Allemagne, il était parfaitement à son aise dans la manipulation des instruments d'investigation dont les laboratoires allemands étaient fort bien équipés. Dans le contexte des études linguistiques en Italie, essentiellement historiques et philologiques, Gemelli fait figure de pionnier en mettant sur pied un appareillage et une méthodologie admirables qui, tout autant que sa formation scientifique décisive, ont en partie assuré sa renommée à l'échelle internationale.

L'adoption des méthodes électroacoustiques rapides et fiables lui permit d'obtenir une grande quantité de données servant de base à des études comparatives originales.

Des appareils étaient construits ou adaptés d'après ses indications dans le laboratoire milanais par le technicien Odaliso Galli. Au début des années 1940, une chambre insonorisée très perfectionnée (qui remplaçait celle de 1936) avait été construite à l'intérieur du laboratoire afin d'obtenir des enregistrements de parole spontanée, fidèles, sans distorsions (Gemelli 1942).

Son génie technologique a su saisir la possibilité offerte par la méthode oscillographique de passer de l'analyse de sons isolés à l'analyse du continuum sonore de la parole, toujours changeant, ouvrant ainsi des perspectives de recherches inédites où une place importante est occupée par la mélodie et l'accent. Le tonomètre et le voltmètre utilisés ont été présentés au congrès des Sciences phonétiques de Gand en 1938 et, en 1939, au Congrès International de psychologie de Zurich.

Selon les buts envisagés, les segments analysés variaient : logatomes, mots, phrases, morceaux de poèmes ou de prose, segments construits (par exemple pour étudier les effets de coarticulation « avvezziamoci a morir se proprio è morte prossima »), phases affirmatives, interrogatives, segmentées.

La perception l'intéressait par-dessus tout : comment l'oreille passe-t-elle de la profusion phonétique à l'austérité phonologique qui gouverne la compréhension ? Quels sont les indices constants de la substance sonore indispensables pour l'identification des unités phonologiques pertinentes et à quoi sert la multitude des autres variations qui se manifestent dans l'onde sonore ? Tous les composants physiques ne sont pas forcément intégrés par l'oreille qui fonctionne comme un filtre et, vice versa, ce qui est perçu n'est pas forcément présent dans la substance physique. Dans de nombreuses expériences, Gemelli avait exploré ces questions touchant la perception des sons du langage.

Dans la définition d'un seuil de durée minimal suffisant pour la perception des voyelles (Gemelli 1934b), cent oscillogrammes de mots bisyllabes avec accent sur la pénultième produits par 4 sujets avaient été analysés et comparés.

Des expériences perceptives pionnières (ayant pour objet des mots italiens et/ou étrangers) faites à l'aide de filtres électriques permettaient de démolir certaines bandes de fréquences des voyelles mettant ainsi en évidence d'un côté la pertinence des paramètres acoustiques dans la reconnaissance des sons et, de l'autre, les mécanismes d'intégration de l'oreille en cas d'altération du signal. Deux lois de la perception se confirmaient opérationnelles : la rectification des données sensorielles et la constance des organisations intuitives (Gemelli 1932). Au début des années 1940, avant l'isolement et la destruction des réseaux de recherche, Gemelli annonçait une publication sur des expériences de synthèse des voyelles auxquelles avait collaboré Annibale Stefanini (1855–1942).[2]

Les résultats de ses recherches, largement diffusés dans la communauté scientifique internationale à travers la publication (ou re-publication) dans des revues de différents pays, (et souvent traduits en allemand et en français), tout comme ses nombreux comptes rendus d'ouvrages (Preto 1981), révèlent une parfaite maîtrise de la littérature spécialisée : Gemelli était au courant de tout ce qui s'était fait et de tout ce qui se faisait à son époque dans les laboratoires du monde entier. Ses résultats s'appuyaient sur les données fournies par une analyse pluri-paramétrique et sur la comparaison d'une extraordinaire quantité d'oscillogrammes en voix parlée, chuchotée ou chantée.

Grâce à son appareillage sophistiqué, Gemelli était intervenu dans le débat sur les composants acoustiques des voyelles (les « formants » qu'il appelle « vocables ») qui avait partagé les spécialistes en deux camps (Helmholtz et Stumpf *vs* Hermann et Scripture). Sont éclairantes, à ce propos, les pages que Laziczius consacre aux arguments avancés dans les deux camps et à l'état de la question dans les années 1940 (Laziczius 1961).

Après la guerre qui avait détruit et effacé tout ce qui avait été fait en Europe, l'appareillage du laboratoire de Milan était destiné à être dépassé par les avancées de la technologie, surtout aux USA. En effet, pendant la deuxième guerre mon-

2. Une correspondance intense entre Gemelli et Stefanini (1930–1937) autour de ce sujet peut être consultée auprès des Archives de l'Université Catholique de Milan. Archivio generale per la storia dell'Università Cattolica del Sacro Cuore, fondo *Miscellanea*, busta 61, fascicolo 10.

diale, dans les laboratoires américains s'étaient développées des techniques de pointe pour l'analyse et la synthèse de la voix. Ces progrès étaient dus aux ingénieurs, qui n'étaient pas linguistes. On considère *Acoustic Phonetics* de Martin Joos (1948) comme la première publication de phonétique linguistique venant d'Outre Atlantique. Gemelli connaissait ces travaux (notamment les recherches « de guerre » menées dans les laboratoires BELL plusieurs fois cités dans ses ouvrages) et avait une avance théorique sur eux car il avait une vaste culture linguistique. Il avait lu tout ce qui avait été écrit d'important dans les sciences du langage de l'époque : Saussure, Bally, Trubeckoj, Rousselot, Grammont, Jones, Bühler, Humboldt, E. et K. Zwirner, Stetson, Fletcher, Sapir, Bloomfield, mais aussi Cassirer, Vossler, Gabelentz pour ne citer que quelques noms (Galazzi 2018a et 2018b). Ces ouvrages étaient disponibles (souvent peu après leur parution) auprès de la Bibliothèque de l'Université dont le Catalogue était mis à jour avec une vitesse impressionnante même en période de guerre (Galazzi 2010b).

Ses recherches phonétiques, bien connues des spécialistes, ont fait l'objet d'appréciations élogieuses, plus souvent à l'étranger qu'en Italie (Galazzi 2012).[3]

3. L'étude des variations et le succès à Gand (1938)

Le vaste projet d'analyse des variations phoniques individuelles et socio-situationnelles, longtemps délaissées par la linguistique structuraliste, était pour Gemelli un objet d'étude prioritaire et pluridisciplinaire, « travail auquel doivent collaborer le psychologue, le phonéticien, le linguiste, car chacun d'eux considère les variations caractéristiques du langage humain d'après son propre point de vue » (Galazzi 1985: 71).[4]

Dès le début des années 1930, les résultats diffusés dans *Ricerche elettroacustiche sopra il timbro di voce nel linguaggio parlato* (1931) basés sur l'analyse comparative de plusieurs centaines d'oscillogrammes de dix sujets différents montrent clairement l'orientation du savant milanais vers les variations qui se manifestent dans la parole vivante.

3. Gyula Laziczius (1896–1957), le grand phonologue hongrois, dans son *Introduction à la phonétique* (1961), cite trois articles de Gemelli. Ivan Fónagy, étudiant la phonétique à Budapest sous la direction de Gyula Laziczius, avait dans la bibliographie du cours les publications de Gemelli sur les variations (1938 ; 1939). Un échantillon de témoignages est reproduit dans Galazzi 1985.

4. Ce sujet, cher aux « jeunes phonéticiens » du dernier quart du XIXème siècle, avait été débattu dans le groupe des pragois puis relégué dans les marges de la recherche linguistique tout au long du XXème siècle.

En 1938 à Gand, au 3ème grand Colloque des Science phonétiques, face à un public admiratif où se trouvaient les plus beaux noms de la phonétique de l'époque, Gemelli illustrait les progrès accomplis depuis les années 1930 (reconnaissance du timbre de la voix) qui lui avaient permis d'aborder le vaste champ des variations individuelles (individualismes). Son appareillage, perfectionné depuis 1934, comportait trois instruments automatiques, fiables et rapides, construits avec la collaboration d'un physicien, Gino Sacerdote : un tonomètre (enregistrement des variations de hauteur) ; un voltmètre (variations de l'intensité)[5] auxquels s'ajoutait un oscillographe qui permettait de visualiser la parole (onde sonore, durée des unités).[6] Pour l'analyse harmonique l'instrument le plus adéquat était, d'après Gemelli, le spectrographe mis au point par les techniciens de la *Bell Telephone Company*, le *Sonagraph* (Gemelli 1937b ; 1938a).

Suivant Humboldt, Gemelli assumait que le langage n'est pas seulement un moyen de communication, mais le reflet de l'âme et de l'opinion du locuteur. La tâche du psychologue consistait à analyser les variations du signal sonore en relation avec les conditions subjectives ou objectives, internes et externes liées au contenu, au contexte, aux émotions. Son idéal de psychologue était d'arriver à une étude comparative objective au moyen de diagrammes et d'analyses algébrique (critiquées par les phonéticiens qui les jugeaient théoriques, non réelles ; Gemelli 1933).

Pour résoudre le problème des temps d'analyse extrêmement longs qui avaient poussé certains (tels que Fletcher) à renoncer, des instruments automatiques avaient été construits qui permettaient d'obtenir les résultats par voie électrique (spectre, variations de la Fo et de l'intensité).

Les données que l'on pouvait obtenir sont en nombre considérable ; pour Fo : la gamme, la fréquence moyenne et les écarts individuels, les fréquences préférentielles, les déplacements des zones de résonance ; pour l'intensité : la moyenne et les écarts de l'intensité syllabique ; pour la durée : les temps d'élocution et de phonation, la vitesse du débit, le nombre, la longueur et la distribution des pauses. D'après ses résultats, les différences individuelles les plus caractéristiques étaient à rechercher dans la vitesse du débit, les mouvements mélodiques, les pauses inter phrastiques, les niveaux d'attaque et de fin de phrase.

---

5. L'analyse de l'intensité a longtemps représenté un obstacle majeur qui était loin d'être résolu dans les années 1940. Gemelli cite les opinions pessimistes de Grammont et Battisti, fait référence à la phonométrie de Zipf et Zwirner avant d'illustrer la méthode mise au point avec Gino Sacerdote, qu'il a appliquée à l'étude des effets de la fatigue, de la conversation ordinaire *vs* la déclamation ; la voix monotone *vs* la voix emphatique (AG *Un metodo per l'analisi statistica dell'intensità sonora*, 1941).

6. La durée des voyelles italiennes a été étudiée par Elise Richter 1938 (Vienne) à partir d'oscillogrammes enregistrés dans le laboratoire de Gemelli.

La prise en compte des variations ouvre un vaste terrain d'investigation et un programme de recherches qui prend en charge : l'état psychique du locuteur ; la microprosodie (contexte phonétique) ; les lois de la structuration des sons ; les individualismes : états émotifs, modalité de la phrase (affirmative, négative, interrogative, ordre) ; les types de discours (monologue, dialogue) ; la mélodie de la phrase ; les applications pratiques (l'enseignement des L2 ; la rééducation, le chant).

Gemelli avait pleine conscience des problèmes techniques qui restaient à résoudre et des difficultés que posait l'étude des caractères individuels.

En 1935, Scripture écrivait que les publications récentes de Gemelli, à savoir ses recherches sur le timbre (1931), y avaient apporté la première contribution positive (Scripture, 1935: 455).

Les résultats d'expériences menées en collaboration avec J. W. Black sur les variations individuelles dans la lecture publiés en 1955 à partir des réalisations de 20 locuteurs des deux sexes, (étudiant.e.s italien.ne.s et américain.e.s) révèlent des différences individuelles dans la distribution des paramètres de fréquence, d'intensité et de durée et dans les niveaux d'attaque et de fin de phrase. La vitesse de débit et la fréquence fondamentale moyenne ont des caractéristiques qui peuvent différer selon le sexe et/ou la nationalité.

Parmi les dernières recherches expérimentales de Gemelli, celles consacrées à l'analyse de la voix chantée ont ouvert un nouveau terrain à travers la comparaison d'extraits d'opéras réalisés par des artistes célèbres (Caruso, Tito Schipa) et par d'autres en formation. Les variations relevées dans l'exécution des notes filées et du vibrato permettent d'étudier le degré de maîtrise des paramètres de la voix et sont une contribution à la didactique du chant (Gemelli, Sacerdote, Bellussi 1954 et 1956; Galazzi à paraître 2025).

Il n'est pas faux d'affirmer que Gemelli a été le héros et le héraut des méthodes élecroacoustiques qu'il a illustrées par ses travaux et dont il a fait sans cesse l'éloge (Galazzi 2010a) car elles permettaient d'étudier dans les détails la morphologie des courbes et témoignaient de l'exceptionnelle plasticité de la parole où chaque variation phonétique a la fonction de transmettre quelque chose.

Une trentaine d'année après le Colloque de Gand, le dernier avant le long silence imposé par la guerre, l'analyse des variations sonores a été reprise et développée avec succès par la phonostylistique (Trojan 1948 ; Léon 1971 ; 1976 ; Fónagy 1977 ; 1982) dont Gemelli peut être considéré, à juste titre, comme un précurseur.[7]

7. Aujourd'hui on ne compte plus le nombre de colloques consacrés aux variations. Parmi les plus significatifs pour notre propos, je citerai celui **organisé par le Laboratoire Ligérien de Linguistique :** ***50 ans de linguistique sur corpus oraux. Apports à l'étude de la variation*****, Orléans 15–17 novembre 2018.**

Références

Fónagy Ivan. 1977. “Le statut de la phonostylistique”. *Phonetica* 34.1–18.

Fónagy Ivan. 1982. “Variation et normes prosodiques”. *Folia linguistica* XVI:1–4.17–39.

Galazzi, Enrica. 1985. *Gli studi di fonetica di Agostino Gemelli.* Milano: Vita e Pensiero.

Galazzi, Enrica. 2010a. “Agostino Gemelli et l’analyse électro-acoustique du langage”. *Un siècle de phonétique expérimentale, fondation et éléments de développement. Hommage à Théodore Rosset et John Ohalan* dir. par Louis-Jean Boë & Coriandre-Emmanuel Vilain, 179–190. Lyon : ENS Éditions.

Galazzi, Enrica. 2010b. “Centralità della voce e punto di vista della Psicologia. Agostino Gemelli e la Scuola linguistica di Praga”. *L’Analisi linguistica e letteraria.* XVIII/2.395–410.

Galazzi, Enrica. 2012. “Les débuts de la phonétique en Italie dans la première moitié du XXe siècle : deux [faux] départs”. Colloque SHESL. Paris. Janvier 2010. *La disciplinarisation des savoirs linguistiques histoire et épistémologie. Dossiers d’HEL,* n° 5. : http://htl.linguist .univ-paris-diderot.fr/dosHEL.htm

Galazzi, Enrica. 2018a. “Karl Bühler et Agostino Gemelli : deux médecins-psychologues cherchant à saisir le langage humain”. *Karl Bühler, une théorie du langage redécouverte, Karl Bühler: 80 Jahre Sprachtheorie.* Internationale Tagung des Prager Linguistenkreises. Prag 9–10.VI 2014. *Travaux du Cercle Linguistique de Prague,* n.s., 7.397–412.

Galazzi, Enrica. 2018b. “Agostino Gemelli e le scienze fonetiche in Europa nella prima metà del Novecento”. *La Cultura linguistica italiana in confronto con le culture linguistiche di altri paesi dall’Ottocento in poi,* 297–312. Convegno SLI Milano. Settembre 2016. Roma: Bulzoni.

Galazzi, Enrica. à paraître (dans un volume éd. par Walter Coppola, *Mimesis.* 2025). “Padre Agostino Gemelli: contributi all'analisi della voce cantata (1951–1956)”.

Gemelli, Agostino, in collab. con Giuseppina Pastori. 1931. “Ricerche elettroacustiche sopra il “timbro di voce” nel linguaggio parlato”. *Regia Accademia d’Italia, Memorie della classe di Scienze fisiche, matematiche e naturali.* Roma. Vol. VI:65–117 avec XII figures hors texte.

Gemelli, Agostino, in collab. con Giuseppina Pastori. 1932. *Recherches et nouveaux résultats dans l’analyse des voyelles. Rapport lu au Congrès de Psychologie – Copenhagen 22–27 août 1932,* (pro manuscripto) pp. 19 avec 19 figures.

Gemelli, Agostino, in collab. con Giuseppina Pastori. 1933. “Quelques recherches sur la nature des voyelles”. *Revue d’acoustique* vol. II/ 3.169–188.

Gemelli, Agostino, Giuseppina, Pastori. 1934a. *L’analisi elettroacustica del linguaggio.* Pubblicazioni a cura della Università Cattolica del S. Cuore di Milano. Vol. in-8 di pp. 250 con 49 fig. nel testo, 4 tabelle e 88 tavole in un volume separato.

Gemelli, Agostino, in collab. con Giuseppina Pastori. 1934b. “La durata minima delle vocali sufficiente alla loro percezione”. *Archivio di Fisiologia* XXIII/3.440–452.

Gemelli Agostino. 1937a. “Nuove applicazioni dei metodi dell’elettroacustica allo studio della psicologia del linguaggio”. *Archivio Italiano di Psicologia* vol. XV/1.82–85.

Gemelli, Agostino. 1937b. “Variations signalatrices et significatives et variations individuelles des unités élémentaires phoniques du langage humain : moyens fournis par l’électro-acoustique pour les déceler et évaluation physio-psychologique des résultats». *Archiv für vergleichende Phonetik* (Berlin). III/3.162–182.

Gemelli, Agostino. 1938a. "Variations significatives et variations individuelles des unités élémentaires phoniques du langage humain : moyens fournis par l'électro-acoustique pour les déceler et évaluation physio-psychologique des résultats". *Proceedings of the third international Congress of Phonetic Sciences (Ghent 18–22 july 1938)*, 355–364. Phonetic Laboratory of the University of Ghent.

Gemelli Agostino. 1938b. Compte-rendu de C. Battisti. 1938. *Fonetica generale*. Hoepli: Milano. Aevum XII/2–3.334–337.

Gemelli, Agostino. 1942. "Criteri fondamentali per la costruzione di una camera isolata acusticamente e schermata elettricamente per ricerche di fisiologia e di psicologia e risultati conseguiti". *La Ricerca scientifica*. XIII/11.619–627.

Gemelli, Agostino, Gino Sacerdote, Giuseppe Bellussi. 1954. "Analisi elettroacustica della voce cantata, Memoria presentata alla Pont. Accademia delle Scienze nella seduta del 9 marzo 1954". *Commentationes Pontificia Academia scientiarum* XVI.[21]–44, 19 tav.

Gemelli, Agostino, Gino Sacerdote, Giuseppe Bellussi. 1956. "Nuovi contributi elettroacustici allo studio del canto – Memoria presentata nella seduta del 7 aprile 1956". *Civitate Vaticana : P. Academia scientiarum*, 13.[1] p., 36 tav. Estr. da: 'Commentationes. P. Academia scientiarum', XVII, 1956, 1. *Rist. in "Bollettino della Società italiana in Fonetica sperimentale, Fonetica biologica, Foniatria, Audiologia"*, a. VI (1956), fasc. 1.3–52 con 11 tavole.

Joos, Martin. 1948. *"Acoustic Phonetics", supplément à la revue Language*, vol 24.

Laziczius, Gyula. 1961 (1944). *Lehrbuch der Phonetik*. Berlin : Akademie Verlag.

Léon, Pierre. 1971. *Essais de phonostylistique*. Studia Phonetica. Paris : Didier.

Léon, Pierre. 1976. "De l'analyse psychologique à la caractérisation auditive et acoustique des émotions dans la parole". *Journal de psychologie* 3–4.305–324.

Preto, Edoarda (a cura di). 1981. *Bibliografia di Agostino Gemelli*. Milano: Vita e Pensiero. Pp. xvi, 467.

Richter, Elise. 1938. "Länge und Kürze". *Archiv für Vergleichende Phonetik*. Bd II.12–29.

doi Scripture, Edward Wheeler. 1935. "Experimental Linguistics". *Nature* 21 Sept. 1935.455.

Trojan, Felix. 1948. *Der Ausdruck von Stimme und Sprache. Eine phonetische Lautstilistik*. Wien : Maudrich.

Abstract

Agostino Gemelli, doctor and psychologist, was involved in the study of phonic variations by avant-garde experimental means which allowed him to perform a multi-parametric analysis hitherto unpublished (Gemelli 1938 and 1939). In a holistic approach to the person that he wished to base on measurable objective data, language was not only a means of communication, but to his eyes, as a psychologist, "the mirror of the soul and attitude of the speaker". The results of his research, published in numerous international journals, were presented at the IIIrd International Colloquium of Phonetic Sciences (Ghent 1938), earning him international renown and recognition. A review of the results he obtained enables us to assess the role that the Laboratory of Università Cattolica in Milan played in the progress of research around the human voice, particularly in the field of nascent phonostylistics (Trojan 1948; Leon 1971; 1976; Fónagy 1977; 1982).

Keywords: experimental phonetics, history of phonetics, Agostino Gemelli, phonetic variations

CHAPTER 17

The structuralist quest for general meanings

Mapping the history of monosemy in grammatical semantics

Lorenzo Cigana & Henrik Jørgensen
Université de Liège | University of Aarhus

This article reconstruct the history and development of the methodology known as "of general meanings", widely adopted in 20th century structural linguistics and grammatical semantics starting from the Thirties onwards, tracking its roots in the framework of German *Allgemeine Sprachlehre* and discussing the debate that it engendered within the structural paradigm, where the notions of "general" vs. "fundamental meanings" (*Gesamt-* vs. *Grundbedeutung*) were defined and gained currency, often marking the competing approaches of Prague vs. Copenhagen schools. In so doing, the paper offers a detailed insight on the philosophical background of such a methodology, reconstructing its epistemological framework and its legacy, contributing in mapping the evolution of one of its most important corollary: monosemy.

Keywords: monosemy, grammatical semantics, general meanings, structural linguistics, system

> Alles Philosophieren über Sprache, wie auch über andere Gegenstände, ist eitel, ja ganz und gar verderblich, wenn nur einzelne Fälle herausgehoben werden, um ihre Bedeutung zu erforschen, und das Ganze nicht berücksichtiget wird: denn er führt zu leerer Tafelei.
> (Wüllner 1827: 3)

1. Introduction

In his contribution to the structure of Russian cases, Roman Jakobson (1936) programmatically wrote:

https://doi.org/10.1075/sihols.133.17cig

> The question of the *general meaning* [*Gesamtbedeutungen*] of grammatical forms is naturally basic to the theory of the grammatical system of language. The importance of this question was fundamentally clear to linguistic thinking associated with the systematist philosophical currents of the first half of the last century, but a comprehensive solution was not possible without further independent development and refinement of linguistic methodology. (Jakobson [1936] 1984: 59)

In so doing, he was acknowledging the existence of an essential ingredient of structural linguistics, namely the research in grammatical semantics concerning the crosslinguistic general meanings assigned to morphological categories. He was also managing to flesh out a manifesto for a long-lasting scholarship that, for many aspects, mirrored the previous investigation of the same issue by Louis Hjelmslev (1935), *La catégorie des cas* I. It's not happenstance that, a few years later, the Norwegian linguist Hans Vogt acknowledged both perspectives on this topic as ushering in a "new era" in linguistics:

> On peut dire, sans exagération, qu'avec la publication de l'ouvrage de Louis Hjelmslev sur la catégorie des cas, ouvrage immédiatement suivi du mémoire du Roman Jakobson sur le système des cas en russe, s'ouvre dans ce domaine, en l'année 1936, une nouvelle ère. (Vogt 1949: 112)

In fact, in their respective works, both Hjelmslev and Jakobson stressed that such a research programme in general grammatical semantics had deep roots in previous linguistic tradition – each pinpointing a different set of notable forerunners – while being taken up and reworked by structural linguistics in a specific and quite new way. Their views, however, differ on some key points, and their discussion took the form of a back-and-forth of critical remarks and responses, turning into yet another battleground for academic positioning.

We will examine this further below, when we present an overview of the most significant approaches on the matter. First, however, we must consider the question: what is a *Gesamt-* or *Grundbedeutung*?

In addressing this issue, it will become clear just how entangled it is with several other theoretical and methodological issues, such as localism, underspecification, markedness, a systemic approach and, to a lesser but still significant extent, grammaticalisation. Accordingly, our reconstruction will at least partially overlap with research in those fields. In fact, the issue of "general meaning" has so far mostly been discussed within the framework of the theories of case and its semantic interpretation (localism).[1] Our claim is that, in order to be properly

1. See, for instance, Ebeling (1957), Fillmore (1968), Kacnel'son (1972), Serbat (1979, 1981), Wierzbycka (1980), van Schooneveld (1983), Kirsner (1985), Bílý (1989), Birnbaum (1998), Danielsen (1980) and, more recently, Anderson (2006) and Fortis (2018). Birnbaum is thus cor-

reconstructed, the issue has to be partially divorced from the domain of grammatical case: the issue of *general* or *fundamental meanings*, despite being formulated in relation to case, was conceived as having a broader reach. Thus, our approach will maintain a different angle, as the investigation is centred on the monosemic claim and aims to disclose its intrinsic theoretical (or epistemological) dimension, from which the other aforementioned issues can be understood as corollaries.

2. Kant, German romantic philology and the motivation of grammatical forms

In a sense, the search for grammatical meanings is as old as grammar itself: after all, the attempt to motivate linguistic forms semantically can be regarded as one of the most basic and intuitive operations of grammar. How these operations were handled, changed from era to era, and so did the types of semantic frames that were called upon.

Such a trend gained great momentum in the late-18th- and early-19th-centuries – when grammar, philosophy and philology were still entangled – mostly within German Romantic philology, taken in what Benes (2008) rightly calls the "linguistic turn in transcendental philosophy" (2008: 46 ff). Such a framework as that fostered by Herder's, Hamann's and Humboldt's (meta)critical reactions towards Kant's *Erkenntnislehre* can be seen as a reinterpretation of the approach maintained in the Port-Royal Grammar (1666) concerning the relationship between language and thought (Burkard 2003, Fortis 2018: 172). It is not by chance that, among the language theorists who figure as representatives of the "first post-Kantian generation" (Benes 2008: 49) and who aimed to reinstate language within the categorical structure of representational thinking, at least four of them – Johann Gottfried Jakob Hermann (1772–1848), Georg-Michael Roth (1769–1817), August Ferdinand Bernhardi (1769–1820) and Franz Wüllner (1798–1842) – were explicitly mentioned by Louis Hjelmslev in his work on grammatical case (1935,

rect when he draws attention to the "existence of a considerable body of secondary literature directly addressing the issue of the perceived merits and/or shortcomings of 'general meaning' as defined, or rather elaborated and redefined, by Jakobson" (Birnbaum 1998: 147), yet this literature is, for the most part, confined to case and does not deal with the perspective of general and theoretical linguistics, epistemology or historiography of linguistics. In some cases, moreover, it resulted in rather biased readings or problematic interpretations, such as Wierzbicka 1980 (see Bílý 1989: 5–6), Bílý 1898 (see hereinafter, Note 24), Serbat 1979, 1981 (see Picciarelli 1999: 41 ff.).

1937) as supporters of the idea of the semantic motivation of linguistic categories[2] (see also Cigana 2019).

It is well known that the aim of the Port-Royal Grammar was to find, for each grammatical operation, its logical counterpart, *i.e.* the act of thought that lay behind it. The simplicity and self-evidence of such a programme was so compelling that its influence lasted more than two centuries: it was taken up once more in the 1930s by Max Deutschbein (1876–1949), mentioned by Jakobson as a final proponent of that approach (see below). Tapping this framework, Reinhold, Roth and Bernhardi

> [...] interpreted language as the external presentation (*Darstellung*) of internal representations (*Vorstellungen*) by articulate sounds. In their view, language was an object of experience, but at the same time it was conditioned by the deep rules of the mind. They set out to discover the capacity of language for shaping the mental faculty of representation and the connections it had to the a priori concepts of understanding. (Benes 2008: 49–50)

In his 1815 *Grundriss der reinen allgemeinen Sprachlehre*, Roth explicitly tried to "deduce" – in the Kantian sense of explaining by justifying (or, should we say, motivating) – the linguistic forms from the hierarchy of logical meanings, by articulating these in usually two or three sub-meanings and matching them to grammatical categories (Cigana 2022: 107 ff.).

This attempt was undertaken in the wake of Bernhardi's *Sprachlehre* (1801–3), the aim of which was to "create a new type of universal grammar that supported the transcendental categories of Kantian philosophy" (Benes 2008: 53). Bernhardi took the same approach as Gottfried Hermann, who tried to use Kant's system of categories as criteria for systematising literary genres and poetic metre (1799), by grounding both poetry and prose, and their fundamental distinction, into thought, feeling and will, on concept, intuition and judgment respectively, as well as for classifying various figures of speech (1803) and even parts of speech (1801; see Couturier-Heinrich 2011: 5; Schramm 2010: 105). For Hermann, the grammarian's task is "to clarify the nature and composition of languages starting from human mind itself, or the source of any spoken language as it were" (Schramm 2010: 107), by discriminating which parts of speech are necessary and which are purely accidental, and by investigating in what way each language employs

2. This is evidence not just of the influence of Kantian philosophy on German philology (Hjelmslev 1935, § 3: 22 ff.) but also of Hjelmslev's own appraisal of – and indebtedness to – those German theoreticians.

and forms these parts, which he conceptualised as in Figure 1 (see Schramm 2010: 110–115; Couturier-Heinrich 2011: 6):[3]

	quantity	**quality**	**relation**	**modality**
noun	number	gender	case	person
particle	interjection	adverb	preposition	conjunction
verb	number	gender	tense	mode

Figure 1. Hermann's table of linguistic categories based upon Kant's system

Hjelmslev reviewed Hermann's thesis in some detail[4] in relation to his treatment of case, explained on the basis of "[...] the first Kantian category ordered under relation, namely the category of inherence and of subsistence, or of accident and substance" (1935: 30; our translation), assigned respectively to accusative and genitive, while resorting to causality and dependence to explain ablative and dative (see Hjelmslev 1935: 29–32). Despite the difficulties in adapting an a priori, logical or intellectual framework for empirical linguistic phenomena (Hjelmslev 1935: 30–31; Schramm 2010: 105; Couturier-Heinrich 2011: 5), Hermann's goal was to prove that language does indeed express the *Geist des Volkes* according to its own rules, while firmly remaining within a representational framework, in contrast to Humboldt's position (Schramm 2010: 109–110).

Franz Wüllner addressed things in much the same way as the other Romantic philologists, except he took more care to clarify the methodological underpinnings of such an approach. In so doing, he was among the first – before Steinthal – to make it clear that the categorical meanings connected with grammatical forms were to be considered *Ideen* or *Anschauungen*, which he dubbed *Grundbedeutungen* (Wüllner 1827, passim) and *Urbedeutungen* (Wüllner 1827: 31, 119) – "fundamental" and "original meanings" respectively – taking into account both panchronic and diachronic nuances. He put forward his semantically motivated theory of grammatical forms in two main works: *Die Bedeutung der sprachlichen*

3. It follows that Hermann's approach cannot be qualified as "original" ("Die Innovation Hermanns als Grammatiker besteht nun darin, dass er konsequent das, was die alten Grammatiker die 'Akzidenten' der Redeteile nannten, den Kantischen Kategorien zuordnet", Schramm 2010: 110): the same stance was shared by the other German Romantic philologists. For instance, the difference between *langue* and *discours*, which, according to Schramm, Hermann had formulated ahead of Saussure, was fleshed out even more clearly by Wüllner, who opposed *Sprachgebäude* with *Sprachgebrauch*.

4. Interestingly enough, Hjelmslev never mentions which work of Hermann he is referring to, not even in the bibliography. In all likelihood, it is *De emendanda ratione graecae grammaticae* (1801).

Casus und Modi. Ein Versuch (1827) and *Über Ursprung und Urbedeutung der sprachlichen Formen* (1831). The latter is a fairly dense treatise which expands on the former without altering its methodological framework. And this methodological commitment is apparent in the first paragraphs of the 1827 volume and was praised by Hjelmslev (1935: 36 ff.), who turned Wüllner into a champion of his own approach. In this respect, it is important to stress that, if Wüllner can indeed be counted among the champions of localism, this is less because he believed in the topical motivation of case, than because he upheld the possibility of a semantic motivation for *any* grammatical form, as a generalised methodological stance.

Wüllner's theory of case takes Greek, German and Latin as its main object languages[5] and assumes that only three original cases exist: genitive, dative and accusative. Nominative and vocative are excluded, as the second is just a disguised form of the nominative, which is, in turn, an inflectional variant of any noun (Wüllner 1827: 4). As Hjelmslev also remarks (1935: 37), Wüllner assumes that linguistic forms are independent of external reality and derive from the representational faculty of the human mind[6] (Wüllner 1827: 1). For instance, the idea of possession expressed by the genitive cannot properly be tracked in the external world (unless perhaps the possessed object is located in the proximity of its possessor, see Wüllner 1827: 2), and so it is necessary to investigate how the relationship between possessed and possessor is conceived [*angeschaut*] from the point of view of the "formal part" of language or the "linguistic edifice" [*Gebäude der Sprache*, passim]. This can be done by turning our attention not outwards, to reality, but inwards, to the workings of the human mind:

> Here, however, one must not content oneself with naming a few general concepts, or even with considering them, which would be nobler, as something objective (since all the substance of thought, be it from the inner or outer world, belongs to the material part of language); rather, one must dissolve the workings of the thinking mind into their most basic building blocks and identify the intuitions that inhabit one's consciousness as guiding principles. (Wüllner 1827: 2)[7]

5. Sanskrit is excluded as Wüllner claims not to be competent enough in that domain.

6. "Alle Sprache ist ja Ausdruck der menschlichen Vorstellung: sie schöpft nicht aus der Außenwelt, sondern aus dem vorstellenden Geiste, der zu seinen Thätigkeiten durch die einwirkenden Gegenstände angeregt und irgendwie bestimt wird" (NB: quotations are given in the original orthography).

7. "Hier darf man sich aber nicht begnügen, einige algemeine Begriffe zu nennen und diese gar, was noch verehrter wäre, als etwas objektives zu betrachten (denn aller Stof des Denkens, sei es aus der inneren oder äusseren Welt, gehört dem materialen Theile der Sprache an); sondern es müssen die Thätigkeiten des denkenden Geistes in ihre Grundkeime aufgelöset und Anschauungen nachgewiesen werden, die als leitende Ideen in dem Bewusstsein liegen". On the link between

These ideas are what Wüllner calls *Gesamtbedeutungen*: meanings that lie at the very core of each grammatical form and are abstract enough to justify the particular occurrences or instantiations of these forms in concrete usage [*Sprachgebrauch*]. In concrete linguistic analysis, it is up to the linguist to recognise and find the formulation for such meanings which fits the structure of the given language. Wüllner's argumentation goes as follows:

a. Any linguistic form, insofar as it is related to the human mind, is linked to space and time as forms of intuition:

> All thought and speech begins with intuition and aims back at it. But all intuition is linked to space and time, and the intuition of these and their possible relationships are, if you like, the forms for any intuition.[8]

b. Case and prepositions are brought together by the act of expressing time- and space-intuitions, so that their specificity cannot lie in what they mean individually, but rather in what they have in common, *i.e.* the spatial *Grundbedeutung*:

> All true prepositions have in common that they originally denoted spatial concepts and differ in that these concepts are different. [...] Consequently, their essence cannot lie in what distinguishes the individual prepositions, but it must denote that which they all have in common, or something even more general that stands above that.[9]

c. The common root of both case and prepositions can then receive a spatial motivation on a phenomenological basis, *i.e.* on how the experience of space and its determinations constitute themselves in the human mind:

> Everything that can be intuited in space is either in motion or at rest. The mind conceives [*anschauet*] what is at rest as a point; whereby no separation or divisions are possible. In the case of movement, however, both the origin and the des-

grammatical meanings and consciousness, which could be at the origin on Hjelmslev's idea of "sublogic" (Cigana 2022: 63), see also the following claim: "die Grundgesetze der Sprache nur dunkel und ohne klares Bewusstsein, bloß im dem Gefühle eines jeden liegen" (Wüllner 1827: 57).

8. "Alles Denken und Sprechen geht von Anschauung aus und zielt darauf zurück. Alle Anschauung aber ist an Raum und Zeit geknüpft und die Anschauungen dieser beiden und ihre möglichen Beziehungen sind gleichsam die Formen für alles Anschauen" (1827: 8).

9. "Alle wahre Präpositionen haben das gemein dass sie ursprünglich Raumanschauungen bezeichnen und unterscheiden sich darin, dass diese Anschauungen verschieden sind. [...] Mithin kann sein Wesen nicht darin liegen, was die einzelnen Präpositionen unterscheidet; sondern er muss das, welches alle gemein haben, oder etwas noch algemeineres, das über jenem steht, bezeichnen" (1827: 7).

> tination can be conceived. Movement is seen as a line, for which the starting point, the end point, or both can be defined. (1827: 7)[10]
>
> The mind first conceives [*anschauet*] the action or the state in itself, without regard to time or space. Once the representation of time and space are introduced to the mind and connected with the action or the state, then these may appear either to coexist peacefully with time and space; or they appear to our intuition to be transient and to extend over time and space; or, lastly, time and space appear to precede the action and the state, which, in turn, derive from them. The first case belongs to the dative, the second to the accusative, the third to the genitive. (1827: 51)[11]
>
> The genitive designates either the point in time from which something is or happens, or it just indicates the "when": according to the latter perspective, both are based entirely on the same intuition. Now the genitive, where it designates the "when", simply indicates the time of the action or the state, regardless of whether this occurs during or within this time: it designates the time without any secondary determinations. The dative, on the other hand, indicates a time during or within which an action takes place or a state occurs. Lastly, the accusative, when it is used without a preposition, always expresses duration. (1827: 52)[12]

Thus, for instance, the *Grundbedeutung* of the genitive was said to cover the meanings of (a) topical origin or provenance (1827: 58); (b) logical source or "validation and justification" (1827: 60); (c) property or "owning" (1827: 62), also nuanced in terms of (d) mereological relation (1827: 67), thus as (e) causality (*ibid.*) and (f) substance (1827: 68). The same treatment is applied to the dative (1827: 77 ff.), the accusative (1827: 99, 107–8) and for the category of grammatical mood (1827: 121 ff.), explained by the dual faculty of recognition [*erkennen*] and desiring [*begehren*] and correspondingly including only two forms: indicative and optative (the imperative and the subjunctive representing two variants in each case, while the infinitive is simply excluded).

---

10. "Alles Angeschaute im Raume ist in Bewegung oder in Ruhe befindlich. Das ruhende schauet der Geist als einen Punkt an; wobei gar keine Spaltungen oder Eintheilungen möglich sind. Bei der Bewegung aber kann das woher oder das wohin angeschauet werden. Die Bewegung ist gleichsam eine Linie, wobei der Punkt des Anfanges oder des Endes oder beide anzugeben sind".

11. "Der Geist schauet zuvörderst die Handlung oder das Sein für sich an, ohne auf Zeit oder Raum Rücksicht zu nehmen. Trit dan die Vorstellung von Zeit und Raum vor die Seele und mit der Handlung oder dem Sein in Verbindung: so erscheinen diese entweder als ruhig zusammenseiend mit Zeit und Raume; oder die Handlung oder das Sein erscheint der Anschauung als übergehend und sich ausdehnend auf Zeit und Raum; oder endlich Zeit und Raum erscheinen als vor der Handlung oder dem Sein liegend und diese aus jenen hervorgehend. Der erste Fall gehörte dem Dative, der zweite dem Accusative, der dritte für den Genitiv".

d. Overall, Wüllner stresses the logical necessity of a monosemic explanation, *i.e.* the fact that the *Grundbedeutung* should be unitary:

> If, as is commonly claimed, the genitive form designates sometimes property, sometimes dependence, sometimes this and that, one should conclude that it basically designates nothing of them. (1827: 9)[13]

> It is sufficiently clear from what has been said that differences may occur in the explanation of a particular case without this being detrimental to the fundamental concept. Some things might perhaps be better explained in a manner different from that which seemed fitting to me. But this is not any kind of lack, since nothing more is required to explain and justify a case than to demonstrate the existence or the possibility of the fundamental concept. It also remains to be determined, in individual instances, how this or that case might be understood in a more abstract way [*geistiger*], or which secondary determination is attached to it. (1827: 11)[14]

> Furthermore, the idea for each linguistic form must be one that encompasses all its occurrences, or at least all its main occurrences, in such a way that it is possible to assess how the ones not covered might easily appear to be motivated through an expanded analogy. Then this idea must be clear in every human mind, even if not clearly consciously, and necessarily inherent in it. Otherwise, the language under its direction would have had to become a chaotic mess, as claimed by many of those who do not wish to investigate the matter. (1827: 3)[15]

12. "Der Genitiv bezeichnet nemlich entweder den Zeitpunkt, von welchem an etwas ist oder geschieht, oder er gibt schlechtweg das wan an: beides beruht nach der lezteren Ansicht völlig auf derselben Anschauung. Der Genitiv nun gibt da, wo er das wan bezeichnet, bloß den Zeitpunkt der Handlung oder des Seins an ohne Rücksicht, ob die Angabe in der Zeit oder während derselben vorfalle: er bezeichnet die Zeit ohne alle Nebenbestimmung. Der Dativ dagegen gibt eine Zeit an, in oder innerhalb welcher eine Handlung vorfält oder ein Sein Statt findet. Der Accusativ aber drückt immer, wenn er ohne Präposition steht, eine Dauer aus".

13. "Wenn, wie man so gemeinlich hört, der Genitiv als Form bald Eigenthum, bald Abhängigkeit, bald dieses und jenes bezeichnet; so sollte man doch auf den Gedanken kommen, dass er im Grunde nichts von dem allen bezeichnet".

14. "Dass also in der Erklärung eines bestimten Falles Verschiedenheit eintreten könnte ohne der Grundansicht zu schaden, geht aus dem gesagten hinlänglich hervor. Und einzelnes wird daher aus andre Weiße vielleicht richtiger können zusammengestelt werden, als es mir gut geschienen. Aber dieses ist auch kein sonderlicher Mangel, da zur Erklärung und Begründung eines Casus nichts weiter erforderlich ist, als das Vorhandensein oder die Möglichkeit der jedesmaligen Grundanschauung darzuthun. Auch bleibt noch übrig zu bestimmen, wie dieser oder jener Casus in einzelnen Fällen geistiger zu fassen sei oder welche Nebenbestimmung ihm beiwohne".

15. "Ferner muss nun die Idee für die jedesmalige Sprachform eine alle ihre Fälle umfassende sein, oder doch so, dass sie alle Hauptfälle umfasst und sich zeigen lässt, wie die, welche nicht darunter gehen, durch eine zu weit geschrittene Analogie leicht gerechtfertiget erscheinen konnten. Dan muss diese Idee eine in jedem menschlichen Geiste klar, wenn auch ohne deutliches

e. It is highly significant that in the monosemic viewpoint proposed in the previous quotation Wüllner seems to recognise the possibility of extending the *Grundbedeutung* by means of metaphor or interpretation (see Widoff 2023). Accordingly, non-spatial meanings could be "reduced" to spatial ones: instrument or causality could be interpreted as abstract/logical nuances of topical proximity, and so forth. This is, of course, a double-edged solution that makes monosemy less problematic, but also, in a way, less monosemic, and can only be warranted through proper metalinguistic justification[16] – something which Wüllner was not concerned about. At any rate, monosemy was maintained as a panchronic hypothesis, generalised beyond the relatively narrow framework adopted in his 1827 work:

> Yes, I would dare to extend to all the languages of the world, even without the slightest historical knowledge of them, the claim that, in general, in their cases, or in that which fulfills their function, there lie the same fundamental ideas that are asserted – and, I believe, really proven – for a number of languages in what follows. (1827: 5)[17]

f. Moreover, this hypothesis is connected to an epistemological requirement concerning how empirical reality needs to be explained: if we have to explain language, then we are forced to assume that it is not randomly or chaotically constituted. Hence the need to subsume the different usage of a form – for instance, a case – into a general meaning linked to that form. In other words, the descriptive (ontic) stance should be coupled with a normative (deontic) one:

> Therefore, if one does not want to accept [...] that the three most noble languages of the western world are unphilosophical in their innermost structure, then there *must be* a fundamental principle, which splits into three and serves the language as guiding intuition when case is used. (1827: 5; our emphasis)[18]

Bewusstsein, und eine nothwendig in ihm liegende sein. Sonst hätte ja freilich die Sprache unter ihrer Leitung ein so wüstes Chaos werden müssen, wie mancher, der nicht prüfen mag, wähnt".

16. For further discussion of Hjelmslev's interpretation see Cigana (2022: 148–149, 181 ff.).

17. "Ja ich möchte von allen Sprachen der Erde auch ohne die geringste geschichtliche Kenntnis derselben die Behauptung wagen, dass in ihren Casus oder in dem, welches deren Geschäft verwaltet, im algemeinen eben dieselben Grundgedanken liegen, die im folgende von einigen Sprachen behauptet und, wie ich meine, wirklich nachgewiesen werden".

18. "Wenn man daher [...] nicht annehmen will, dass die drei edelsten Sprachen der Westwelt in ihrem innersten Baue unphilosophisch seien; so muss es einen Grundgedanken geben, welcher sich in eine Dreiheit spaltet und der Sprache bei dem Gebrauche der Casus zur leitenden Anschauung dient".

If Franz Wüllner was counted by Hjelmslev among the champions of grammatical semantics, Max Deutschbein was quoted by Jakobson as the most (at that time) recent representative of that same tradition (Jakobson [1936] 1984: 61–62).

In 1933, at the 3rd International Congress of Linguists in Rome, Deutschbein gave a talk on the *Bedeutung der Kasus im Indogermanischen* in which he really tapped the aforementioned tradition of speculative grammar, revamping it in the light of Otto Jespersen's terminology (1924). Syntax is defined as the expression of the synthetic function of human consciousness, through which the speaker puts together different conscious content by giving it a linear order. Three kinds of connections might be envisioned (Deutschbein 1935: 141): "simple connection" [*Verknüpfung*] (giving rise to a nexus), "combination" [*Verbindung*] (giving rise to a junction or nominal phrase) and "crystallisation" or "fusion" [*Verschmelzung*] (giving rise to complex constructs and word-groups). In each case, however, it is only the internal representation of external reality, i.e. "thingness" [*Dingheit*] and "activity" [*Tätigkeit*], which is combined, and this correlates with the traditional coupling of a noun and a verb, both reciprocally transposable via adjectivisation (participles).

Under this approach, grammatical number offers a way of synthetising two or more "thingnesses" by quantitative organisation. Each meaning has its own syntactic construction: "plural" (connection: a simple sum of entities), dual and possibly trial (combination) and singular or collective (a cohesive unity). The same approach holds for grammatical case, which offers another possibility for synthesis, expressing the dependency between two objects. Wüllner's influence is patent here, as Deutschbein identifies three main cases: genitive, dative and accusative. The degree of dependency between two objects expressed by each of these cases – and called "coherence" by Deutschbein (1935: 142) – can be either "dynamic" (the accusative expresses the governed object as reaching out to encroach the logical sphere of the governing object, representing simple connection), "kinetic" (the dative expresses the tension or orientation towards the indirect object, which stands for a syntactic combination) or "static" (the genitive, which expresses pure belonging and thus a state in which the governed object is conceived as included, thus "fused", in the governing one). Cases also express how the "logical domains" [*Dingheitssphären*] of two objects interact, by subsumption [*Unterordnung*] (accusative), juxtaposition [*Nebenordnung*] (dative with instrumental and sociative variants), interpolation [*Einordnung*] (genitive) or extrapolation [*Ausordnung*] (ablative). The particular functions of each case are then analysed in more detail (Deutschbein 1935: 143–145).

One cannot fail to recognise, in those classifications, the same principles as those operating in the other speculative grammars, and most notably in those of Roth and Wüllner. Given the strong a priori nature of such attempts, which often symptomatically bore the label "rational",[19] "logical" or "philosophical" in their titles, one may well ask why they were taken up by structuralists such as Hjelmslev and Jakobson. If an approach retained so many characteristics of the structuralistic framework, what did this framework fall short of? And where did the need to distinguish between *Grundbedeutungen* and *Gesamtbedeutungen* come from? The answer is not a simple one, and it requires careful distinctions to be drawn between the levels of theoretical assumption, methodology and empirical description. In short, while the theoretical framework, *i.e.* the monosemic semantic motivation of categories, was indeed consistent with the structuralist one, this cannot be said for either the methodological ground chosen – which, for structuralism, comprised systems and oppositions – or for the broader empirical and comparative coverage. More on that below.

Overall, the pervasiveness of the *Grundbedeutung*-hypothesis cannot be overlooked, especially when considering it not from the point of view of case, but from that of the classic stumbling block for such endeavours: grammatical gender. Here, any such hypothesis had to stand its own against the counterargument (endorsed, among others, by Meillet 1903, Marty 1910, Wackernagel 1924 and Potebnja 1888), according to which grammatical gender was a luxury, a vestige of diachronic evolution, and thus devoid of semantic motivation. One would have had to push a motivationally-driven hypothesis to its limits in order to turn it into a fully methodological principle with heuristic power and systematic reach: this was first achieved by structuralism.

3. The structuralist turn

In many ways, the structural take on the *Grundbedeutung*-tradition didn't consist of rejecting such a framework, rather reversing it: the starting point was no longer the logical or representational workings of thought, but the structure of grammar. Hence, the morphosyntactical definition of grammatical categories has priority over semantic meaning. However, when it came to establishing semantic values, the efforts and findings of the previous tradition came in useful. This is especially clear in the case of the debate initiated by Hjelmslev and Jakobson. From a historiographical point of view, it is tempting to assume their respective reconstructions in the light of Vogt's quotation given above, *i.e.* as a sort of compass, to keep the focus of our investigation on the *Grund-* or *Gesamtbedeutung*. Yet it must be borne in mind that both linguists tackled the tradition of speculative grammar in

19. The abuse of such labels might also be deemed symptomatic of a certain take on the matter: cf. Brøndal 1940, Holt 1946.

an ideological way, *i.e.* in order to simultaneously provide their own narratives for their analyses, as well as to distance themselves both from it and, possibly, from each other. Moreover, their terminological "rebranding" of the previous tradition had the effect of overshadowing a number of similar attempts that flourished between 1920 and 1930, including those by Gustave Guillaume (1883–1960), Jacques van Ginneken (1877–1945) and Viggo Brøndal (1887–1942) (see §3). Yet, the debate around *Grund-* or *Gesamtbedeutung* was a way for both Hjelmslev and Jakobson to make their point, in order to catalyse further research in the domain of structural linguistics.

The debate took the form of a back-and-forth between the two linguists.

Hjelmslev theorised the necessity of postulating a meaningful unitary ground for grammatical categories in 1928, applying it to the category of articles, and he extended this revamped method of *Grundbedeutungen* to the category of case in 1935, also reviewing Wüllner's principles.

The term *Grundbedeutung* was, however, first used by Jakobson in his criticism of Deutschbein's proposal during the Congress in Rome (1935):

> The basic[20] meaning [*Grundbedeutung*] of each case is determined by the entire case system of a given language and can be established only by investigating the structure of this system. One cannot however establish general and universal case-meanings. An example: contrariwise to the definition of genitive formulated in [Deutschbein's] talk, the genitive of Russian means that the thingness of B lies at least partially outside the domain of A.
>
> (Jakobson 1935, see also Jakobson [1936] 1984: 61–62)

It might be of some interest, then, that in 1936, after Hjelmslev's publication, Jakobson dropped the term in favour of the relatively freshly coined *Gesamtbedeutung* (1936). In fact, the two terms were *meant* to mean the same thing, only connoting a different personal take on the matter. Nowadays, they are used synonymously. However, at the time, both linguists took great care to keep them distinct, as their two notions stood worlds apart. Hence the controversial status of this terminological couple.

In their respective papers, both Hjelmslev (1935) and Jakobson (1936) react against earlier tradition: while it succeeded in stressing the need for such unitary meanings in grammar, it did so only at the cost of systematicity. In fact, despite what Wüllner and Deutschbein claimed,[21] the whole they spoke of was rather the

20. We would prefer "fundamental meaning", however, in the English translation of 1936, the term *Grundbedeutung* has been translated as "basic meaning" (see Jakobson [1936] 1984: 62).

totality of *each form taken in itself*, not one stemming from the mutual relationships occurring between these forms. Not that this was faulty per se, but it was highly insufficient to account for the organic nature of a linguistic system: a structural description needed to describe each form 1) as a totality supporting multiple and different contextual meanings (*Einzel-* or *Sonderbedeutungen*, see Jakobson [1936] 1984: 59), and 2) as a part of a bigger totality (namely: the paradigm of belonging), contracting mutual relationships with other forms. In Jakobson's and Hjelmslev's frameworks, *both* these levels were deemed to carry a unitary meaning (a relatively concrete one in the first case, and a quite abstract one in the second) – an idea that was left implicit or explicitly denied in earlier scholarship.[22]

The difference between Hjelmslev's *Grundbedeutung* and Jakobson's *Gesamtbedeutung* lies in how such a hierarchy was conceived and is thus a matter of mereology rather than semantics. Hjelmslev suggested that the "value" of a given grammatical form (for instance: a case) is conceived as a nuance of the "fundamental value" assigned to the corresponding category. Theoretically speaking, the value of each contextual meaning (*Einzelbedeutung*) that a form may have in speech form depends on the value of this form, and this, in turn, depends on the fundamental meaning (*Grundbedeutung*) of the relative category: and while the fundamental meaning is panchronic, the value of each form depends on each language, so that the ablative in a language A may mean a topical distancing, in a language B it may mean logical proximity (instrumental function), and in a language C it may be completely absent (in cases where its semantism may be taken up and redistributed by other collateral forms, or converted), while still being interpreted on the basis of a common semantic parameter, namely "direction" (the content-substance associated with case in general; on this, see Cigana & Polis 2023).

In Hjelmslev's view, the monosemic approach requires the reduction of the multiplicity of contextual meanings to a single unitary meaning by interpretation or metaphorical extension (see above). The justification for this is that the *Grundbedeutung* is so abstract that it works on multiple phenomenological levels at the same time. For instance, grammatical case is said to work on both logical *and* topical levels. This means that it is acceptable to interpret causality (abstract, logical), for example, in terms of proximity (concrete, topical), and vice versa.

21. See, for instance, Wüllner: "So wird mich dieses ermuntern, einst meine geringen Kräfte an einem größeren Werke über das gesamte Sprachgebäude zu versuchen" (Wüllner 1827: Vorrede).

22. "Es ist aber auch kein Grund vorhanden anzunehmen, dass die einzelnen Casus noch etwas algemeineres bedeuteten, als aus dem gesagten folgt" (Wüllner 1827: 7).

This sounds quite pretentious, yet the point here is that Hjelmslev took great care in formulating this requirement explicitly, not implementing it implicitly. This is why Jakobson's 1936 criticism must have hit him especially hard.

While remarking that Hjelmslev's 1935 work marked "a considerable step forward toward a scientific solution to case" (Jakobson [1936] 1984: 62), he also stressed that "the author does not sufficiently adhere to his own principles in his own concrete studies of case system" (Jakobson [1936] 1984: 63). Jakobson could hardly have said anything that would have upset Hjelmslev more! What he meant was that Hjelmslev was reverting to the old tradition by confusing the morphological (paradigmatic) value of a form with the enumeration of its syntactic (syntagmatic) meanings in speech:

> Here, the problem of general meanings is clearly pushed aside, on the one hand, in favor of the traditional list of individual meanings, or of the list of syntactic functions of each of the two cases (e.g. nominative as the case of the subject and of the predicate, as a predicate-less form, and as an address form) and, on the other hand, in favor of establishing the principal meaning of each case. *(ibid.*: 65)

Jakobson warned that:

> The question of the general meanings of cases belongs to morphology while the question of particular meanings belongs to syntax, since the general meaning of a case is independent of its environment, while its particular meanings are defined by various combinations of surrounding words involving both their formal and their real reference – the particular meanings are therefore, so to speak, *combinatory variants of the general meaning.* (*ibid.*: 69)

Of course Jakobson is perfectly right. The point is that Hjelmslev was trying to do exactly the same. What the claim that "in the nominative 'the value of «subject» predominates', while in the accusative 'the value of «object» predominates' and is often the only one envisaged" (Jakobson [1936] 1984: 66, quoting Hjelmslev 1935: 116 ff., *passim*) really shows is that, in Hjelmslev's view, syntactic meanings are not conceived as independent functions but as contextual variants that a given invariant (a case form) assumes in speech. The whole point is then how to subsume and map these contextual variants under their general – or fundamental – value, and the answer Hjelmslev came up with was: according to a given set of marked-unmarked configurations.[23] Thus, while the terms "*Gesamt-*" and "*Grundbedeutung*" basically denoted the same idea – a common push towards monosemy –, they came to connote rather different things:

23. More precisely, insistence – something that was completely disregarded by Jakobson.

a. the relationship between morphology and syntax, or how these were conceived in relation to each other, either as two independent levels (Jakobson and Brøndal, see Jakobson [1936] 1984: 62–63, 99) or as unilaterally dependent (Hjelmslev);
b. Hjelmslev's and Jakobson's willingness to make a statement.

In fact, in Jakobson's eyes, Hjelmslev's *Grundbedeutung* [*signification fondamentale*] was too close to "principal meaning" [*signification principale*], while clearly "what the author has in mind is more accurately expressed by the term general meaning" [*signification générale*] ([1936] 1984: 62). Hjelmslev did not delay in responding to this criticism. In his second volume on case, in 1937, he took up the debate from where Jakobson had left it:

> Pour fixer la signification fondamentale d'un élément il faut tenir compte de l'ensemble des emplois qu'il contracte dans l'usage, mais la valeur n'est pas identique à la somme de ces emplois : la valeur est une signification fondamentale (grundbedeutung), nullement une signification générale dans le sens d'une gesamtbedeutung ; (Hjelmslev 1937: 45)

also rebounding in 1939:

> une variante (aussi bien qu'une qualité) est toujours une fonction d'une forme; une signification particulière (ou une qualité sémantique) – qu'elle soit « principale » (« pertinente ») ou non – est toujours fonction d'une signification fondamentale, qui ne se confond pas avec la signification « générale », mais qui en diffère par son plus haut degré d'abstraction, et dont on peut, non pas trier mécaniquement, mais déduire logiquement les significations particulières .
> ([1939] 1970: 115)

The crux of the matter can be represented as in Figure 2, where the three levels belong respectively (1) to a given grammatical paradigm (e.g. inflectional case), (2) to its members (e.g. nominative, accusative, dative, etc.), (3) to the particular meanings and instantiations of a given member (e.g. the instrumental, provenience, comitative etc. functions of ablative):

Was it a mere terminological issue? Only partially, since the two methods yield quite different applications. The reasons for this are simple.

Firstly, Hjelmslev's monosemy consisted of attaching a single value to a given category *as a whole*, while Jakobson attached the single value to a given opposition between two members *within* said category. So, a category has only one *Grundbedeutung* (Hjelmslev's monosemy) but multiple *Gesamtbedeutungen*, each attached to a single opposition between terms (Jakobson's monosemy). From this perspective, Hjelmslev was right in claiming an essential difference between the two terms.

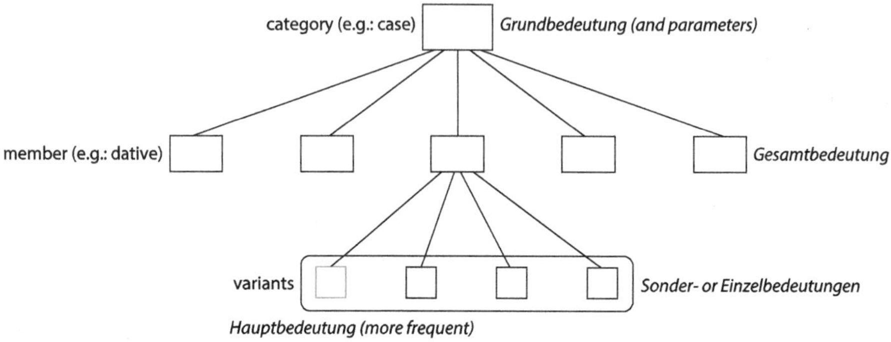

Figure 2. Tentative representation of the relationship between *Grundbedeutung* and *Gesamtbedeutung*

Secondly, the two concepts rely on a different take on the notion of "opposition" – and, to illustrate this, it is worthwhile considering the methodological aspects involved. In a significant shift from previous scholarship, in structuralism it was maintained that linguistic elements do not acquire a meaning "positively", by the simple fact of existing, but rather "negatively", by contracting mutual oppositions. Jakobson took the notion of opposition quite literally, by postulating a strict binary framework: an opposition occurs between two elements. More complex systems, then, need to be described in terms of branching oppositions. This, however, eventually leads to the impossibility of maintaining a monosemic approach. In fact, if each opposition of a given system represents a general meaning, the ratio between elements and possible oppositions (and thus oppositional meanings) increases geometrically:

> Between 16 terms – the number of simple Greek prepositions reported by Bortone (2010) – there are 120 possible oppositions, and between 181 terms – the total count given for Swedish above – there are a whopping 16.290 possible oppositions. (Widoff forthcoming)

Hjelmslev's take was different, leading to a less explosive result:[24] the oppositions (or "correlations") between elements are said to occur on parameters, called dimensions, that work as Cartesian coordinates. Each dimension represents a different nuance of the *Grundbedeutung*, in relation to which each element behaves oppositely, according to six (or seven) logical configurations. Despite its convolutedness, the whole theory was devised to make a monosemic approach viable

24. Despite what Bílý claims (Bílý 1989: 15, § 4.5): his calculus is simply faulty because of an erroneous interpretation of Hjelmslev's assumptions (notably, on the orientation of dimensions; see Cigana 2022: §§ 2.5.8 and 2.5.9 for a detailed discussion).

without having to give up the possibility of accounting for multiple contextual variants.

A thorough comparison of Jakobson's rendering of Russian cases (1936) and its transposition into Hjelmslev's theory was carried out by Sørensen (1949), who showed that, while Jakobson operated with four correlative meanings (1. transitivity [*Bezug Korrelation*], 2. extension [*Umfang Korrelation*], 3. shaping [*Gestalt Korrelation*], 4. position [*Rand Korrelation*]), Hjelmslev's model only required two semantic parameters of the fundamental meaning of case (1. proximity/distancing, 2. degrees of contact). Sørensen links the differences between the two models to the debate about *Grund-* or *Gesamtbedeutung*:

> C'est cette différence qui fait que M. Hjelmslev parle de « signification fondamentale » ou de « valeur », tandis que M. Jakobson préfère parler d'une signification générale (Gesamtbedeutung) dont les différents sens particuliers seraient une sorte de variantes combinatoires. Selon M. Jakobson, il n'y a pas plus dans la signification générale que dans l'ensemble de sens particuliers, bien qu'il ne conçoive pas le rapport entre les sens particuliers et la signification générale comme un rapport d'addition mécanique, puisqu'il parle d'une hiérarchie régulière de sens particuliers. M. Hjelmslev voit la chose autrement [here Sørensen quotes the citation reproduced above: Hjelmslev 1937: 45].
>
> (Sørensen 1949: 127–128)

Of course, the catch in Hjelmslev's theory is that the model performs well when it comes to systems that are (relatively) limited, such as the paradigms of inflectional fundamental nominal or verbal morphemes, while, for open or productive systems, such as lexical categories (where such categories can be established), the calculus requires many more dimensions, and thus the monosemic approach remains in question.[25]

4. Extending the count

At any rate, the importance of Sørensen's comparison lies not just in having shown how the two models capture the same facts and where they overlap or differentiate, rather, it shows that, at least around 1949, such a comparison was felt to be relevant and necessary, and that the debate around those issues was still lively and productive.

25. In this case, Hjelmslev's approach is slightly different, as the whole lexical level is not deemed to form a single system.

To understand to what extent, it is worthwhile considering two sources: firstly, the *Proceedings* of the Sixth International Congress of Linguists, held in Paris in 1948; secondly, the volume in homage to Louis Hjelmslev on the occasion of his 50th birthday, *Recherches structurales* (1949), in which the aforementioned paper by H. C. Sørensen is included. During the 6th ICL, Hjelmslev presents the activity of the Copenhagen school as a cohesive group focused on general grammar and morphology, and he portrays the research of Viggo Brøndal, Paul Diderichsen, Jens Holt, Hans Christian Sørensen and himself, each as devoted to the illumination of the structure and semantism of a specific grammatical category (see Sørensen 1949: 126–135). While the picture is slightly exaggerated, the scholars mentioned are indeed those who were – at different points in time – closest to Hjelmslev's preoccupations and methods. The volume *Recherches structurales* (1949) confirms this, adding even more names to the group, including:

- Hans Vogt (1949), *L'étude des systèmes de cas*. Much like Sørensen, Vogt compares Jakobson's and Hjelmslev's methods (as applied by Sebeok and Lotz, respectively) in relation to case, pinpointing their underpinnings (segmentation and establishment of the inventory; oppositions vs. dimensions), and stressing the methodological originality of the *Grundbedeutung* scholarship (see also here, Introduction);
- Émile Benveniste (1949), *Le système sublogique des prépositions en Latin*. This contribution must be understood as one of the most dedicated homages to Hjelmslev, as the author does not simply focus on the issues of case and prepositions, describing – in a somewhat old-fashioned way – the functions of Latin *prae*, rather he goes so far as to adopt Hjelmslev's rather idiosyncratic term of *sublogic*: "La solution doit découler des conditions posées à la signification générale[26] de la préposition. Le *prae* causal et le *prae* comparatif doivent s'expliquer par le même schème sublogique qui est à la base des emplois communs de *prae*" (Benveniste 1949: 181). He concludes that: "Tous les emplois de *prae* se tiennent ainsi dans une définition constante. Nous avons voulu montrer sur un exemple que, dans l'étude des prépositions, quels que soient l'idiome et l'époque considérés, une nouvelle technique de la description est nécessaire et devient possible, pour restituer la structure de chacune des prépositions et intégrer ces structures dans un système général" (Benveniste 1949: 183–184). Of course, this method was not new to Benveniste: just a year earlier he had published one of his most significant works, "Noms d'agent et noms d'action en indo-européen" (1948), in which he participates in this debate in a quite literal sense: he and Holt had a lively argument concerning the semantism of agentive suffixes (see Cigana 2018: 29). In light of this, the technique presented by Benveniste in 1948, although foreshad-

owed in his 1935 research on the value of Indo-European roots, can hardly be said to be a "new theory and method for the study of suffixes and suffixal junction" (Fruyt 1992: 159): its importance was rather in having extended the framework to the domain of derivation and suffixes, consolidating the structural method in general grammar and grammatical semantics (see also Benveniste 1956, 1958 and 1959). Incidentally, it is worth noting that, based on the Jakobson-Hjelmslev discussion, Benveniste's description wouldn't respect either criterion: *against* Jakobson's requirement, Benveniste was too prone to consider a single preposition along with its *Einzelbedeutungen*; *against* Hjelmslev's requirement, Benveniste's *signification générale* pertains to the chosen preposition (*prae*) rather than the category of preposition;
- John Lotz (1949), *The semantic analysis of the nominal bases in Hungarian.* This contribution touched on one of Hjelmslev's most pressing concerns – to avoid any a priori limitation of his theory to IE languages. Lotz worked for some time with Hjelmslev and presented a description based on 14 bases (14 suffixes added to the stem) and four semantic relations (1. aggregation or consistence in terms of countable/uncountable quantification, 2. dependence, 3. inclusion/exclusion in reference to communication, 4. address). While detailing the correlative meanings, Lotz's model does not commit itself to monosemy: the fact that the inventory of nominal bases is closer to the lexical domain rather than to morphology reduces this necessity (see here Note 25);
- Paul Diderichsen (1949), *Morpheme categories in modern Danish.* Diderichsen reviews the table of categories given in Hjelmslev 1936 and both their morphosyntactic and semantic definitions (case, person, diathesis, emphasis, comparison, number/gender, aspect/tense/mood, article), tweaking the model, while overall complying with its monosemic foundation, e.g. by suggesting the adoption of the previous semantic definition of an article as based on the *Grundbedeutung* "abstraction-concretisation" given by Hjelmslev in 1928 and "obviously inspired by Guillaume's famous book, *Le problème de l'article et sa solution dans la langue française*, Paris 1919)" (Diderichsen 1949: 149, see below); or by adding an 11th category of negation/affirmation as a "nova stella" (Diderichsen 1949: 151) in Hjelmslev's categorial firmament, which shares the semantic content of "reality" with mood;
- the article by Hans Christian Sørensen (1949), *Contribution à la discussion sur la théorie des cas*, mentioned above.

Of course, the actual breadth of research within the framework of *Grund-* or *Gesamtbedeutung* was significantly greater. Hjelmslev's theory inspired still further

26. Here, Benveniste uses this term as unmarked in relation to the Hjelmslev-Jakobson debate.

research that was carried out relatively autonomously, including by Gunnar Bech (1949, see especially: 38–39), Anders Bjerrum (1949), Holger Steen (1949) and, to some extent, Schmitt-Jensen (1970). Moreover, other important contributions were formulated outside of the Hjelmslev-Jakobson debate – and even predating it. The theories of Gustave Guillaume, Jacques van Ginneken and Viggo Brøndal were constructed in the wake of Michel Bréal's programmatic lecture at the Collège de France (1868), much like Hjelmslev's and Jakobson's.

Gustave Guillaume had already been working on the category of articles (1919) and on the verbal categories of tense, mode and aspect (1929, 1933),[27] elaborating a unified framework for these investigations known as psychomechanics (see Monneret 2012, Cusimano 2012: 80 ff.), focused on the identification of the preconscious operations that form the meaningful ground of linguistic categories, creating a mental representation which then seeps into speech. In this sense, for instance, the cognitive operations of "particularisation" and "generalisation", which, according to Guillaume, characterise the categories of article and number (Guillaume 1945b: 166), can be seen as two sides, or "tensions" (1945a: 159 ff.), of a single and fundamental semantic parameter. It is also worthwhile mentioning that, in 1944, Guillaume spoke of a "signification première", which German translators deemed appropriate to translate as *Grundbedeutung* (Guillaume 2000: 67):

> [...] we do not see how thought could arrange itself in order to apply something that does not signify anything by itself: an application in the order of signification is only possible through a given *basic signification*; a zero meaning has no possible application. (our translation and emphasis)[28]

Elsewhere, Guillaume distinguishes a "valeur d'emploi" (Guillaume [1944a] 1973: 141–142) from a "valeur en système" (*ibid.*) or "valeur essentielle" (*Id.*: 140); later he also referred to an "idée de base" or "signification fondamentale" (1944c [1973]: 201) intended as an "opération primordiale de la pensée" (1947 [1973]: 186). His insight,[29] however, remains the same, and it is consistent with Hjelmslev's definition of *Grundbedeutungen* as "significations fondamentales" or "valeurs" (Hjelmslev 1935: 84):

27. Guillaume kept on working on his psychomechanics for the following twenty years: see Guillaume 1937, 1939, 1942–43, 1944b, 1945a, 1945b.

28. "[...] on ne voit pas sur quoi la pensée se réglerait pour faire application de quelque chose qui ne signifierait rien par soi-même: une application dans l'ordre de la signification n'est possible qu'à partir d'une signification première donnée, une signification zéro n'a pas d'application possible" (Guillaume [1944a] 1973: 141).

29. Blumenthal speaks of an "Idealistische Neuphilologie" taken up by Guillaume and Weinrich (Blumenthal 1985: 84).

> It cannot be over-emphasised that the *systemic value* of a form is fully acquired in the language, whereas the value of usage remains to be acquired […]. *The systemic value* of a form is flexible with respect to its use-values in discourse (Guillaume [1944a] 1973: 141; our translation and emphasis).[30]
> […] the current urgent challenge for linguistic science is to steer research in the direction followed here, in which, before any examination of the usage-value of a form, care is taken to reconstitute the system of which it is integral part and where it acquires its *essential value* – a value that exists in the mind (without our being able to realise it directly, since we don't have direct access to these deep operations) before any usage-value is attested in speech.
> (Guillaume [1944a] 1973: 143; our translation and emphasis)[31]

Here, again, the particular meanings that linguistic forms acquire in speech are said to stem from (and be subsumed under) a fundamental meaning, which serves as the invariant to which particular meanings can be reduced (see Guillaume 2000, xiii).

Jacques van Ginneken also participated in reviving this methodology. In his case, however, there was a twist: the *Grundbedeutungen*, instead of being conceptual or logical (representational), were said to be of affective nature, resulting either from an original act of consciousness dubbed "assent" (van Ginneken 1907, see Cigana 2017), deemed to be at the source of *declinabilia*, or from feelings and emotions, at the basis of *indeclinabilia*. Van Ginneken's rather peculiar theory resulted in an attempt to classify linguistic elements according to the various forms of assent they included – real or potential, absolute or relative, significant or indicative – and it can thus be situated in the wake of speculative grammar.[32] This tradition was, in fact, never rejected by Van Ginneken, but rather tweaked in the light of the research on linguistic feeling and the affective roots of language developed in French experimental psychology by, for instance, Henri Delacroix, Théodule Ribot, Alfred Binet and Jean-Martin Charcot. Van Ginneken's ideas –

30. "On ne saurait trop souligner que la valeur d'une forme en système est totalement acquise dans la langue, alors que la valeur d'emploi, elle, y reste tout entière à acquérir […]. La valeur d'une forme en système est permissive à l'endroit de ses valeurs d'emploi dans le discours".

31. "[…] la tâche actuelle urgente de la science du langage est de porter ses recherches dans une direction qui est celle suivie ici, où, avant tout examen de la valeur d'emploi d'une forme, on prend soin préalablement de reconstituer le système dont elle fait partie intégrante et où elle prend sa valeur essentielle, valeur préexistante dans l'esprit – sans que nous nous en puissions rendre compte directement (nous n'avons pas un accès direct à ces opérations profondes) – à toute valeur d'emploi attestée dans le discours".

32. Hence his interest in Brøndal's and Hjelmslev's theories – interest that was reciprocated, at least to some extent.

in all their flamboyancy – were instrumental in the fight against representationalism and catalysed the advent of the structural paradigm.

Last but not least, Viggo Brøndal's concept of meaning journeys through the same realms of linguistic tradition as Jakobson's and Hjelmslev's, yet his does so with a very different attitude, and it achieves radically different goals. Looking at his work objectively, it may appear that he is more dependent on the tradition than Jakobson and Hjelmslev, constructing his counterparts of *Gesamtbedeutungen* for only a narrow set of categories derived from Aristotle and Kant (Brøndal 1928: 63–73, 1932: 19–20). In the introductory chapter of *Ordklassserne* (Brøndal 1928: 1–62), he demonstrates how his four categories are always at the centre of the discussion of the parts of speech in the tradition. This way of conceiving the fundamentals of linguistic analysis seems to construct the credibility of its claims on the grounds that linguistic analysis has revolved around these concepts since the origin of European thought. Yet, what he does when he builds his analytic concepts from his fundamental structures takes him to a position quite remote from the tradition due to the fact that he conceives the set of categories as manifestations of some kind of structured meta-level. His four fundamental concepts, the *Relatum* (R) and the *Relator* (r), the *Descriptum* (D) and the *Descriptor* (d), are organised as a system defined by two binary oppositions, 'Subjective | Objective' and 'Active| Passive' (Brøndal 1928: 70), portrayed in Figure 3:

	Passive categories	Active categories
Subjective categories	*Descriptum*	*Descriptor*
Objective categories	*Relatum*	*Relator*

Figure 3. Brøndal's categorisation

In this way, Brøndal changes the table of categories, *i.e.* the possible predicates of things in the Aristotelian approach, into an interdependent binary system. It is worth noting that his stance is to be understood as an explicitly and fully abstract[33] attempt to reduce the multiplicity of linguistic phenomena to a set of unitary parameters. This is most clear in Brøndal's *Præpositionernes Theori* (1940), which represents, in many ways, an endeavour parallel to Hjelmslev's (1935–1937) on grammatical case. Here, Brøndal puts forward the methodological tenets that guide his idea of reduction, which, in principle, is not restricted to prepositions but holds at any linguistic level – lexical, morphological, syntactic, etc. Among

33. For instance, localistic approaches are discarded with the argument that meaning always derives from the most abstract level of structural organisation (see Brøndal 1940, §§ 8, 26).

those tenets, monosemy clearly plays a central role. Besides repeatedly speaking of a "primitive or original" meaning of prepositions (Brøndal 1940, § 26), also called "fundamental" (§ 8) or "central" (§ 27), Brøndal assumes this meaning to provide the unitary definition[34] that cuts through, as it were, the multiple particular usages of a given linguistic element and accounts for their being variants (§ 24):

> What is needed to replace the tentative traditional definitions – whether these are based on syntax or morphology – are the means that allow us to define both the specificity of a class of prepositions with respect to other classes of words, and each preposition with respect to the other. As regards the class as such, it seems sufficiently defined if we say that it expresses the relation in general; within this framework, it will therefore be necessary to define each particular preposition as the sum of special relations. (Brøndal 1940, § 12; our translation)

> Here it is necessary to establish the principle that all intuitive forms are equivalent, *i.e.* that they are parallel and equally legitimate facets of the same common definition. A preposition has a central meaning, and it has only one, whatever the object or purpose for which it is used: physical, biological or psychic phenomena (all real), political, aesthetic or religious entities (all ideal), logical objects or mathematicians (all formal). The decisive point for a theory of language is that within usages [...] it is at any rate necessary to abstract from all the intuitive, formal, ideal and real elements. This abstraction will not generally lead to one type, but to several parallel types, more or less (but always to a certain degree) related to each other. These types, independent of any form of intuition, will appear in each of these as regular and analogous forms: they will form analogous series or semantic spectra, constantly recurring. The recognition of this series or spectra seems to me to be the most suitable way to reach the goal that we have set ourselves here: to establish definitions of prepositions.
> (Brøndal 1940, § 26; our translation)

5. Perspectives and conclusions

In what precedes, we have presented a few approaches which tackle the issue at stake: linking the structuralist take on *Gesamtbedeutungen* to its pre-structuralist background and its later reception. Connecting the dots is especially challenging since structuralism transformed the hypothesis of *Gesamtbedeutungen* to the point of turning it into a characterising feature of its own scholarship. Furthermore, the successive developments of this trend pushed it in a different direction,

34. The reduction of the multifarious to a unitary definition is, according to Brøndal, "always possible and necessary" (1940, § 78).

namely towards cognitive naturalisation, synergising with the mentalistic implications at the foundation of this scholarship and often dropping the monosemic approach altogether[35]; others scholars delved deeper into the issue[36] although remaining somewhat bound to the domain of case and localism: the articles by Kuryłowicz (1949) and de Groot (1956), along with several works that followed that line of criticism (see here Note 1), reviewed Jakobson's and Hjelmslev's models, focusing on their applicability to case theory, highlighting various (presumed)[37] shortcomings, such as the vagueness of the semantic values adopted, the limited predictive power, the distinction between primary and secondary functions and between the morphological and syntactic contexts of cases and prepositions (see 162–164), skipping the historical and epistemological dimensions of the issue.

Mapping the full extent of the monosemic approach in structural linguistics and beyond (see for instance Lévi-Strauss 1967), connecting it with its later developments, is, in our eyes, a long-term yet worthwhile challenge for the historiography of language science: the completion of such a mapping would permit a better understanding of the basic underpinnings of the monosemic hypothesis beyond the special domain of theories of case, in relation to which it has traditionally been discussed, leading to a challenge to the claim that "general-meaning analyses are not particularly helpful if one wants to know in what way languages differ from each other" (Haspelmath 2003: 214). After all, the hypothesis of general meanings was formulated as a prerequisite for linguistic comparison, leading to a method for consistently capturing both typological differences and identities across different languages.

35. As in Langacker's analysis of English prepositions (Falkowska 2014; Jansen 2001; see also Langacker 1985), in Anderson's localistic grammar (Fortis 2018), or, more generally, in the semantic maps method (Haspelmath 2003; François 2008: 165–166; Cigana & Polis 2023).

36. This would be the case of Eugenio Coseriu's notion of "unitary meaning" (Coseriu 1992 [1988]: Chapter 7; see Willems & Munteanu 2021: 31–34, 42–43; Widoff 2021: 248 ff.), through which he explicitly took a stance on the issue of *Grund-* or *Gesamtbedeutung*, bringing to the foreground another central aspect – underspecification (Willems 2022: 47).

37. "Presumed" in the sense that the reviews have been quite unilateral, and very few attempts have been made so far to submit them for serious criticism (see here Note 1).

References

Anderson, John M. 2006. *Modern Grammars of Case. A Retrospective.* Oxford Oxford University Press.

Bech, Gunnar. 1949. *Das semantische System der deutschen Modalverba* (*Travaux du Cercle Linguistique de Copenhague IV*), 3–45. Copenhagen: Einar Munksgaard.

Benes, Tuska. 2008. *In Babel's Shadow: Language, Philology and the Nation in Nineteenth-Century Germany.* Detroit, Mich.: Wayne State University Press.

Benveniste, Émile. 1935. *Origines de la formation des noms en indo-européen.* Paris: Maisonneuve.

Benveniste, Émile. 1949. "Le système sublogique des prépositions en latin". *Recherches structurales* (*Travaux du Cercle Linguistique de Copenhague, V*): 177–184. Copenhagen: Einar Munksgaard.

Benveniste, Émile. 1956 [1966]. "La nature des pronoms". *Problèmes de linguistique générale*, I, 251–257. Paris: Gallimard.

Benveniste, Émile. 1958 [1966]. "Catégories de pensée et catégories de langue". *Problèmes de linguistique générale*, I, 63–74. Paris: Gallimard.

Benveniste, Émile. 1959 [1966]. "Les relations de temps dans le verbe français". *Problèmes de linguistique générale*, I, 237–250. Paris: Gallimard.

Bílý, Milan. 1989. "The Case of the Invariant Case Reconsidered". *Slovo: Journal of Slavic Languages and Literatures* 37.5–33.

Birnbaum, Henrik. 1998. "Jakobson's Concept of General Meaning". *Sketches of Slavic scholars,* § 9. Indiana: Slavica Publisher.

Bjerrum, Anders. 1949. *"Verbal Number in the Jutlandic Law" (Travaux du Cercle Linguistique de Copenhague, IV)*, 156–176. Copenhagen: Einar Munksgaard.

Blumenthal, Peter. 1985. Review of *Textgrammatik der französischen Sprache* by Harald Weinrich. *Zeitschrift für französische Sprache und Literatur* 95:1.82–95.

Bréal, Michel. 1868. *Le idées latentes du langage. Leçon faite au Collège de France pour la réouverture du cours de grammaire comparée.* Paris: Hachette.

Brøndal, Viggo. 1928. *Ordklasserne. Partes orationis. Studier over de sproglige Kategorier.* Copenhagen: G. E. C. Gad.

Brøndal, Viggo. 1932. *Morfologi og Syntax.* København: Bianco Lunos Bogtrykkeri.

Brøndal, Viggo. 1940. *Præpositionernes Theori. Indledning til en rationel Betydningslære.* Copenhagen: Munksgaard.

Burkard, Thorsten. 2003. "Die lateinische Grammatik im 18. und frühen 19. Jahrhundert. Von einer Wortarten- zu einer Satzgliedgrammatik. Ellipsentheorie, Kasuslehre, Satzglieder". *Germania Latina – Latinitas Teutonica. Politik, Wissenschaft, humanistische Kultur vom späten Mittelalter bis in unsere Zeit* edited by Eckhard Keßer & Heinrich C. Kuhn, 781–830. Munich: Wilhelm Fink.

Cigana, Lorenzo. 2018. "La forma del mondo. L'analisi glossematica del contenuto tra linguistica e filosofia". *Rivista Italiana di Filosofia del Linguaggio* 1.22–36.

Cigana, Lorenzo. 2019. "The Formalisation of Grammatical Meanings in Copenhagen Structural Linguistics. Some Remarks". *History and Philosophy of the Language Sciences* (online), https://hiphilangsci.net/2019/06/14/formalisation_copenhagen

Cigana, Lorenzo. 2022. *Hjelmslev e la teoria delle correlazioni linguistiche.* Roma: Carocci.

Cigana, Lorenzo & Stéphane Polis. 2023. "Hjelmslev, a Forerunner of the Semantic Maps Method in Linguistic Typology?". *Acta Linguistica Hafniensia* 55:1.93–118.

Coseriu, Eugenio. 1988 [1992]. *Einführung in die allgemeine Sprachwissenschaft.* Tübingen: Francke.

Couturier-Heinrich, Clémence. 2011. "Gottfried Hermann, un philologue kantien". *Revue germanique internationale* 14.73–90.

Cusimano, Christophe. 2012. La sémantique contemporaine. Du sème au thème. Paris: Pups.

Danielsen, Niels. 1980. "The 'Cases', Hjelmslev, and the Cases". *Linguistic studies,* 84–113. Heidelberg: Winter.

de Groot, A. Willem. 1956. "Classification of the Uses of a Case illustrated on the Genitive in Latin". *Lingua* 6.8–65.

Deutschbein, Max. 1935. "Bedeutung der Kasus im Indogermanischen". In *Atti del III Congresso internazionale dei linguisti (Roma, 19–26 settembre 1933)* edited by Bruno Migliorini & Vittorio Pisani, 141–146. Firenze: Felice le Monnier.

Ebeling, Carl L. 1957. "On Case Theories". *Museum* 62.129–145.

Falkowska, Marta. 2014. "Subjectivity and Objectivity in Language as Seen by Louis Hjelmslev and Ronald W. Langacker". *Cognitive Linguistics in the Making* edited by Kinga Rudnicka-Szozda & Aleksander Szwedek, 41–51. Frankfurt am Main & Bern: Peter Lang.

Fillmore, Charles J. 1968. "The Case for Case". *Universals in Linguistic Theory* edited by Emmon Bach & R. Thomas Harms, 1–88. New York: Holt, Rinehart & Winston.

Fortis, Jean-Michel. 2018. "Anderson's Case Grammar and the History of Localism". In (eds.), *Substance-based Grammar – The (Ongoing) Work of John Anderson* edited by Roger Böhm & Harry van der Hulst, 113–198. Amsterdam: John Benjamins.

François, Alexandre. 2008. "Semantic Maps and the Typology of Colexification: Intertwining polysemous networks across languages". *From Polysemy to Semantic Change* edited by Martine Vanhove, 163–215. Amsterdam: John Benjamins.

Fruyt, Michèle. 1992. "Les principes méthodologiques d'Emile Benveniste dans *Noms d'agent et noms d'action en indo-européen*", in *Linx* 26.159–171.

Guillaume, Gustave (1944c) [1973], *Un déterminant de l'espèce de mot: l'incidence. Leçon du 13 janvier 1944*, série A, in Guillaume, 1973, 201–205.

Guillaume, Gustave. 1919. *Le problème de l'article et sa solution dans la langue française.* Paris: Hachette.

Guillaume, Gustave. 1929. *Temps et verbe. Théorie des aspects, des modes et des temps.* Paris: Honoré Champion.

Guillaume, Gustave. 1933. *Immanence et transcendance dans la catégorie du verbe ; esquisse d'une théorie psychologique de l'aspect.* Paris: Alcan.

Guillaume, Gustave. 1937. "Thèmes de présent et système des temps français ; genèse corrélative du présent et des temps". *Journal de Psychologie* 34.161–178 (Rep. in *Langage et science du langage* edited by A.-G. Nizet, 59–72. Québec & Paris: PUL, 1964.)

Guillaume, Gustave. 1939. "Esquisse d'une théorie psychologique de la déclinaison". *Acta Linguistica* 1.167–178 (Rep. in *Langage et science du langage* edited by A.-G. Nizet, 99–107. Québec & Paris: PUL, 1964.)

Guillaume, Gustave. 1942–43. "L'Architectonique du temps dans les langues classiques". *Acta Linguistica* 3:2–3.69–118.

Guillaume, Gustave. 1944a–[1973]. *Nature de l'acte du langage. Leçon du 27 avril 1944*, série A, in Guillaume, 1973, 137–143.

Guillaume, Gustave. 1944b. "Particularisation et généralisation dans le système des articles français". *Le Français moderne* 12.143–156.

Guillaume, Gustave. 1945a. "La question de l'article: d'une raison qui s'est opposée jusqu'ici à une coopération étroite et fructueuse des linguistes historiens et des linguistes théoriciens". *Le Français moderne* 13.1–2.

Guillaume, Gustave. 1945b. "Logique constructive interne du système des articles français". *Le Français moderne* 13.3–4.

Guillaume, Gustave. 1947 [1973]. *Découverte du système: technique d'analyse appropriée. Leçon du 12 décembre 1947*, série C, in Guillaume, 1973, 185–187.

Guillaume, Gustave. 1973. *Principes de linguistique théorique de Gustave Guillaume*. Québec: Presses de l'Université Laval & Paris: Klincksieck.

Guillaume, Gustave. 2000. *Grundzüge einer theoretischen Linguistik*. Tübingen: Max Niemeyer Verlag.

Haspelmath, Martin. 2003. "The Geometry of Grammatical Meaning". In *The New Psychology of Language: Cognitive and Functional Approaches To Language Structure*, vol. II, edited by Michael Tomasello, 211–242. Mahwah, New Jersey & London: Lawrence Erlbaum Associates.

Hermann, Gottfried. 1799. *Handbuch der Metrik*. Leipzig: Fleischer.

Hermann, Gottfried. 1801. *De emendanda ratione graecae grammaticae*. Leipzig: Fleischer.

Hermann, Gottfried. 1803. *De differentia prosae et poeticae orationis*. Leipzig: Fleischer.

Hjelmslev, Louis. 1935. *La catégorie des cas. Étude de grammaire générale*, I (Acta Jutlandica, 7, 1). Aarhus: Universitetsforlaget.

Hjelmslev, Louis. 1937. *La catégorie des cas. Étude de grammaire générale*, II (Acta Jutlandica, 9, 2). Aarhus: Universitetsforlaget.

Hjelmslev, Louis. 1939 (1970). "La structure morphologique". *Essais linguistiques* (*Travaux du Cercle Linguistique de Copenhague XII*), 113–138. Copenhagen: Nordisk Sprog- og Kulturforlag.

Holt, Jens. 1946. *Rationel semantik (pleremik)*. Aarhus: Aarhus Universitetsforlaget.

Jakobson, Roman. 1935. Reaction to Deutschbein (1935). In *Atti del III Congresso internazionale dei linguisti (Roma, 19–26 settembre 1933)*, edited by Bruno Migliorini & Vittore Pisani, 146. Firenze: Felice le Monnier.

Jakobson, Roman. 1936 [1984]. "Contribution to the General Theory of Case: General Meanings of the Russian Cases". *Roman Jakobson, Russian and Slavic Grammar: Studies 1931–1981* edited by Linda R. Waugh & Morris Halle, 59–103. Berlin: Mouton de Gruyter. (Translation of "*Beitrag zur allgemeinen Kasuslehre: Gesamtbedeutung der russischen Kasus*". *Travaux du Cercle Linguistique de Prague*, 1936, 4.240–288).

Jansen, Hanne. 2001. "Brøndal og Langacker: Omkring ordklassers semantik". *Ny forskning i grammatik: Fællespublikation 8 Gilbjerghovedsymposiet 2000*, 127–148. Syddansk: Universitetsforlag.

Jespersen, Otto. 1924. *Philosophy of Grammar*. Allen & Unwin: London.

Kacnel'son, Solomon Davidovich. 1972. *Tipologija jazyka i rečevoe myšlenie*. Leningrad: Nauka.

Kirsner, Robert S. 1985. "Iconicity and grammatical meaning". *Iconicity in Syntax* edited by John Haiman, 249–270. Amsterdam: John Benjamins.

Kuryłowicz, Jerzy. 1949. "Le problème du classement des cas". *Bulletin de la société polonaise de linguistique* 9.20–43.

Langacker, Ronald Wayne. 1985. "Observations and Speculations on Subjectivity". *Iconicity in Syntax* edited by John Haiman, 109–150. Amsterdam: John Benjamins.

Lévi-Strauss, Claude. 1967. "Le sexe des astres". *To honor Roman Jakobson. Essays on the occasion of his seventieth birthday, 11 october 1966*, 1163–1170. La Haye: Mouton.

Marty, Anton. 1910. *Zur Sprachphilosophie. Die „logische", „lokalistiche" und andere Kasustheorien*. Halle: Max Niemeyer.

Meillet, Antoine. 1903. *Introduction à l'étude comparative des langues indoeuropéennes*. Paris: Hachette.

Monneret, Philippe. 2012. "D'une psychomécanique à une neurolinguistique". *Repenser la condition humaine. Gustave Guillaume et Jean Piaget* edited by André Jacob. Paris, Riveneuve.

Picciarelli, Massimiliano. 1999. "Topologia, sistema sublogico e rappresentazione schematica nella teoria hjelmsleviana dei casi". L. Hjelmslev, *La categoria dei casi. Studio di grammatica generale*, 31–56. Lecce: Argo.

Potebnja, Alexander A. 1888. *Iz zapisok po russkoj grammatikě*, I-II. Poluechtov.

Schmitt-Jensen, Jørgen. 1970. *Subjonctif et hypotaxe en italien. Une esquisse de la syntaxe du subjonctif dans les propositions subordonnées en italien contemporain*. Odense: Odense University Press.

Schooneveld, van, C.H. 1983. "Contribution to the Systematic Comparison of Morphological and Lexical Semantic Structures in the Slavic Languages". *American Contributions to the Ninth International Congress of Slavists, Kievi, September 1983, I: Linguistics and Poetics*, 579–615. Columbus, Ohio: Slavica.

Schramm, Michael. 2010. "Hermann und Kant: Philologie als (Kantische) Wissenschaft". *Gottfried Hermann (1772–1848). Internationales Symposium in Leipzig 11.-13. Oktober 2007* edited by Kurt Sier & Eva Wöckener-Gade, 83–121. Tübingen: Narr.

Serbat, Guy. 1979. "L. Hjelmslev et la 'Catégorie des cas': contradictions et apories d'une pensée 'totaliste'". *L'Information Grammaticale* 1.11–15.

Serbat, Guy. 1981. *Cas et fonctions. Étude des principales doctrines casuelles du Moyen Âge à nos jours*. Paris: PUF.

Sørensen, Hans Christian. 1949. "Contribution à la discussion sur la théorie des cas". *Recherches structurales* (*Travaux du Cercle Linguistique de Copenhague V*), 123–133. Copenhague: Nordisk Sprog- og Kulturforlag.

Steen, Holger. 1949. "Le nombre grammatical". *Travaux du Cercle Linguistique de Copenhague* IV, 47–59. Copenhague: Einar Munksgaard.

van Ginneken, Jac[ques]. 1907. *Principes de linguistique psychologique. Essais de synthèse*, Amsterdam, Paris & Leipzig : Van der Vecht, Rivière & Harrassowitz.

Vogt, Hans. 1949. "L'étude des systèmes de cas". *Recherches structurales* (*Travaux du Cercle Linguistique de Copenhague, V*), 112–122. Copenhague: Nordisk Sprog- og Kulturforlag.

Wackernagel, Jacob. 1924. *Vorlesung über Syntax: mit besonderer Berücksichtigung von Griechisch, Lateinisch und Deutsch.* Basel: E. Birkhaüser.

doi Widoff, Andreas. 2021. "System, Norm and Meaning". *Eugenio Coseriu: Past, Present and Future* edited by Klaas Willems & Cristinel Munteanu, 245–260. Berlin: De Gruyter.

doi Widoff, Andreas. 2023. "On the feasibility of general meanings in prepositional semantics", *Acta Linguistica Hafniensia* 55:1.16–36.

Wierzbicka, Anna. 1980. *The Case for Surface Case.* Ann Arbor: Karoma Publishers.

doi Willems, Klaas. 2022. "Norms, Language-specific Meanings and Schemas. A Coserian Perspective on Contemporary Concepts in Linguistics". *Energeia. Online Journal for linguistics, language philosophy and history of linguistics,* VII.1–62 [https://energeia-online.org/article/view/3653/2764].

Wüllner, Franz. 1827. *Die Bedeutung der sprachlichen Casus und Modi. Ein Versuch.* Münster: Coppenrath.

Name index

Subject index